TODAY'S ELECTRONIC OFFICE

PROCEDURES AND APPLICATIONS

Dorothy A. Neal
Instructor of Business Education
Sacopee Valley High School
South Hiram, Maine

Rosemary T. Fruehling
Director of Office Technology and Skills
Market Segment, McGraw-Hill Book Company

Constance K. Weaver
Director, Planning Systems
McGraw-Hill, Inc.

Gregg Division
McGRAW-HILL BOOK COMPANY

New York   Atlanta   Dallas   St. Louis   San Francisco
Auckland   Bogotá   Guatemala   Hamburg   Lisbon
London   Madrid   Mexico   Milan   Montreal   New Delhi
Panama   Paris   San Juan   São Paulo   Singapore
Sydney   Tokyo   Toronto

Sponsoring Editors ■ Roberta Moore and Marilyn Sarch
Editing Supervisor ■ Nicola von Schreiber
Design and Art Supervisor ■ Caryl Valerie Spinka
Production Supervisor ■ Frank Bellantoni
Photo Editor ■ Rosemarie Rossi

Cover Designer ■ Sulpizio Associates
Technical Art ■ Burmar Technical Corp., Interactive Graphics, Inc.
Interior Design ■ MKR Design

PHOTO CREDITS

ACME Visible Records, Inc.: page 218; **Jules Allen:** pages 13, 21, 24 (left), 36, 37, 38, 39, 47, 63, 88, 89, 97, 99, 105, 167, 169 (right), 219, 240, 251, 262, 286, 333, 339, 342, 348, 349, 397, 405, 409, 422, 423, 424, 437; **AT&T, Bell Laboratories:** pages 94, 323, 329, 330, 342 (top); **Audio Visual:** page 388; **BASF Systems Corporation:** pages 68 (bottom left), 215; **Andy Canfield (The Image Bank):** page 69 (top middle); **John Cavanagh:** pages 259, 260, 276, 278, 279, 362; **Control Data Corporation:** page 168; **Culver Pictures, Inc.:** page 6; **James D'Addio:** page 1; **Devoke Data Products:** page 222; **Will Faller:** pages 69 (top left and bottom), 188, 220, 222, 299, 305, 313, 314, 402, 403; **Fugitsu Imaging System of America:** page 166; **Richard Hackett:** pages 24 (right), 47 (left), 83, 85, 86, 91, 162, 209, 241, 266, 270, 274, 284, 291, 331, 332, 337, 391; **David W. Hamilton (The Image Bank):** page 69 (top right); **Erich Hartmann/Magnum Photos:** pages 150, 153, 154, 233; **Hayes Microcomputer Products:** page 261; **Michael Heron:** pages 80, 93, 98, 327; **Honeywell Information Systems, Inc.:** pages 9, 35; **Houston Instruments:** pages 169 (left), 237; **IBM Corporation:** pages 26 (top), 68 (top and middle), 180; **Interleaf, Inc.:** page 246; **Ted Kawalerski:** page 242 (middle); **Les Morsillo:** page 78; **Moog, Inc.:** page 2; **Panel Concepts, Inc.:** page 10; **Pitney-Bowes:** page 243 (left); **Ricoh Corporation:** page 265; **Bob Rogers:** pages 66, 158, 217, 247, 261 (right), 297, 315, 348 (right), 363, 437; **Sepp Seitz/Woodfin Camp & Associates:** pages 27, 350; **Sperry Corporation:** pages 18, 25, 26 (bottom); **Texas Instruments:** page 235; **3M Corporation:** pages 68 (bottom right), 227 (right); **Wang Laboratories:** page 390; **Xerox:** pages 242 (top and bottom), 343 (right)

Library of Congress Cataloging-in-Publication Data

Neal, Dorothy A.
    Today's electronic office.

    Includes index.
    1. Office practice—Automation. 2. Business—
Data processing. 3. Electronic office machines.
I. Fruehling, Rosemary T. II. Weaver, Constance K.
III. Title.
HF5548.N37   1989   651.8   87-34241
ISBN 0-07-046146-5

The manuscript and line art for this book were processed electronically.

Today's Electronic Office: Procedures and Applications

  2 3 4 5 6 7 8 9 0   VNHVNH   8 9 5 4 3 2 1 0 9

ISBN 0-07-046146-5

Dorothy A. Neal is currently an instructor of Business Education at Sacopee Valley High School in South Hiram, Maine.

In addition to her teaching responsibilities at the secondary level, Ms. Neal has served as President of the Business Education Association of Maine, President of the New England Business Educators Association, and President of both the Eastern and National Business Education Associations.

Ms. Neal is coauthor of *English Style Skill-Builders,* Fourth Edition, and has also written numerous articles for professional publications in the area of office education.

Ms. Neal received her B.S. degree from the University of Maine at Machias, and her M.A. degree from the University of Southern Maine.

Dr. Rosemary T. Fruehling is an internationally known educator and lecturer in the field of business education. Dr. Fruehling has taught office education at both the high school and the postsecondary levels. She has also conducted business education teacher-training seminars for the McGraw-Hill International Division and for the U.S. Department of Defense.

Dr. Fruehling has served as a consultant to such business firms as International Milling, General Mills, Honeywell, and Warner-Lambert Pharmaceutical Company. She has also served as Postsecondary Vocational Education Section Manager, in the Division of Vocational-Technical Education of the Minnesota State Department of Education.

Dr. Fruehling is coauthor of other publications with McGraw-Hill, among them, *Business Correspondence: Essentials of Communications,* Sixth Edition; *Business Communication: A Problem-Solving Approach,* Third Edition; and *Psychology: Human Relations and Work Adjustment,* Sixth Edition.

Dr. Fruehling received her B.S., M.A., and Ph.D. degrees from the University of Minnesota in Minneapolis.

Constance K. Weaver is currently Executive Director, Business Week, Executive Programs Week and Services, for McGraw-Hill, Inc.

In addition to her extensive experience in business, Ms. Weaver has spent several years developing and marketing educational materials in the field of business education. She has conducted business education teacher-training seminars for McGraw-Hill in the areas of office automation and microcomputer applications. She has also taught at the postsecondary level.

Ms. Weaver has a wide-ranging background and practical experience in microcomputer applications and office systems and has recently completed coordinating the implementation of an integrated office system within the Corporate Planning Department of McGraw-Hill.

Ms. Weaver received her B.S. degree from the University of Maryland, College Park, Maryland.

CONTENTS

PART

III BUSINESS SKILLS
FOR THE ELECTRONIC
OFFICE 284

PART

MANAGEMENT SKILLS
FOR THE ELECTRONIC
OFFICE 388

Rapid new developments in technology have propelled us very quickly into the age of information sharing. Today microcomputers, satellite tele-communications, desktop publishing, local area networks, and optical disks have pushed office automation technology into a new and exciting age of information sharing.

This text will prepare you for entering the business world where you can have an exciting and interesting career in the business office of today and the constantly changing one of tomorrow.

THE TEXTBOOK

Today's Electronic Office is designed for use by high school students in the office technology curriculum and can serve as a reference book once you start working. It reviews the concepts of information processing and presents information processing tasks and procedures within the context of a total office system. The textbook is built around five distinct phases of information processing: (1) Data Creation and Input, (2) Processing, (3) Storage, (4) Output, and (5) Distribution/Communication.

Today's Electronic Office is divided into four parts.

Part I, The Worker and the Workplace, deals with the changes automation is bringing to the business office. Although it focuses on the new technology, this part emphasizes the role of human relations skills in the electronic office.

Part II, Information Processing Procedures, shows how modern offices gather, process, and distribute information. The importance of basic communication skills is stressed as well as the technology.

Part III, Business Skills for the Electronic Office, describes the multifaceted role of office workers in the electronic office.

Part IV, Management Skills for the Electronic Office, explains why office workers today need to be aware of the different functions in the electronic office. It ends with a review of job opportunities in the electronic office.

Each of the four parts of *Today's Electronic Office* is divided into chapters. Each chapter begins with a brief section that introduces the material covered in the chapter and highlights the main ideas. Headings emphasize the major ideas of the chapter and help you follow the main points as you read the text. Technology tips are boxed, and important terms are highlighted in bold print and explained in the text.

End-of-Chapter Materials

Each chapter concludes with a summary that provides a point-by-point review of the chapter's highlights in a concise list format. The vocabulary section lists all new terms defined within the chapter in the order in which they appeared in the text. Each chapter concludes with a series of review questions that enable you to determine how much of the material you remember and how well you understand it, and with skillbuilding activities that give you a chance to exercise your problem-solving, organizational, and communication skills.

THE APPLICATIONS MANUAL

The exercises and activities in the Applications Manual are designed to reinforce the procedures covered in the textbook. They give you an opportunity to apply the concepts you learned and to practice the skills you acquired. The manual is organized by chapter, with an average of five activities or applications for each chapter of the textbook. It contains a variety of work situations that require students to work independently and in groups. The applications reflect the kind of work that one would do in a business office.

ACKNOWLEDGMENTS

For their reviews of the manuscript, we wish to thank Carol Baker, formerly Instructor of Office Procedures, Taylor Business Institute, Paramus, New Jersey; Daphne Robinson, Instructor, R. J. Reynolds High School, Winston-Salem, North Carolina; and Georgina L. Seals, Instructor, Illinois Valley High School, Cave Junction, Oregon.

A personal tribute to the late Dr. Phyllis Morrison for her encouragement and support.

For their input and interest during each stage of this book's production, we wish to recognize the students at Sacopee Valley High School, South Hiram, Maine.

Many other people have also contributed their time and technical expertise to the development of this book. To all of them we extend our grateful acknowledgment.

Dorothy A. Neal
Rosemary T. Fruehling
Constance K. Weaver

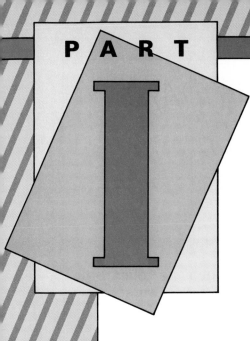

PART I

THE WORKER AND THE WORKPLACE

*T*he business office is rapidly changing from a manual-based system to an electronic computer-based system. Using sophisticated equipment in the electronic office, office workers will make decisions, analyze data, organize information, create graphics, and set up conferences.

In the transition period, businesses will continue to use traditional equipment, such as the electric typewriter, the U.S. Postal Service, and telephones, along with computer systems. Obviously, there will always be a need for some traditional equipment, but electronic systems will increasingly dominate.

The chapters in Part 1 tell you how automation is affecting the basic office function of information processing and describe the electronic office of today. You will see why these are exciting times to start a business office career and why additional skills are important for advancement.

WORKING IN TODAY'S CHANGING OFFICE

In the past office work was fairly predictable and unchanging. For years office workers performed the routine tasks of answering the telephone, taking dictation, transcribing and typing letters and reports, and filing. While the introduction of electric typewriters and photocopying machines made a job easier to complete, there was little opportunity to learn new skills or to advance to higher-level positions.

All that has changed. Today the basic office skills remain. They include filing, keying, dictating and transcribing, communicating effectively, computing, practicing positive human relations, and making decisions. In addition to these basic skills, new skills are required. For example, learning how to use the computer for electronic tasks such as electronic filing must be learned. Never before have office workers been expected to deal with changes as rapidly as those that have taken place in the last few years. It is likely that the rate of change will continue to increase in the future.

Office workers must be well-informed about individual job requirements. They must understand new equipment and procedures and be able to make good decisions and to avoid errors.

Today businesses have the *tools* necessary for their employees to do all of these things well. Businesses need employees with a positive work attitude—employees who can adapt easily to change. The easier it is for you to adapt to change, the greater your chances are of being successful on the job.

When businesses were introduced to computers in the 1970s, major changes in the way information was processed began to occur. This chapter will focus on the ways in which new technology is changing today's office.

As a result of studying this chapter, you will be able to:

- Explain how today's electronic office has changed the way information is processed.
- Define and give an example of office functions, tasks, and procedures.
- Be aware of the need to develop mature decision-making and human relations skills.
- Understand how traditional office skills are used along with electronic office skills in the processing of information.
- Explain the changing roles of workers in today's office.

 HANGING INFORMATION PROCESSING TECHNOLOGY

What do we mean when we talk about **information processing**? Essentially, we are talking about taking raw data and turning it into useful information. We should begin by defining data. **Data** is usually in the form of unorganized facts, such as words or figures. **Information** means facts (data) that have been organized in a way so that they can be used. In a business environment, information is chiefly used to make decisions. For example, when a list of names and addresses is prepared in alphabetic order, or when a chart is prepared showing average monthly sales figures, the data has been organized into useful information. Once organized, the information is much easier to communicate and to use in decision making.

Another example illustrating the difference between data and information is the United States census. Every ten years, the U.S. Census Bureau counts the population of the country by conducting a census. To do this, the Census Bureau collects data such as the number of people in each household; their ages, incomes, and occupations; and other vital facts. These facts, or data, can then be grouped together to communicate such information as

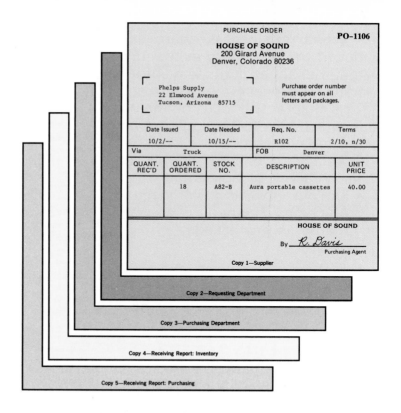

| PURCHASE ORDER | | | | PO-1106 |

HOUSE OF SOUND
200 Girard Avenue
Denver, Colorado 80236

Phelps Supply
22 Elmwood Avenue
Tucson, Arizona 85715

Purchase order number
must appear on all
letters and packages.

Date Issued	Date Needed	Req. No.	Terms
10/2/--	10/15/--	R102	2/10, n/30

| Via | Truck | FOB | Denver |

QUANT. REC'D	QUANT. ORDERED	STOCK NO.	DESCRIPTION	UNIT PRICE
	18	A82-B	Aura portable cassettes	40.00

HOUSE OF SOUND

By _R. Davis_
Purchasing Agent

Copy 1—Supplier

Copy 2—Requesting Department

Copy 3—Purchasing Department

Copy 4—Receiving Report: Inventory

Copy 5—Receiving Report: Purchasing

Fig. 1-1   These purchase orders contain data on customers, product sales, dates, geographic area, and many other facts. This data can be processed to provide information for use within the organization. One common format for providing information in business offices is the preparation of reports.

the average household income in a particular city, or a list of the fastest-growing cities. This information can then be used to determine future needs of different regions of the United States. Examples of processed information are memorandums, letters, reports, financial statements, invoices, purchase orders, and schedules.

OFFICE FUNCTIONS, TASKS, AND PROCEDURES

Business managers need to find efficient ways to handle rapidly growing amounts of business information. Modern offices are automating many functions previously performed manually. When people use the term **office automation**, they are talking about the use of computers and other electronic equipment to perform tasks that used to be done manually. Using technology for routine office tasks—preparing documents, storing information, and transferring information from one place to another—frees workers to spend time on more challenging tasks. Automated technology allows work to be done faster and more efficiently. For example, if a series of tasks, such as keyboarding, formatting, editing, and revising a document, is automated, the efficiency of the entire function of processing written documents will improve. In turn, automation will change the procedures that are followed in performing these functions and tasks. Let us define these terms:

Functions   A set of actions expected from a person or machine; functions are composed of a series of tasks or responsibilities. For example, one of your functions as an administrative assistant might be *scheduling meetings.*

Tasks   Individual assignments or jobs that are necessary to complete a function of your job. For example, *setting up staff meetings* is one *task* you would perform as a part of your job function: *scheduling meetings.*

Procedures   A series of steps that must be followed in a regular, definite order to complete a task.

For example, to set up a staff meeting, you would follow these procedures:

- Prepare materials needed for the meeting.
- Check your supervisor's calendar.
- Reserve a meeting room.
- Call the staff members to announce the time and date.
- Distribute a memo confirming the date, time, and place.

By studying office procedures, you will learn not only *how* office tasks are done but also the materials and equipment to be used, as well as other aspects of accomplishing tasks and functions. Through the use of office procedures, you will be able to carry out your job functions in a predictable and orderly way.

Keep in mind that while there are certain general standards, each office will have its own procedures that workers must follow to accomplish their tasks and functions. The procedures you learn here may or may not be exactly like those you will find on a job. You must learn to adapt what you study here to your particular work situation.

HE CHANGING OFFICE

More than a century ago, office workers felt threatened by the introduction of a new machine into the office. This machine was called a typewriter. Workers were afraid that the machine would make their skilled handwriting unnecessary. And if their skills became unnecessary, so would they. As time passed, they learned that—on the contrary—the typewriter helped them complete their work faster and more easily. With greater capabilities, the need for office workers increased.

This same suspicious reaction occurred when businesses began to **automate**, which means using machines

The introduction of the typewriter created many new jobs and soon came to be thought of as a basic requirement for an office.

instead of people to perform certain tasks. Many workers were afraid that computers would soon do away with the need for people in the office. Instead, the demand for office workers has increased in spite of automation. The Bureau of Labor Statistics estimates that the number of office workers in the United States, which was *approximately 38 million in the 1970s*, will *rise to more than 55 million in the 1990s*. While some jobs are being eliminated, many more are being created. The way jobs are done will continue to change. No matter how much electronic equipment is installed in an office, people will still be needed to operate that equipment, to collect and organize facts, and to arrive at the decisions required to make the information meaningful.

PRODUCTIVITY

Businesses have automated their operations and procedures in order to take advantage of the efficiency offered by the use of technology. When people talk about automating an office, what they are really talking about is creating a workplace where computers and other electronic equipment can carry out as many routine jobs as possible. The goal of doing this is to increase productivity.

In a narrow sense, **increased productivity** means that more work can be done by fewer employees or that the same amount of work can be done in less time. Increased productivity can also mean that workers have greater flexibility in how they go about doing individual tasks. The quality of their work can be improved as well as the efficiency with which the work is completed.

Until the 1980s the major application of technology to improve productivity was in the shop or factory, not the office. One reason for this is that the need for efficiency in the factory is greater than in the office. Another important factor is that in the shop and factory it is easier to identify those jobs that can be broken down into step-by-step procedures that can more easily be computerized. Assembly line jobs, such as measuring foods to fill bottles, can more easily be computerized than office jobs that require more individual decisions for each task.

It is not surprising that the first computers to enter the office were used to automate routine business functions in accounting and financial operations. Now advancements in information processing technology have resulted in automation of many office jobs. The way office jobs are done will continue to change with each technological development. These changes will require that future office workers become more adaptable and willing to learn new skills and new ways of doing their jobs.

ASTERING CHANGE

Change should always be seen as an opportunity for both personal and professional growth. Many people tend to cling to the familiar and to resist the unfamiliar. It is important to accept that some changes are inevitable. You can build on each successful experience to help yourself master whatever changes are necessary for your job.

Learn to accept the truth, even if it is unpleasant. Although we would like to think that certain aspects of our lives are permanent, this is never the case. The ability to cope means looking at things objectively. We need to be able to recognize the need for change and act upon it when it comes.

Mastering change also means that we have to accept errors as a natural part of risk taking. Being willing to take risks encourages future risk-taking behavior. This willingness can lead to many new opportunities. A failure, though disappointing, does not have to mean defeat. If you ask yourself "What's the worst thing that would happen?", you may be surprised. Even the worst thing is often not as bad as it seems.

Learn to recognize your own lack of knowledge. It is always easy to see weaknesses in others, but it is not always as easy to admit our own ignorance. Yet admitting ignorance gives you a chance to change, to learn, and to grow.

People who master change successfully are able to understand and explain what is happening around them. You will find that this book helps you to understand the changes taking place in the business world. If you know what to expect in your future office job, you will be able to adapt to its requirements so that you can achieve your future career goals.

The use of electronic technology is causing a change in the roles of office workers. Secretarial responsibilities will change to reflect the new skills required in today's office.

USING TRADITIONAL AND ELECTRONIC OFFICE SKILLS

You will find that the English and math skills which you learned from the time you entered school until now will continue to be important to you in today's electronic office. A working knowledge of arithmetic, grammar, spelling, and punctuation will always be essential in a business office. Learning to follow instructions, to think clearly, and to organize materials is equally essential. Even though computers process words and numbers automatically, you need to be able to check your results as well as evaluate material.

As you have just learned, information processing is dynamic. Data in its original form is often combined with other data and processed using a variety of equipment and procedures to form new information. Because business functions are combined, or integrated when processing data in the electronic office, one small error can affect not only your own work but also the work of others throughout the business. If you do not check your work carefully, an incorrect figure can easily be stored. For example, suppose that you are helping to prepare a budget. If you keyboard a decimal figure with the decimal point in the wrong place, the computer will then use this incorrect number in calculating budget figures automatically, and these figures also will be incorrect.

Many business offices today are a mix of traditional and electronic equipment, so that workers must be familiar with procedures used in both.

When people talk about "computer errors," they usually mean mistakes such as the one just described. Computers do give incorrect information on occasion. When this happens, it is almost always because a person gave the computer incorrect data to begin with. If what we send into a computer is wrong, what we get out will also be wrong. This idea is sometimes referred to as **GIGO**, which stands for "garbage in, garbage out." Many errors can be prevented by proofreading all work carefully.

Word processing in the electronic office is a good illustration of why you need basic office skills as well as additional new skills. To be good at word processing, you must have good keyboarding skills. You also need to know more than just how to operate the equipment. You need to know the functions and capability of the software program that you are using. Furthermore, when storing a letter electronically on a computer disk, you will be using the same organizational and filing skills that you would use in storing a hard copy in your file drawer. No matter how much processing you do with computers, you will find that the basic skills that you have learned in school are essential for you to be successful in today's office.

EVELOPING MATURE DECISION-MAKING SKILLS

Because computers perform so many tasks automatically, you might think that there are fewer decisions to be made in the electronic office than in the traditional office.

Ergonomics

Today's office has also brought major changes in the way people have to adapt to their work environment. Standard desks are being replaced by work areas designed to accommodate a computer and a printer. These work areas are known as **workstations**. While the traditional typewriter is still found in many offices, it is fast being replaced by the computer. Traditional files are similarly being replaced by electronic storage. Saving space is a major factor in the reorganization of filing system procedures.

An entirely new field of study called **ergonomics** has come into existence. Ergonomics is devoted to examining how the physical work environment affects the worker and his or her job performance. The goal of ergonomics is to focus on adjusting workstations to meet the changes taking place in the office environment as well as to meet the needs of its workers.

People who study the field of ergonomics are called **ergonomists**. Employers realize that people are most productive when they are physically comfortable. More attention is being given to designing workstations, furnishings, and equipment with the workers' well-being in mind.

Actually, just the opposite is true. Technology can help managers and other office workers make faster and better decisions because they can obtain and organize information to meet their specific needs more quickly and efficiently. At the same time, technology presents us with more choices than we have in traditional offices. Thus there are more decisions to be made. In the electronic office, decision-making skills are more important than they have ever been.

Decision making is a major part of a manager's job. Managers must decide how to achieve the goals of the business while at the same time serving as the link between management and staff. To make decisions wisely, managers need information. Technology has given managers access to vast amounts of information that might otherwise have taken them weeks or months to gather by traditional methods. It has also given them access to some information that they might otherwise not have been able to obtain.

The choices presented by technology have increased the importance of decision-making skills for secretaries,

The mix of equipment in offices today makes it necessary for the worker to decide which piece of equipment is the best to use for a particular task. In this office, the worker has the choice of sending a memo or letter electronically over the computer or conventionally through the U.S. Postal Service. Before making a decision, the worker will have to answer such questions as: How quickly does the information need to reach the recipient? Which is the least expensive way to send this information? Is an immediate reply necessary?

Productivity in the Office

How do office workers choose the best way to do a particular job? Often they have to make a decision about the best equipment or tools to use for a particular task or function. In order to make correct decisions, they need to understand the four factors of cost, speed (efficiency), quality, and security. These factors must be considered together to bring about a meaningful equipment decision.

Cost. Choose the method of work that allows you to accomplish your goal with the lowest possible cost to your employer.

Speed (Efficiency). In some cases speed is more important than saving money. Find out how quickly an item needs to reach the party you are dealing with.

Quality Standards. Knowing what quality standards to meet will help you decide which technology to use. For example, a computer system may include several printers, some faster than others. However, the output from the fast printers may not be as presentable as the documents from the slower printers. You would choose a higher-quality printer for documents intended for customers and others outside your organization. A lower-quality printer is a better choice for internal memos.

clerks, and other members of managers' support staffs as well. Selecting the right type of equipment, deciding on the order in which to perform tasks, and choosing the proper format for written documents are just a few examples of the decisions made by support staffs.

UMAN RELATIONS SKILLS

While office technology can save time and help you process information, it may also reduce your opportunity for human interaction. Sending interoffice messages electronically will save on telephone calls, and teleconferencing will save on meetings in person. If customers can order merchandise from your company by electronic mail, your employer's representative will spend less time in face-to-face contact with the customers. There is no doubt that technology allows an employer to carry out business more efficiently. However, when the amount of human contact in business is reduced, human relations may suffer.

Becoming aware of the role people play in total office operations has led to new approaches in determining office policies and procedures. Involving employees in the decision-making process is an example. This eliminates the possibility that office employees will feel that their concerns are not being considered. When employees feel involved, a more productive working atmosphere is created.

Of course each employee must take responsibility for making the work environment a pleasant one by making a special effort to have good human relations on the job. Keep in mind the following:

- Remember that the key to good human relations is your attitude toward yourself. If you feel good about yourself, it is easier to get along with others.
- Try to understand others and to care about what they are thinking or feeling.
- Practice behaving toward others as you would like to have them behave toward you.

The changing roles and responsibilities of workers in the electronic office makes the development of good human relations skills as important as ever.

- Define goals for yourself so that you will feel positive about your work. Make an effort to relax at work and put enthusiasm into your job.

HANGING OFFICE ROLES

Technology in today's offices has changed the roles of the workers in those offices. What once was handled by a worker known as a "secretary," today may be handled by several workers with different job titles and different job descriptions.

The term *office worker* is a very broad term covering every kind of job title and job classification. Depending on the size of the office, the term might include a file clerk, a mail clerk, a receptionist, a secretary, an information processing specialist, an executive assistant, or an administrative assistant.

Today's secretaries and other office workers are members of a growing and essential occupation. A term that is being used to describe people who work with information is **knowledge worker**. This term can be applied to lawyers, managers, insurance adjusters, clerical workers, and secretaries, to name just a few. Throughout this book, the terms *secretary* and *office worker* will be used wherever appropriate, unless a specific job (such as file clerk) is being discussed.

The office worker of the future will need to have a broad base of knowledge, with emphasis on specific skills in order to perform his or her job at top efficiency. More sophisticated technology will continue to be introduced into the business world. This technology will mean further specialization.

The role of the secretary will continue to be upgraded, allowing a secretary the opportunity to use creativity and initiative. Secretaries will continue to handle new tasks. This will make a secretary's work more challenging!

- Office work and the way it is done are changing greatly.

- Information is data that has been organized in a manner that makes it useful for making decisions.

- Office technology or office automation involves using computers and other electronic equipment to perform tasks that were done manually in the past.

- Through the use of office procedures, business workers can carry out their functions and tasks in an orderly way.

- Changes in the way information was processed began to occur in the 1970s, when computers began to be used in business offices.

- The Bureau of Labor Statistics estimates that the number of office workers will rise to more than 55 million in the 1990s.

- Businesses need employees with positive work attitudes who can adapt easily to change.

- The chances of being successful are greater if you can master change.

- In today's office basic and traditional office skills are an essential part of understanding and working with electronic technology.

- Standard desks are being replaced by workstations designed to hold a computer, software, and a printer with various types of paper use options.

- Basic English and math skills are essential in today's electronic office, as are mature decision-making skills and organization skills.

- Cost, speed, quality, and security are related to getting a job done effectively and efficiently.

- Learning to handle human factors has led to new approaches in dealing with work in the electronic office.

- Today's office workers are continuing to take on changing roles as the needs of technology change.

information processing
data
information
office automation
function
task
procedure
automate
increased productivity
GIGO
workstation
ergonomics
ergonomist
knowledge worker

R EVIEW QUESTIONS

1. Why is it so important to be able to master change in today's electronic office?

2. What major invention transformed the way in which businesses carried out their work?

3. Give a brief explanation of office automation as it applies to the electronic office.

4. What are the benefits of using procedures in an office?

5. Explain what is meant by the term *ergonomics*.

6. What role do environmental factors play in today's changing office?

7. Discuss the importance of developing the ability to make mature decisions in today's office.

8. What are the four factors to be considered in selecting the best technology for a task?

9. Why are human relations skills of major importance in today's changing office?

10. How have roles continued to change in today's electronic office?

1. Select a personal experience that has required you to deal with change within the last year. Write a paragraph describing how you have handled this change. What have you learned from this life experience that you can share with your classmates?

2. Talk with someone you would feel comfortable talking to who is working in an office. Ask this person what changes he or she has had to deal with on the job. How has the person coped with these changes? Be as specific as possible. Write a brief summary of your discussion, and share the information by giving a report in class.

3. Compose a list of items which you use on a daily basis and which are more efficient because they are automatic. For example, do you use a microwave oven as opposed to an electric stove? Once you have made your list, talk with the office worker you interviewed in the activity above. How has automation affected the office where he or she works? Finally, on the basis of your discussions with the office worker and your study of Chapter 1, make a list of changes that you think might occur within the next five years in office automation.

4. Find several magazines or catalogs that contain information and pictures relating to today's changing office. If possible, cut out pictures of the changing office environment and design a poster showing the changes in a creative manner. Explain your creation to your classmates.

5. Select one article from a business magazine that relates to changing office roles, and write a brief summary of the article. Highlight the important points as well as your personal thoughts about possible changes for the future.

MODERN OFFICE TECHNOLOGY

*I*n Chapter 1 we said that businesses want to automate office functions and tasks in order to increase productivity. We also said that it is likely that you will have to adapt to changes brought about by technology after you are on the job.

Your first office job may not require you to operate any equipment more complicated than an electric typewriter, but sooner or later you may be required to use an electronic typewriter, a word processor, or a computer. The technology for processing information is changing rapidly. If you are to keep up with these changes, you need to understand information process-ing equipment and how it works.

This chapter will trace the development of modern office technology from the typewriter to the computer. You will see how computers, word processors, and other types of electronic equipment have allowed busi-nesses to automate many of the functions, tasks, and procedures used for processing information. As a result of studying this chapter, you will be able to:

- Describe how word processing technology evolved.
- Describe how computer technology evolved.
- Understand how information processing technology functions.

OW WORD PROCESSING EVOLVED

When Christopher Sholes, a printer and inventor from Milwaukee, Wisconsin, invented the typewriter in the 1800s, no other communication device made more of an impact on the office. By 1909 no fewer than 89 separate manufacturers were turning out these popular machines.

The typewriter business in the early part of this century was much like the computer business today. People wanted to use typewriters, and manufacturers kept introducing machines with improvements. Buyers were bewildered and often frightened because there were so many different models to choose from. No one could be sure which type of writing machine was best. After several years, many manufacturers went out of business, and a standard typewriter emerged, which was produced by the few companies remaining.

The purpose of the typewriter was to speed up the process of putting words on paper. Using a typewriter to prepare documents was a revolutionary improvement over handwriting documents or having documents set in type.

The typewriter also produced a revolution as hundreds of schools began to spring up to train workers to use the typewriter. When it became obvious that most students in these schools were women, learning to use the typewriter was promoted as a way to help women win economic freedom. Within a decade or two, the male clerks in most offices were replaced by women, and secretarial and clerical work became, by tradition, a woman's occupation. Today that tradition is changing as automation elevates the status of all office workers.

HE ELECTRIC TYPEWRITER

A few years after the introduction of the manual typewriter, an electric typewriter was introduced by E. Remington & Sons, manufacturers of sewing machines and guns. This took place in 1925. In 1934 the International Business Machines Company (IBM) brought out an improved electric typewriter.

Electric typewriters made typing faster and easier, since typists need to apply only a little pressure to depress the keys. Another major change was the introduction of the "RETURN" key. Instead of having to reach up and push a bar at the end of every line, typists merely had to hit an extra key. They no longer had to take their fingers off the keyboard to make the carriage return.

This capability was improved with word processors when **word wrap** was introduced. *Word wrap* means that it is not even necessary to hit the "RETURN" key at the end of every line, because the computer automatically starts a new line. It is only necessary to hit the "RETURN" key to start a new paragraph.

By the 1950s electric typewriters had replaced most manual typewriters. The pace of change accelerated phenomenally during this period of time, and each succeeding development took the typewriter a step closer to word processing.

Self-correcting typewriters were yet another major advancement for typists. A typewriter with this capability allows the user to simplify the correction process. The typist can use a special key and an erasing tape to correct a mistake on the original copy without having to erase by hand or retype the entire page.

Electric adding machines and calculators also joined the electric typewriter in the office, thus providing more automated equipment in the office.

*T*HE ELECTRONIC TYPEWRITER

Electronic typewriters were still another major step in the evolution toward word processing. **Electronic typewriters** are electric typewriters with a number of computerized functions. The functions available depend on the model. The electronic typewriter bridges the gap between the electric typewriter and the computer. More sophisticated electronic typewriters are often called **text-editing machines** because a machine of this type will allow the user to alter the copy. The commonly used term **word processing** was first used to describe some of the functions electronic typewriters could perform.

In 1964 IBM developed a machine known as the Magnetic Tape Selectric Typewriter (MT/ST). When IBM marketed this particular typewriter, it referred to the machine as an electronic typewriter. The MT/ST allowed the user to store keystrokes by recording them on magnetic tape. When corrections were typed, the MT/ST automatically made a new recording of the text. This allowed the user to make a tape that was free of errors and replay it to produce a perfect copy of the text. The entire tape—or section of it—could be replayed any number of times, causing the machine to type copies automatically at 150 words a minute. With this machine, multiple original copies could be produced much faster than with a standard typewriter.

Unlike today's modern word processors, the MT/ST did not have the feature of **random access**, which is the ability to retrieve a document electronically without looking at any of the other documents recorded on the storage medium. If the third document on an MT/ST tape was desired, it was necessary to play through the first two.

Three stages in the evolution of the typewriter were *(top left)* manual, *(top right)* electric, and *(bottom)* electronic.

In 1969 IBM introduced the Magnetic Card Selectric Typewriter, commonly referred to as the **Mag Card**. The first Mag Card typewriters worked like the MT/STs except that they recorded keystrokes on magnetically coated cards instead of tape. Each card held one page of text. By separating the stored text into pages, it was possible to print any single document or page without replaying the others.

A later version, the Mag Card II, was the first word processor with an internal electronic memory as well as an attached storage unit. The memory could retain up to 8,000 characters as long as the typewriter was turned on. Revisions could be made before transferring the text from the internal memory to the storage card.

The Mag Card II also included a correcting ribbon that lifted errors from the page as you struck over them. It was now possible to produce a usable copy of the corrected text as it was typed in instead of having to print out a corrected version.

Today it is possible to buy electronic typewriters that have large storage capacities, on-line display screens, and a limited ability to communicate with each other over telephone lines or cables.

*T*HE WORD PROCESSOR

The mass production of word processing equipment began in the 1970s. Major manufacturers such as Olivetti, Royal, Lanier, and Digital Equipment Corporation began to manufacture word processing equipment, and the technology began to advance rapidly. With the introduction of the IBM Displaywriter in 1980 and the entry of major computer manufacturers such as Burroughs and Honeywell, the merging of computer technology and word processing technology became complete.

Today word processing and computers are viewed as one. Actually, word processing is just one major function of a computer.

When copy is keyboarded on a word processor, the strokes appear as characters on a **display screen** that looks something like a television screen. This screen is used to display information. It is possible to go to any point on the screen by using keys that move a **cursor**, which is a spot of light or some other symbol. Whatever appears on the screen can be changed, corrected, and edited without having to rekey the entire document. Words, sentences, and paragraphs can be moved easily and can be underlined, deleted, inserted, or keyed in boldface type.

As work is completed, the document can be stored in the word processor's memory and can easily be retrieved from memory when a paper copy is desired. When the document is displayed on the screen, the copy is known as **soft copy**. When the copy is produced on paper, it is known as **hard copy**.

A word processor has enormous advantages over any other machine previously used in the office for similar purposes. Word processors perform major **formatting** tasks almost effortlessly, such as numbering pages, setting margins, centering titles, highlighting passages, and dividing copy into multiple columns.

A word processor saves a great deal of time because it is not necessary to retype a document once it is keyboarded and stored in memory. All this means that businesses can become more productive because their employees can accomplish more work in less time. Greater job satisfaction will result as well when office workers do not have to repeat so many tedious, mechanical tasks.

Word processing has created a whole new concept in office operations. Desks have become workstations, and typewriters have become word processors. The term *workstation*, introduced in Chapter 1, refers to a work area that contains all the equipment, furnishings, and accessories needed to perform a job in an electronic environment. The major changes brought about by the introduction of word processing include:

- Increased productivity through increased speed and better quality.
- Reduced keying and proofreading time.
- Reduced time spent on repetitive tasks.
- Increased efficiency through the use of office equipment.
- Greater opportunities for office workers in all aspects of their work.

When word processing was first introduced into the office, manufacturers produced specialized machines designed specifically for word processing functions, such as text editing, formatting, and document merging. These machines are called **dedicated word processors** and are still used in some offices. Most computers today combine word processing capabilities with other capabilities, providing a broader range of functions.

Word processing equipment can be found in most offices today. Microcomputers are now replacing dedicated word processors because the computer can be used for a wider variety of functions.

OW COMPUTERS EVOLVED

As the word indicates, computers were originally designed to "compute." The first electronic automatic computer was known as ENIAC, which stands for Electronic Numerical Integrator and Computer. It was developed at the University of Pennsylvania in 1945. ENIAC filled a room 50 by 30 feet and cost more than $400,000. Today a computer with similar capabilities would fit on your desk.

The first computer designed to process business data was called the Universal Automatic Computer (UNIVAC I). It was developed in 1951 by the Remington-Rand Corporation (the same company that introduced the first commercial typewriter). In 1952 the CBS broadcasting network used UNIVAC I to predict the results of the U.S. presidential election. After analyzing only 5 percent of the vote, UNIVAC I correctly predicted that Dwight Eisenhower would defeat Adlai Stevenson. This feat made the general public conscious of computers and their power. Some people even feared these machines that could "outthink" them.

The second generation began about 1959 with what is called "solid-state" circuits, or transistors. **Transistors** are electronic devices consisting of substances that conduct electricity. Invented at Bell Laboratories in the late 1940s, transistors were already used in radios and television before being used in computers.

Computers using transistors were smaller, faster, and more reliable than first-generation computers. They were also less expensive, and so more businesses could afford them.

Third-generation computers were introduced in April of 1964 when IBM launched its new System/360 computer using the latest technological development: microchips. **Microchips**, known formally as **microprocessors** or informally as **chips**, are slivers of silicon about the size of a baby's fingernail. Unlike other computer circuits, chips can be mass-produced, making them less costly. Chips are also more reliable than transistors. With the advent of microchips, computers became practical and affordable for small businesses as well as for government and large corporations.

First-generation computers such as ENIAC, shown above, used vacuum tubes. They were large and generated a lot of heat.

The IBM System/360 was one of the first computers to use the microchip. This launched a new generation of computer technology.

Today computers are classified in three broad categories, depending on how powerful they are.

Mainframe Computers. Mainframe computers have larger storage capabilities and can process information faster than any other category of computers. Mainframes are so fast that they can process about 5 million instructions a minute. Mainframes are used primarily by the government, by universities, by institutions such as hospitals, and by companies that sell computer time to other smaller companies.

Minicomputers. Smaller and usually less powerful than mainframes are minicomputers. Because of the inven-

Modern computers use the microchip, which is very small but which can store tremendous amounts of data.

Microcomputers, the smallest, least expensive computers, are found in offices of all sizes.

tion of the microchip, many minicomputers are actually more powerful than first-generation mainframes. Because they are less expensive and easier to operate than mainframes, minicomputers are used by moderate- and large-sized companies as well as the government. They perform the same kinds of tasks that mainframe computers do in processing data. Minicomputers are designed to do a wide variety of tasks—with word processing being a major task.

Microcomputers. The smallest computer, taking its name from the microchip that made it possible, is the **microcomputer**. It can perform a wide variety of functions, including word processing. Microcomputers, also called **personal computers**, are the computers that individuals keep on their desks and use in their homes.

Microcomputers are found in all kinds of offices. A physician's office, for example, may use a single microcomputer for word processing, billing, and storing patients' medical records. A small real estate sales company might use a microcomputer to keep track of houses for sale, sales commissions, and other data. The real estate office might have its microcomputer connected via a telephone line with a minicomputer or mainframe computer so as to receive information about houses for sale in a particular area of the region, state, or country.

COMPUTERS AND INFORMATION PROCESSING

What do we mean when we talk about information processing? Essentially, we are talking about transforming data into useful information. This process can be broken down into five steps:

- **Input.** The preparation and keyboarding of data.
- **Processing.** The organization and calculation of words and numbers.
- **Storage.** The recording of information so that it can be recalled and used again.
- **Output.** Display of the processed information in soft-copy or hard-copy format.
- **Distribution/Communication.** The transfer of information from one location to another.

The advancements technology has brought in the processing, storage, and communication steps of information processing have had the most impact on changing office functions, tasks, and procedures. While the input and output steps have also changed, the changes in these steps have really happened as a part of the advancements in processing technology. Processing, storage, and distribution/communication technology developed separately, but at the same time. Let's take a brief look at the technology in each area.

Processing. Automation was first applied to the data processing function in the office. This is because data processing tasks could more easily be broken down into step-by-step procedures for computerization. In fact, it was the use of the computer in business data processing that led to the information explosion. Because computers could perform at astounding speeds, businesses could process more data and therefore generate much more information than before.

The next major area of use for computer technology was *word processing*, which is the manipulation of text. The term word processing was first applied to an electronic typewriter. Today, though, the term has come to mean using a computer to create, edit, revise, format, or print text.

Word processing is the cornerstone of the electronic office. For a time many people developed the impression that word processing was all there was to office automation. Now systems have been developed that allow word processing and data processing to be done on one piece of equipment. This breakthrough in processing technology has allowed data and word processing to merge into one function called *information processing*. But the ability to process more information faster is only part of the story. The capability of computers to store more and more information in smaller and smaller spaces is also changing the way offices carry out their operations.

Storage. Today's personal computers can perform the same functions as a computer that used to take up a whole room. Why? Because the instructions the computer needs to perform complex functions can now be stored in a space the size of a fingernail. It is this capacity that allowed manufacturers to produce the computers that can sit on a desk top, bringing technology to the office worker's fingertips.

Anyone in the office who has the equipment can obtain information that is stored electronically. Managers and professionals with computers on their desks can retrieve information with the push of a button. Secretaries can store forms and documents that have to be used over and over again, cutting back on hours spent rekeyboarding. And more important, information that has been collected and stored can be quickly retrieved for use in making business decisions and improving business operations.

Distribution/Communication. There would be little point in having so much information stored in a computer if we could not easily retrieve it in order to distribute and communicate it. The big technological breakthrough in communications was the telephone, followed by radio, television, and communications satellites. This technology has evolved to the point where computer communication is becoming commonplace today.

Linking computers or word processors for the purpose of enabling people to share equipment and information is not a brand new development. Terminals tied to large computer or word processing systems have done this job for years. An example of one of the early systems used in this way is the IBM 360 computer system, discussed earlier in this chapter.

Computer communication is common today in companies that have mainframe and minicomputer systems. Now, microcomputer systems can be set up so that different departments located throughout a company can be connected to each other. This type of linkage is called an **electronic network**. In an electronic network, computers and other devices located in various places are connected so that data and other computer resources can be shared and exchanged. Workers can access internal files, that is, data held on the computer system within the organization, or external files, data held on computer systems outside the organization.

Components of Information Processing Systems.
Regardless of what functions computers perform, all computers have the same basic units or physical components, which are called **hardware**. See Fig. 2-1 for the basic units of all computer systems.

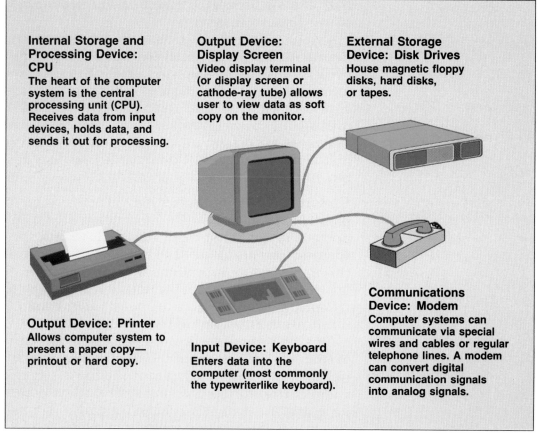

Internal Storage and Processing Device: CPU
The heart of the computer system is the central processing unit (CPU). Receives data from input devices, holds data, and sends it out for processing.

Output Device: Display Screen
Video display terminal (or display screen or cathode-ray tube) allows user to view data as soft copy on the monitor.

External Storage Device: Disk Drives
House magnetic floppy disks, hard disks, or tapes.

Output Device: Printer
Allows computer system to present a paper copy—printout or hard copy.

Input Device: Keyboard
Enters data into the computer (most commonly the typewriterlike keyboard).

Communications Device: Modem
Computer systems can communicate via special wires and cables or regular telephone lines. A modem can convert digital communication signals into analog signals.

Fig. 2-1.

In Chapter 3 we will take a closer look at each of the stages of information processing and see how each stage works in the electronic office.

- Using a typewriter to prepare documents proved to be a revolutionary improvement in processing words as opposed to handwriting documents or setting documents in type.

- The first electric typewriter, introduced by E. Remington & Sons, made typing faster and easier.

- Electronic typewriters are electric typewriters with a number of computerized functions. They bridge the gap between the electric typewriter and the computer.

- The mass production of word processing equipment began in the 1970s. Today word processing and computers are viewed as one.

- When a document is displayed on the screen, it is known as soft copy.

- When a document is produced on paper, it is known as hard copy.

- Word processors perform major formatting tasks almost effortlessly, such as numbering pages, setting margins, centering titles, highlighting passages, and dividing copy into multiple columns.

- Word processing has created a whole new concept in office operations.

- The first electronic automatic computer was known as ENIAC, which stands for Electronic Numerical Integrator and Computer. It was developed in 1945.

- The first computer designed to process business data was called the Universal Automatic Computer (UNIVAC I). It was developed by the Remington-Rand Corporation in 1951.

- Microchips, or slivers of silicon about the size of a baby's fingernail, were introduced in April 1964 when IBM launched its System/360 computer.

- Mainframe computers have larger storage capacities and can process information faster than any other kinds of computers.

- Microcomputers, or personal computers as they are known today, are smaller and less powerful than mainframe computers and are used in many businesses and homes today.

- Today it is possible to communicate with other computers if proper equipment is attached to the computers involved.

- The advancements technology has brought in the processing, storage, and communication steps of information processing have had the greatest impact on changing office functions, tasks, and procedures.

- The basic units of all computer systems are an input device, a central processing unit, a storage device, an output device, and a communications device.

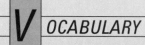

VOCABULARY

word wrap
electronic typewriter
text-editing machine
word processing
random access
Mag Card
display screen
cursor
soft copy
hard copy
formatting
dedicated word processor
transistor
microchip
microprocessor
chip
microcomputer
personal computer
input
processing
storage
output
distribution/communication
electronic network
hardware

1. Give a brief description of how the concept of word processing evolved.

2. What are the differences between electric and electronic typewriters?

3. What role did the Mag Card typewriter play in automating office operations?

4. How does a word processor aid the user in the preparation, storage, and retrieval of information?

5. Explain the difference between soft copy and hard copy.

6. Describe the concept of working at a workstation as opposed to "just a desk" in today's automated office.

7. Give a brief history of how computers have evolved.

8. List and briefly describe the three basic types of computers used today.

SKILLBUILDING ACTIVITIES

1. Go to your school or local library and, using the Reader's Guide to Periodical Literature, look up articles written from 1950–1955 in national magazines about computers, even UNIVAC 1, by name. Read about business and public reactions to the new technology. Look especially for predictions of what computers would do in the future. Write a one-page essay on your findings, including which predictions have come true or been exceeded.

2. As you already know, the five steps in the information processing cycle are: Input, Processing, Storage, Output, and Distribution/Communication. Write a

brief paragraph explaining the technology in each area.

3. Read two articles concerning office automation. Ask your teacher to suggest magazines that would have such articles. Write a summary of the two articles. Use a word processor, if possible, to complete this activity.

4. Ask your teacher if a manual typewriter, an electric typewriter, an electronic typewriter, and a word processor are available for your use. Write a one-page report on how automation is affecting office work. Prepare the report on each piece of equipment, noting the changes brought about by each piece.

AUTOMATION OF INFORMATION PROCESSING

The automation of an office means using technology to change the way in which information is processed. Chapters 1 and 2 discussed how raw data is converted into useful information and the evolution of information processing technology. This chapter will go into some detail about information processing **systems**. A system is an organized set of procedures. Few businesses would survive if they did not use systems to function.

As you have already learned, all offices process information. There are more similarities than differences in the ways businesses do this. Office workers in the sales office of a major hotel chain perform functions that are similar to those performed by office workers in a small-town insurance sales office.

It should be noted that every office is also unique, with its own procedures, personnel, and challenges.

Currently, offices are also in widely varying stages of adapting the technology to meet their individual needs. Some offices are using almost exclusively traditional methods of carrying out office functions; others have integrated certain electronic functions; and still others are functioning as fully electronic offices.

This chapter takes you on a guided tour of information processing from the initial gathering of data to the final stage of sending the information. You will see how various office functions fit together into a systematic flow, and you will learn more about the technology that is changing the way businesses operate today.

After studying this chapter, you will be able to:
- Name the five stages of the information processing cycle and explain how information is processed through each phase.
- Understand the differences between the information processing cycle in the traditional office and the cycle in the electronic office.
- Understand the importance of combining traditional office procedures with electronic office procedures.

THE INFORMATION PROCESSING CYCLE

The flow of information through an office is known as the **information processing cycle**. Thinking of information processing as a cycle helps us to understand how data is processed through a series of logical steps to become useful business information. These five basic steps are input, processing, storage, output, and distribution/communication.

In the traditional office, the flow of information through the information processing cycle flows in a step-by-step process, beginning with input and ending with storage. In the past the order of this five-step sequence never varied. But modern technology has made some important changes in this cycle.

In the traditional office the typewriter is used for keyboarding *input* taken from shorthand dictation.

In *processing* the document, editing changes must be marked on the draft copy.

The entire copy is then retyped and *output* in final form for signature.

Distribution is handled manually through postal services or interoffice mail.

Storage of file copies in file folders is the final stage of the cycle.

To understand how the information processing cycle is changed by technology, let us look at each phase of the cycle and see how these steps work when you process a letter in a traditional office.

Information Processing Cycle	Traditional Office Function
1. **Input**: Preparation and keyboarding of data	Transcribe, using proper format; type letter, using a typewriter keyboard.
2. **Processing**: Organization and creation of words or calculation of numbers. In the traditional office each keystroke is simultaneously processed and output.	Creation of draft, edit, make corrections, and proofread.
3. **Output**: Display of processed information	Produce original and carbons or photocopies. Collate, fold, bind for distribution.
4. **Distribution/Communication**: Transfer of information from one location to another.	Send original and copies, using U.S. Postal Service and interoffice mail.
5. **Storage**: Recording of information so that it can be retrieved.	File copies as appropriate.

Now let us look at how technology has changed the information processing cycle from a step-by-step process, where the next step cannot take place until the previous one is completed, to a dynamic integrated process. When electronic technology is used, the job of processing a letter is no longer a straight series of steps.

Assume that you work in an electronic office and your boss has asked you to prepare a letter. You may organize the data by taking dictation, just as you would in a traditional office. You would then transcribe the letter using a computer keyboard instead of a typewriter. As you keyboard the data into the computer, you are not simultaneously creating hard-copy output as you would on the

During *processing* the document is stored temporarily in the computer's memory. Editing can be done on the soft copy; then a command is used to tell the computer to save the final copy of the document.

In the electronic office the document is *input* using the computer keyboard. Copy is transcribed from shorthand notes, the same as in the traditional office.

The final document can be *output* in soft copy form and *distributed* electronically through an electronic mail system.

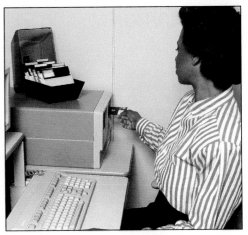

The document is permanently *stored* on a floppy disk which can be kept at the workstation for easy retrieval.

typewriter. Rather, your data is being stored in the temporary memory of the central processing unit (CPU), allowing you the option of changing the data before saving it and outputting it as hard copy.

Once you have finished keyboarding your letter, you have several options available to you: You might store the document externally on a disk and return to complete the task at a later time. You may electronically check for misspelled words; you may proofread and edit the document in soft-copy format, or print out a hard-copy draft of the document to give to your boss to edit. You might even send the letter electronically from your computer to the person or persons to whom it is addressed without ever printing a hard copy.

As you can see, in this example you would have processed the document, stored it, and communicated the information almost at the same time. This is why we can say that information processing is no longer a series of steps that take place one after the other. Input, processing, storage, output, and distribution/communication are now integrated through the use of technology.

Let us compare more closely the information processing cycle in the traditional office and the information processing cycle in the electronic office.

TRADITIONAL AND ELECTRONIC INFORMATION PROCESSING

As we go through the steps in the information processing cycle, remember that the basic functions remain the same regardless of the type of office. What changes are the tasks and procedures, as well as the way they are performed with different types of equipment.

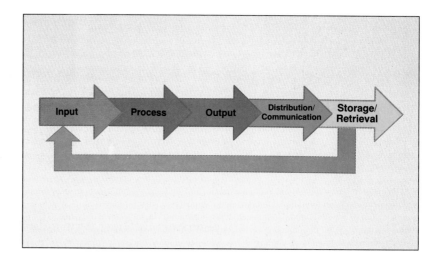

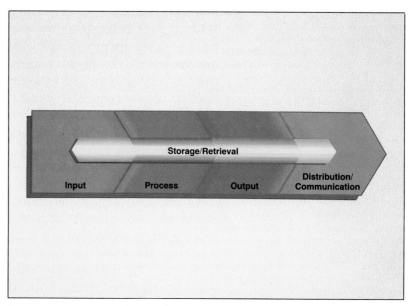

Fig. 3-1 Information processing in the traditional office happens in a linear process where one step cannot be done until the prior step is completed. In the electronic office information processing is a dynamic, interactive process with many options.

INPUT

Input is a very important step in the processing of information in both the traditional and the electronic office. Often when people think about input procedures they mainly focus on the task of keyboarding. This is, in fact, a narrow view because the tasks of gathering and organizing data to be processed is a very important part of the input step.

Many methods for gathering and organizing data are the same in the traditional and electronic office. For example, most managers find it efficient to provide verbal input in the form of machine or shorthand dictation. Some managers prefer to prepare handwritten drafts. In the electronic office managers who have their own computers may prefer to use the keyboard to create drafts. The draft can then be formatted, edited, and proofread by their secretaries. This is called **originator-generated input**.

Fig. 3-2 In a traditional office, printed and verbal data is gathered and input through the use of various input media. The typewriter is both the input device and the processor. After the information is typed and corrected, it is copied and made ready for distribution by hand or by mail. A copy is then filed by hand for office records.

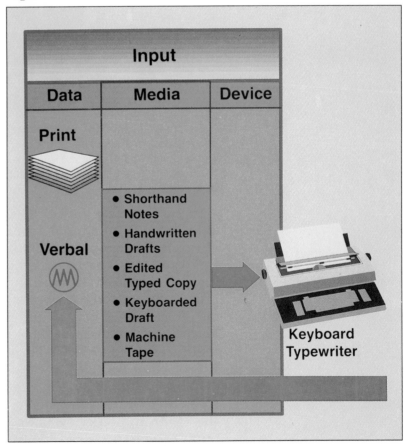

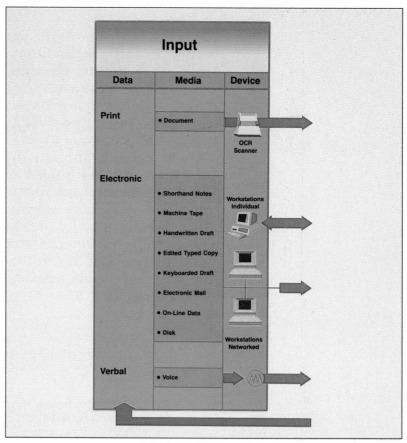

Fig. 3-3 In the electronic office options for handling input are greatly expanded. Data is created electronically, in print, and orally. Types of input media include those used in the traditional and word processing offices, plus more. Different types of equipment and equipment configurations are available.

In an electronic office, it is possible that some of the data you need for input has already been prepared and stored in the computer system on a diskette or on tape. In this case the data could be retrieved electronically and revised without rekeying. In the traditional office this previously created data would have to be retrieved manually from the file, edited, and then rekeyed. Data can also be retrieved from an outside source that supplies information to users for a fee. These services are called **on-line information services**.

In the traditional office, the primary input device is the typewriter which will usually be electric or electronic. In the electronic office, you would most often use a computer or word processor. In the electronic office, there are devices other than the computer keyboard that may be used to input data. One of these is the **optical character reader** (or **OCR**), a device that can scan a printed or typed document electronically and transfer the characters to the computer system.

Another form of input is **voice-activated input**—an exciting technology that allows a computer system to "translate" human speech into signals that can be "read" or understood by a computer program. These voice activated systems have a programmed vocabulary of words that can be understood. Current developments are taking place to enable these systems to distinguish differences in pronunciation, voice inflection, and the use of words that sound alike but are spelled differently. Voice-activated input technology will continue to be developed because of its exciting potential.

P ROCESSING

As you study the illustrations of the processing phase in the electronic office, you will see a major difference. In the traditional office, the typewriter serves as both the major input device and the processing device. In the electronic office, the keyboard of the computer, which is used for input, is a separate device from the **central processing unit (CPU)**, which is the heart of the computer system.

The CPU contains the instructions that carry out the input, processing, storage, output, and distribution/ communication functions of the computer. It handles the arithmetic-logic calculations as well as the storage of instructions and data in "memory" until they need to be called up and used.

The processing phase as we have traditionally known it involves completing both typing and nontyping tasks. Nontyping tasks include setting format specifications, such as those for margins, tab stops, line spacing, and positioning of the first line of text. Once these steps are completed, the document is prepared, with all needed corrections. The next step is to proofread and edit the document. Errors can be corrected with an automatic correction key on the typewriter or by using correction tape, correction fluid, or some other form of manual correction. If the errors are major, the document may have to be redone entirely, which takes a great deal of time. Also, all copies must be corrected.

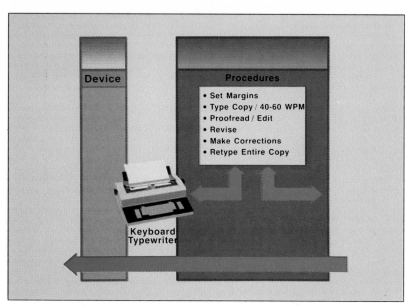

Fig. 3-4 In the traditional office the typewriter is the input device and the processor. Formatting and editing procedures are done manually.

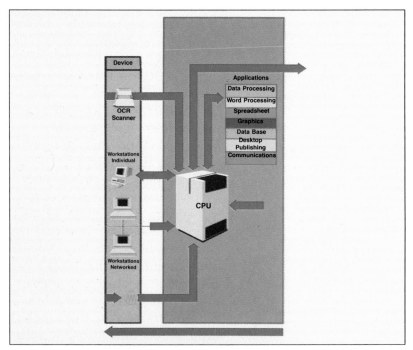

Fig. 3-5 Processing in the electronic office differs from word processing in that systems are networked and there are many more processing applications.

CENTRAL PROCESSING UNIT

The heart of a computer system is the central processing unit (CPU). The CPU receives data from the input devices, carries out the various operations, and sends the results to output devices. The CPU consists of three principal parts:

- **Control Unit**. This is the part of the CPU that causes the system to carry out instructions. It is a kind of internal "police officer" that routes information here and there within the computer for processing, storage, and communication.
- **Arithmetic-Logic Unit**. This unit does the arithmetic functions of adding, subtracting, multiplying, and dividing. It can determine if a number is larger or smaller and if it is negative or positive. In that way it is able to make a logical decision.
- **Memory**. This is sometimes called **main memory, temporary memory,** or **internal memory**. The memory in the CPU holds data that is input and sends it out as necessary to the arithmetic-logic unit or to input devices. It also holds the instructions, or program, to carry out the function.

With word processing in the electronic office, much of the above will be eliminated. Through the use of command keys on the keyboard, also called function keys, margins, tabs, and line spacing can be set or changed easily. The text can also be easily adjusted to fit new specifications automatically. If the document length changes, the computer will provide the new, correct page numbers. Editing tasks such as adding or deleting one or more words can be completed easily without doing the whole page over. It is possible through certain commands to insert headings for each page. The computer will even proofread your work for spelling errors if it has the software capability to do so. It will still be necessary for you to read the work. The computer cannot discriminate between homonyms such as *there* and *their*, nor can the computer know if you left out a word or if you used punctuation incorrectly.

Once you have printed a hard copy and submitted it for approval, any other needed changes can be made easily and quickly. This is done by editing the soft copy stored in memory and printing out a revised hard copy. It does not matter how many revisions the document has been through: revised hard copy can still be generated easily.

It is also possible to perform other processing applications if proper software is used.

Merging Information. With a computer, information from different computer files can be merged, or combined. For example, if you have to send the same letter to ten different individuals, it is possible to merge the letter with a file that contains a list of names, addresses, and salutations. The computer will then print the same letter ten times, and each letter will have a different inside address and salutation.

Data Analysis. In an electronic office where all data is stored electronically, it is easy to use the computer to make comparisons of all stored data. This data can be easily retrieved and converted into different formats, such as bar graphs or variable two-line charts for easy analysis. In a traditional office, such tasks would be done manually and would often be assigned to a professional such as an accountant. In an electronic office, any office worker who has been trained to use the computer would be able to prepare the required information.

Databases. In an electronic office, you can use the computer to gain access to databases. An **electronic database** is a collection of data on a particular subject which is stored on electronic media. For example, a retail company can create a computerized database containing the selling prices of its products. The database might also list the names, sizes, and locations of all its retail outlets. The benefit of an electronic database is that the data can be manipulated in many ways to show different aspects of the same information then output as a report or as part of another document. Tasks such as this take many hours of concentrated work if done manually.

Decision-Support Applications. As has been suggested, in an electronic office, a wide variety of applications can be performed. These are often referred to as **productivity tools** or **decision-support tools**, because they allow complex, time-consuming tasks to be done in a fraction of the time it takes to do them manually. The applications might include:

- **Data processing**—the manipulation of alphanumeric data.
- **Spreadsheeting**—the use of a grid or matrix (similar to a ledger), in the form of columns and rows on the screen, to perform mathematical calculations and analysis.
- **Graphics**—the creation of charts, graphs, and other types of pictorial images.
- **Database management**—the entering, organizing, storing, and retrieving of data in a format and order specified by the user.
- **Composition**—electronic typesetting of words and images. Desktop publishing is a common form of composition today.

 TORAGE

In a traditional office, the storage phase of the information flow does not come until the very end of the process, after the data has been inputted, processed, outputted, and distributed or communicated. In an electronic office, storage is an automatic part of the input and processing phases. Whenever a document is keyboarded, it is stored by the computer. It is first stored temporarily in the elec-

Hard disk

5¼″ floppy disk

3½″ floppy disk

Floppy disks and hard disks are the most commonly used storage devices for microcomputers.

tronic circuits of the system. Then it is stored permanently when the computer is commanded to save it. Data can then easily be retrieved and reused for input.

Data is stored on magnetic disks, called **data disks**, which are either soft, **floppy disks**, or hard disks. Data may also be stored on magnetic tape. The size and individual needs of a business will determine the type of disk used for storage.

One major difference between storing data on disks and storing data as hard copy is in the amount of physical space required. A single data disk can hold many letters, depending on their length. It would be easy to file 100 disks, holding many hundreds of letters, memos, and reports, in 2 small boxes that could sit on your desk. It would take several full-sized file drawers to hold the same amount of hard-copy information.

Traditional and electronic offices both keep paper records of many documents. Many individuals feel that this is necessary in case of accidental erasure of data or in case of a power failure. In a power failure, whatever is stored in the temporary memory of the computer is lost unless it has been stored on a disk. Also, data already stored on a disk can become garbled or confused if a power surge precedes the power failure. Many larger companies that rely heavily on their computers have backup power generators for precisely this reason. One way to

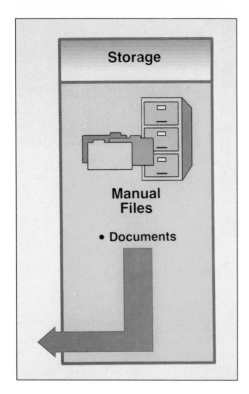

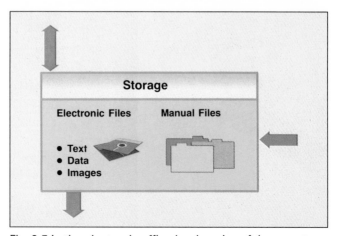

Fig. 3-7 In the electronic office hard copies of documents are greatly reduced. Text, voice, and images can be stored on a variety of storage media and can be retrieved at any time.

Fig. 3-6 In the traditional office hard copies of documents are stored in paper folders. Filing is a time-consuming procedure and frequently information is lost or misplaced.

reduce the problem of accidental loss of electronically stored data is to make **backup copies** of all disks and update those copies regularly.

But even barring these problems, many companies store hard-copy records because they do not feel completely comfortable with the concept of electronic storage of data.

In an electronic office where some of the office workers may not yet be completely familiar with computers, hard copy may be filed for use by those workers. Also, there are still some types of documents that may not be stored electronically for a variety of individual reasons.

Retrieval involves locating the appropriate disk and then having the computer locate the information desired in the right place on the disk. This step is similar to the retrieval phase in a traditional office, where the hard-copy document must be found in a file drawer. The main difference is that with disks you usually do not have to get up from your workstation to retrieve the information.

Electronic filing solves many of the problems associated with traditional filing. For example, files stored on a computer's hard-disk unit can be protected so that only certain individuals have access to them. Instead of having to lock file cabinets and sign documents in and out of files, users of a word processing system can secure their files by using a **password system**. Under this system, all individuals who are allowed to use the files are assigned a password. This means that they must enter the code word, or password, into the computer before they can gain access to any of the information stored there. To achieve additional security, it is not unusual for a company to change passwords on a regular basis.

UTPUT

In a traditional office, the output is the finished document and the main output device is the typewriter. Every keystroke on the typewriter simultaneously creates output. If duplicates of the finished product are needed, a photocopier or carbon paper (because of its low cost) may be used.

In an electronic office, the hard copy is produced by a printer. There are different types of printers, and the output they produce will differ in quality. Because information can be communicated electronically, output in the electronic office can also be in soft-copy form only. For example, brief messages sent from one computer to another may simply be read by the recipient and then deleted from the system.

Some electronic offices use laser printers. A laser printer uses a combination of electronics and photography to produce beautifully printed originals with incredible speed. Because the laser printer is very fast, it can be used instead of a photocopier to make duplicates. While a laser printer can collate material automatically, most printers cannot.

In most cases photocopiers are still used for duplication. It is still necessary to collate and bind hard copies of documents manually.

ISTRIBUTION/COMMUNICATION

The distribution/communication phase of information processing involves getting the information that has been prepared out to the individuals who need it. As with other stages in the process, the way this is done will depend

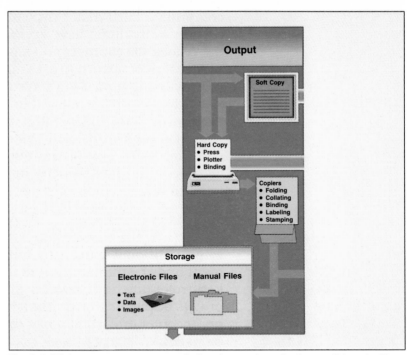

Fig. 3-8 All documents are output in hard copy form in the traditional office and manually prepared for distribution.

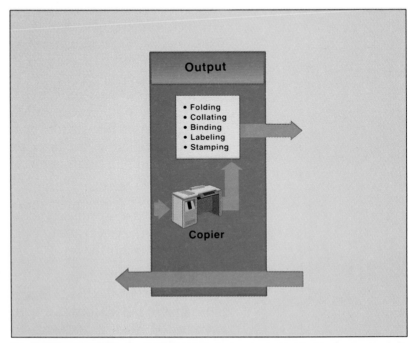

Fig. 3-9 The capability for both local and remote output in hard copy or soft copy form is a major change from the traditional to the electronic office.

greatly on the type of office you are working in. In a traditional office, output is distributed within the office via interdepartmental mail. For distribution outside of the office, either the U.S. Postal Service or a private courier service such as Federal Express could be used.

Electronic Mail. In the electronic office, information can be communicated electronically through the use of an **electronic mail** system which allows communication within local areas. Electronic offices still need to distribute information manually, because not all offices are able to communicate electronically. Communication can also take place through telecommunication systems, which allow people and computers to communicate with others in remote locations.

An electronic network provides instant communication of three kinds: between one person and another, between a person and a computer or some other piece of equipment, and between two pieces of equipment. These kinds of instant communication can save at least several days and even weeks in the distribution/communication phase of the information processing cycle. Instant communication helps people to receive immediate feedback to help them make decisions. This timesaving dimension of the electronic office has the potential of revolutionizing the ways in which people make decisions that affect basic business operations.

Electronic mail can be most useful when information is needed immediately. Imagine that you needed the most recent sales figures from ten branch offices. In a traditional office, you would have to make ten phone calls or write ten memos requesting the information. Even if you used an express mail service, you would have to wait at least one day to get the information. With electronic mail, you can send the requests for information to each office simultaneously. In seconds all ten offices would have your request. If no one is attending one of the machines to which the mail is being sent, the computer will store the information until the person returns and turns on the system. The information you require will be sent to you as quickly as the people on the other end can command their computers to supply it, usually in a short period of time.

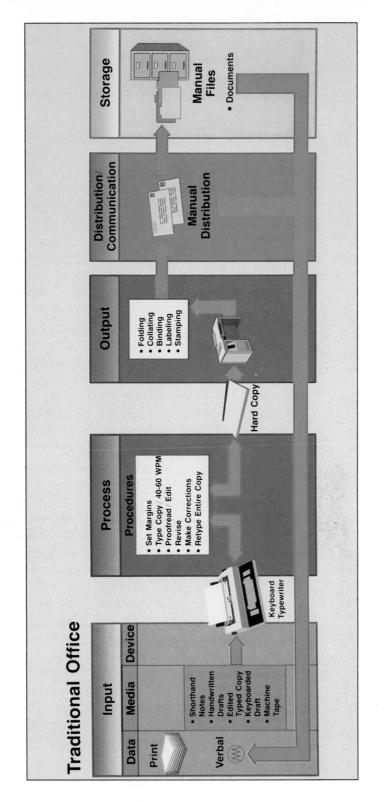

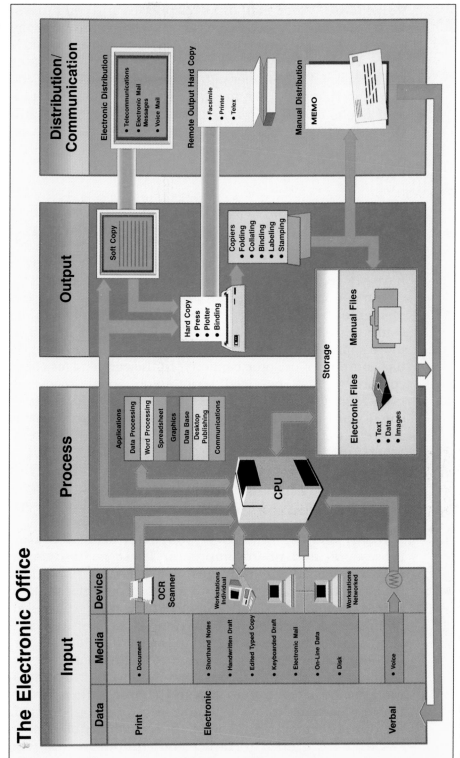

Fig. 3-11 Compare the flow of information through the traditional office and the electronic office. In the electronic office there are more options available for the input of data. In the processing phase applications that go way beyond text manipulation can be accessed through the CPU. The storage/retrieval phase is moved to the middle of the process. In the electronic office, all data can be accessed electronically and paper and traditional files are greatly reduced. Output can be in soft-copy or hard-copy form and distribution can be instantaneous through the use of local and remote networks.

Voice Mail. **Voice mail** links telephones and computers. With voice mail it is not necessary to key in your message or request for information. You can telephone a branch office in another time zone, where a computer will answer the phone, take your message, and use a signal to tell the manager that there is a message waiting. When the manager opens up the office, he or she will see the light and can respond immediately to your message.

THE ELECTRONIC OFFICE

Today there is really no such thing as a "typical" office. Some businesses still use traditional equipment and procedures, while others have brought in all the latest electronic equipment. In between are those offices which have started to automate but are not fully electronic.

In most offices the first phase of automation is the implementation of some type of word processing system. As computers have become smaller, less expensive, and more sophisticated, more and more offices have begun to use computers in some capacity. In the early stages these computers may be used strictly for word processing tasks, usually taking the place of the typewriter or dedicated word processing systems. As offices become more aware of the wide variety of the capabilities of computers, other functions, such as database, spreadsheet, graphics, and electronic communication are combined with word processing to form an "integrated system" of functions. The "integrated system" concept will be discussed further in Chapter 4.

Today many offices have typewriters, dedicated word processors, and microcomputers. These computers do not interact with mainframes or other systems and do little communicating with other microcomputers. Many offices do not take full advantage of their computer's ability to store and retrieve information. In these offices hard copy is still generated and filed in the traditional manner.

There will continue to be a mix of traditional and electronic office systems as businesses move toward maximum usage of computers so that the processing of information becomes almost totally electronic. One major factor in this movement will be the availability of employees who are trained to utilize the equipment and who understand its capabilities.

In an electronic office, workers have access to more information than that which exists in their own computer files. The computers have the ability to communicate with computers in other offices, giving the workers access to information in those offices' files as well. In networked systems data retrieval from remote locations is possible. It is the use of these networking capabilities that most distinguishes the electronic office from offices that mainly utilize computers for one specific function.

Chapter 4 will examine in greater detail the components of electronic information processing systems and the specific skills that will prepare you for whatever stage of automation you encounter on the job.

S UMMARY

- The steps in the information processing cycle are input, processing, storage, output, and distribution/communication. The order of these steps varies, depending on the equipment used.

- In the traditional office, the main forms of input are shorthand notes, handwritten drafts, and machine dictation. In the electronic office, additional forms of input are available. They include data that is already stored in the computer system, data from on-line information services, originator-generated input, and voice-activated input.

- In the traditional office, the typewriter is both the input and the processing device. In the electronic office, the computer's central processing unit (CPU) does the processing.

- In the electronic office, formatting and editing and some proofreading tasks are handled automatically by the computer through the use of command keys on the keyboard.

- Computers can also be used to merge information, analyze data, gain access to a database, and provide decision support.

- In the traditional office, storage takes place at the end of the information processing cycle. In the electronic office, storage is an automatic part of the input and processing phases.

- In electronic systems, most data is stored on disks. However, many electronic offices still maintain hard-copy files.

- In the electronic office, output may be in the form of hard copy or soft copy. Hard-copy output is generated through the use of printing devices.

- Electronic mail systems and electronic networks allow people and computers to communicate in both local and remote locations.

- Electronic mail allows office workers to revise information quickly and to receive immediate feedback.

- Voice mail links telephones and computers.

- Offices are in various stages of automating their information processing systems. They range from using mostly traditional or word processing equipment to being fully electronic with sophisticated communication capabilities.

VOCABULARY

information processing
  cycle
input
processing
output
distribution/
  communication
storage
originator-generated input
on-line information service
optical character reader
  (OCR)
voice-activated input
central processing unit
  (CPU)
database
productivity tool
decision-support tool

data processing
spreadsheeting
graphics
database management
composition
control unit
arithmetic-logic unit
memory
main memory
temporary memory
internal memory
magnetic disk
data disk
floppy disk
backup copy
password system
electronic mail
local area network (LAN)
voice mail

REVIEW QUESTIONS

1. List the five phases of the information processing cycle.

2. What are the major forms of input used in both the traditional office and the electronic office? What additional forms are available in the electronic office?

3. How does word processing assist the user in the processing stage of the information processing cycle?

4. What additional processing functions can be performed when proper software is used?

5. List and explain five decision-support applications.

6. What are the three principal parts of the central processing unit?

7. What is the most common storage medium used in the electronic office?

8. How can electronic filing aid the user?

9. Computers can be invaluable in the business office because they satisfy the security demands of a good filing system. How do they do this?

10. What are the forms of output in the electronic office?

11. Give a brief description of the most important forms of distribution/communication in today's automated office.

12. What is the main advantage of using electronic mail?

13. Explain how voice mail works.

14. What is the main factor that distinguishes an electronic office from other offices that have electronic equipment?

S KILLBUILDING ACTIVITIES

1. Design a chart illustrating the five phases of the information processing cycle. Follow a business letter that you might be sending through these five phases. Give special emphasis to the role of automation in completing this activity. Share this information with your classmates.

2. Read two magazine articles on the fast growing technology of voice-activated input. Develop and present a short presentation on this important technology.

3. Check with your school office to determine how it handles a major report, such as an attendance report. Try to identify the various stages of the information flow in relation to the preparation of the report. How is input accomplished? What processing is done and how is it done? What form does the output take? At what point does storage/retrieval take place? How is communication/distribution carried out? Into which of the three categories of offices does your school office fall?

4. Prepare a report showing the advantages and disadvantages of electronic mail versus the traditional method of mailing. Be prepared to make a short presentation.

WORKING WITH COMPUTERS AND SOFTWARE

As workers become more and more skilled at working with computer hardware and software, they are able to utilize these tools to find new ways of accomplishing their job functions and tasks. These new procedures will make it possible for offices to operate more efficiently.

Because offices are at different stages of automation, it is impossible to predict what situation you will encounter on your first job. You may be using a typewriter which is electric or electronic. It is very likely that you will be working with computers in performing office tasks.

Because technology for processing information is changing rapidly, you need a basic understanding of how the most up-to-date equipment works and how it is used. Chapter 4 focuses on the knowledge you need to work with the technology successfully in today's modern office.

After studying this chapter, you will be able to:

- Understand the importance of integrating automated systems in the office.
- Name the basic components of a computer system.
- Describe the equipment that is used at an electronic workstation.
- Understand the three main categories of computer software used in business offices.
- Understand how software packages are set up to be used on the computer.

*I*NFORMATION PROCESSING SYSTEMS

In Chapter 3 you learned how information flows through an electronic office system. Now you need to take a closer look at the kinds of tasks that you will be performing on the computer and the kinds of equipment you will be using on the job.

In the business office, computers were first used almost exclusively for large data processing jobs, such as processing payrolls, updating inventory, and filling orders. These data processing functions were handled for the most part by computer experts. Later computerized word processing equipment became available and was mainly used by office support staff.

Today many companies continue to handle data processing and word processing as separate functions. With electronic technology, data processing and word processing tasks can be performed by using the same equipment. As a result, some businesses are able to integrate

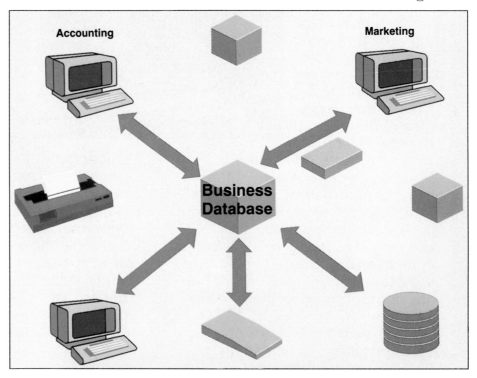

Fig. 4-1 Integrated information processing systems allow users in different departments within an organization to share and have access to a centralized source of information.

Data Processing and Word Processing

Some data processing tasks must still be handled by computer specialists because of the technical knowledge required. Most of these specialized tasks include writing computer programs. **Programs** are the sets of instructions that enable computers to carry out specific applications. Computer specialists include systems analysts, who decide how computer programs can be applied to specific business problems; programmers, who design, test, and maintain computer programs; and database administrators, who define, update, and control access to databases.

Other data processing responsibilities are handled by computer operators and data entry clerks. Their jobs require less technical training. People in these positions must have good keyboarding skills and be able to key in data quickly.

Like data processing, word processing is often handled by specialists. Some organizations have word processing centers staffed by word processing operators, individuals who are highly skilled at operating the equipment and processing complex documents. Input is sent to the center from various departments in rough-draft form or as recorded dictation.

many of the tasks and functions performed by their processing departments and equipment. In an **integrated information processing system**, data processing, word processing, and other applications can all be performed on one machine at the individual workstation.

To understand how an integrated system works, think about how a letter is processed in an office with word processing equipment only. Suppose that your boss dictates a letter to customers giving them information on current prices obtained from this month's price list. From your notes you transcribe the letter. Then you proofread it and present it to your boss for signing. At this point the afternoon mail arrives, and it includes an updated printout from the data processing department. This new report shows price increases that went into effect since the last monthly report. Your boss asks you to change the figures in the letter.

In addition, you are asked to find the price history of the products listed in the letter and to make a chart of the price increases for a report your boss is preparing. When this is completed, the chart needs to go to the art department to be typeset.

If your workstation had word processing capabilities only, you would revise the letter, proofread it, and print out a copy. You would distribute the letter via the U.S. Postal Service and interoffice mail. For the report, you would call the data processing department or write a memo to request the price history. You would send a second memo to the art department explaining what you want done with the chart.

Each aspect of your boss's request would be handled as a separate task. There would be a time lag in completing the assignment while you waited for information from the data processing department. You would then wait for a while longer for the typeset chart to be returned from the art department. If errors occurred in the typesetting process, the chart would have to be returned for corrections.

Now let us see how these same tasks could be handled with an integrated information processing system.

1. Your boss could call up price information on a computer. The latest figures would be in front of your boss as a reply is prepared.

2. You could distribute the letter through an electronic mail system.

3. Your computer would be connected to the central data processing computer. You could request the price history data for the report by using your keyboard. You would be able to get the information immediately on the screen of your computer.

4. You would have access to spreadsheet and graphing applications. You could perform the necessary calculations to create the chart, convert the numbers to graphic form, and print out the chart without the art department's help.

With an integrated information processing system, you could complete the entire assignment in one afternoon.

From this example, you can see that integrated information processing at the electronic workstation has several advantages:
- Employees have ready access to up-to-date information.
- Workers have more control over their work, and so fewer revisions are necessary.
- Managers have more control over the order in which work is done and the amount of time needed for each task.
- Administrative support staff can use their computers for many applications other than word processing.
- Administrative support staff can take more responsibility for gathering, processing, analyzing, and distributing information.

Before studying the specific tasks and procedures you will perform in an integrated information processing system, you need to understand more about the hardware and software you will be using.

 # THE ELECTRONIC WORKSTATION

Regardless of what functions they perform, all computers have the same basic physical components. These physical components are known as the **hardware**. To make all the hardware work, the computers must be given programs, or instructions. These programs are called **software**.

COMPUTER HARDWARE

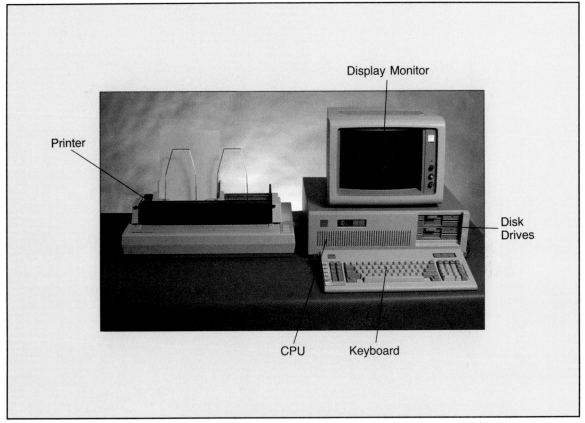

Printer

Display Monitor

Disk Drives

CPU Keyboard

A typical standalone microcomputer system has all of its basic components at the workstation.

A typical electronic office workstation consists of a microcomputer central processing unit, a disk drive, a keyboard, a display screen, and a printer—all at one location. Generally, microcomputers are self-contained, that is, all their components work together as one unit. Because they are self-contained, they are called **standalones**. The equipment that forms a computer system can be set up in many different ways. The components of minicomputers and mainframe computers are often spread over many different offices or buildings. The CPU may be in one building, a keyboard and display screen in another, and the printer in the same building, but perhaps in another room. Figures 4-2 and 4-3 show how these systems may be set up. Now let us look at the individual hardware components in detail.

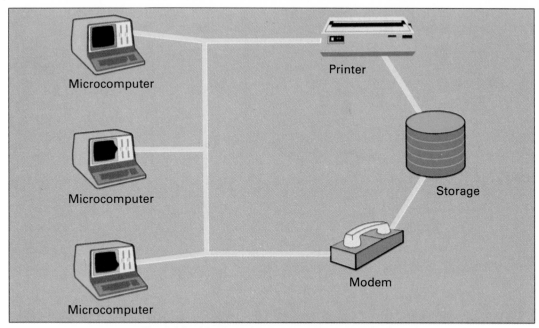

Fig. 4-2 In this shared resource system, each microcomputer has its own CPU and shares the printer, storage, and modems.

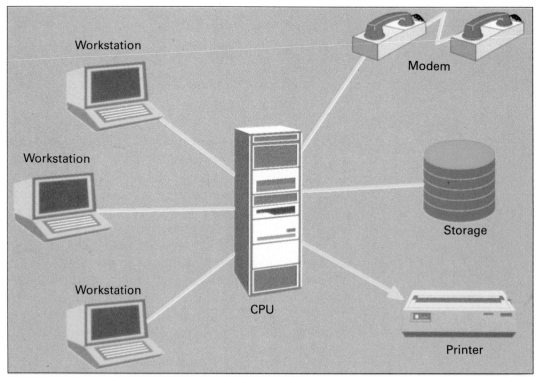

Fig. 4-3 The central processing unit in a shared logic system is bigger and far more powerful than CPUs for standalone equipment.

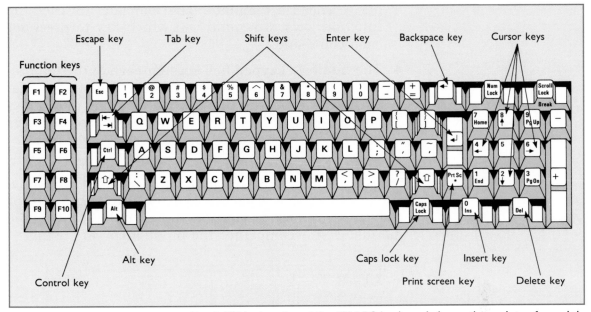

Fig. 4-4 This drawing of the IBM PC keyboard shows the variety of specialized function keys common to many computers systems.

The Keyboard. There are many new devices that can be used for inputting data into the computer. The keyboard is still the one that is the most frequently used. Most keyboards have four main parts:

1. The **alphanumeric keypad** is very similar to a standard typewriter keyboard. Depending on the type of computer, some alphanumeric keys have uses other than those related to typing. There may also be some special keys.

2. The **cursor control keypad** controls the symbol (the cursor) that marks your position. You use a cursor control key to move the cursor in the direction of the arrow that is pressed.

3. The **function keys** located on the left side of the keyboard are used to activate specific commands that the computer system can perform. These commands are different, depending on the program that is being used. Many programs come with a plastic or cardboard

device called a **template**. The template fits over the function keys to remind you which key to press for each command.

4. The **numeric keypad** has keys for each of the ten arabic digits and is usually set up like a calculator keypad. On most keyboards this keypad also has more than one function. For example, the cursor control keys may be on the numeric keypad.

In addition to the above, electronic keyboards have a number of other keys that perform specialized functions, such as those that allow you to insert text within copy or delete text. You will learn to operate these by studying the manual that accompanies the product you are using.

The templates shown here are for two different word processing programs. You can see from the templates that the function keys operate differently from one program to the other.

Software and Processing

Software programs are written in special languages. Computer programmers need to know these languages to write software programs. They use basically two types of languages: low-level and high-level.

Low-level languages direct the computer through each step that it has to take in order to perform a particular operation. **Assembly** is an example of a low-level language.

High-level languages use symbols that represent a series of steps. They save the programmer from having to input each individual step. Most high-level languages use symbols that are similar to words with which people are familiar. Among the most common high-level languages are **BASIC, COBOL, FORTRAN,** and **Pascal.**

Today there is a new level of computer language called **user-level language.** Little formal training is needed to write programs in user-level languages because they allow the use of everyday terms rather than computer codes. An example of a user-level language is dBaseII.

The Processor. You cannot see the processor, or central processing unit, of a microcomputer because it is inside the computer. In Chapter 2 we discussed the microprocessor, or microchip, which enables the microcomputer to process as much information as the earlier mainframe computers. In addition to controlling the computer's processing instructions, the processor determines the amount of memory the computer has.

Computer memory is measured in **kilobytes** (usually abbreviated as **K**). A kilobyte represents roughly 1,000 alphabetic or numeric characters. A computer that can retain about 64,000 characters in its CPU at one time is said to have 64K memory. Just a few years ago, the most popular office microcomputer came with 64K as a standard feature. Since then manufacturers have developed models with greater memory capacity. Most office computers being installed today have memories of 128K, 256K, or more. The more memory a computer has, the more power it has to run complex programs.

If your computer system is a standalone, its CPU will be contained within the equipment at your workstation. The computer will be equipped with **disk drives**, which are devices into which disks are placed so that they may be "read" or "written on" by the system. Some computers have similar devices for use with tape cassettes.

If your equipment is part of a minicomputer or mainframe system, the workstation—consisting of a monitor and a keyboard—will be connected to the minicomputer or mainframe CPU. This type of workstation consisting of a monitor and a keyboard is also called a **terminal**.

Storage Media. The computer stores data in its temporary memory. When the computer has finished processing the data, it must be given instructions to store or "file" it permanently. The most commonly used storage medium for computer files is a magnetic disk or tape.

Disk Drives. The disk drive is a device that is either built into the computer terminal or contained in a small, separate, boxlike plastic case. This drive contains a small electromagnetic head that is capable of reading, writing, or erasing information on a disk. Standalone computers have one or two disk drives. A second disk drive can be added to any system that has only one.

Portable microcomputer with two floppy disk drives.

Microcomputer with one floppy and one hard disk.

This microcomputer may utilize two input devices: either a mouse or a keyboard.

If you need to work with large amounts of data, your computer may have a **hard disk** drive for storage. This kind of drive stores about ten times as much information as compared with a floppy disk.

Terminals may also be equipped with disk drives so that information can be transferred from the main system's storage unit to a floppy disk to be stored at the individual workstation. This procedure is known as **downloading** of data or information.

Floppy disk

Hard disk

Magnetic tape

Printer. The printer is the most commonly used output device. Because most offices still output the majority of documents in hard-copy format, printers are frequently found at the individual workstations. Printers are also a frequently shared resource in a computer system. Because different printers provide different levels of quality of output, businesses typically buy several types of printers, and workers share the most costly models.

Laser printer

Dot-matrix printer

Letter quality printer

Display Monitor. All computers have a display screen. Depending on its size, the display area will show anywhere from a few lines to a complete page of text. For example, a display monitor on a microcomputer might display 80 characters on each line and 24 lines, which is considered a half-page display.

Display screens may be color screens or monochrome screens. **Monochrome screens** are available in various two-color combinations. (They are called "monochrome"

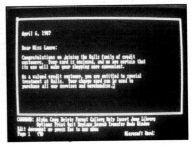

The three most common color combinations for monochrome screens are green/black, amber/black, and white/black.

because all the characters appear on the screen in only one color against the background screen color, which is usually black.) Ergonomists have spent a lot of time studying color combinations to determine which colors are best for the characters and background on the screen. Common color combinations are green on black, amber on black, and white on black.

Communication Devices. Computer systems can be connected to each other by special wires and cables so that they can communicate. When computer systems are connected by wires for communication within the same office or between offices in the same building, they are said to form a local area network (or LAN). Through telecommunications, communication can take place between computers in different buildings, even those separated by great distances.

Even if they are not hooked up with special wires and cables, computer systems can communicate with each other over regular telephone lines. To do this, the systems need a device called a **modem**. A modem is a device that can be connected to a computer and connected to a telephone system. You can then telecommunicate. You will learn more about this when you study Part II of this text.

A modem.

OMPUTER SOFTWARE

Computers are relatively useless pieces of machinery without software. Without software a computer is like a camera without film or a car without an engine.

Software can be divided into three distinct categories: programming software, operating systems software, and applications software.

ROGRAMMING SOFTWARE

Programming software consists of the instructions of programs that are implanted in the circuits of the CPU.

These instructions make the computer operate. The ordinary user does not interact with this software.

PERATING SYSTEMS SOFTWARE

Operating systems software has two major functions: to operate the computer equipment and to translate programs into machine-readable instructions. You can think of an operating system as the set of instructions that enables your computer to perform certain basic maintenance functions. These functions include loading and running a program, copying a file or disk, or checking the files on a disk. Think of the operating system as playing a similar role to your car key when used to start the car. This software does most of its work behind the scenes. With some computers, especially mainframes, office workers may not even be aware of the systems software. It performs such jobs as assigning places in memory and controlling input and output.

Computers with different operating systems are said to be **incompatible**. This is why software that runs on one computer might not necessarily run on another.

The operating system for microcomputers is provided on a disk and is referred to as the **disk operating system** or **DOS**. The DOS disk must be placed in the computer disk drive when the machine is turned on or the computer will not operate. This procedure is called **installation**. When you purchase a software program to run on your computer, you will have to install DOS on the disk or install it in the computer each time you want to run the program. The computer manufacturer's manual will give you specific instructions on how this is done.

APPLICATIONS SOFTWARE

Applications software consists of the programs that instruct computers to execute specific tasks. As an office worker processing data into business documents, you may use many applications programs or only a few, depending on your job. For example, an administrative assistant in a large law firm might use word processing software to produce memos, communications software to send memos to branch offices, and a spreadsheet program to keep track of expenses. In a business's order fulfillment department, an office worker might use only two

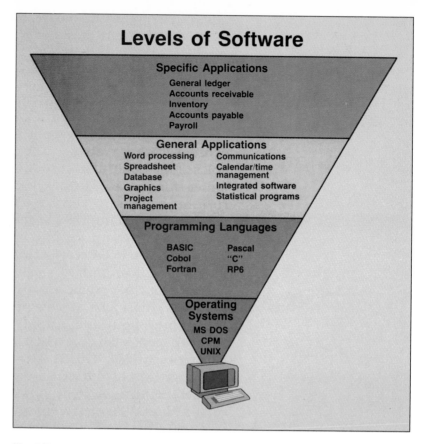

Levels of Software

Specific Applications
General ledger
Accounts receivable
Inventory
Accounts payable
Payroll

General Applications
Word processing   Communications
Spreadsheet   Calendar/time
Database   management
Graphics   Integrated software
Project   Statistical programs
management

Programming Languages
BASIC   Pascal
Cobol   "C"
Fortran   RP6

Operating Systems
MS DOS
CPM
UNIX

Fig. 4-5

applications programs: one to store information in and retrieve information from the company's database and one for sending electronic messages.

There are thousands of specialized applications programs on the market for use in offices today. The most commonly used applications programs are for word processing, spreadsheets, database management, graphics, and communications. These programs are called **horizontal applications software** because they can be applied to general office functions and are used in almost all types of businesses. In addition, there are **vertical applications software** programs which are specialized designs for medical and legal office uses, accounting and data processing applications, and computer-aided drafting and design.

Applications programs are designed with the purpose of the user in mind. For this reason they are typically judged on the basis of whether or not they are "user-friendly." If users can learn to operate a program within a short period of time and with a minimum amount of instruction, it is said to be **user-friendly**.

Applications programs use menus and commands to carry out their functions. A **menu** is a list of operations that can be performed with an applications program. These operations are usually listed as options on a separate screen at the beginning of the program or at the top or bottom of the screen containing the data.

For example, a word processing applications menu might include such options as Edit, Save, Print, and Delete. Each of these selections may have a submenu. Menu selections are usually made by pressing a letter, a number, or a combination of keys.

In addition to using menus, applications programs use many **commands** to carry out their functions. The software manual explains which keys operate specific commands. These commands are not always displayed on the screen while the program is operating, so it is necessary to memorize them in order to operate the program efficiently.

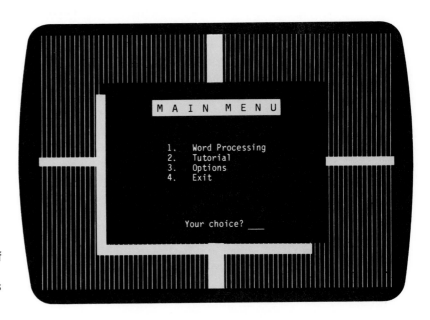

Fig. 4-6 Typically, software menus are set up like a table of contents. The *main menu* lets you select from the major parts of the program.

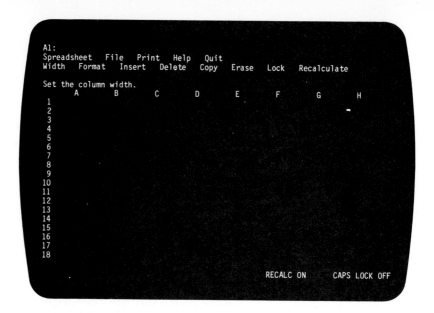

```
A1:
Spreadsheet   File   Print   Help   Quit
Width   Format   Insert   Delete   Copy   Erase   Lock   Recalculate

Set the column width.
        A       B       C       D       E       F       G       H
  1
  2                                                                  -
  3
  4
  5
  6
  7
  8
  9
 10
 11
 12
 13
 14
 15
 16
 17
 18
                                        RECALC ON      CAPS LOCK OFF
```

Fig. 4-7 Each main part has a
submenu from which to select.

/NTEGRATED APPLICATIONS PROGRAMS

In recent years software producers have been concentrating on the development of **integrated applications programs**, or a package of programs for several applications that are designed to work together. The purpose of integration is to bring the major business computing applications together. A typical integrated software product includes spreadsheet, database management, graphics, and word processing programs in a single package. Many products also include a communications program. With an integrated package, you can quickly switch from one application to another when the need arises. You can also move data from one application to another.

All the programs in an integrated software package use similar menus and commands, enabling you to switch from one application to another without having to remember an entirely different set of procedures for operating the software.

As you study the chapters in Part II of this book, you will examine in greater depth the five basic business software applications and learn how you will use them on the job.

S *UMMARY*

- In the business office, computers were first used for data processing and then, later on, for word processing.

- Today, instead of being handled as separate functions, data processing and word processing applications can be combined in integrated information processing systems.

- All computers have the same physical components, called "hardware."

- The term *software* is the name for the programs, or instructions, that make computer hardware work.

- Microcomputers are generally self-contained and for this reason are called "standalones."

- A typical microcomputer workstation consists of a CPU, a keyboard, a display screen, one or more disk drives, and a printer—all at one location.

- The CPU manages the computer's internal processing instructions, as well as the amount of memory the computer has.

- Computer memory is measured in kilobytes (K); 1K equals approximately 1,000 characters.

- The most commonly used storage medium for computer files is a magnetic disk or tape.

- Computer systems can be connected to each other through local area networks, through telecommunications, or by means of a modem.

- There are two main types of computer languages: low-level and high-level.

- Computer software can be divided into three types: programming software, operating systems software, and applications software.

- Recent integrated applications programs are combining the major business computing applications in a single package.

integrated information
  processing system
program
hardware
software
standalone
alphanumeric keypad
cursor control keypad
function key
template
numeric keypad
kilobyte (K)
disk drive
terminal
low-level language
Assembly
high-level language
BASIC
COBOL
FORTRAN
Pascal
user-level language

hard disk
downloading
monochrome screen
modem
programming software
operating systems
  software
incompatible
disk operating system
  (DOS)
installation
applications software
horizontal applications
  software
vertical applications
  software
user-friendly
menu
command
integrated applications
  programs

1. Contrast data processing and word processing.

2. Give a brief explanation of integrated information processing systems.

3. What are some of the advantages of integrated information processing at the electronic workstation?

4. Explain the difference between hardware and software.

5. What are the standard devices in a typical electronic workstation?

6. What is the most commonly used storage medium for computer files?

7. How does a modem assist in electronic communications?

8. Describe the three chief categories of software.

9. Describe the two basic items used by applications software to carry out their functions.

10. Explain what is meant by the term *integrated applications programs*.

S KILLBUILDING ACTIVITIES

1. Look through business magazines that deal with office design. From this activity, design a typical office workstation that you might be using when you begin your first job. Write a brief report accompanying the design to explain the design.

2. Select two stores that sell two different kinds of computers. Obtain information on the two kinds of computers describing things that both kinds of computers have in common as well as things that both kinds of computers do not have in common. Share this information with your classmates.

3. Investigate the possibility of installing a modem either at home or at school. What important points must you keep in mind? Write a report giving this information.

4. Visit a store that sells a wide variety of software. Select a software package that you might be interested in purchasing for personal use. What factors should you consider before purchasing? Write a report giving this information.

5. Prepare a demonstration to a person who is unfamiliar with computers. Include information you have studied in Chapter 4.

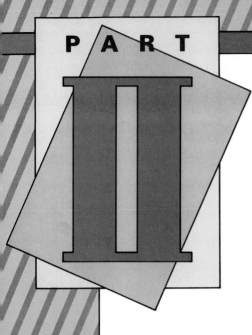

PART II

INFORMATION PROCESSING PROCEDURES

*I*nformation is valuable, but only according to how we use it. Business offices exist to use information for the benefit of the business. The more effectively they process information, the more effective their business is.

Part 2 shows how a modern office gathers, processes, and distributes information. In the electronic office sophisticated machines facilitate the information cycle. You will learn about how that cycle operates in both the traditional and the electronic office.

Regardless of how extensively we use computers, the starting point of the information cycle is always a person. And the ending point is also a person. A person's actions result in the creation of data. A person's use of the data justifies gathering and distributing it. So the human factor remains important. For that reason Part 2 covers such basic human interactions as speaking, listening, and writing.

DEVELOPING COMMUNICATION SKILLS

Communication is the basis of all human interaction. We communicate to others through both the spoken and the unspoken word. The unspoken word may be communicated by nodding your head, extending your hand, or looking directly into the eyes of the person you are communicating with. The spoken word requires that you select the proper words to convey your message. Words control a large part of our lives, for words spoken in certain combinations are what makes each of us unique in communicating. Being able to communicate your thoughts to convey messages and to have them understood is a skill that you can develop.

In the business world, a person who cannot communicate effectively using both the spoken and the written word will find it difficult to succeed. Communication is a necessary "tool of the trade." In this chapter we look at the basic communication skills—speaking, listening, writing, and reading—and see how they are used in business. We also will examine the use of nonverbal communication, an important aspect of the communication process. Learning how to communicate effectively has always been one of a business person's biggest challenges. In today's technological business world, the area of communication has become even more complex and even more important than in the past.

As a result of studying this chapter, you will be able to:
- Describe the communication process.

- Understand the difference between verbal and nonverbal communication.
- Understand the steps required to prepare an oral or written message.
- Understand the skills needed for effective oral and written communications in business.
- Understand how communication skills are used in different types of business situations.

HE COMMUNICATION PROCESS

Communication is a two-way process in which information is exchanged. This exchange may take place between an individual and a group or between an individual and a machine. The process of communicating in the business world is referred to as **business communication**. Developing the art of effective business communication is an important skill for success on the job.

Wherever you work, there will be a standard way of communicating certain things. For example, if you answer the telephone, you may be required to answer by saying the name of the company or the department in which you work. If you prepare a written communication, such as a letter or a memo, that written communication must follow an established format. Every business will have specific procedures and guidelines for these and other types of situations and tasks.

All communication requires a sender, a receiver, and a message. The **sender** is the person who creates and sends the **message**, or information. The **receiver** is the person who receives and interprets the message. In order for information to be exchanged, it is necessary for the receiver to respond. The terms given to this process of speaking, writing, listening, and responding are **encoding** and **decoding**.

Encoding occurs when the sender constructs the message to be sent. The sender may choose the verbal form, using written or spoken words to communicate, or the nonverbal form, using symbols, pictures, or body gestures. Nonverbal communication that depends on behavior such as gestures, facial expressions, and posture is called **body language**. Body language is a very important part of the communication process.

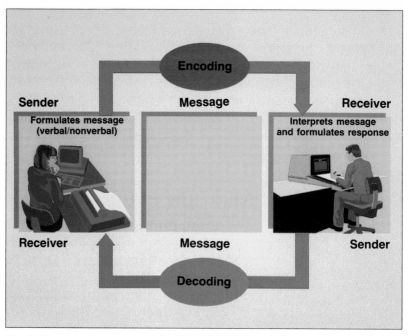

Fig. 5-1 People communicate by encoding and decoding messages. The sender encodes the message; the receiver decodes it.

Once the message is encoded, it is sent from the sender to the receiver for decoding, or interpretation. Interpretation involves all the ideas, facts, attitudes, emotions, experiences, and memories in the receiver's mind. They cause the receiver to interpret the message in a particular way. The decoding process results in a response that begins the sender-message-receiver cycle again.

In order to communicate effectively, you have to think clearly, speak and write well, and demonstrate good interpersonal skills. You must be understood in the business office, and good communication skills make that possible.

Miscommunication occurs when something goes wrong between the sender and the receiver. The sender may send a message that is confusing or that contains inaccurate information, or the receiver may not hear or understand the message correctly. With the amount of information being communicated, it is highly likely that on occasion a message will be miscommunicated. Miscommunication in the business world can cause serious errors that result in lower productivity and an increased business expense.

Try these techniques for improving message communication and preventing miscommunication:

- *Concentrate.* It can be difficult to read, listen, and respond accurately when there is a lot of noise or when you are thinking about something else. Work hard to concentrate on one thing at a time. Try to tune out distractions.
- *Be aware of your own mental blocks.* All people have certain "mental blocks" that prevent them from communicating effectively. For example, some individuals might be uncomfortable about using a computer because they are afraid that they will not be able to understand how to operate such a complex piece of equipment. This fear may actually interfere with their ability to concentrate on listening to the instructions being given, and the result will be the very outcome that they are afraid of. Telling yourself that you can overcome a mental block as well as really concentrating to do so will help eliminate this problem.
- *Be aware of the other person's mental blocks.* You may discover that your supervisor does not respond with sympathy when you say that you "can't" do something. To many people the words *I can't* really mean *you haven't tried.* You might find that using words such as *I need help* results in a warmer, more positive response.

Trying to interpret too many signals at once leads to miscommunication.

If you make a practice of paying attention to other people's responses to the words you use and the way you use them, you will find it a good way of detecting the mental blocks of others.

- *Ask for and give feedback.* Giving **feedback** to another person means responding in a way that lets the person know that you have received the message and that you understand the message. Feedback can be as simple as repeating the message you have just heard in order to confirm that you understood it. When you are on the job, you should make sure that you get feedback from your supervisor so that you know how well you are performing a particular assignment and where improvements are needed.

 REPARING MESSAGES FOR COMMUNICATION

Preparing messages to be communicated to one person or a group of people requires careful planning. Follow these steps in preparing a message to be communicated:

1. Develop your idea.

2. Identify your audience.

3. Gather the necessary information.

4. Process the information.

5. Select the method of communication.

Develop Your Idea. First, have a clear idea of what you want to say. Do you want to explain a new office procedure? What points will you need to cover? What is the most logical order in which to cover the points? How much detail do you want to devote to the explanation of each step in the office procedure that is being discussed?

Identify Your Audience. Next, consider the audience that will be receiving the information. Will it be your supervisor, your coworkers, or people under your supervision?

Ask yourself these questions:

1. Who needs this information?

2. What do they already know about this matter?

3. What will be the best way to send this message?

4. Will I need a response from the receivers of this information?

Gather the Necessary Information. You want to make sure that the information you present is accurate. Examples of ways to gather the necessary information are reading information on file, using reference materials, and consulting with individuals whose knowledge you respect and value.

Process the Information. Processing the information means organizing the information in a way that allows your reader or listener to understand it. One of the best ways to organize information is to develop an outline. Outlines are helpful whether you plan to speak or write your message. Writers always make sure that they have answered the five Ws: Who? What? When? Where? and Why? Another question that might have to be answered

Practicing good communications by preparing messages accurately is a very important skill in the electronic office.

Hands-on practice can be the best way to show a coworker how to operate a new piece of equipment. Choosing the right method for communication information is an important office skill.

in business is, How? These are five guidelines for anyone to use in preparing an outline. Ask yourself these questions as you begin to organize your information.

Select the Method of Communication. Certain kinds of information require certain methods of communication. It would be inappropriate to write a memo and send it through interoffice mail when a quick phone call would serve the purpose. On the other hand, it would be difficult to communicate a detailed statistical report by telephone. Written communication would be more appropriate for this type of information.

In an office with limited electronic communications equipment, you would most likely communicate face-to-face, over the telephone, or through written messages such as letters or memos. In a fully developed electronic office, you will have computers and other electronic equipment to help you send messages. Because individuals understand information in different ways, it is a good idea for message senders to use as many methods of communication as they may need to get the job done. For example, conducting a hands-on demonstration or using a procedures manual with illustrations can be very helpful in teaching people to use equipment.

DEVELOPING COMMUNICATION SKILLS

ORAL COMMUNICATION

Oral communication is the most important human relations skill. What you say to visitors in the office or what you say to your coworkers creates impressions and attitudes that are difficult to change. The saying "We never get a second chance to make a good first impression" is very true.

One major factor affecting the impression you make in the business world is your use of language. Notice the way you speak at home and among your friends. Would this same manner of speaking be understood and accepted by people in the business world? For example, at home or at school, when you greet your friends or are introduced to someone, it is perfectly acceptable to say "Hi." In a business setting, this type of greeting would be inappropriate, especially if you were speaking to someone outside the company or to someone at a higher level in the company. The appropriate greeting in this situation would be "How do you do?" While this is a very common greeting in the business environment, it may sound strange and you may feel very uncomfortable when you hear yourself say it, especially if you are not accustomed to speaking this way. Speaking standard business English will make your message clearer to others and will communicate the message much more quickly and effectively.

Speaking. Oral communication occurs in both formal and informal situations. Practice these guidelines for preparing and sending messages orally in formal and informal situations:

- *Be sure that your message is worthwhile.* In the business office, time is money. Remember, the time someone spends listening to you is valuable. Be sure that what you say is appropriate for the occasion, is direct and clearly stated, and will be of value to the listener.
- *Be sensitive to your audience.* From the moment you begin speaking, be aware of those listening to you. Be sure your audience can hear you. Notice their facial expressions and other body language signals. Adjust your speaking to meet their needs. If you feel that it is

necessary to obtain feedback from your audience for any reason, stop and do so. For example, it is often necessary to ask, "Can everyone hear me?"

- *Develop voice control and quality.* Consider the size of your audience, and speak so that you can be heard. The tone of your voice should be well modulated. Maintain audience interest by speaking expressively and emphasizing appropriate words. Rehearse a presentation to be made to a group of people. Practice your presentation under conditions that are as realistic as possible. If you can, tape your voice and listen to its control and quality.
- *Use correct English.* There is no substitute for good grammar and an appropriate vocabulary for the situation at hand. Using correct English creates an impression of authority and professionalism. Be very much aware of your sentence structure, including correct subject-verb agreement, parts of speech, mood, and tense. Misuse of grammar can change the entire meaning of a sentence and result in a serious miscommunication. Words that are mispronounced will confuse your listener and seriously affect your credibility. Be especially careful with proper names. Learning to pronounce a person's name correctly demonstrates that you have taken a personal interest in that person.
- *Be sensitive to timing.* Choose a time to speak that is not hectic or stressful to the listener. Be aware of the

Presenting the appropriate image is a key to success in any communication situation.

amount of time allotted to the particular speaking situation. If necessary, save questions for a time when you have the listener's full attention. If you are using the telephone to communicate, think of the person at the other end of the line as your audience. Avoid interrupting unless you do it with extreme tact.

- *Present and maintain a good appearance.* Dressing appropriately will make you feel confident when you speak. Dressing appropriately will also demonstrate your professionalism. You can look like an office superstar in your best professional attire and spoil that image by using poor grammar or speaking in some other unprofessional manner.

Study the illustration below listing several common formal and informal situations encountered by office workers.

Study the facial expressions indicating understanding.

Listening. Listening involves hearing something with thoughtful attention and understanding what you have heard. While we may hear words spoken, we quite frequently do not listen as well as we could or should. Keep in mind the following techniques that will help improve your listening skills:

- *Listen actively.* Concentrate on what the speaker is saying. Draw up a mental summary as each major thought is presented.

- *Interact with the speaker.* Use appropriate body language; for example, nod or shake your head and make appropriate comments as needed to give the speaker feedback.
- *Take notes.* Write down important notes for later reference. Be careful not to take too many notes. Write only the main ideas. If you know shorthand, practice using it. Doing so will force you to listen better.
- *Sit in a comfortable position.* Sit where you can hear and see the speaker. Try to avoid distractions such as glaring lights or noises.
- *Take time to review the message.* Taking time to review the message with the speaker can often prevent a time-consuming phone call or a costly error.
- *Complete follow-up work right away.* Except for your notes, your only record of the message is in your head. Do any follow-up work immediately, before you forget what you heard.

ERSON-TO-PERSON COMMUNICATION

Most person-to-person communication in the business office is informal. The kinds of person-to-person situations you are most likely to deal with include greeting visitors, answering the telephone, responding to questions and requests for information, and giving and receiving instructions.

If you will be greeting visitors, try to become familiar with their names, their titles, and the organizations or companies they represent. Be aware of frequent office visitors. Make coworkers aware of this information so that they are also prepared to greet and help visitors. Unless you are asked to do otherwise, you should always use a visitor's last name and his or her title—Mr., Mrs., Dr., and so on.

Always take the time to acknowledge visitors or callers, even if you are on the telephone. A simple smile and a nod to visitors will put them at ease and let them know that you have communicated the fact that they are there.

Know how to shake hands and formally introduce people. Offer a visitor refreshments if they are available. Be aware of special needs of disabled visitors. These are all common courtesies that convey your sense of professionalism.

As an office worker you can expect to greet many visitors and clients. Often these situations require that you make introductions.

On occasion you may have to deal with an angry or upset visitor. When you have to communicate with an angry or upset visitor, try first to identify the visitor and find out the purpose of the visit. Be as tactful as possible. Tact is the ability to avoid offending or embarrassing people.

Always try to remain objective in any situation where you may encounter an angry or upset person. Do not take the person's behavior personally. Be courteous and calm while trying to help the person handle the situation. Once you feel that you have all the facts of the situation, it may be necessary for you to ask your supervisor or another person to assist you in solving the problem.

There are a number of person-to-person exchanges that are more formal in nature. For example, if you were a doctor's medical assistant, you might be asked to talk with a patient to obtain specific information before the patient actually meets with the doctor. This type of oral communication is formal in nature because of the type of situation and the fact that you are meeting the person for the first time and asking for personal information. You want to come across as being positive, supportive, and respectful of the patient while still obtaining the necessary information.

Before beginning a formal exchange, make sure that you know the person's name and the purpose of the meeting. Be prepared with any questions you want to ask. Try to respond clearly and concisely to questions that the person asks you. When you are near the end of the meeting, summarize the main points. Give feedback, if appropriate, to let the person know how you felt about the discussion. For example, a good way to end a formal discussion is by saying, "It was a pleasure talking with you."

After the meeting is over, think back over the conversation, and make notes concerning the things that you need to remember to follow up on.

As was mentioned earlier, many of your person-to-person exchanges will be by telephone. You may have to screen telephone calls for your supervisor and others. You may also have to make arrangements for meetings over the telephone. It is extremely important that you find ways to communicate effectively over the telephone, because your voice is your only means of contact with the other person. Your voice must convey your warmth, your sincerity, and your mood. Write notes to yourself, and attach them to your telephone as reminders to be aware of these qualities if you are having a problem in this area. Try to think of a phone call as a speech in which you must be prepared to convey certain messages and ideas. Write down the items that you want to cover when communicating over the telephone to avoid wasting time and miscommunicating. This will keep you on track and help you act positively in this type of person-to-person communication.

Here are some typical formal communication situations in which office workers most often find themselves:
- Presenting information or a report to a supervisor or colleague.
- Having a job interview.
- Conducting a training program.
- Making a sale to a customer.
- Participating in staff meetings.
- Participating in seminars or workshops.

Some typical settings in which information is communicated are:
- Answering the telephone.
- Greeting visitors or customers.
- Receiving instructions from your supervisor.

- Handling inquiries from colleagues or subordinates in your own department or in other departments.
- Training a new staff member.

Person-to-Group Communication. When one person is speaking to a group of people, the process is known as **person-to-group communication**. Examples of person-to-group communication are staff meetings, seminars, and any other kinds of situations where you are asked to speak to a group or participate in a group discussion. Meetings such as these usually involve the exchange of large amounts of information. Keep these guidelines in mind for successful person-to-group communication:

- *Be prepared.* Always be prepared by being very familiar with the material to be covered. Do your homework for the meeting thoroughly. Prepare an agenda to give to your audience. An **agenda** is a sheet containing a list or a plan of the items to be covered in the presentation. With an agenda, your audience will easily be guided through the presentation and will be more receptive to

It is easy to see that this person is communicating her message to her audience.

what is coming. The members of your audience will be able to develop their questions prior to the meeting, on the basis of the agenda they receive. Occasionally you can make use of materials such as charts, graphs, diagrams, and other drawings. These types of visual aids can help clarify your message and make it more interesting for your audience. Always be looking for additional techniques that demonstrate complete preparation for any presentation you make.

- *Be sure that your audience is comfortable.* Is the room large enough? Are there enough chairs appropriately arranged for positive interaction? Can everyone see you and hear your presentation? Is all the necessary equipment placed in the proper arrangement? All of these factors contribute greatly to making the audience more receptive to your presentation. When an audience is not comfortable, it will be much more difficult for you to communicate your presentation in a positive manner.
- *Be sure to summarize and ask for questions.* At the end of your presentation, summarize the main points. If you use the words *in summary* when you are at that point in your presentation, your audience will be aware that your presentation is nearly over, and the members will be ready to ask their questions. Always try to allow some time for questions. This is often one of the best ways to get information communicated on the basis of the needs of your audience and as a result of your pre-

As the cost of using electronic technology decreases, more and more businesses will use video teleconferences to conduct meetings.

sentation. Questions also allow you to evaluate and further clarify certain points you have made in your presentation.

Teleconferences. **Teleconferencing** is a form of electronic communication that allows you to conduct a presentation or group discussion using a television, a video, or any other electronic communications device that can transmit pictures. It is also possible that you may be part of a teleconference without a video. This will require additional preparation, similar to the steps previously discussed for effective telephone conversations. In all cases be sure that you are thoroughly familiar with the equipment being used. Rehearse carefully all details of the communication process before beginning. Incorporating all the previous points of oral communication will aid you greatly in refining skills used in teleconferencing.

RITTEN COMMUNICATIONS

When you communicate in writing, usually you have time to think about what you will say and how you will say it. The amount of time you have to prepare a written communication from the moment you receive the task until the task is completed is known as **turnaround time**. Offices can vary greatly in terms of required turnaround time, most of which is determined by individual office needs. Having electronic equipment to help you meet deadlines and shorten turnaround time certainly can improve office productivity.

When you communicate in writing, you always have a permanent record of the information that was exchanged. If there is a question concerning the information, the written communication is readily available, and you can refer to it to answer the question.

Because written communications are permanent, they should always reflect your best efforts. Keep in mind that the written communications you prepare represent not only your skills but also the company's work. Your reputation and your company's reputation go hand in hand in the total written communication process.

Writing is a skill that can be learned, practiced, and improved with concentrated effort. Many of the same techniques discussed for improving oral communication can be used to improve written communication. Preparation is the most important technique for writing. Be comfortable, have the right tools or instruments available, and be sure your message fits the situation you are writing about.

Writing Skills. There are also general techniques that can be applied specifically to improving writing skills. Keep these techniques in mind at all times:

- *Be yourself.* Use words that fit your personality and your style. Do not use words that you are unfamiliar with or words that are too long. Avoid long sentences. Long sentences will confuse the reader and often cause miscommunication.
- *Know your reader.* Whenever you are writing, you should have an idea of who will be reading your message. This will allow you to aim your message in the right direction. The same holds true if more than one person will be reading your message.
- *Demonstrate empathy.* Empathy is the ability to understand and feel what others feel. Put yourself in the reader's position as you compose messages. Putting yourself in the reader's position helps you to communicate your message in a positive and meaningful manner.
- *Be courteous.* Be especially careful to always be respectful in your written communications. A message written quickly and without much thought can often be interpreted incorrectly. Messages communicated electronically often are not written as courteously as they might be because they are too brief.
- *Keep to the point.* Keep your messages to the point being communicated without being rude. Rambling on and on wastes valuable reading time and causes confusion.
- *Be results-oriented.* Know what you want your message to achieve, and write the message accordingly. Although you must be courteous in both instances, you might adopt one tone when writing to a valued client about a missed payment and another tone when writing to a problem client who misses payments.
- *Organize your message.* Organize the points you need to cover by listing them or preparing an outline if the

Editing changes can be made on hard copy.

message will be longer than a few sentences. Organization is an important key to effective written communications.

- *Be clear and concise.* Give the reader the facts of the message in clear, understandable words that will convey the message efficiently. For example, if you need 25 desks in a room, state that you will need 25 desks, not that you will need "*around* 25 desks."

- *Be complete.* Include all necessary information. Have you included who? where? when? what? and why? All messages will require answers to each of these questions, so using these questions as a guide will help you check your message to ensure that nothing has been left out.

- *Be accurate.* Always cross-check and verify your data. Use a dictionary or other reference materials to make sure that words are spelled correctly and used in a meaningful manner.

- *Avoid jargon.* **Jargon** is a specialized technical language; usually, it is not used in everyday communication. In this book we have referred to *hard copy* and *soft copy.* These terms represent the jargon of the electronic office.

- *Proofread.* Proofreading is one of the most important skills you must develop. If you do not proofread your written messages carefully before you send them, you waste the effort you put into improving your writing. You also waste the advantage of having time to prepare that writing gives you over speaking.

An example of careful proofreading.

Usage Skills. The most important usage skills are knowing grammar, understanding punctuation rules, and spelling correctly, as well as having a good vocabulary. Keep the necessary reference materials readily available. Examples of reference materials that are used frequently are a dictionary; a reference manual such as *The Gregg Reference Manual, Sixth Edition*; and a thesaurus. A **thesaurus** is a book that lists synonyms, or words that can be used for other words.

Listed below are principles of good usage that you should always be aware of when preparing a written message. Some of these principles will reinforce what has already been discussed.

- *Be consistent.* Once you decide on the format for your message, stick with it throughout. In writing, **format** means the general appearance of your message. If you decide to indent the first line of each paragraph, do so throughout.

- *Use the active voice.* You can write in either the active voice or the passive voice. Experts recommend using the active voice as much as possible in writing. The active voice is direct and to the point. *We value your interest* is better than *Your interest is valued.* The former is the active voice, and the latter is the passive voice.

- *Be concise.* Some people believe that their writing appears more formal when they use long sentences and many words. This is not true. Inserting useless words in written communications causes confusion. For example, the phrase *the general consensus of opinion* is wordy and also redundant. *Consensus* means *collective opinion* and gains nothing from the modifier *general.* Keep an eye out for useless words when you write. Edit them from your written message before you send it.

- *Do not overexplain.* Some writers believe that adding a lot of extra details will help make the subject clearer to the reader. Too much detail causes confusion.

- *Remember the second comma.* Parenthetical expressions should be set off with commas. If the parenthetical expression is in the middle of the sentence, be sure to insert the second comma. This rule also applies to the year in a date and to the state in an address when they are contained in a sentence—for example, "On June 25, 19——, we received your request for information. We sent the information to you at your Teaticket, Massachusetts, address."

- *Use positive expressions.* Be positive and firm in your written messages. For example, instead of writing, "We do not believe we will be able to attend the special session for new staff personnel on August 4," write, "We will not be able to attend the special session for new staff personnel on August 4."

- *Use the first or the third person.* Using the first or third person is related to using the active or passive voice. Many writers of business messages begin sentences with the word *it,* as in "It has been found that . . . ." This is a weak way to state something, and you should avoid it when possible. Instead, try to be more direct and say, "We have found that . . . ."

Reference materials that are used frequently.

Reading Skills. Knowing how to read critically and interpret written communications is an important aspect of developing good communication skills. Many of the skills applied to reading are the same skills applied to listening.

Keep these techniques in mind and practice them when you are reading:

- *Be comfortable.* Sit in a comfortable chair, and be sure it is adjusted in a comfortable position. If your back hurts or your leg is falling asleep, your mind will be on your physical discomfort rather than on what you are reading. If you are sitting at a desk, be sure the desk is also comfortable.

- *Have adequate lighting.* All companies are required by law to provide adequate and safe working conditions. Lighting falls into this category. One problem with reading in the electronic office is glare on display screens. The position of a display screen should be adjusted to avoid glare. If glare is still a problem, you can put an antiglare screen over the display screen.

- *Have a noise-free environment.* Minimize noise in your office. Take whatever steps are necessary to guarantee that your work area will be relatively noise-free.

Reading written communications in a pleasant environment helps produce a positive result.

- *Keep eyeglasses clean.* If you wear glasses to read and write, make sure that they are always clean. Dirty glasses will contribute greatly to increased eyestrain.
- *Highlight important points.* As you read letters, memos, and reports, highlight important points with a colored marker or underline the important points so that you can see them quickly.

If your job involves reading many long reports or books, learn to skim the material by speed-reading. Speed-reading can be learned through a speed-reading course. Catching the main points quickly and then returning to those in question for in-depth reading can save you much time in reading written communications in the office.

SUMMARY

- Communication is the basis of all interaction. Communicating effectively is a skill that can be developed and used to achieve success in the business world.

- Communication is a two-way process. In the business world, this process is called business communication.

- Businesses have standard procedures for handling both oral and written communications.

- The basic parts of any communication are the sender, the receiver, and the message.

- The process of communication is known as encoding and decoding.

- Nonverbal communication is called body language.

- Miscommunication can cause serious problems in business situations.

- The five basic steps in preparing a message for communication are: (1) develop your idea, (2) identify your audience, (3) gather the necessary information, (4) process the information, and (5) select the method of communication.

- Oral communication is the most important human relations skill. It will have the greatest impact on the impression you make on others.

- Listening means hearing with thoughtful attention and understanding what you have heard.

- Most person-to-person communication in the business office is informal. Informal situations include answering the telephone, responding to questions and requests, greeting visitors, and giving and receiving instructions.

- Formal person-to-person exchanges include interviews, meetings, and telephone calls.

- Person-to-group communication is done in meetings, seminars, and any other kinds of situations where you are a part of a group.

- Written communications are very important because they represent not only you but also your company.

- Proper usage skills and the ability to read critically and interpret will help you prepare good written communications.

business communication   feedback
sender   person-to-group
message   communication
receiver   agenda
encoding   teleconferencing
decoding   turnaround time
body language   jargon
miscommunication   thesaurus
               format

REVIEW QUESTIONS

1. Explain the three basic components of any communication.

2. What is the meaning of *encoding* and *decoding* in the communication process?

3. Define the term *body language*.

4. Name and describe four techniques for avoiding miscommunication.

5. Discuss the five basic steps for preparing a message.

6. Why is oral communication so important to human relations?

7. Name the basic guidelines for effective oral communication. Are they all of equal importance? Why or why not?

8. What are the basic techniques for good listening?

9. Give three examples of business situations where person-to-person communication would be considered informal. Name three situations where formal communication would be used.

10. Explain the importance of written communications in the office.

1. You are composing a report describing a visit you have made to an office. You are searching for synonyms for the following words: people, steps, setup, style of print, and designs. Use a thesaurus to find synonyms. Compose a sentence illustrating each synonym you use.

2. Develop a poster collage showing an example of positive body language on one side of the poster and an example of negative body language on the reverse side. Present this information to your classmates. What effect does body language have in the business world?

3. List the qualities you feel are essential to effective oral communications. From these qualities, compose a checklist that can be used by your classmates when preparing to speak orally. Check with your teacher for additional specific directions on this project. Use the checklist the next time an oral presentation is made in your class. Evaluate its effectiveness at the end of the presentation.

4. You are in charge of introducing a speaker. You have information on the speaker written down, but you do not want to read word for word. What steps could you be sure to use in making a positive introduction?

6 CREATING INFORMATION FOR INPUT

*T*oday it is possible to communicate information electronically or in printed form. Although electronic communication is becoming more widely used, printed copy is still used most often.

Information in a hard copy format is needed for several reasons. It is easier to read, especially if the information is complex. Reading long documents from a computer screen can be tedious and a strain on the eyes.

Whatever form of input is used to communicate, excellent written communications skills are needed.

Every written communication that you prepare is a reflection of you and your organization. Knowing which format to use as well as when and how to write the communication will make you a very desirable office worker.

After studying this chapter, you will be able to:

- Prepare interoffice memos.
- Prepare business letters for personal and professional use.
- Develop an awareness of the standard types of letters that businesses use and be able to compose them.
- Prepare formal and informal reports for personal and professional use.

ORMS OF WRITTEN COMMUNICATION

The three major forms of written communication used in offices today are interoffice memorandums, letters, and reports.

Interoffice memorandums are formal or informal written communications for circulation within the company, between and among individuals.

Letters are formal or personal written messages directed to a person within the company or a person, group, or organization outside the company.

Reports are formal written messages communicating information in detail. These may be directed to people both inside and outside the company.

NTEROFFICE MEMORANDUMS

Interoffice memorandums are used for communications among employees within the same organization, whether or not they are in the same building. Interoffice memorandums are usually referred to simply as **memos**.

Memos have many uses in the office: they are used to transmit information or materials; to make announcements, requests, and recommendations; and to provide a record of agreements and decisions that are made. While many interoffice communications could be handled by telephone or in person, sending memos helps prevent misunderstandings and misinterpretations. This is particularly important in a large organization where information must be exchanged among larger numbers of people. By using memos to avoid misunderstandings, employees are actually contributing to greater efficiency and productivity in the organization.

Many businesses provide printed memo forms in a standard, easy-to-use format, with slight variations depending on the individual business. Memos may also be formatted on plain paper if printed forms are not available. In either case simplicity of use makes the memos a popular form of communication within the company.

The interoffice memorandum has three major parts: the heading, the body, and the closing.

The *heading* contains the company's name or logo (identifying symbol), the title *Interoffice Memorandum*, and the guide words *To*, *From*, *Subject*, and *Date*. If guide words are not printed on the form, they must be formatted and keyed on plain paper.

The *body* contains the message.

The *closing* contains the sender's signature or initials. Since the sender's full name is keyed at the top after the guide word *From*, it is rarely keyed again at the bottom. The person preparing the interoffice memorandum should key his or her reference initials at the lower left.

Electronic messages may follow a similar format. Once completed, the interoffice memo can be stored electronically for easy distribution and retrieval. If electronic transmission is not available, hard copies will have to be prepared for distribution. If interoffice memos are not communicated electronically, special interoffice mail envelopes are used.

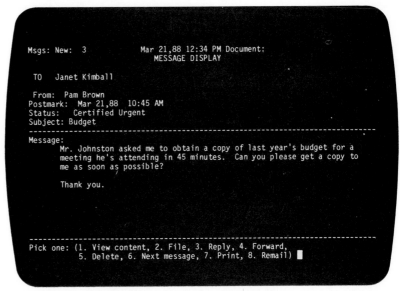

Fig. 6-1 Once you select the view option, the complete message will appear on your screen. You then decide which of the other options is appropriate for each message. The option to forward the message to another person was chosen here.

Formatting a Memo on a Printed Form

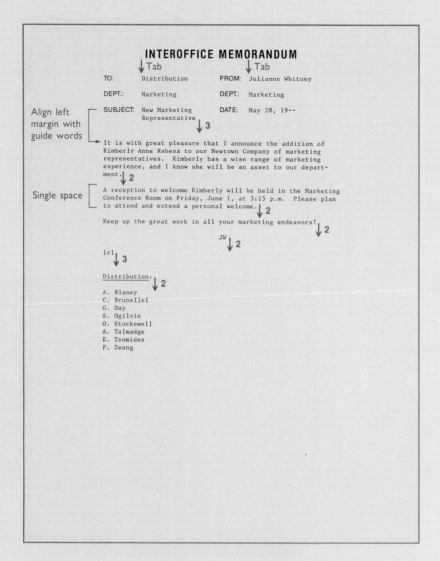

Fig. 6-2 Memo on printed form

1. Set a tab stop 2 spaces after the longest guide word on the left and right sides of the printed heading.

2. Align the left margin with the left margin of the guide words.

3. Key the appropriate information after each printed guide word, using capital and lowercase letters.

4. If the interoffice memorandum is being sent to more than one person, it may be possible to fit two or three names in the space following *To*.

5. If it is not possible to fit the names of all individuals after the guide word *To*, key the word *Distribution*. On the third line after the reference initials (or the enclosure notation, if there is one), key *Distribution:*. Double-space, and then list the names of the individuals who are to receive a copy of the memo. Arrange the names either in order of company rank starting with the highest or in alphabetic order, and block the names at the left margin. For purposes of distribution, place a check mark next to one name on each copy or use a colored highlighter to indicate who is to receive each copy.

6. Begin the message on the third line below the last line in the heading. Set the margins for a 50-space (10-pitch) line or a 60-space (12-pitch) line.

7. Use single spacing. Paragraphs may be either blocked or indented.

8. Key the writer's name or initials on the second line below the last line of the message, beginning at the right tab stop that was set in step 1. Although memos do not require a signature, many writers prefer to sign or initial them. If this is the case, key the writer's name or initials on the fourth line below the end of the message.

9. Key the reference initials at the left margin on the second line below the writer's name or initials.

10. Key an enclosure notation, if needed, on the line below the reference initials, beginning at the left margin.

11. Key a copy notation, if needed, on the line below the enclosure notation, if used, or on the line below the reference initials. If the addressee of the memo is not intended to know that a copy of the memo is being sent to one or more other persons, use a blind copy notation. Refer to the "Letters" section for an explanation of this.

12. If the memo continues beyond the first page, key a continuation heading on a plain sheet of paper. Continue keying the message on the third line below the last line of the continuation-page heading.

Formatting a Memo on Plain Paper

1. Set left and right margins for a 50-space (10-pitch) line or a 60-space (12-pitch) line.

2. Center the heading *MEMORAN-DUM* on line 7 in all-capital letters.

3. On the third line below the heading *MEMORANDUM*, begin keying the guide words *DATE:*, *TO:*, *FROM:*, and *SUBJECT:*, as well as any others you may wish to add. Double-space the guide words and

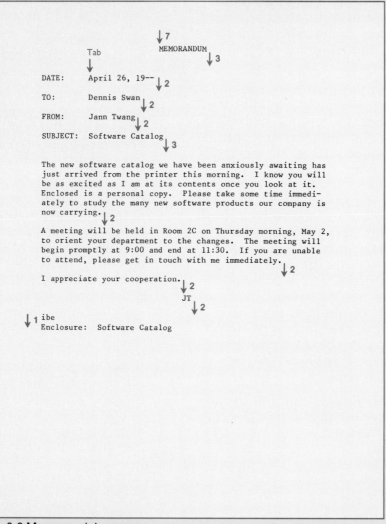

Fig. 6-3 Memo on plain paper

block them at the left margin. Use all-capital letters, and follow each guide word with a colon.

4. Key all the information that follows the guide words so that they block at the left, 2 spaces after the longest guide word. If *SUBJECT:* is the longest guide word, set a tab stop 10 spaces from the left margin.

5. Follow the same guidelines used for printed interoffice memorandums for the message, the closing, the reference initials, the enclosure notation, and distribution.

State Utility Company	INTEROFFICE ENVELOPE (FOR ALL INTEROFFICE AND BRANCH OFFICE MAIL)		1. PLEASE WRITE LEGIBLY NAME AND COMPLETE ADDRESS. 2. USE ONLY ONE CONSECUTIVE LINE AT A TIME. 3. CROSS OUT ALL PREVIOUS ADDRESSES. 4. USE ALL SPACES BEFORE DESTROYING ENVELOPE.		
NAME	DEPT. OR BRANCH OFFICE CITY	LOCATION	NAME	DEPT. OR BRANCH OFFICE CITY	LOCATION
A. Young	Art Dept.	39			
C. O'Brien	Human Resources	22			
D. W. Brown	Marketing	25			

Fig. 6-4 Interoffice mail envelope

LETTERS

Letters can be classified as either personal-business letters or business letters. A **personal-business letter** is a letter which is sent by an individual to a business or another person and which deals with matters of a personal nature. A **business letter** is similar to a personal-business letter except that the format varies slightly, and the letter is written on behalf of the business.

Letters follow a standard format, with slight variations in style depending on the sender's preference and the purpose of the letter. The basic format of a letter includes the following sections: the heading, the opening, the body, and the closing.

PERSONAL-BUSINESS LETTERS

Study the illustration of a personal-business letter below, giving special attention to each section of the personal-business letter.

The Heading. The **heading** contains the address of the person sending the letter. This is called the return address. The last line of the heading always contains the current date.

The Opening. The **opening** contains the inside address and the salutation. The inside address contains the name and address of the person you are sending the letter to. The salutation is a greeting such as *Dear Mrs. Lord* or

PERSONAL BUSINESS LETTER

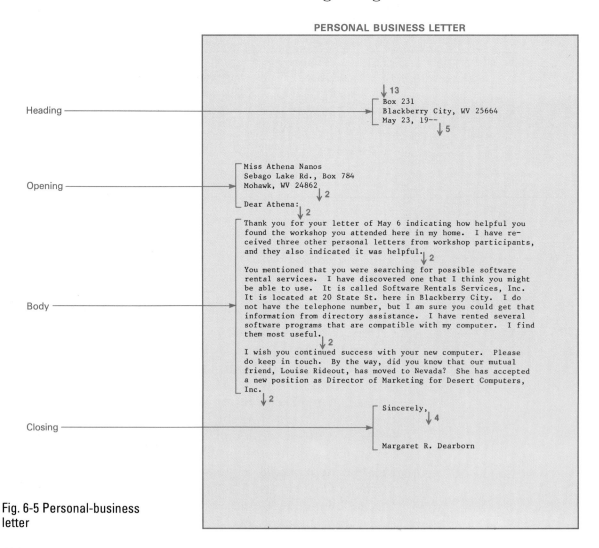

Heading

↓ 13
Box 231
Blackberry City, WV 25664
May 23, 19--
↓ 5

Opening

Miss Athena Nanos
Sebago Lake Rd., Box 784
Mohawk, WV 24862
↓ 2
Dear Athena:
↓ 2

Body

Thank you for your letter of May 6 indicating how helpful you found the workshop you attended here in my home. I have received three other personal letters from workshop participants, and they also indicated it was helpful.
↓ 2
You mentioned that you were searching for possible software rental services. I have discovered one that I think you might be able to use. It is called Software Rentals Services, Inc. It is located at 20 State St. here in Blackberry City. I do not have the telephone number, but I am sure you could get that information from directory assistance. I have rented several software programs that are compatible with my computer. I find them most useful.
↓ 2
I wish you continued success with your new computer. Please do keep in touch. By the way, did you know that our mutual friend, Louise Rideout, has moved to Nevada? She has accepted a new position as Director of Marketing for Desert Computers, Inc.
↓ 2

Closing

Sincerely,
↓ 4

Margaret R. Dearborn

Fig. 6-5 Personal-business letter

Dear Rowena, depending on how well you know the individual to whom you are sending the letter.

The Body. The **body** contains the message in paragraph form. Usually, the body of the letter is more than one paragraph, depending on the nature of the message.

The Closing. The **closing** contains a closing phrase known as the complimentary closing. This is followed by the written and printed name of the sender.

 USINESS LETTERS

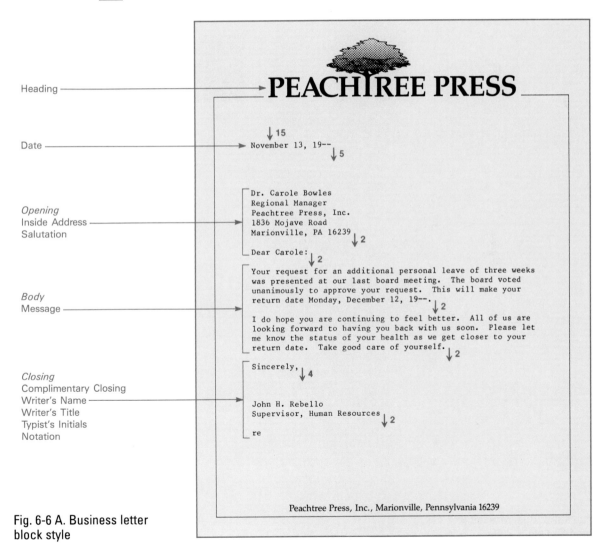

Heading

Date

Opening
Inside Address
Salutation

Body
Message

Closing
Complimentary Closing
Writer's Name
Writer's Title
Typist's Initials
Notation

PEACHTREE PRESS

↓ 15
November 13, 19-- ↓ 5

Dr. Carole Bowles
Regional Manager
Peachtree Press, Inc.
1836 Mojave Road
Marionville, PA 16239 ↓ 2

Dear Carole: ↓ 2

Your request for an additional personal leave of three weeks was presented at our last board meeting. The board voted unanimously to approve your request. This will make your return date Monday, December 12, 19--. ↓ 2

I do hope you are continuing to feel better. All of us are looking forward to having you back with us soon. Please let me know the status of your health as we get closer to your return date. Take good care of yourself. ↓ 2

Sincerely, ↓ 4

John H. Rebello
Supervisor, Human Resources ↓ 2

re

Peachtree Press, Inc., Marionville, Pennsylvania 16239

Fig. 6-6 A. Business letter block style

A business letter is similar to a personal-business letter in many ways, but the major difference lies in the message of the letter and the changes in formatting the letter. A business letter is sent on behalf of a business and is signed by an individual who represents the business in some capacity. Most large businesses use a standard letter format for increased efficiency. Study the illustrations and parts of a business letter on page 113 and below.

The Heading. The heading contains the letterhead and the date line. The letterhead, already printed at the top of the stationery, contains the company's name and address, along with other pertinent business information.

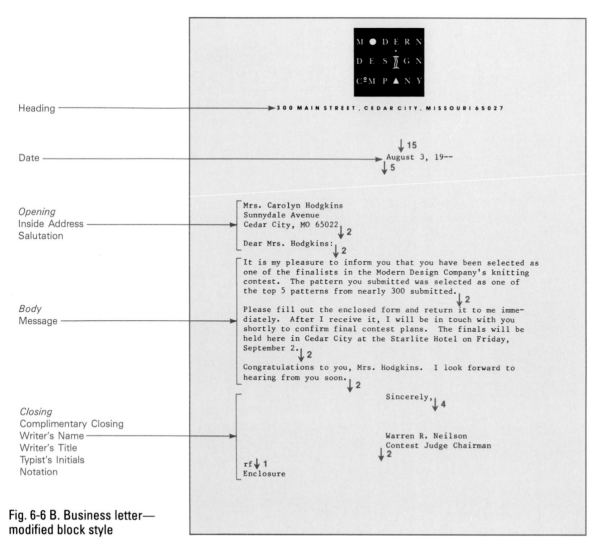

Heading

Date

Opening
Inside Address
Salutation

Body
Message

Closing
Complimentary Closing
Writer's Name
Writer's Title
Typist's Initials
Notation

Fig. 6-6 B. Business letter—
modified block style

The letterhead may also include the company's identifying symbol or drawing, known as a logo. The date line contains the current date.

The Opening. The opening contains the inside address and the salutation. The inside address contains the name and address of the person you are sending the letter to. It is important to note that the inside address is the same as the address that will be printed on the envelope.

The salutation is an opening greeting such as *Dear Mr. Jacques* or *Dear Mrs. Morse*.

The Body. The body contains the message in paragraph form. Usually, the body of the letter is more than one paragraph, depending on the message.

The Closing. The closing contains a closing phrase, known as the complimentary closing, and the sender's name and title, as well as reference initials. The reference initials are the initials of the person who prepared the letter. Study the illustration of these closing parts on page 114.

PROCEDURES

Formatting Letters

1. Prepare personal-business and business letters on stationery of a good quality and weight. You will not get the best results with stationery which is too light or too heavy and which has a poor-quality finish. If a letter is being prepared electronically, the printer should be a letter-quality printer that produces high-quality copy. The stationery used for letters is usually the standard letter size ($8\frac{1}{2}$ by 11 inches).

2. Margins will vary depending on the size of the stationery and the size of the print being used. The two most common sizes of print are 10-pitch (10 spaces to the inch) and 12-pitch (12 spaces to the inch). Set margins for a 50-space line if you are using equipment with 10-pitch print. Set margins for a 60-space line if you are using equipment with 12-pitch print.

Use these steps to determine the margin settings for letters prepared on standard size stationery:

a. Subtract the line length being used (50 or 60) from the total number of spaces available (85 or 102).

b. Divide the difference by 2 so that the margins will be uniform on each side, and round to the next highest number if there is a remainder of more than $\frac{1}{2}$. This number is the LM (left margin).

c. Add the number of line spaces (50 or 60). The number you get is the RM (right margin).

3. On a personal-business letter, begin the return address on line 13 at the center point of the paper. This is on space 42 if 10-pitch print is being used or on space 51 if 12-pitch print is being used. The return address is formatted with single spacing.

4. Begin the current date of a business letter between line 12 and line 15 at either the left margin (block style) or the center of the paper (modified-block style). Leaving 12 to 15 lines allows for flexibility in balancing the letter, depending on its length.

5. For both personal-business and business letters, begin the inside address 5 lines below the date line. The inside address is formatted with single spacing, as shown in the illustration on page 113. The same address goes on the envelope.

6. Begin the salutation 2 lines below the inside address. The salutation is followed by a colon (:). If the sender knows the person well, he or she may use the person's first name in the salutation, as shown in the illustration below.

7. Begin the body of the letter 2 lines below the salutation. The body of the letter is formatted with single spacing, except for double spacing between paragraphs. Paragraphs may be formatted either even with the left margin or with a first-line indention of usually 5 spaces. Study the illustrations Figs. 6-5 and 6-6A.

8. Begin the complimentary closing 2 lines below the last line of the body of the letter. The complimentary closing is formatted at either the left margin (block style) or the center of the page (modified-block style). The complimentary closing may or may not be followed by a comma depending on the sender's preference. It is important to point out that if a colon is used after the salutation, a comma should be used after the complimentary closing (this is known as mixed punctuation). If a colon is not used after the salutation, a comma should not be used after the complimentary closing (this is known as open punctuation). *It is important to be consistent in following this procedure.*

9. Begin the name of the sender of the letter 4 lines below the com-

plimentary closing, either at the left margin (block-style) or at the center of the paper (modified-block style). The sender will sign his or her name in the space between the complimentary closing and the keyed name. The sender's

business title, such as Executive Director, should be keyed on the line below the keyed name.

10. Format the initials of the person who prepared the letter at the left margin.

PECIAL NOTATIONS

Because business people who write letters have individual preferences, there are certain parts of a letter that they may wish to format in a special way. These special parts are known as **notations**. The most commonly used notations are explained and illustrated below. Study these special letter parts to improve your skill in preparing business letters.

Attention Line. An **attention line** is used when a letter is addressed directly to a company. An attention line will route the letter to a specific person or to a specific department within the company. An attention line may be addressed to a specific person by name or title. Using an attention line stresses that the letter deals with a business matter and may be handled by another person or department rather than the one named in the attention line. It is important to emphasize that it is usually easier to place the name of the person or department above the company name in the inside address and omit the attention line.

- The attention line should be placed on the second line below the inside address, beginning at the left margin.
- The attention line may be prepared in capital and small letters or in all-capital letters.
- The word *Attention* should not be abbreviated. Use a colon after the word *Attention*.

- If extra emphasis is desired for the attention line, it may be underscored.

```
Schmidt & Bryant Industries
8510 Thrasher Boulevard
Potlatch, ID 83855

Attention: Mr. Walter Ridlonsky


Merrymeeting Manor
675 South Main Street
San Manuel, AZ 85631

ATTENTION: SALES MANAGER
```

- If electronic equipment is being used and you plan to prepare the envelope address by repeating the inside address, insert the attention line in the inside address between the name of the addressee and the street address or box number. Doing so eliminates the need to add the attention line manually.

```
SCHMIDT & BRYANT INDUSTRIES
ATTENTION MR WALTER RIDLONSKY
8510 THRASHER BOULEVARD
POTLATCH ID 83855


MERRYMEETING MANOR
ATTENTION SALES MANAGER
675 SOUTH MAIN STREET
SAN MANUEL AZ 85631
```

Subject Line. A **subject line** is used to place emphasis on a particular topic being discussed in the letter. Using a subject line allows the reader to zero in immediately on the topic of the letter.

- The subject line appears between the salutation and the body of the letter, with 1 blank line above and below.

```
Dear Mr. Curran:

Subject: March 15 Workshop Schedule
```
or

```
Dear Mr. Curran:

SUBJECT: MARCH 15 WORKSHOP SCHEDULE
```

- Usually, the subject line begins at the left margin. The subject line may be centered for special emphasis if desired. If paragraph indentions are used in a letter, the subject line may also be indented the same number of spaces.
- The subject line may be prepared in capital and small letters or in all-capital letters. The subject line is usually prepared without underscoring, but for special emphasis the complete subject line may be underscored.

```
Subject: March 15 Workshop Schedule
SUBJECT: MARCH 15 WORKSHOP SCHEDULE
SUBJECT: MARCH 15 WORKSHOP SCHEDULE
```

Reference Initials. **Reference initials** are used to indicate who prepared the letter. In most cases this is a secretary or a person in a similar position. The examples below indicate the variety of styles in the preparation of reference initials. While all the examples given are acceptable, the first one shows the style that is preferred, primarily because it is easy to prepare.

- Key the initials of the person who prepared the letter at the left margin, 2 lines below the writer's name and title. If the writer's name is keyed in the signature block, the writer's initials are unnecessary in the reference initials section of the letter. If the writer wants his or her initials used, they should precede the initials of the person who keyed the letter.
- Reference initials may be keyed in either capital letters or lowercase letters. When giving two sets of initials, key them both the same way for efficiency. Use a colon to separate two sets of all-cap initials and a diagonal to separate two sets of small-letter initials.

```
aem    jeh/aem

AEM    JEH:AEM
```

Enclosure Notation. An **enclosure notation** indicates that one or more items are being sent with the letter. The enclosure notation is formatted on the line below the reference initials. It is extremely important to make sure that the correct number of enclosures shown in the notation agrees with the number specified in the message section of the letter and also with the number of items actually enclosed.

Study the styles of enclosure notations illustrated below.

```
aem
Enclosure

aem
Enc.

aem
Enclosures:
1. Check for $685
2. Invoice B3452

jeh/aem
Enclosures: 2
```

Copy Notation. A **copy notation** is used to let the addressee know that one or more other persons will be sent a copy of the letter. The copy notation is formatted 1 line below the reference initials or 1 line below the enclosure notation, whichever is last on the page. The copy notation is placed at the left margin and is followed by a colon, 2 spaces, and the names of the persons the copies are going to. (The colon may be omitted.) Notations for the commonly used reprographic methods are *cc* for *carbon copy*, *c* for *copy*—these are used for both carbon copies and photocopies—and *pc* for *photocopy*.

```
JEH:AEM
cc: Steven Haukklah

jeh/aem
c Steven Haukklah
  Doris Haukklah
```

```
jeh/aem
pc Steven Haukklah
```

Blind Copy Notation. A **blind copy notation** is used when the addressee is not intended to know that one or more other persons are being sent a copy of the letter. The blind copy notation is placed on all copies except the original. The original copy (top copy) must be removed before the blind copy notation is keyed on the remaining copies. The blind copy notation is keyed in the top left corner of the letter starting at the left margin, 7 lines from the top of the letter, or it is keyed 2 lines below the last item in the letter at the left margin. Study the illustrations below. Use of the colon is optional but does improve readability.

```
JEH:AEM

bcc: Mr. Dunne


JEH:AEM

bc: Mr. Dunne


JEH/AEM

bpc: Mr. Dunne
```

Postscript. A **postscript** is usually an afterthought but may also be used to express a thought deliberately not placed in the body of the letter. The postscript is placed 2 lines below the reference initials, enclosure notation, or copy notation, whichever is last on the page. The postscript is formatted at the left margin with single spacing and with the initials PS as illustrated. Leave 2 spaces after the colon or period, whichever is used. Study the illustrations.

PS: Think about the possibility of scheduling your flight later in the evening. We could have dinner together.

PS. Best wishes for the best in the coming year!

Estimating the Length of Letters

Letters are classified into three categories when length is being considered:

1. Short letters: 75 words or less

2. Average letters: From 75 to 225 words

3. Long letters: Over 225 words

Much time can be saved if you learn how to estimate the length of the letter you are preparing, whether you are using shorthand notes, handwritten rough-draft copy, or rough-draft copy prepared electronically. Use the following guidelines in this process:

1. Choose one average line from your draft or shorthand notes.

2. Count the number of words in the line.

3. Count the total number of lines in your draft or shorthand notes. Combine partial lines in this counting process.

4. Multiply the total number of lines by the number of words in the average line you selected.

5. Set the margins according to the length of the letter and the size of the stationery you are using.

6. If you are using transcribing equipment or some other piece of electronic equipment that involves working with recorded dictation, use a dictation slip (illustrated below) to estimate more accurately the length of the dictation.

Formatting Continuation Pages

When it is necessary to use a second page for a letter, keep the following points in mind:

1. Use plain stationery (without a letterhead) of the same quality and color as the letterhead stationery.

2. Use the same margins and line spacing that you used on the first page.

3. Begin on the seventh line from the top of the page. Study the two illustrations below for correct formatting of the continuation page.

4. Try to begin a continuation page with a new paragraph. If this is not possible, try to bring forward to the new page at least two lines of the previous paragraph. Do not divide a paragraph that contains three or fewer lines. Do not divide the last word on any page.

5. Use the same format for the closing that you would use on a one-page letter.

Formatting Envelopes

Envelopes may be classified as either large (No. 10) or small (No. 7). A third type of envelope that is also used often is the window envelope. Window envelopes vary in size, depending on the needs of the businesses using them. See the illustrations below. Note their major differences. The U.S. Postal Service prefers that all envelopes be formatted with all-capital letters and no punctuation. The major reason for this is that its electronic equipment reads envelopes formatted this way faster. Keep the following points in mind as you format envelopes:

1. Use single spacing, and block each line at the left.

2. Place the city, state, and ZIP Code on the last line.

3. Leave 1 space between the state name and the ZIP Code.

4. The state name may be spelled out or given as a two-letter abbreviation.

5. When using a large envelope (No. 10), begin the address on line 14, approximately 4 inches from the left edge. When using a small envelope (No. 7), begin the address on line 12, approximately 2 inches from the left edge.

6. When the envelope contains a printed return address for a company or an organization, key the

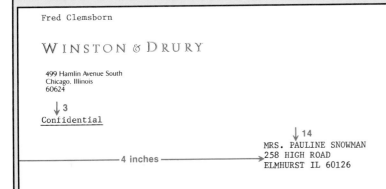

Fig. 6-7 A. Envelope with printed return address

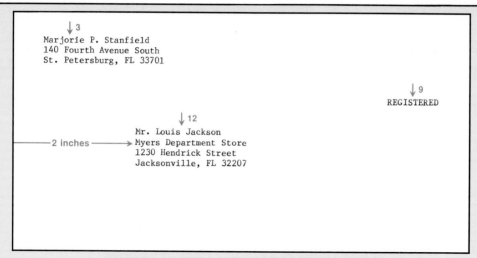

Fig. 6-7 B. Envelope without printed return address

name of the writer on the line above the return address. If all the lines in the printed return address are blocked at the left, align the writer's name at the left (as shown in the illustration). If all the lines in the printed return address are centered on the longest line, center the writer's name accordingly.

7. If a printed return address does not appear on the envelope, key a return address in the upper left corner, beginning on line 3 about a half inch in from the left edge. The return address should contain the following information, arranged on separate lines: (1) the name of the writer; (2) the name of the company (if appropriate); (3) a street address or post office box number; and (4) the city, state, and ZIP Code. See the illustration.

8. A notation such as *Personal, Confidential, Please Forward,* or *Hold for Arrival* goes below the return address. It should begin on the third line below the return ad-dress and align at the left with the return address. Begin each main word with a capital letter, and use underscoring. Do not allow any notations or graphics to fall alongside or below the area established for the mailing address. Copy placed in these locations will interfere with optical character reader processing.

9. If an attention line was used within the letter itself, it should appear on the envelope as well. The attention line may be created exactly like a personal or confidential notation, or it may be keyed within the address block—between the name of the addressee and the street address or post office box number.

10. If a special mailing procedure is used, key the appropriate notation (such as *SPECIAL DELIVERY* or *REGISTERED*) in all-capital letters in the upper right corner of the envelope. Many offices have stamps that can be used for mailing notations.

Folding and Inserting Letters

Study the illustrations below to learn the proper methods for folding letters and inserting them into large and small envelopes.

FOLDING AND INSERTING FOR LARGE ENVELOPES

Fold up
bottom third.

Fold down to within
1/2 inch of crease.

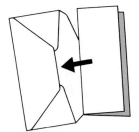
Put last crease
in envelope first.

Fig. 6-8 A. Folding and inserting for large envelopes

FOLDING AND INSERTING FOR SMALL ENVELOPES

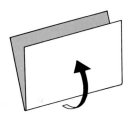
Fold bottom up to
1/2 inch from top.

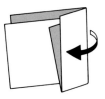
Fold right to
left 1/3.

Fold left to right
to within 1/2 inch
of edge.

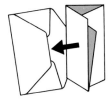
Put last crease
in envelope first.

Fig. 6-8 B. Folding and inserting for small envelopes

TYPES OF BUSINESS LETTERS

Because every business is unique, so are the types of letters a business might send. When you begin working in a business, your job responsibilities might include composing letters for various reasons. Your company may have a procedures manual that will help you in composing and preparing the most commonly used types of business letters. It is also possible that you might have to compose letters without the assistance of a procedures manual, relying on your own individual knowledge instead. Whatever the situation, knowing the major types of business letters will help you greatly.

Jessie Jones College
Singleton, Texas 77831

September 1, 19--

Miss Lori Howard
38 Stone Hill Drive
Singleton, TX 77831

Dear Miss Howard:

Congratulations! I just heard that you have been selected to represent the Broward House Book Company as a member of a special task force to study young writers.

When you were in my classes here at Jessie Jones College, I knew you were especially interested in working with young writers. I also remember how well you were able to compose and edit. The experience you have acquired in working with young people in your athletic activities will also assist you in this important assignment.

Please let me know if I may help you as you begin this important assignment. I know you will do a fine job.

Sincerely,

Louise Fosterville
Teacher, Business Communications

si

Fig. 6-9 Letter of goodwill

Letters of Goodwill. What is goodwill? Goodwill is a business's individual prestige that goes beyond the value of what the business sells. Goodwill is the intangible part of the business that cannot be spelled out in words or given a monetary value. Examples of letters of goodwill are announcements, invitations, and messages of sympathy, appreciation, congratulations, praise, or recognition. Letters of goodwill should be written promptly and should be composed in an enthusiastic and sincere style. Study the illustration of a letter of goodwill in Fig. 6-9.

Letters of Response. Letters of response are written to answer requests for information or materials. These letters should be direct and be handled promptly.

THE PALAMOUNTAIN ORCHARD
ZENITH, WASHINGTON 98073

July 17, 19--

Mr. Elwyn P. Dinegard
Berry Hill Apple Orchards
RR 4, Box 2830
Corinna, ME 04928

Dear Mr. Dinegard:

Thank you for your recent letter requesting information about videotapes on improving apple production. I remember your speaking to me after my presentation at our conference here in Zenith.

I obtained those videotapes from Apple Training Videos. The address is:

                    3500 North Bend Road
                    Redwood Valley, CA 95470

Best of luck to you as you undertake your project. Let me know if I may be of further assistance.

Cordially,

THE PALAMOUNTAIN ORCHARD

Abel Palamountain
President

AP:WO

Fig. 6-10 Letter of response

Businesses that receive many letters requesting the same type of information often have a form letter that can be used. Form letters contain the response message, and they can be individualized in order to assure the reader that personal attention has been given to the matter.

Study the illustration of a letter of response in Fig. 6-10.

Letters Requesting Information. Letters requesting information make up a large portion of business correspondence. Letters requesting information should be clear and concise, and they should be worded in a way that encourages an immediate response. Study the illustration of a letter requesting information in Figure 6-11.

July 13, 19--

Mr. Abel Palamountain
The Palamountain Orchard
8562 McIntosh Lane
Zenith, WA 98073

Dear Mr. Palamountain:

Last fall I attended a conference in Zenith dealing with the improvement of apple production. You spoke at one of the sessions I attended, and I enjoyed it very much.

Currently, I am in the process of trying to organize a similar program here for the improvement of my apple business. You gave out a list of videotapes you felt were of great assistance to you. Could you send me specific information on where I might obtain this information? It would help me greatly.

I will be looking forward to hearing from you soon concerning this matter. Please feel free to call me. My business card is enclosed.

Sincerely,

Elwyn P. Dinegard
Orchard Owner

ro
Enclosure

Fig. 6-11 Letter requesting information

Letters of Refusal. Letters of refusal say no to a specific request or situation in as positive a manner as possible. Great tact must be used in writing a letter of refusal because of the importance of maintaining goodwill.

Study the illustration of a letter of refusal in Figure 6-12.

Three other types of business letters that are used less frequently than those mentioned and illustrated are letters of claim or adjustment, letters of credit or collection, and letters selling products or services. These types of letters are used less frequently by the beginning worker in a business because of their complexity. You should also be familiar with these types of letters as well as what they represent.

```
                                        February 22, 19--



Mrs. Mary Ellen Moon
Manager, Clover Acres Kennel
694 Chute Street
Gandy, NE 69137

Dear Mrs. Moon:

It was wonderful to hear from you last week inviting me to
consider working at your kennel.  I very much appreciate your
faith in me as a potential worker.

Unfortunately, I will have to say "no" to your offer for the
job.  I have just accepted a position as dog groomer with
another kennel near my home.  Please keep me in mind for the
future if such an opportunity might come up again.  You know
how much I love animals.

Best wishes to you in your most important work.

                         Sincerely,


                         Gary P. Mingo
```

Fig. 6-12 Letter of refusal

Letters of Claim or Adjustment. Letters of claim and/or adjustment indicate a complaint about a specific matter such as slow service, an error made on an invoice, or discourteous service. When this happens, it is appropriate to write a letter of adjustment giving an explanation of the matter and possibly promising compensation to the individual or replacement of the item involved. Keep letters of this type short, direct, and specific. Be familiar with the policies and procedures of your company when writing this type of letter. Customer satisfaction must be your major goal.

Letters of Credit or Collection. Letters of credit or collection are used to indicate that credit is being given to the applicant for a product or service. Credit letters should be written in a positive, friendly tone.

A collection letter is written when a credit customer does not make a prompt payment. A company usually uses a series of collection letters, and each succeeding letter is stronger in tone. Most companies have form letters for this purpose.

Sales Letters. Sales letters that are written to sell a service or a product have a positive, catchy tone to encourage the reader to take immediate action. Sales letters often contain graphics to further motivate the reader into action. Many businesses have a special department, such as advertising or promotion, to handle this type of correspondence.

With electronic equipment, all of the above letters can be easily prepared and stored. Also, with proper electronic equipment, a company can make excellent use of graphics and photographs in selling a service or product.

EPORTS

Reports serve many purposes. Reports can be simple or complex, depending on the nature of the information to be communicated. For example, a report may simply communicate information on sales quotas or present a detailed analysis of sales quotas over a period of time. From a detailed report, decisions on future sales actions may be made.

Reports may be prepared in a variety of formats. A report may be part of a letter or memo. Reports may be generated on a regular basis and prepared on printed forms, with the necessary information inserted in the appropriate spaces. Other types of reports are prepared more formally. The way a report is prepared is usually determined by the individual needs of the person completing the report and the nature of the information being reported.

PROCEDURES

Selecting Report Formats

Keep the following points in mind when you select a report format:

1. *Who will read the report?* Can it be prepared as an interoffice memorandum or as an enclosure for an interoffice memo? Is the report going to a person or group in high-level management? If this is the case, the report will require a more formal format.

2. *What is the desired result of the report*? If you are simply providing information, a simple, easy-to-understand presentation is all that is needed. If you are attempting to persuade the person reading your report to accept a particular viewpoint, you will need to use a structure in your report that is a bit more detailed.

3. *What is the present mind-set of the person who will receive the report?* If it is necessary to provide detailed reasoning for your reader, perhaps you will need to do extensive research. If you already know that the reader agrees with your point of view, a simpler approach can be used.

ARTS OF A FORMAL REPORT

A **formal report** has three parts: front matter, body, and back matter.

The **front matter** precedes the main text of the report and contains the following elements.

Title Page. In a *business* report, the title page includes the full title; the subtitle (if any); the writer's name, title, and department; and the date of submission. The title page may also indicate for whom the report was written, such as a department manager.

In an *academic* report (such as a research paper), the title page includes the full title, the subtitle (if any), the name of the writer, the instructor, and the course, along with the date of submission.

Table of Contents. The table of contents includes a list of all the sections by number and title, along with the opening page number of each section. Main headings within the sections can also be listed.

Lists of Tables and Illustrations. Separate lists of tables and illustrations are included if there are many tables and illustrations and if they are likely to be used frequently by the reader.

Foreword or Preface. The foreword or preface indicates for whom the report is written, the objectives of the report, and the methods used to assemble the material in the report. It is in this section that acknowledgments of help received may be given. Acknowledgments may also be treated as a separate part of the front matter, placed immediately after the foreword.

Summary. The summary is a statement of the conclusions and recommendations. It precedes the body of the report.

The body is the main part of a formal report. It contains the following elements.

Introduction. The introduction includes the objectives, the methods, and an overview of the topic being reported (in greater detail than in the foreword). If a report has several sections, the introduction may precede Section 1 of the text or be labeled "Section 1."

Main Discussion. The main discussion includes all the important data, evidence, analyses, and interpretations needed to fulfill the purpose of the report. The main discussion may consist of several sections or one long section that opens with an introduction and closes with conclusions and recommendations. Different levels of headings may be used throughout the text of the main discussion to make the text easier to follow.

Conclusions. The conclusions section presents the key points and recommendations that the writer hopes the reader will be persuaded to accept. If several sections are contained in the report, the conclusion is the final section.

The **back matter** follows the body of the report. It contains the following elements.

Appendixes. Appendixes include a collection of tables, charts, or other data too specific to be included in the body of the report. These items are provided in this section as supporting details for the interested reader.

Endnotes. Endnotes take the place of footnotes placed at the bottom of individual pages in the report. Using endnotes simplifies the preparation of the report.

Bibliography. The bibliography is a list of all the sources that were consulted in the preparation of the report and from which material was derived or directly quoted.

Glossary. The glossary is a list of terms (with definitions) that the reader may not easily understand.

ARTS OF AN INFORMAL REPORT

An **informal report** has no front matter. The information that would go on a title page appears at the top of the first page and is immediately followed by the body of the report.

An informal report usually contains no back matter except a list of endnotes and a bibliography.

Formatting Formal and Informal Reports

Side Margins

Prepare all reports on a 6-inch line (60 spaces with 10-pitch print, 72 spaces with 12-pitch print). If a report is unbound and will remain that way, it may be stapled or clipped with a device in the upper left corner.

If you are placing the report in a binder or binding it in any other manner along the left edge, increase the left margin by 3 spaces. This will allow for the binding on the left edge.

Top and Bottom Margins of Formal Reports

Use the following guidelines for preparing the opening pages and other pages:

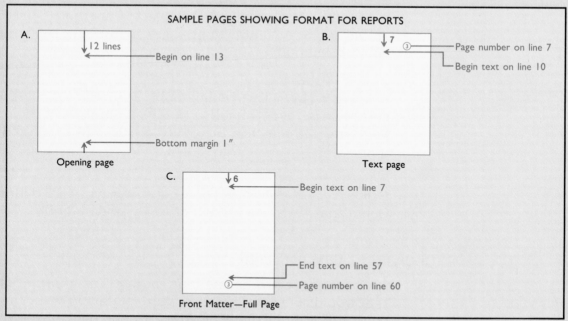

SAMPLE PAGES SHOWING FORMAT FOR REPORTS

A.
12 lines
Begin on line 13
Bottom margin 1″
Opening page

B.
↓7
③ Page number on line 7
Begin text on line 10
Text page

C.
↓6
Begin text on line 7
End text on line 57
③ Page number on line 60
Front Matter—Full Page

Fig. 6-13 Formats for reports: A. Opening page
B. Text page
C. Front matter—full page

1. On opening pages, leave a top margin of 12 lines (2 inches) and a bottom margin of 6 lines (1 inch). On all other pages, a minimum of 6 lines should be left at the bottom. On a full page of copy, the last line of text typically falls on line 57 and the page number on line 60.

2. Leave 6 blank lines at both the top and bottom of other pages in a report.

3. In the *body* and *back matter* of the report, place the page number on line 7 at the right margin and continue the text from the preceding page on line 10.

4. In the *front matter* of the report, the page number is always placed at the bottom of the page. Begin the text on line 7. On a full page of text, place the last line of text on line 57. Study the illustrations below.

Top and Bottom Margins of Informal Reports

Use the following guidelines when preparing the opening page:

1. Leave a top margin of 12 lines (2 inches). On line 13 key the title of the report; center the title, and use all-capital letters. If there is a subtitle, center it in capital and small letters on the second line below the main title. If the title or subtitle is too long, break it into sensible phrases and arrange them on two or more single-spaced lines.

2. Key *By* and the writer's name in capital and small letters, centered on the second line below the title or subtitle.

3. Key the date on which the report is to be submitted on the second line below the writer's name, and center the date. Additional details that appear on a title page, such as the writer's title and affiliation or the name and affiliation of the person or group for whom the report has been prepared, are omitted when the title begins on the same page as the body. If these details need to be provided, you will have to prepare a separate title page.

4. On the third line below the date, begin the body of the report. On the first page of an informal business report, no page number should appear. Continue the text to line 60. Count this first page as page 1, but do not number it as page 1. Study the illustration below.

```
                              ↓ 13
line 13        COMPACT DISKS--THE NEW RECORDING WONDER
                                                      ↓ 2
line 15                 By Stephanie Durwood
                                             ↓ 2
line 17                  January 15, 1988
                                          ↓ 3
line 20      Are you aware of the latest sound recording wonder?  If you are not,
          you should be!  Today's technology has now provided us with an exciting
          new dimension in recording sound with the introduction of compact disks.
          The compact disk will indeed revolutionize the recording business
          industry.
line 30      A compact disk is a round disk similar to what we used to use, often
          called a record.  The compact disk is a bit smaller and is extremely
          sensitive to touch and heat.  In order to be used, the compact disk must
          be inserted into a compact disk recorder which will then allow the user
          to simply press a button and play the recording.  The sound is phenome-
          nal!  You must not touch the compact disk recorder with your fingertips,
          for you can damage the compact disk because of its composition.
line 44      Compact disks are being produced in all types of music tastes.
          Last night I played one of my all-time favorite groups that just has had
          a compact disk produced with its greatest hits.  The sound was great!  I
          have just received two new sound speakers which really help, too.
line 52    I recommend that if you love music as much as I do you check out
          the possibility of getting one of these recorders that will play this
          new exciting wonder--compact disks!
```

Fig. 6-14 Short report

If the report requires more than one page, leave 6 blank lines at the top of each additional page. Key the page number on line 7, and resume keying the text on line 10. Place the last line of text on line 60.

If the report requires one or more elements of back matter, such as endnotes or a bibliography, follow the style established for a formal report.

Formatting the Front Matter of Formal Reports

Title Page

There is no one correct arrangement for the parts listed on a title page. Study the two acceptable formats below.

```
                    PRODUCT DEVELOPMENT STRATEGIES
                                               ↓ 2
                An Analysis of Research and Development
                         From 1987 to 1989



                              ↓ 4 (minimum)




                            Prepared by
                                       ↓ 2
                           Rita H. Smith
                          Research Department



                              ↓ 4 (minimum)




                             Submitted to

                       Product Evaluation Committee
                          Alpha Products, Inc.

                            June 1, 1988
```

Fig. 6-15 A. Three-block arrangement

1. *Three-Block Arrangement.* Group the material into three blocks of type, and leave equal space (at least 3 blank lines) above and below the middle block. Position the material as a whole so that it appears centered horizontally and vertically on the page.

2. *Two-Block Arrangement.* Group the material into two blocks of type, and leave at least 6 blank lines between the blocks. Position the material as a whole so that it appears centered horizontally and vertically on the page.

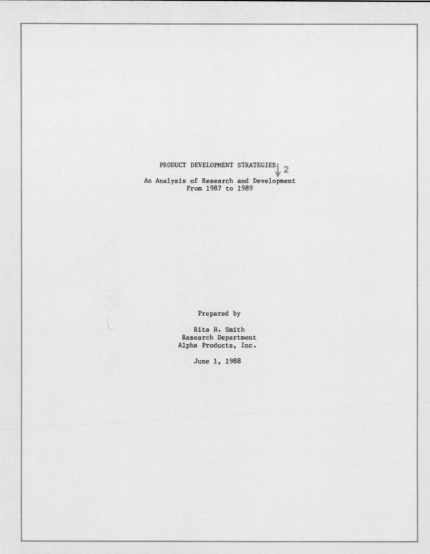

PRODUCT DEVELOPMENT STRATEGIES ↓ 2

An Analysis of Research and Development
From 1987 to 1989

Prepared by

Rita H. Smith
Research Department
Alpha Products, Inc.

June 1, 1988

Fig. 6-15 B. Two-block arrangement

Table of Contents

The table of contents is prepared on a separate sheet of paper. Key the word *CONTENTS* or the words *TABLE OF CONTENTS* in all-capital letters, centered on line 13. On the third line below, begin keying the table of contents. Double-space the entries. Use the same side and bottom margins as for the text pages in the body of the report.

↓13

CONTENTS ↓3

I.	Factors Affecting the Growth of Software Market	1 ↓2
II.	Statement of Purpose	6
III.	Marketing Strategies	9
IV.	Research Strategies	14
V.	Production Strategies	16
VI.	Financial Analysis of the Plan	19
VII.	Summary	24

Fig. 6-16 Contents page

Foreword or Preface

Keep the following points in mind when you prepare a foreword or preface:

1. If a foreword or preface is to be prepared, use a separate sheet of paper. Key the appropriate title in all-capital letters, centered on line 13.
2. On the third line below, begin keying the actual text. Use the same side and bottom margins as for the text pages in the body of the report. Follow the same guidelines for spacing, indentions, and headings given for the body of the report.

3. The foreword or preface should cover the following points:

Audience. Who will be reading the report?

Motivation. What motivated the writer to prepare the report?

Objectives. What does the writer hope the report will accomplish?

Methods. How was the information gathered and how were the conclusions arrived at?

Acknowledgments. Which individuals and organizations need to be recognized for their help and contributions? This element may also be treated as a separate section.

Summary

If a summary is used, follow the same guidelines provided for a foreword. Keep it short, not more than one or two pages. The summary may be organized into paragraphs or as a set of numbered paragraphs.

Numbering Front Matter Pages

On all pages of the front matter except the title page, center the page number on line 60, the seventh line from the bottom of the page. Key the page numbers as small roman numerals. Count the title page as page i, even though no number is keyed on that page. Leave 2 blank lines above the page number—more if the text above runs short.

TEXT SPACING AND INDENTATIONS IN FORMAL AND INFORMAL REPORTS

Running Text. In most cases *double-space* text. Use single spacing or 1½-line spacing in business reports when the costs of paper, reproduction, storage, and mailing are important considerations.

Paragraphs. Indent text paragraphs 5 spaces. At the bottom of a page, do not divide a paragraph with only two or three lines; always leave at least two lines of the paragraph at the bottom of one page and carry over at least two lines to the top of the next page.

Quoted Material. If a quotation will make four or more printed lines, use single spacing. Indent the quoted material 5 spaces from each side margin, and leave 1 blank line above and below the quoted material. If the quoted matter represents the start of a paragraph in the original, indent the first word an additional 5 spaces.

Items in a List. Use single spacing, and leave 1 blank line above and below the list as a whole. Either key the list on the full width of the 6-inch line, or indent the list 5 spaces from each side margin. If any item in the list requires more than one line, leave a blank line after each item in the list. If an item continues on to a second line, align the turnover with the first word in the line above.

If the items each begin with a number or letter, key a period after the number or letter and leave 2 spaces before the first word. Align the numbers or letters on the period. If an item continues on to a second line, align the turnover with the first word in the line above.

Tables. Tables may be keyed with single, double, or $1\frac{1}{2}$-line spacing. Establish one style of spacing for all tables within a given report.

TEXT HEADINGS

Headings are the key elements for letting readers see at a glance the main topics of the writer's discussion and the way in which the discussion is organized. It is important that heads be used throughout the report to reflect the coverage and the structure of the material. It is also essential that the heads be keyed in a way that clearly indicates different levels of importance. Keep the following points in mind when determining headings:

- Try to limit yourself to three levels of text heads, not counting the section title. If you use more than three, it will be difficult for the reader to grasp their distinction.
- Before keying the final draft of the report, make an outline of the heading structure as it then stands and analyze it for:

Comprehensiveness. Does it cover all aspects of the discussion, or are some topics not properly represented?

Balance. Is one section loaded with heads, while a comparable section has only one or two?

Parallel structure. Are the heads all worded in a similar way, or are some complete sentences and others simply phrases?

FORMATS FOR THE BACK MATTER IN FORMAL AND INFORMAL REPORTS

The back matter in both formal and informal reports is located at the end of the report and may include appendixes, endnotes, a bibliography, and a glossary. Begin each of these sections on a separate sheet of paper. Use the same margins as for other pages in the report, and treat the numbering of the back matter pages as discussed earlier in this chapter.

Appendixes. Use the following guidelines when you prepare appendixes:

- Key the word *APPENDIX* (plus a number of letter, if appropriate) and the appendix title in all-capital letters, centered on line 13. If the title is long, key it in two or more centered lines, single-spaced.
- Leave 2 blank lines before keying the body of the appendix. Choose the format that displays the copy in the most effective way.

Footnotes and Endnotes. *Notes* serve two major functions in reports:

1. They provide *comments* on the main text, communicating additional thoughts on the topic that might be distracting if placed in the main text of the report.

2. They serve as *references*, identifying the source of a statement quoted or cited in the text.

When notes appear at the foot of a page, they are called *footnotes*. Study the illustration of a footnote.

When notes appear all together at the end of a complete report or manuscript, they are called *endnotes*. Study the illustration of an endnotes section.

Footnotes or endnotes are usually keyed by number to a word, phrase, or sentence in the main text. Endnotes are used more and more because they are easier to prepare and allow for easier reading through the main text of the report. One drawback is that the reader does not know in each instance whether the endnote will contain a comment worth reading or a simple reference note.

When using a typewriter, indicate either a footnote or an endnote, by inserting a *superior* (raised) number after the appropriate word, phrase, or sentence in the text.

```
52          the year.1  This unique invention was not accepted until Germantown        15
53                                                                                      14
54          Software introduced it in 1983.2                                            13
55                                                                                      12
56          _____                                                            11
57              1Frank Bowles, "The Distant Land," The National Software Journal,       10
58          April 1986, pp. 21-25.                                                       9
59                                                                                       8
60              2Ibid., p. 30.                                                           7
61                                                                                       6
62                                                                                       5
63                                                                                       4
64                                                                                       3
65                                                                                       2
66                                                                                       1
```

Fig. 6-17 A. Footnote

```
                                    ↓ 13
                                   NOTES
                                       ↓ 3
            1.  "The Age of Information," Business Week, September 3, 1986,
        p. 13.↓ 2
            2.  Ibid., p. 51.
```

Fig. 6-17 B. Endnote

If you are using electronic equipment, indicate a footnote or endnote by enclosing the number in brackets or parentheses. Try to position the number so that it *follows* the end of a sentence or the end of a paragraph. Leave 1 space before the opening bracket or parenthesis. Leave 2 spaces after the closing bracket or parenthesis if a new sentence begins on the same line. Study the example below:

```
. . . as ''the age of innocence.'' (3) She went on . . .
```

If the number must go *within* a sentence, leave 1 space before the opening bracket or parenthesis and 1 space after the closing bracket or parenthesis. To avoid confusion, try to place the enclosed number so that it is not next to any other punctuation mark in the sentence. Do not use a number enclosed in parentheses within a sentence where it could be mistaken for a number that accompanies an enumerated item.

Formatting Footnotes

1. Key an underscore 2 inches long (20 10-pitch strokes or 24 12-pitch strokes) to separate footnote material from the main text. Key the underscore 1 line below the last line of text, beginning at the left margin.

2. If the text runs short on a page, the footnote is still placed at the bottom of the page.

3. Begin the first footnote on the second line below the underscore.

4. Single-space each footnote. Leave 1 blank line between footnotes.

5. Indent the first line of each footnote 5 spaces. Key the footnote number on the line or as a superior figure. Key any additional lines within the footnote beginning at the left margin. Study the illustration on page 143.

6. Allow three to four lines for each footnote. This will make it easier for you to estimate and allow for at least 1 inch at the bottom of your paper.

Formatting Endnotes

1. On a new page key *NOTES* or *ENDNOTES* in all-capital letters, centered on line 13.

2. Begin keying the first endnote on the third line below the title.

3. Single-space each endnote, and leave 1 blank line between endnotes.

4. Indent the first line of each endnote 5 spaces, and key any additional lines within the same endnote beginning at the left margin.

5. Key the identifying number for each endnote on the line, not as a superior figure.

6. Use the same margins as for other pages in the body of the report.

Bibliography. Use the following guidelines when you prepare a bibliography:

- Use a separate sheet of paper for the bibliography. Key the word *BIBLIOGRAPHY* in all-capital letters, centered on line 13. Leave 2 blank lines, and begin keying the first entry on line 16.
- Use the same margins as for other pages in the body of the report.
- Begin each entry at the left margin. Single-space each entry, and leave 1 blank line between entries.
- Indent turnover lines 5 spaces so that the first word in each entry will stand out.
- List the entries in a bibliography alphabetically by the author's last name. When a bibliography contains more than one work by the same author, replace the author's name with a long dash (six hyphens) in all the entries after the first. List the works alphabetically by title.

Study the illustration of a bibliography in Figure 6-18.

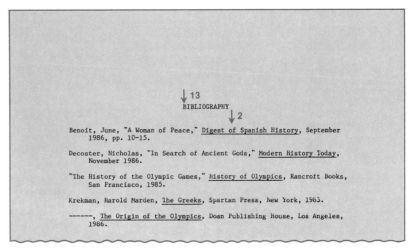

Fig. 6-18 Bibliography

Composing Interoffice Memorandums, Letters, and Reports Electronically

If you are composing interoffice memorandums, letters, and reports electronically, keep the following points in mind:

1. Be sure that you are sitting in a comfortable chair, and be sure that the lighting is good. These factors will help you to work at top efficiency as you compose.

2. Know what you have to compose. Be sure that you have all reference materials and other necessary information at your fingertips to save time.

3. Be sure that you are thoroughly familiar with the software package you are using. This will save you a great deal of time. If you are not familiar with your equipment and software, much time can be wasted, and much frustration can and will occur. Try to utilize all special keys as you compose.

4. Know what format you want to use for an interoffice memorandum, a letter, or a report.

5. Check your printer before you begin to compose. Is it ready to print? Much time can also be wasted when the printer is not ready.

6. When you begin to compose, key quickly and do not worry about making keying errors. Simply key your ideas. Once these ideas are on the screen, you can proofread and edit before you print the document. Or you can print a draft copy and edit from the draft. Some users prefer this method because it is easier to read printed copy than to read the material in soft-copy form on the screen. This is strictly a personal preference.

7. If the document runs more than one page, print out a copy after you key each page. Save your document material after every few paragraphs, and print the copy after you complete each page. This will ensure that you will have one hard copy at your fingertips for reference, and this copy will also serve as a backup if there should be a power failure. While most large offices have backup power systems, this is not always the case, and there is no guarantee that you won't accidentally hit a plug. Electronic equipment is sensitive to certain vements.

8. Classify and store your completed work in an organized manner so that it will be easy to retrieve the items. This can be done by reading the software procedures manual carefully and then devising a system so that your business will have a specific procedure to follow.

- The three major forms of written communication used in offices are interoffice memorandums, letters, and reports.

- Interoffice memorandums are referred to by the simple term *memos*. Memos are used for communications among employees within the same organization.

- The main parts of a memo are the heading, the body, and the closing. Formatting of memos varies, depending on whether they are keyboarded on preprinted forms or on plain paper.

- Letters are classified as either personal-business letters or business letters. The main parts of a letter are the heading, the opening, the body, and the closing.

- Special notations on letters include the attention line, the subject line, reference initials, the enclosure notation, the copy notation, the blind copy notation, and the postscript.

- The most common types of letters used in business include letters of goodwill, letters of response, letters requesting information, letters of refusal, letters of claim or adjustment, letters of credit or collection, and sales letters.

- Business reports may be simple or complex, depending on the nature of the information to be communicated. When you are determining the format to use for a report, ask yourself these questions: Who will read the report? What is the desired result of the report? What is the present mind-set of the person who will receive the report?

- The parts of a formal report are the front matter, which consists of a title page, a table of contents, lists of tables and illustrations, a foreword or preface, and a summary; the body, which includes an introduction, the main discussion, and conclusions; and the back matter, which may have appendixes, endnotes, a bibliography, and a glossary.

Interoffice Memorandum	subject line
memo	reference initials
personal-business letter	enclosure notation
business letter	copy notation
heading	blind copy notation
opening	postscript
body	formal report
closing	front matter
notation	back matter
attention line	informal report

REVIEW QUESTIONS

1. Why are written documents such an important form of communication in business?

2. What are some common uses for memos in business offices?

3. What is the difference between a personal-business letter and a business letter?

4. Why are attention lines sometimes used on letters? What other special notations are frequently used?

5. Explain the importance of using an enclosure notation when materials are sent with a letter.

6. What is the difference between a copy notation and a blind copy notation?

7. Name and briefly discuss the major categories of letters used by businesses.

8. What is one purpose of a business report?

9. Explain the difference between a formal report and an informal report.

10. What are the main parts of a formal report? Which parts are optional?

1. Proofread the two addresses below. Prepare large envelopes in an appropriate format acceptable to the U.S. Postal Department.

   Envelope 1

   Mr. Kenneth R. Finley
   3541 Pine Avenue
   Livermore Falls, ME 04264

   Envelope 2

   Mrs. Jeanette L. Kinsey
   90 Park Avenue
   New Scotland, NY 12127

2. List the advantages of using special notations in business letters. When would it be most appropriate to use special notations?

3. Compose a letter requesting information on a new type of desk your company is considering buying. Compose an appropriate inside address. Prepare your letter electronically, save the letter, and print out a rough draft copy. Check with your teacher after you have composed the letter for possible changes. Then return to your word processor, make any necessary corrections, and print a final copy. Pass in your final copy to your teacher for evaluation.

4. Read some articles in magazines. Look for examples of wordiness or imprecision. Decide how the wordy phrases can be reduced to one word. Edit the articles to eliminate poor writing practices. Explain your editing.

INPUT

*C*reating data involves organizing thoughts into an appropriate format and then communicating these thoughts. This is known as preparing **input** and represents the first step in the IPSOD (input, process, storage, output, distribution) cycle. These skills were covered in detail in Chapters 5 and 6.

Input preparation will vary depending on the type of data and the input device used by the sender. Office workers with a broad range of skills to handle this input phase are very valuable in today's electronic office.

Chapter 7 focuses on the importance of understanding data creation and the role of input in the information processing cycle.

As a result of studying this chapter, you will be able to:

- Identify the major types of input media and input devices.
- Determine the appropriate form of input to use for increased office efficiency.
- Develop a continuing awareness of data creation and its contribution to effective input in the information processing cycle.

Before input can occur, the necessary data must be collected. Data comes from several sources. Dictation is one source. You might take dictation directly from a person, or you might take previously recorded dictation from a machine. Data can also come from previously stored information in the computer, face-to-face discussions, telephone calls, or electronic messages. The data may be in the form of hard copy or soft copy. As technology develops, more and more offices will be able to collect verbal data electronically—directly on the computer. **Voice input**, as it is called, will speed up both data collection and communication.

In order to collect the necessary data, you must know how to gather and organize appropriate materials. This skill might simply mean retrieving the necessary file from a manual or electronic file, or it might mean completing research through an electronic database.

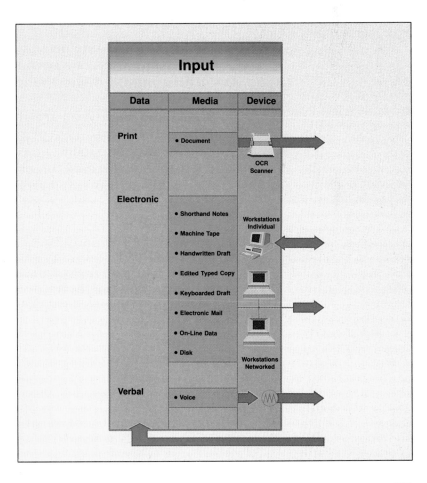

Fig. 7-1 Data that is to be input can appear in a variety of forms and in many different media.

You will also need to know how to manage your time. Learning how to manage time wisely is extremely important and contributes greatly to overall productivity on the job. Inputting requires that today's office worker possess excellent language skills as well. This is necessary when data must be recorded, for the message must be clear to the reader. Without excellent language arts skills, it is difficult to transcribe messages accurately, no matter what form of input is used.

NPUT MEDIA

It is essential for you to become aware of the various types of input media and to understand which type is best for a specific situation.

HORTHAND DICTATION

Dictation involves one person speaking and another person recording what has been said. The person doing the recording may use shorthand notes or work from machine dictation.

Shorthand is still regarded as an extremely valuable skill for several reasons. A person who can use shorthand to take dictation usually can command a higher salary in the job market because he or she is considered to be a more highly skilled employee. Many executives prefer to dictate directly to a person rather than speak into a piece of equipment or use handwritten notes to draft material. A machine can be cumbersome, and it can disrupt the thought patterns of the speaker. Using shorthand to take dictation can preserve confidentiality, because the message exists only in the mind of the speaker and in the form of the shorthand specialist's hard-to-read shorthand symbols. Above all, using shorthand to take dictation allows for human contact, which continues to be a priority in the process of communicating information.

TAKING SHORTHAND DICTATION

If you work in an office where shorthand is used, always be prepared to take dictation.

Face-to-face dictation is an excellent method of input.

Supplies. Keep a supply of shorthand notebooks, pens, and pencils available. Use a rubber band or a large paper clip or clamp to mark your place in your dictation notebook. Keep a red pencil handy to take down instructions. Use a folder to carry any papers connected with the dictation. Special brightly colored paper clips can be used to code special items such as "rush" items.

Separation of Items. The date and time of dictation should be placed at the bottom of the page. This will help you transcribe efficiently later. A space between each item of dictation will allow you to add special instructions in red pencil. Another efficient way to separate dictation is to take the dictation in only the first column and save the second column for special notes. The advantage is that any special notations will be near the actual dictation.

Changes. Changes can be handled as you take the dictation or at the end of the dictation by adding a special note at the bottom. If your supervisor frequently makes changes, allow ample space in the second column of your notebook for these changes.

Spelling. All unfamiliar names should be verified and spelled out in longhand. It is also essential that names and other important information be taken directly from incoming documents to avoid misspelling or confusion.

End Marks. Mark the end of each separate item of dictation with some distinctive symbol so that you can tell at a glance where each item begins and ends.

Numbering. If you number each memo and letter requiring an answer and then number your shorthand response with the same number, you can easily coordinate your dictation with related correspondence. Using this numbering system saves time.

Questions. Mark an item of dictation in your notebook with a large "X" when you need to ask a question. The "X" will serve as a reminder that you want to ask a specific question about that point in the dictation. Ask the question when the dictation is finished.

Transcribing shorthand notes using a word processor enables the secretary to edit material twice: once when it is being keyboarded, and again when it is proofread before printing out a hard copy.

Complete Information. It is possible that on occasion you may have to take dictation on something other than a notebook. In this situation, take the dictation and staple it to your shorthand notebook as soon as possible so that you avoid confusion and do not lose information. It is also advisable to obtain copies of all printed forms that you may have to use to complete your dictation tasks. Attach the forms to your shorthand notebook for easy reference.

P R O C E D U R E S

Transcribing Shorthand Dictation

It is important to transcribe shorthand dictation in an efficient manner so that the message can be transferred at the right time. Keep the following procedures in mind.

1. Organize all materials and information before you begin to transcribe so that you will not have to interrupt your work to look for what you need.

2. Prioritize the dictation that you have to transcribe. Transcribe the "rush" items first.

3. Check the specific instructions for each item before you begin to transcribe it. Make at least one duplicate of each item you transcribe.

4. Carefully verify the spelling of any special words and names before you begin each item. Also check the accuracy of addresses, times, dates, and other pertinent information.

5. Transcribe directly from your notes, checking carefully for correct grammar and sentence construction.

6. Proofread the document before you remove it from the typewriter or word processor. Make all necessary corrections.

7. Draw a diagonal line through each shorthand item after it has been transcribed. Keep a rubber band around the last page that has been transcribed so that you will immediately be ready to pick up your transcribing where you stopped.

8. Check your notebook carefully at the end of the day for any items that have not been transcribed. Plan to transcribe this dictation the next day after completing that day's "rush" items.

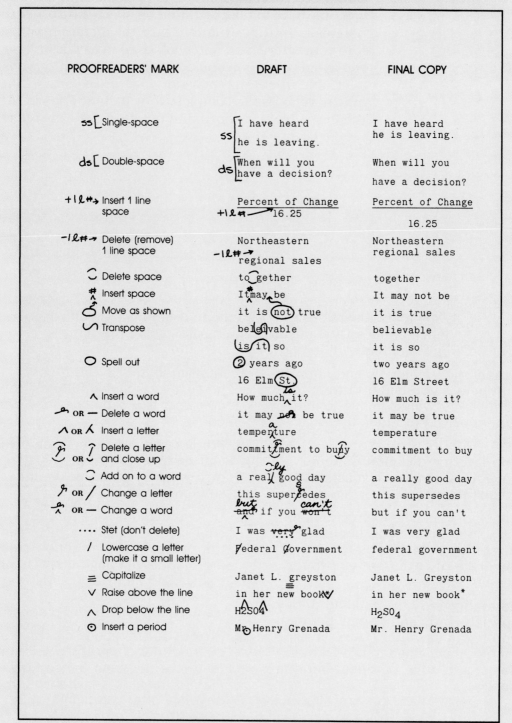

Fig. 7-2   Proofreaders' marks and what they mean

PROOFREADERS' MARK	DRAFT	FINAL COPY
˄ Insert a comma	a large⌄old house	a large, old house
˅ Insert an apostrophe	my children's car	my children's car
˅˅ Insert quotation marks	he wants a loan	he wants a "loan"
= Insert a hyphen	a first⸗rate job	a first-rate job
	ask the co̅owner	ask the co-owner
OR ⊥/M Insert a dash or change a hyphen to a dash	Success⊥at last! Here it is⊥cash!	Success--at last! Here it is--cash!
___ Insert underscore	an issue of <u>Time</u>	an issue of <u>Time</u>
Delete underscore	a <u>very</u> long day	a very long day
( ) Insert parentheses	left today(May 3)	left today (May 3)
¶ Start a new paragraph	¶ If that is so	If that is so
Indent 2 spaces	Net investment in tangible assets	Net investment in tangible assets
⊐ Move to the right	$38,367,000	$38,367,000
⊏ Move to the left	Anyone can win!	Anyone can win!
= Align horizontally	Bob Muller TO:	TO: Bob Muller
‖ Align vertically	‖Jon Peters ‖Ellen March	Jon Peters Ellen March

MACHINE DICTATION

There may be times when the originator needs to dictate messages and no one is available to take notes. In these situations a dictation machine can be used. Dictation machines allow the originator more flexibility in choosing when to give dictation (for example, after office hours or on a business trip). Some of the machines available for machine dictation are described on the next page.

Desk-Top Dictation Machines. Desk-top dictation machines record dictation on standard-size cassettes or on minicassettes. These machines are used by persons who dictate frequently.

Desk-top dictation machines are equipped with many capabilities for ease of use, such as indexing of the dictation and automatic scanning of the tape. Automatic scanning allows the user to move the tape backward for repetition of the message.

Desk-top dictation machines can be purchased as strictly dictation units or as **combination units** with both dictation and transcription capabilities.

Portable Dictation Machines. Dictation machines that are small, portable, and lightweight are also available. These dictation machines run on batteries, so they can be used in automobiles and in other places where electricity is not available. A portable dictation machine is ideal for the person who travels a great deal and needs the freedom to dictate anywhere. Portable dictation machines do not usually have as many features as the larger desk-top machines.

A portable dictation machine

Centralized Dictation Systems. Large businesses often use centralized dictation systems, which let the user call a central recording device to dictate. When a centralized dictation system is used, the dictation is usually recorded on one of two devices, either an endless loop or a multiple-cassette machine. An **endless loop** is a long tape, joined at the ends, that stays inside the recording device and stores the dictation for hundreds of documents. As the device records the latest dictation, the oldest input is automatically erased. An endless loop allows many operators to transcribe different documents simultaneously.

Unlike endless loops, cassettes can be removed from the recording device. Cassettes are used with a **multiple-cassette dictation machine** and can be distributed to the transcribers who are free to handle them. This system allows for greater flexibility in transcription.

With most centralized dictation systems, a supervisor assigns the dictation to be transcribed to the operators. The supervisor may use a computer to track work load, turnaround time, priority of tasks, and overall productivity.

Transcribing Machine Dictation

Keep the following procedure in mind when you transcribe dictation from a machine.

1. Set up the machine for efficient use. Dictation machines usually have hand or foot controls that allow the user to play back dictation in order to check information. If you are using hand controls, place them near your keyboard for maximum efficiency.

2. Read the operator's manual for the dictation machine *before* you begin to operate the machine. Each dictation machine has unique features, and knowing how to operate the machine properly can save time.

3. Use indicator slips when you transcribe. An **indicator slip** is a specially marked slip of paper designed to fit into a section of the machine. The originator can use this to indicate where each recorded item ends. The slips can also be used to indicate where special instructions are located on the tape.

4. Listen to all instructions before you begin to transcribe. Prioritize the items so that you will transcribe the most important items first. If you fail to listen carefully for all detailed instructions, you will find yourself wasting a great amount of time.

5. Listen to several sentences before you begin to transcribe. (When you actually start transcribing, you will, of course, return to the beginning of the item.) If necessary, complete a draft of the document being transcribed. It is often necessary to complete a draft when you are first beginning to use a dictation machine to transcribe. Be sure to mark each draft with the word *draft* and with the date. As you become more familiar with the equipment and the originator's style, fewer drafts will be necessary.

6. Review and proofread each piece of work carefully before you remove it from the typewriter or print it out.

7. Ask questions whenever you are uncertain about anything. Doing so can actually save time and result in increased productivity, since you will make fewer mistakes.

SHORTHAND MACHINES

A **shorthand machine** is a portable machine with keys similar in construction to the keyboard of a typewriter or word processor. When taking dictation, the user presses the keys of the shorthand machine to produce several letters for each word heard. A person who uses a shorthand machine is specially trained and can record up to 250 words a minute, which is twice as fast as most people can take shorthand notes manually.

Shorthand machines are especially useful in situations where many people are speaking. These machines are used most frequently in the courtroom during trials, at public hearings, and at special business meetings where official records of the proceedings are required.

Computer-aided Transcription. Shorthand machines linked to computers are now able to produce edited transcripts. This new technology is known as **computer-aided transcription**. In computer-aided transcription, the operator inserts a cassette into a special section of the computer that converts the keystrokes into actual words and then displays these words on the computer's screen. The computer operator then edits and formats this transcript on the screen and prints out a hard copy. Computer-aided transcription can save much time in the transcription process when used appropriately and efficiently.

DRAFTS

A **draft** is a preliminary, rough copy of a document. A draft may be either handwritten or keyboarded and is prepared in a format that allows the user to proofread the material and edit it for final preparation. Drafts may be prepared in soft-copy or hard-copy form.

Handwritten Drafts. Fifty percent of all documents today are originated in handwriting. Handwriting drafts gives the user the advantage of convenience and privacy. Executives can compose while traveling without disturbing others, and confidentiality of correspondence can be maintained.

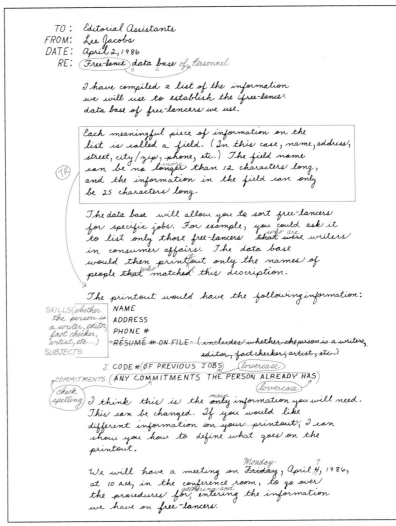

Fig. 7-3 Handwritten documents are the most popular way of originating data in the business office. This sample of a handwritten draft has been marked up to indicate changes and corrections.

Keyboarded and Printed Drafts. More drafts are being generated electronically than ever before. Keying electronic drafts allows for much easier editing and also saves time in the revision process.

Drafts are also prepared on the typewriter. A typed draft can be edited for revision, and paragraphs can be cut and pasted to refine the document. Occasionally it is necessary to prepare a second draft before the final copy.

Originator-Keyboarded Input. Executives are increasingly using their own computers to prepare input. This input can then be formatted and edited by the administrative assistant. **Originator-keyboarded input** saves time if the proper equipment linkages exist. Executives can use portable computers to transfer drafts electronically when they are away from the office.

This executive travels with a portable computer. She keyboards material and sends the disk to her secretary.

Boilerplate. Frequently used paragraphs that are stored electronically are called **boilerplate**. These electronically stored paragraphs can be retrieved easily from memory and used as needed. These paragraphs can be combined with additional paragraphs to produce an original document.

Stored Documents. **Stored documents** are similar to boilerplate. All systems allow the user to store documents (form letters, memos) electronically in their entirety and then retrieve an entire document as needed. Revisions can be made to individualize a document, avoiding having to rekey the document.

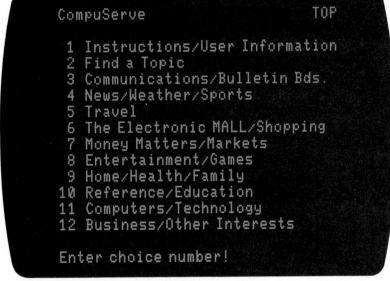

```
CompuServe                          TOP

    1 Instructions/User Information
    2 Find a Topic
    3 Communications/Bulletin Bds.
    4 News/Weather/Sports
    5 Travel
    6 The Electronic MALL/Shopping
    7 Money Matters/Markets
    8 Entertainment/Games
    9 Home/Health/Family
   10 Reference/Education
   11 Computers/Technology
   12 Business/Other Interests

   Enter choice number!
```

Fig. 7-4 External data banks provide many different types of information for businesses that subscribe to their services.

Databases. As you learned in Chapter 3, a **database** is a collection of information that can be obtained from a computer's memory. Data from a database can be used to produce a new document, or it can serve as information for parts of a document.

Examples of a business database are a stored inventory and a list of customer names and addresses.

On-Line Information Services. Many companies choose to subscribe to outside services to collect data. An **on-line information service** allows the user to obtain a variety of data from a special collection of information known as a **data bank**. A code to access the appropriate telephone line by means of a modem can be used. The modem connects the user's computer to the data bank. Using data banks allows businesses to have fast access to much up-to-the-minute information, such as stock prices or the availability of airline reservations.

Data Forms. Data forms are various blank business forms stored in a computer's electronic memory. The appropriate information for each individual use (a customer's name and address, as well as information about his or her purchases, for example) can be keyed into the

```
                    Thank you for taking the time to write us.  We like to keep
                    in close touch with our customers.

                    We were very sorry to hear of your problem with

                    Morrison Industries uses only the finest materials and takes
                    every possible step to ensure that products reach the store
                    in perfect condition

                    In some cases, problems in shipping can affect the condition
                    of a product.

                    We feel it may account for the problem you described.

                    Please accept our apologies.
          01
                    We enclose a check for the amount of purchase.

          02        Thank you again for the information you have provided.
          03
                    Thank you for your concern.

                    Please contact us again should you have any questions about
          04        Morrison Industries.

          05

          06
          07
          10
```

appropriate places on the form as it appears on the computer screen. When the final form is printed out, it is an individualized one. Each customer, in effect, has an original form printed out just for him or her, though all forms follow a designated format.

INPUT DEVICES

Several input devices are used in today's electronic office. Your choice of which input device to use will depend primarily on what is readily available to you as well as on what you feel will most productively accomplish the task.

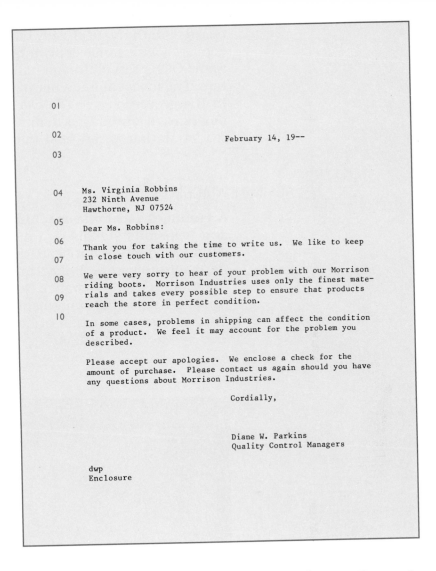

Fig. 7-5 "Boilerplate" paragraphs and complimentary closings are shown on the page on the left. Above is a sample of the kind of individualized letter that can be prepared by selecting an appropriate paragraph.

You are already familiar with the most frequently used input device: the keyboard. There are many other input devices available in the electronic office. It is quite possible that you will use some of these in addition to your electronic keyboard.

OPTICAL CHARACTER READERS

An **optical character reader (OCR)** scans typed or printed pages and converts the text into electronic signals that the computer can understand. As an OCR scans a page, the typed or printed contents are transferred to a computer storage device. An OCR eliminates the need to keyboard data that has already been printed. Most OCRs can convert a wide range of print faces into electronic signals. Some OCRs can even read handwritten numbers and letters. The most common use of optical character readers is in the grocery store. The clerk at the checkout counter moves each purchased item across the optical character reader so that it can read the price.

FACSIMILE MACHINES

A **standard facsimile machine** scans a document page and transmits signals to a receiving facsimile machine, which produces a duplicate document. A **digital facsimile machine** can be linked to a computer so that it can function as a long-distance OCR. The receiving computer converts the signals and displays them as soft copy, permitting easy production of hard copy. The soft copy can also be stored on a disk.

Facsimile machines can send documents electronically over long distances.

OTHER INPUT DEVICES

Computers are available that allow the user to input data without keyboarding, using special input devices. Users who do not have keyboarding skills can use these devices to manipulate text already entered by someone else, but the users cannot create text copy with most of them.

Mouse. A microcomputer terminal may have a special attachment called a **mouse**, a small hand-operated device that allows the user to move the cursor and to input processing commands without using the keyboard. The mouse can be moved around on a special tablet or on the desk top.

This hand-operated mouse allows the operator to move the cursor to any point on the screen. Mice are useful input devices for computer operators who are not comfortable with keyboarding.

Touch Screen. Computers that have a feature called a **touch screen** allow the user to enter commands by touching the screen. Such a system displays a menu with a list of functions or pictures. By pointing at the desired option and touching the screen, you can make another menu appear that displays various tasks included in that particular function. Again, you touch the screen to make the file you want to use appear. These types of screens are used a great deal for computer-assisted learning programs, where users touch the screen to answer questions.

Graphics Tablet. A **graphics tablet** is a board that creates images on the screen. To create graphics, you may use your finger, a special pen, or a mouse to draw the image on the board. The image then appears in the same

Graphics tablet

Light pen

position on the computer screen. Graphics tablets require special software to convert hand movements into digital signals, which are then converted into pictures.

Light Pen. You can also create images on a computer screen with a light pen. A **light pen** is a penlike device connected to the computer terminal by a flexible wire. As the pen is moved against the screen, the movements appear as light on the screen. A light pen can be used to trace drawings or maps on the screen or to create your own drawings.

Digital Scanner. A **digital scanner** is similar to an OCR except that a digital scanner can read charts, blueprints, and pictures and convert them into digital data to be reproduced on the computer screen. Digital scanners are most widely used in architectural and engineering firms where employees frequently work with complex technical drawings.

Digital Cameras. Some computer systems can use a **digital camera** to accept input. A digital camera is wired to the computer and converts photographic images into computer signals. This capability allows engineers, designers, and others who work with photographs to produce them on documents. Office workers can also use digital cameras to create documents and slides for meetings and presentations.

Digital scanner

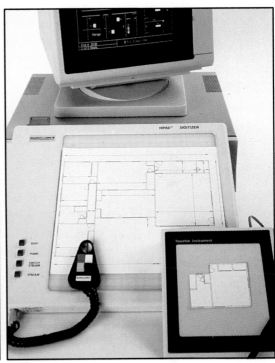

Digital camera

NPUT PREPARATION PROCEDURES

Using efficient procedures when preparing input information will result in increased productivity, whatever medium or device is being used for input. Preparing to input data on a computer terminal connected to a mainframe or minicomputer requires fewer steps than preparation with a microcomputer. With a mainframe or mini-

DOS Commands

The internal commands are:

- COPY Copy specific files from one disk to another.
- CLR Clear the screen.
- DEL Delete files.
- DIR List the names of the files that are on the disk.
- RENAME Change the name of a file.

The external commands are:

- FORMAT Make a disk compatible with the operating system so that it can be read and written on.
- DISKCOPY Copy an entire disk.
- COMP Compare the contents of two files.
- DISKCOMP Compare the contents of two disks.
- CHKDSK Check a disk and show the amount of memory remaining.

computer, all you need to do is turn on your terminal and select the appropriate processing application from the menu. If there is a security system to protect private files, users may have to use a "log on" procedure. This usually involves keying in one or two names or codes, usually called a **user ID** or **password** so that the computer will recognize you as a valid user. In order to input data on a microcomputer, you will need to have a disk that contains the disk operating system (DOS) for your hardware, a program disk that contains the applications program you will be using, and a data disk on which to store the files you will create as you process the data. You will need a copy of the user's guide or operations manual for the software package, and if you are not completely familiar with the computer system, you should have a copy of the computer operations manual also.

The first thing you will do is **load** the DOS disk in order to **boot** the system. The terms *load* and *boot* are used to describe the procedure that makes the system ready to run a software program.

As you become more familiar with your manual and with the disk operating system of your computer, you will be better able to understand problems that may arise and solve them without help.

PROCEDURES

Booting Up the System

Because the IBM Personal Computer and its compatibles are so common in the business world, we will use this system as an example in explaining how the boot procedure works.

1. Remove the DOS disk from its paper sleeve, and place it with the label side up in drive A, which will be the drive on your left as you face the computer. Close the door of the disk drive.

2. Turn on the printer, the monitor, and the computer. Depending on the setup of your equipment, these will have separate switches, or they may be plugged into a single switch.

```
Current date is Tue  1-05-1988
Enter new date:
Current time is   0:00:09.66
Enter new time:


The IBM Personal Computer DOS
Version 2.10 (C)Copyright IBM Corp 1981, 1982, 1983

A>  diskcopy a: b:

Insert source disk into drive A:

Insert target disk into drive B:

Strike any key when ready
```

DOS diskcopy command

```
Current date is Tue  1-05-1988
Enter new date:
Current time is  0:00:09.83
Enter new time:

The IBM Personal Computer DOS
Version 2.10  (C)Copyright IBM Corp 1981, 1982, 1983

A> dir


ANSI     SYS    1664  10-20-83  12:00p
FORMAT   COM    6912  10-20-83  12:00p
CHKDSK   COM    6400  10-20-83  12:00p
SYS      COM    1680  10-20-83  12:00p
DISKCOPY COM    2576  10-20-83  12:00p
DISKCOMP COM    2188  10-20-83  12:00p
COMP     COM    2534  10-20-83  12:00p
EDLIN    COM    4608  10-20-83  12:00p
MODE     COM    3139  10-20-83  12:00p
FDISK    COM    6369  10-20-83  12:00p
BACKUP   COM    3687  10-20-83  12:00p
RESTORE  COM    4003  10-20-83  12:00p
PRINT    COM    4608  10-20-83  12:00p
RECOVER  COM    2304  10-20-83  12:00p
ASSIGN   COM     896  10-20-83  12:00p
TREE     COM    1513  10-20-83  12:00p
GRAPHICS COM     789  10-20-83  12:00p
SORT     EXE    2408  10-20-83  12:00p
FIND     EXE    5888  10-20-83  12:00p
MORE     COM     384  10-20-83  12:00p
BASIC    COM   16256  10-20-83  12:00p
BASICA   COM   26112  10-20-83  12:00p
       23 File(s)     28672 bytes free

A>
```

DOS directory command

DOS disk format command

```
Current date is Tue  1-05-1988
Enter new date:
Current time is  0:00:08.84
Enter new time:


The IBM Personal Computer DOS
Version 2.10 (C)Copyright IBM Corp 1981, 1982, 1983

A> format
Insert new disk for drive A:
and strike any key when ready
```

Fig. 7-6   These screens show examples of three common DOS commands.

3. Wait. It will take 15 to 45 seconds for the power to activate the system. You will hear either a "beep" sound first or a whirring sound from the disk drive. A red dot light on the disk drive will go on. This means that the disk is being read. *Do not open the disk drive door when the red light is on.*

4. A **prompt**, which is a message from the computer system to the user, will appear on the screen. In Fig. 7-7 the operator has entered the date and time.

5. If you do not get the proper system boot prompts, it may be because of a minor problem. If there is a problem, you will get prompts similar to those shown in Fig. 7-8. The most common error at this point is placement of the wrong disk in drive A.

6. Once you have corrected the problem, you can restart the boot procedure by pressing the keys marked "Ctrl," "Alt," and "Del" simultaneously. This is an awkward maneuver of the fingers, and it is purposefully arranged this way to avoid accidental rebooting while inputting, which could lose information in the temporary memory.

7. When the "A" prompt appears on the screen, you are ready to begin input. Remove the DOS disk from drive A, replace it with your applications program disk, and key in the appropriate command (this will vary with the applications program you are using). If your system has two disk drives, you can put your data disk in drive B. Otherwise, you will have to switch disks when you are ready to save the files you create.

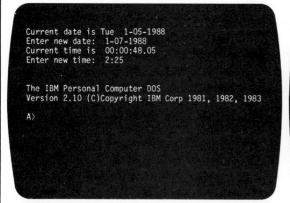

Fig. 7-7   The DOS program asks you to enter the date and time. These prompts can be bypassed by hitting the "enter" key. When the "A" prompt appears, the computer is ready to accept your program disk.

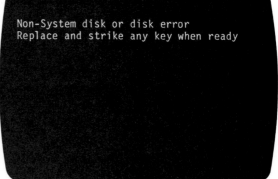

Fig. 7-8   This screen shows that the wrong disk is in drive A.

WORKING WITH DISKS

A floppy disk is a round, flat, double-sided sheet of pliable plastic that is magnetically treated and coated and kept in a protective vinyl jacket or a jacket composed of a hard material. Floppy disks come in three basic sizes: 8 inches, 5¼ inches, and 3½ inches in diameter.

Some microcomputers have a hard disk, which is a storage device made of magnetically treated plastic, aluminum, or ceramic. It is sealed directly inside the computer's cabinet. The storage capacity of hard disks is much greater than that of floppy disks that may be inserted individually into the computer.

FORMATTING FLOPPY DISKS

Every manufacturer designs its hardware and software differently. For this reason you will need to prepare every disk used to store the document files that are input on your system. This preparation procedure is called **formatting**.

Formatting a disk is different from formatting a document. To format a data disk, you load the DOS disk and then insert the data disk into the drive of the computer and keyboard the formatting commands of your disk operating system. The operations manual for your system will tell you specifically how to do this.

TAKING CARE OF AND HANDLING FLOPPY DISKS

TECHNOLOGY NOTE

Floppy Disks

Here are some technical terms that you will need to know when you work with floppy disks.

- **Double-sided**. The disk can store twice the amount of data that can be stored on a single-sided disk.

If you work with floppy disks, you need to learn how to use, store, and protect them. They are delicate and are very easily damaged. Carelessness can also lead to the accidental loss of important data. The following guidelines can help you guard the disks against damage and accidental loss of data.

- Apply write-protect tabs to any disks containing data that should not be changed.
- Handle a floppy disk only near the label at the top of its rigid protective cover.
- Never remove a floppy disk from its protective cover, and never touch the parts of the disk that are exposed through openings in the cover.
- Do not bend a floppy disk.

- **Double-density**. The disk can store twice the amount of data that can be stored on a single-density disk.
- **Write-protect notch**. This is an indentation on the outside edge of a floppy disk. When the notch is uncovered, you can add new data to the disk, erase data, or replace data already on the disk. A **write-protect tab** (a small sticker) can be placed over the notch to prevent storage of new data or changes in the existing data on the disk. The main purpose of the write-protect notch is to prevent you from accidentally writing over or erasing data that is important.
- **Hub ring**. This is placed in the ring of a disk to protect the disk from damage while it is in the disk drive.

- Do not use pens, pencils, or erasers on the surface of the protective cover of a floppy disk. Instead, write on an adhesive-backed identification label before you apply it to the disk cover. Remove any old labels, if possible, instead of adding new labels on top.
- Keep floppy disks out of direct sunlight and away from radiators, lamps, and other sources of heat.
- Store floppy disks at room temperature.
- When they are not in the disk drive, keep disks protected in a box or a protective jacket.
- Store floppy disks, in their paper jackets, so that they are standing on their edges, not in stacks, in specially designed containers. These are available from computer supply dealers.
- Keep magnets away from floppy disks and hard disks, because magnetism can erase data. Keep metal paper clips away from disks too, because many office workers use magnetic paper-clip containers that magnetize the clips themselves.
- A ringing telephone can create a magnetic field, so don't leave your disks near telephones or set a telephone on top of a disk drive.
- Be careful when you insert floppy disks into disk drives.
- Keep floppy disks away from water and other liquids. If they should get wet for some reason, dry them with a lint-free cloth.

PROCEDURES

Guidelines for Keyboarding

Keep the following guidelines in mind as you keyboard input.

1. *Posture.* Sitting correctly in your chair will reduce the back strain and fatigue that can easily occur after sitting in front of a typewriter or computer terminal for several hours.

2. *Your Chair.* Be absolutely certain that the chair you are using is comfortable for you. Adjust the chair for your height and your position at the keyboard. Your chair is properly adjusted and your sit-

ting position is correct if your feet reach the floor and rest there without pushing up your knees, if your spine is straight, and if your hips are placed firmly against the back of the chair. You should not have to move your upper arms away from your sides in order for your hands to reach the keyboard.

3. *Your Computer Terminal.* Placing the keyboard and computer terminal correctly can also help you to avoid poor posture and the fatigue and tension that result from it. Adjust your keyboard and terminal at a height that allows you to reach the keyboard comfortably and to look at the screen without slumping in your chair or straining your neck. The screen should be just below your eye level so that you look slightly downward at it.

4. *Your Furniture.* Be absolutely certain that the furniture upon which your computer terminal or typewriter is sitting is comfortable for you to work. Check for tables and/ or desks that provide ample space for needed materials as well as space in which your body can be comfortable.

5. *Your Copyholder.* A **copyholder** is a device that holds hard copy at an angle from which you can read the copy easily while you are keyboarding. You can choose from a wide variety of copyholders. Be certain you have selected a copyholder that fits your individual needs. You should be able to use a copyholder without having to move your head back and forth constantly in order to shift your eyes. The proper placement of a copyholder also prevents fatigue, back strain, and eyestrain.

6. *Lighting.* Proper lighting contributes to your comfort and your productivity when you are keyboarding. Proper lighting enables you to read both your screen and your hard copy without eyestrain. Be sure that the overhead light and/or desk lamp is properly placed so that it does not cause glare on your screen. If your workstation area is lighted by natural light through windows or skylights, place your computer screen so that the windows are behind it. This will ensure that the screen won't reflect light. Adjust your screen for brightness and contrast. Turn up the brightness as much as you can without hurting your eyes. Then adjust the contrast so that bright characters appear on the screen against a dark background.

- Before you can perform the first step in the IPSOD process—inputting—you need to gather data and prepare it for processing. You gather data from many sources, and you collect it in three different formats—print, electronic, and verbal.

- An important part of an office worker's job is to gather data and prepare it for processing. Office workers need to be knowledgeable in language arts and office procedures.

- As an office worker, you need to be familiar with many different kinds of input media. The most common input medium is shorthand dictation, and shorthand is a highly valued skill.

- Taking and transcribing shorthand dictation requires that you follow several basic rules—such as keeping your materials at hand and organizing them—so that you can perform your work efficiently and with a minimum of delays and errors.

- Dictation machines are convenient because you don't have to be present when your supervisor wants to dictate. Some dictation machines are portable or desk-top units, while others are large centralized units. Shorthand machines allow the users to speed up the recording of words, and computer-aided transcription machines convert keystrokes into soft copy.

- Drafts are rough or working copies of documents from which you produce finished documents. Drafts can be in hard-copy form (such as handwritten, keyboarded, or printed drafts) or in soft-copy form (originator-keyboarded input, boilerplate, stored documents, and electronic messages).

- The most common way to input on a computer is through the use of a keyboard. You can also use an OCR to read typed or printed words or codes, or you can use a digital facsimile machine to reproduce a page of text on a computer screen.

- Other input devices include mice, touch screens, graphics tablets, light pens, digital scanners, and digital cameras.

- When preparing to input data on mainframe or mini-computer systems, you may have to log on by keyboarding a code called a user ID or password.

- The disk operating system performs important functions that are represented by internal commands and external commands.

- When you use a microcomputer, you need to boot up the system by loading the DOS disk and you must format your floppy disks to prepare them for recording the files that you create.

- Floppy disks are delicate and must be handled carefully in order to avoid damage to the disks or accidental loss of data stored on the disks.

V OCABULARY

input
voice input
combination unit
endless loop
multiple-cassette dictation
  machine
indicator slip
shorthand machine
computer-aided
  transcription
draft
originator-keyboarded
  input
boilerplate
stored document
database
on-line information service
data bank
optical character reader
  (OCR)
standard facsimile
  machine

digital facsimile machine
mouse
touch screen
graphics tablet
light pen
digital scanner
digital camera
user ID
password
load
boot
prompt
formatting
double-sided
double-density
write-protect notch
write-protect tab
hub ring
copyholder

1. List the major sources from which data is collected for processing.

2. Describe the skills an office worker must possess in order to process data efficiently.

3. List the most commonly used forms of media for dictation.

4. What details need to be reviewed before beginning the transcription process, no matter what input medium is being used?

5. What steps would you take if you could not understand either your own shorthand notes or information on a cassette?

6. Explain computer-aided transcription.

7. How can the special microcomputer attachment called the mouse serve as an input device?

8. What is the role of the disk operating system in the input phase of information processing?

9. Explain the purpose of a user ID or password.

10. List the precautions you can take to protect the data stored on a floppy disk.

SKILLBUILDING ACTIVITIES

1. Select a partner to dictate a short letter requesting information about a new video product. Determine which input medium you will use. After you have transcribed the letter, evaluate it. Then reverse roles with your partner and repeat the same activity. Make a list of suggestions that will help you and your partner become more efficient at dictation and transcription.

2. Your company is developing a new procedures manual for its workers who originate information. You have been given the responsibility for writing the section of the procedures manual called "How to Use Dictation Equipment Efficiently." Prepare an outline of what you would include in this section.

4. Using a word processor or typewriter, transcribe the longhand draft shown in Fig. 7-3.

5. Get a computer supplies catalog from a dealer, a library, or someone you know. Look in the section that shows disks and related supplies. Make a list of the items you would need for ideal care of your disks. Include prices and brief descriptions of the items.

PROCESSING

*D*uring the processing phase of the IPSOD cycle, data is manipulated, transforming it into useful information. Electronic processing allows tasks that would be completed manually to be completed much more quickly. Examples of these tasks might involve revising and editing text, calculating figures, generating reports from recorded information, and creating charts and graphs.

Learning how to use computers efficiently continues to be a major training goal in business. What options are available when handling these tasks? How do you decide which software package is the most efficient when completing a task? Knowing how to make wise decisions when working with computers and software will give you an edge in moving forward in your job.

Because of the new technologies, office workers must assume more responsibility. No longer do they sit behind a desk waiting for their supervisor to tell them what to do and how to do it. They are now expected to make many decisions on their own. Managers are delegating more tasks to their support staff.

This chapter will give you a detailed look at the four major software applications—word processing, spreadsheet, database, and graphics. You will also learn how integrated software programs are used to process information. Also included is information that will help you learn to make decisions about selecting the appropriate software tool for the specific task.

After studying this chapter, you will be able to:

- Name and describe the four major software applications.
- Describe the major steps in creating documents, spreadsheets, databases, and graphs.
- List and describe the word processing functions that are common to most word processing programs.
- Describe a spreadsheet and explain its major uses.
- Describe a database and explain its major uses.
- Describe the types of graphs that a graphics program can produce.
- Describe the advantages of using integrated software.

PPLICATIONS SOFTWARE

The great feature of using **applications software** is that by changing the software, you can completely change the personality of the computer. The same computer that does word processing can prepare budgets and perform statistical analyses with spreadsheet software, keep records of data and generate reports using database software, prepare business graphs using graphics software, and do much, much more. As you can see, the microcomputer is indeed a very flexible tool. As an office worker, you will decide which software to use to complete your daily tasks. This is both the challenge and the opportunity that applications software provides.

OMMON FEATURES OF APPLICATIONS SOFTWARE

Function Keys. Regardless of the type of software you are using, the function keys of your microcomputer will be used to execute the functions provided by the software.

Template. Because the functions performed by each function key change from program to program, most applications programs include a template for the user. A

template is a card or plate that is placed over the function keys of the microcomputer keyboard. This plate labels each key with its use within the applications program.

Command-Driven Programs. Not all features of an applications program are completed with a function key. With a **command-driven program,** you will request other functions by pressing keys in a designated sequence.

Menu-Driven Programs. If a program is not command-driven, then it will be menu-driven. A **menu-driven program** displays a **menu** on the screen, which is a list of the functions the user can select from. After making a selection from the menu, you may be given another menu, called a **submenu,** which is a detailed list of the choices within the first function you chose.

Help Features. Many applications programs have on-line help features. Some display a **help screen** that can be accessed to see which commands or keys are used to complete each function provided by the program. More sophisticated **help facilities** are somewhat "intelligent" in that they follow the steps you are taking to complete a function. If you need additional help, you will be told what to do next to complete what you started.

C REATING DOCUMENTS, SPREADSHEETS, DATABASES, AND GRAPHS

The functions will vary from program to program, but the basic steps in creating a document, spreadsheet, database, or graph are the same.

Booting the Computer and Loading the Software. Boot the computer first, loading your operating system, then your applications software. Chapter 4 covers the boot procedure and how to load software. Refer to this discussion if necessary.

Formatting. Regardless of the program you are using, some formatting will be necessary. With word processing it will involve setting margins and tabs. With spreadsheet and database programs, it will involve establishing column and field widths. With graphics, it will involve selecting the type of graph to be produced.

Inputting and Editing. When you are ready to begin inputting, make sure that your chair and your computer keyboard and screen are at a comfortable level for you. Check that the lighting in the room does not cause too much glare on the screen and that the screen brightness is set at a proper level. This can decrease the chance of eyestrain.

Saving. Periodically throughout the format and the input and edit stages, save your work. This will ensure that you do not lose too much work should the computer experience a failure. Once you have completed inputting and formatting and are ready to print, you will want to save your work for a final time to be sure that the most updated version of your work is stored.

Proofreading. It is best to proofread your work while it is on the screen—that is, before printing it.

Printing. If your work is already formatted, all you will need to do to print it is to select the print option used for your software.

Proofreading. Regardless of whether or not you proofread your work before printing it, you must still proofread it after you get the printout. Errors that you might miss on the screen will be obvious once they are printed.

Making Revisions. If you find that you need to make additional revisions after printing your work, you will have to:
- Retrieve the file.
- Revise.
- Save the file.
- Proofread.
- Print.
- Proofread.

This is called the **revision cycle** and takes a fraction of the time it would take to redo your work.

Now that we have reviewed the major similarities that you should be aware of when using any of the four types of applications programs covered in this chapter, let us take a closer look at each type individually to see how the four types differ.

WORD PROCESSING

Word processing today can best be defined as the use of a computer and software in creating, organizing, formatting, editing, printing, and storing all types of documents, such as memorandums, letters, charts, and reports. Some of the most basic word processing functions are listed below.

- *Center.* Automatically centers text between the right and left margins.

- *Copy.* Designates a block of text, such as a paragraph, that needs to be duplicated in another place or in several other places within the document.

- *Delete.* Designates a character or block of text that needs to be removed from the document. This type of delete function will require fewer keystrokes in removing large portions of text than the delete function listed below.

- *Global search and replace.* Finds every occurrence of a selected word or phrase in a document and replaces it with new copy. For example, if the words *United States of America* appear in many places in a document and you decide to change them in each place to the abbreviation *U.S.A.,* you can use the global search and replace function.

- *Help.* Lists on the screen the functions that the software can perform and details on how to use them.

- *Indent.* Automatically sets up a temporary left margin for keying indented text.

- *Insert.* Allows text or space to be inserted in the middle of existing text without altering any of that text.

- *Merge.* Inserts a document that has already been stored or filed into the document being edited.

- *Move.* Designates a block of text that needs to be moved from its original location to another place.

- *Save.* Stores or files a portion of the document being edited as a separate document in itself.

- *Search.* Locates a specific text sequence that you wish to get to quickly.

ICROCOMPUTERS VERSUS DEDICATED WORD PROCESSORS

Most of the word processing programs available today are used on microcomputers. Although word processing on microcomputers is most common, there are also machines called **dedicated word processors** that are designed solely for the function of word processing. This means that they cannot do spreadsheet or database tasks or perform any other applications program functions. One example of a dedicated word processor found in offices today is the Wang Alliance, whose keyboard is pictured in Fig. 8-1. An important advantage of using a dedicated word processor is that the keyboard is designed for one purpose: word processing.

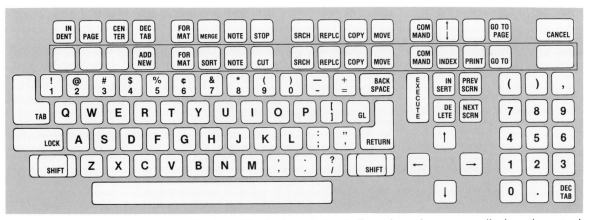

Fig. 8-1   The keyboard of a dedicated word processor displays the actual commands right on the keys. This makes it somewhat easier to use than a microcomputer with word processing capabilities because you do not need to memorize all the different commands for editing functions.

Microcomputers, on the other hand, are designed to be effective in a variety of applications in addition to word processing. Although this allows them to be more flexible, it also means that their keyboard layout is appropriate for most applications, but ideal for none.

A major factor in deciding whether to get a dedicated word processor or a microcomputer with word processing software is whether or not other applications, such as spreadsheet or graphics, will be needed. Most offices today require workstations that can do more than word processing and are purchasing microcomputers rather than dedicated word processors.

As we discussed in an earlier section, there are several steps in creating documents, spreadsheets, databases, and graphs that apply to all of these programs. The following additional information is specific to using word processing software on a microcomputer.

CREATING DOCUMENTS

Formatting a Document. The layout of the document on the printed page is very important in word processing and is the result of document formatting. One of the most dramatic benefits of word processing is the ability to quickly and easily change the appearance of a document with a few keystrokes.

The following paragraphs will give you an overview of the various types of word processing formatting functions.

- *Setting margins, tabs, and indentions:* Many word processors also provide **decimal tabs,** which will align columns of numbers on the decimal points. Setting margins, tabs, and indentions is usually done before the document is input, just as you would at a typewriter. Most systems display a **format line,** sometimes called a **format ruler,** which is a line at the top or bottom of the screen that shows where your margins and tabs are set.

On the word processor screen shown in Fig. 8-2, the

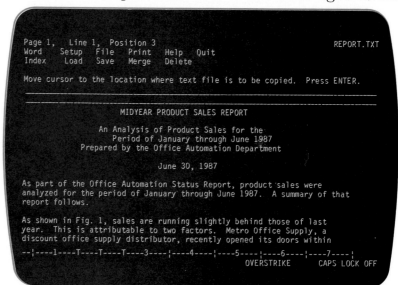

Fig. 8-2 This word processor screen shows the format line at the bottom. The right margin is set at 70. The *T* stands for each tab set; the tabs are set at 15, 20, and 25.

format line runs from left to right along the bottom of the screen. It indicates the left and right margins and the width of the text line. The left margin is set at 10, and the right margin is set at 70 (the zeros have been omitted). This would allow for a text line of 60 characters.

The format line also shows the location of the tab settings. In this example, the tabs are set at 15, 20, and 25. This means that they are 5, 10, and 15 spaces from the left margin.

- *Highlighting text:* Features such as underscores, boldface print, italics, and superscripts and subscripts are usually added as the text is being inputted.
- *Establishing page design:* The final stage of formatting that establishes certain page design parameters is sometimes done just before printing. This formatting usually includes the following functions:
  Line spacing: Selects single or double spacing. Triple spacing and other variations are sometimes an option.
  Page length: Defines the number of lines per page.
  Page numbering: Numbers pages automatically.
  Headers and footers: Allows for headings at the top (headers) or bottom (footers) of each page.
  Justification: Aligns text at the right margin, giving a flush appearance similar to the appearance of text in a newspaper or magazine.
  Font: Selects type styles on the printer being used when more than one style is available.
  Print size: Selects the size of type when the document is being printed.

Some programs may provide other formatting functions as well.

Inputting and Editing the Document. As you key, if you need to correct mistakes or wish to revise anything on the screen, use the appropriate word processing functions to do so.

Saving and Proofreading the Document. Follow the procedures for saving and proofreading outlined earlier in this chapter. These procedures apply to all applications programs.

Printing the Document. You should follow the procedure given for the program you are working with.

Spelling Checkers. Many word processing packages have an **electronic dictionary** or **spelling checker.** An electronic dictionary compares the words in the document with those in the dictionary. When a word in the document does not match any word in the dictionary, it will be highlighted so that the user can correct any errors. Many spelling checkers will allow users to enter additional words, including frequently used proper names, so that they are not flagged by the electronic dictionary.

Some spelling checkers have a "replace" feature that will automatically replace the misspelled word with the correct word. Some word processors today include a *Thesaurus.* Figure 8-3 illustrates how a spelling checker highlights words in question.

Even after you use a spelling checker, it is important to proofread all documents. Spelling checkers cannot catch errors in the usage of words.

Mail Merge. Many word processing programs have a **mail merge,** or **list processing,** feature that can create personalized form letters for any number of people. These letters can be prepared in a fraction of the time it would take to type each letter individually, because you input the letter once, omitting the name, the address, and other variable information. This letter without the varia-

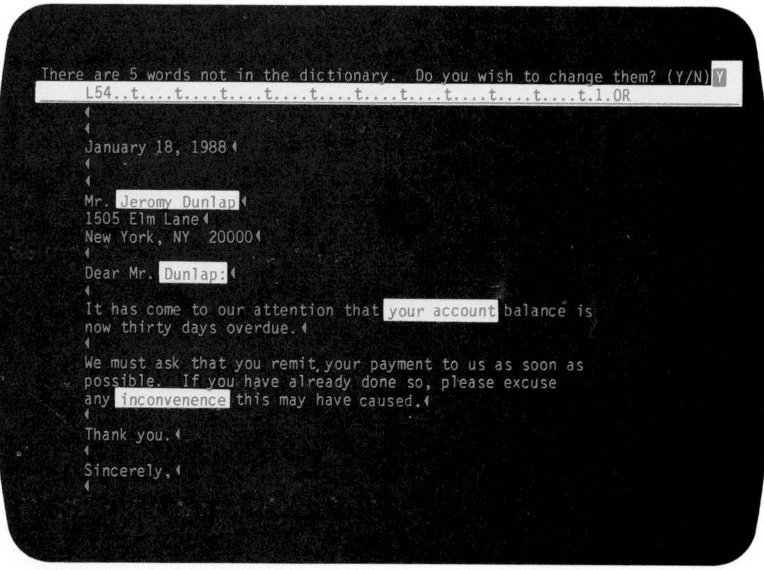

Fig. 8-3   The spelling checker highlights misspelled words.

ble information is sometimes called the **merge document.** You then input a list of names and addresses and whatever variable information you want inserted in the letter. This is sometimes called the **list document.**

The program does the rest, automatically.

Now we will look at another popular type of applications program.

PREADSHEETS

A **spreadsheet** is an electronic worksheet, similar in layout to an accounting ledger sheet and is arranged like a grid in columns and rows. Values are entered in these columns and rows, and calculations are performed on them.

Spreadsheet software increases the decision-making powers of the user. Spreadsheet software allows you to play "what if" scenarios with the figures you are working with. For example, your teacher might have your class grades on a spreadsheet. It is the end of the school year, and you have only one more test to take before your final grade for the course is determined. You ask your teacher what your final grade would be if you got an 80 on the last test. Your teacher enters 80 in the column for the last test, and your final grade is calculated. This is shown in Fig. 8-4.

```
To 4:80                                           1COMMAND.SPD
Spreadsheet   File   Print   Help   Quit
Width   Format   Insert   Delete   Copy   Erase   Lock   Recalculate

Press ENTER to accept highlighted option.  Press F2 or Esc to input data.

        A                  B          C  °      D          E
1  NAME                  Test 1     Test 2    Test 3    Final Grade
2
3  Adam Smith              75         80        -          -
4  Jane Doe                70         75       80         75
5  Julie Dobson            85         80        -          -
6  Tyrone Jackson          85         90        -          -
7
8
```

Fig. 8-4 A teacher can use spreadsheet software to keep track of students' grades. If one test score must be changed, the spreadsheet software automatically recalculates the final grade.

You can see that a spreadsheet is a lot more than just an advanced electronic calculator. It is also a powerful decision-making tool, often called a **decision-support tool.**

It is obvious that the spreadsheet has many uses in today's offices. These include not only analyses for tasks such as budgeting, sales projections, expense report calculations, and project planning but also analyses for broader tasks such as calendaring and the creation of forms.

*T*HE ANATOMY OF A SPREADSHEET

Now that you understand some of the benefits from using spreadsheet software, we will study the parts of a spreadsheet.

Columns, Rows, and Parameters. As was mentioned earlier, a spreadsheet is arranged like a grid in columns and rows. The **parameters,** or maximum number of columns and maximum number of rows, vary from program to program.

Cells and Cell Addresses. The place where a column and a row intersect is called a **cell.** Each cell is identified by its column letter and row number. This is called a **cell address.** For example, the cell address for the cell highlighted in Fig. 8-5 is E14.

Cell Reference and Active Cell. The cell address of the highlighted cursor block is usually located on the top line of the screen. This is called the **cell reference.** The user can always refer to this to quickly identify where he or she is in the spreadsheet. The cell upon which the cursor block is located is called the **active cell.**

Labels. The entries in the columns and rows of a spreadsheet are described by **labels.** A label can be made up of letters or a combination of letters and numbers. The label for column B in Fig. 8-5 is "STANDARD PRODUCTION EXPENSES." Labels are simply identifying names that categorize the data within the same row or column.

Values. A **value** is a number that is entered in a column or row of the spreadsheet.

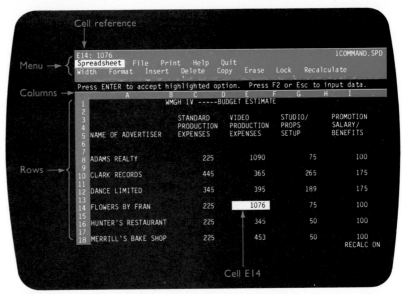

Fig. 8-5 The grid of a spreadsheet contains individual cells where the information is input. The computer will automatically recalculate all variations you wish to explore.

S PREADSHEET FEATURES, FUNCTIONS, AND COMMANDS

Formulas. A **formula** is an entry that will make the spreadsheet program perform an arithmetic operation on the cells identified. It is the formulas that give the spreadsheet its power to perform calculations, using the values entered in its cells.

A	B	C
1 WORLD TRAVEL AGENCY		
2 INCOME STATEMENT DECEMBER 31, 198X		
3		
4 REVENUE	$350,000	100.0%
5		
6 TOTAL EXPENSES	$290,000	82.9%
7		
8 NET INCOME	$60,000	17.1%

Value Formula
$$\frac{Net\ Income}{Revenue} = 17.1\%$$

Place Formula
$$\frac{+\ B8}{+\ B4} = 17.1\%$$

Mathematical Operations. Spreadsheet programs will perform all basic mathematical operations. These operations and their corresponding symbols are addition (+), subtraction (−), multiplication (∗), and division (/). Some programs will also find exponential values (multiplying a number by itself; for example, 5 squared, or 5 raised to the 2d power, is 25). Different mathematical operations can be combined within a single formula.

Functions. Some formulas can become very long when mathematical operations are performed on many cells. Spreadsheet programs have several functions that simplify the way in which formulas can be entered. The @SUM function represents "the sum of" and is used when strings of cells are added. The @AVG function is used in the same way to calculate the average of a string of cells. There are other functions available as well, and these will vary from one program to the next.

Commands. All spreadsheet programs include basic commands for manipulating the data entered. These **commands** are instructions that tell the spreadsheet program what to do. Spreadsheet programs will differ in the commands that they have, but most usually include at least the basic commands listed below.

Move: Allows a group or range of cells to be moved.

Copy: Allows a group or range of cells to be copied from one part of the spreadsheet to another, leaving the original range of cells where it was.

Insert: Allows rows or columns to be inserted anywhere in the spreadsheet.

Delete: Allows rows or columns (or a block of rows and columns) to be deleted from the spreadsheet.

Save: Will save, or file, a spreadsheet onto a hard disk or diskette.

Load: Retrieves a spreadsheet from a disk. It is then possible to view, edit, or reformat the original spreadsheet.

Print: Prints the entire spreadsheet or just a portion of it.

Some additional information specific to spreadsheet software is presented below.

CREATING A SPREADSHEET

The main difference you will find when creating a spreadsheet, as opposed to a document, is that you are working with cells of data organized in rows and columns rather than strings of text. For this reason formatting and editing functions differ in how they are performed.

Formatting a Spreadsheet. Since a spreadsheet contains columns, you must first set the width of the columns. On the basis of the information you wish to place in each column, you will estimate how many characters long each column should be. If you find later that a column is not wide enough to accommodate an entry you wish to make, you can easily increase the column width. Just as margins and tabs are set before a document is inputted, column widths are established before spreadsheet data is entered.

Spreadsheets also have options for the format in which values are displayed. For example, numbers can be displayed with or without decimal points and places, dollar signs, percent symbols, or commas. Also, cell entries can be right-justified or left-justified.

Inputting and Editing the Spreadsheet. Enter the values in the columns that you have formatted. As with word processing, if you make any errors in values, labels, or formats, you can correct them using the functions and commands provided by your spreadsheet program.

Saving and Proofreading the Spreadsheet. Follow the procedures for saving and proofreading outlined earlier in the chapter that apply to all applications programs.

Printing the Spreadsheet. Before printing the spreadsheet, you will probably have to specify whether you wish to print the entire spreadsheet or just a portion of it. If you want to print just a portion of it, you will specify the cell at which printing should begin and the cell at which printing should end.

DATABASES

Information that can be manipulated is even more useful. For example, suppose that your address book contains 500 names, addresses, and telephone numbers. You are planning a party, and you want to send invitations to only those people in your book who live in your town. It would take you a very long time to flip through each page and write down the information you need for each person who should receive an invitation. A database can do this for you.

THE ANATOMY OF A DATABASE

A **database** is a stored collection of data whose structure allows the data to be manipulated in a variety of ways.

The strength of database software is its ability to record, manipulate, select, sort, calculate, and retrieve data on the basis of criteria that the user selects. Before you can understand how database software manipulates data, you must first understand the components of a database. In defining each part, we will refer to the discussion of your address book.

Data File. The collection of records on a particular subject is called a file, or **data file.** The entire address book discussed earlier is a data file.

Record. A **record** is all the data for an individual entry within a data file. In your address book, the entry for each individual includes the name, address, and telephone number. These items make up the record for that individual.

Field. A **field** is each category of information within a given record. For example, in the record for a person listed in your address book, the name, the street address, the city, the state, the ZIP Code, and the telephone number are individual fields.

Field name. A **field name** is the title used to categorize, or identify, a listing of fields. In the address book, as shown in Fig. 8-6, the field names are *NAME*, *ADDRESS*, *CITY*, *STATE*, *ZIP*, and *ACCOUNT*. The list of names has the heading *NAME*—this is a field name.

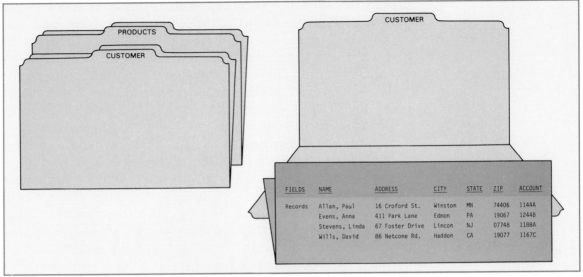

Fig. 8-6 Most businesses organize data into files. The customer file contains individual records about each customer, which are organized into fields.

DATABASE FEATURES AND FUNCTIONS

Three basic forms of data can be stored in a database. Alphabetic data, numeric data, and alphanumeric data.

Customer File

FIELDS	NAME	ADDRESS	CITY	STATE	ZIP	ACCOUNT	ACCOUNT BALANCE
Records	Lee, Rosemary	14 Elm St.	Atlanta	GA	33601	1140A	$16.50
	Smith, Roger	16 Rosemont St.	Parktown	MN	22010	1160B	$27.40
	Tally, Sue	241 Circle Dr.	Oakmont	SD	17070	1611C	$41.30
	Vern, Tom	1100 Redmont St.	Culver	TX	06107	1662A	$12.00
alphabetic	alphanumeric	alphabetic	alphabetic	numeric	alphanumeric	numeric	

A customer file may have several different fields, each of which has been identified as either an alphabetic field, numeric field, or alphanumeric field.

Sort. The sort feature of a database program is one of the two most powerful features for manipulating data. **Sort** will allow the entries in a data file or database to be reordered, usually alphabetically in ascending or descending order; numerically in ascending or descending order or alphanumerically in ascending or descending order. A specific field is used as the basis for sorting. This field is called the **sort key.** For example, if you entered your address book in an electronic database and you wanted to get a list of all records in alphabetic order by the name of the city rather than the name of the individual, you could have the database program prepare the list. You would tell the program to sort the database by the field *CITY*, in alphabetic order. The field *CITY* is the sort key in this case.

Some database programs will allow two levels of sorting. This enables you to select a second field to sort on in cases where there is more than one entry for each item identified by the first sort key. For example, there might be several entries for the city *Detroit* in your address book, and within this listing you may want the entries alphabetized by name. The *NAME* field in this case is called the **second sort key.** The sort keys are sometimes called the **primary sort key** and the **secondary sort key.** The results of sorting on the two keys described here are shown in Fig. 8-7. Keep in mind that each program may have a different procedure for instructing the computer to perform the sort function. If this is the case, you will use either menus or commands, which were discussed earlier in this chapter.

Select. The select feature is the second of the two most powerful features of database programs. **Select,** sometimes called **get** or **search,** allows you to select a portion of the database—a group of records—that meets the criteria you specify. This feature differs from the sort feature in that it does not reorganize data. It simply retrieves selected data.

Formatting a Database. Before you can begin working on a database, you must define the record structure. How many fields will make up each record? What will each field name be? Some database are arranged in columns for each field, you must also set the width of each field that you will be working within. On the basis of the information you wish to place in each field, you will estimate how many characters long each field should be. If you find later that a field is not wide enough to accommodate an entry you wish to make, you can easily increase the width.

Fig. 8-7 The complexity of your search will vary depending on the number of variables you are searching for. Suppose you work for a travel agency and are planning to mail a brochure promoting a new hang gliding vacation in the Rockies. First you must build a mailing list. To do so you could search through your database to locate individuals who fit the following criteria: 1) are between the ages of 25 and 50, and 2) have incomes of over $30,000 a year.

NAME	AGE	INCOME	OCCUPATION	YEARS	ADDRESS
Clay, AM	42	35,000	programmer	16	6637 N Bou
Clay, Agnes S	35	60,000	banker	18	1634 N Bou
Clay, Albert	60	25,000	mechanic	12	5422 Mulbe
Clay, Alice Mrs	54	40,000	accountant	16	900 E Vern
Clay, Amos	36	18,000	teacher	16	5360 Hunte
Clay, Annie	41	23,400	phone repair	16	2201 N 51
Clay, Calista	23	15,000	student	13	315 N 60
Clay, Catherine	27	19,500	bus driver	12	912 Sanger
Clay, Chas	71	8,000	retired	9	613 S Lehi
Clay, Clarence	51	28,000	postal worker	11	1211 W 82
Clay, DE	36	15,000	actor	16	1229 Chest
Clay, Dresner O	45	75,000	lawyer	19	5040 Balti
Clay, Elsie	54	36,500	engineer	20	2025 Kimba
Clay, Frances	52	29,000	sales	16	3810 N 15
Clay, Geo	47	17,000	painter	9	5457 Spruc
Clay, H Mrs	53	32,000	programmer	16	5022 Locus
Clay, Harrod E	38	45,000	florist	13	257 W Cumb
Clay, Irma V	38	33,000	designer	14	515 N 58
Clay, Jeannette	49	28,000	teacher	16	1320 Ridge
Clay, John H Jr	51	27,400	sales	12	8347 Templ
Clay, Kayoung	34	24,000	cook	10	3025 N 22
Clay, LF	41	33,000	researcher	20	2201 N 51
Clay, Leon	27	19,400	admin. asst	14	1313 E Mt
Clay, Leonard J	31	21,000	typesetter	12	6133 Cobb
Clay, Leroy	44	25,600	nurse	15	1400 N 16
Clay, M	36	18,300	tour guide	12	1632 W But
Clay, M	41	38,000	tailor	10	767 S 12th
Clay, Martha E	24	10,000	student	14	3435 Ormes
Clay, Mary	28	26,000	insurance	16	4117 Michi
Clay, Nathan	35	32,000	word process.	16	6049 Irvin
Clay, Nathl B	42	26,100	sales	16	6216 Lands
Clay, Roger	37	23,500	machinist	12	10101 Nort
Clay, Thos H Jr	33	40,000	reporter	18	1340 W Wha
Clay, William	36	34,600	writer	16	456 Washin
Claybon, Ann	41	20,000	secretary	12	110 Elmhur
Claybourne, E	23	18,500	paralegal	14	8 Oak Plac
Claycomb, B	27	21,500	sales	12	1254 W 68
Claydon, B	32	36,600	plumber	14	996 Queens
Clayman, M	50	45,000	supervisor	12	1000 Bruns
Clayton, Wm	65	57,000	pharmacist	20	555 Essex

AGES – 25 TO 50
INCOME – OVER $30,000

NAME	AGE	INCOME	OCCUPATION	YEARS	ADDRESS
Clayman, M	50	45,000	supervisor	12	1000 Bruns
Clay, Dresner O	45	75,000	lawyer	19	5040 Balti
Clay, AM	42	35,000	programmer	16	6637 N Bou
Clay, M	41	38,000	tailor	10	767 S 12th
Clay, LF	41	33,000	researcher	20	2201 N 51
Clay, Harrod E	38	45,000	florist	13	257 W Cumb
Clay, Irma V	38	33,000	designer	14	515 N 58
Clay, William	36	34,600	writer	16	456 Washin
Clay, Agnes S	35	60,000	banker	18	1634 N Bou
Clay, Nathan	35	32,000	word process.	16	6049 Irvin
Clay, Thos H Jr	33	40,000	reporter	18	1340 W Wha
Claydon, B	32	36,600	plumber	14	996 Queens

Inputting and Editing the Database. Enter the data in the fields that you have formatted. If you make any errors, you can correct them by using the functions and commands provided by your program.

Saving and Proofreading the Database. When using database software, you should follow the procedures for saving and proofreading outlined earlier in the chapter that apply to all applications programs.

GRAPHICS

You have probably already heard the expression "A picture is worth a thousand words." This expression is usually used in describing how a work of art can express many things that the artist wants to say. When taken a step further, this expression can apply to any other type of pictorial representation, such as a photograph or a business graph.

Statistics show that we comprehend and retain much more information if it is given to us in graphic form rather than in the form of written words alone. We can also see and understand trends more quickly through a graph than through text. For example, suppose that you own a video store. When the amount in stock of any video item falls below 40, you reorder the item to maintain an adequate inventory. If you study the graph in Fig. 8-8, you can determine which items need to be reordered more quickly than if you study the chart alone. In the graph the reorder point is clearly illustrated. All you have to do is pick out the bars that fall below the reorder line.

Computer graphics software is used to create business graphs from numeric data that is entered. It has completely automated the manual task of drawing graphs on graph paper, and it prepares graphs quickly and accurately.

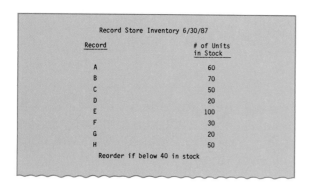

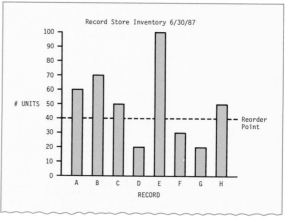

Fig. 8-8   The graph clearly illusrates the reorder point.

 THE ANATOMY OF A GRAPH

Before you can understand how to graph data using a graphics program, you must first understand the anatomy, or "skeleton," of a graph.

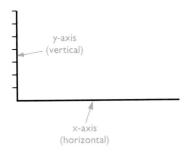

Axes. As Fig. 8-9 illustrates, most graphs are created within the boundaries of two axes. These **axes,** or reference lines, act as yardsticks or rulers for drawing and measuring the data. The horizontal axis is usually called the **x-axis.** The vertical axis is called the **y-axis.** These two axes create the work space in which the graph is drawn.

Labels. When creating a graph, it is very important to label it clearly so that it is easy to understand. Figure 8-10 shows the labels that are important for most graphs.

Fig. 8-10 The number of units is within the boundary of the y-axis. The x-axis shows the months of the year.

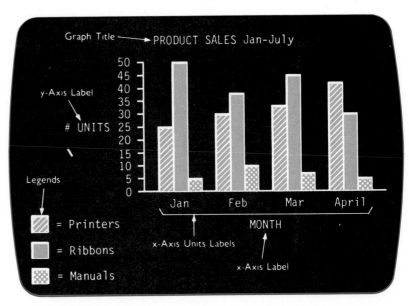

TYPES OF GRAPHS

Bar Graphs. A **bar graph** has vertical bars that are measured by the y-axis. There are three different types of bar graphs—single bar, stacked bar, and side-by-side bar—as shown in Fig. 8-11. Stacked and side-by-side bar graphs are used to compare two or more items in terms of given axis units. When creating stacked or side-by-side bar graphs, it is important to use clear **legends,** which

Pie Chart

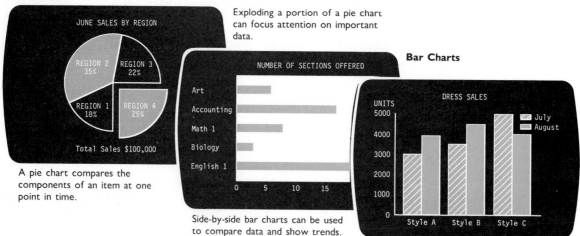

Exploding a portion of a pie chart can focus attention on important data.

A pie chart compares the components of an item at one point in time.

Side-by-side bar charts can be used to compare data and show trends.

Bar Charts

Bar charts can be used to show a trend over time. Using a pattern, such as crosshatching, a bar can highlight a specific point.

Line Graphs and Area Charts

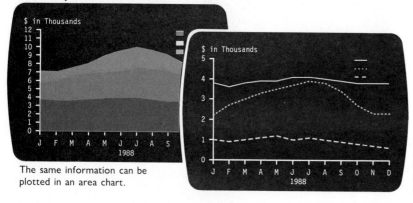

The same information can be plotted in an area chart.

Line graphs, like bar charts, plot independent variables. When several data points must be shown, it is safe to use a line graph.

Scaling Your Axes

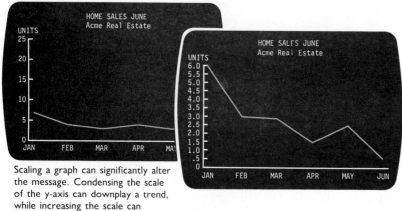

Scaling a graph can significantly alter the message. Condensing the scale of the y-axis can downplay a trend, while increasing the scale can highlight it.

Use familiar numbers when scaling axes. Use of decimals, or negative numerals can be confusing.

Fig. 8-11   Different types of graphs.

identify the items represented by the bars. Legends are also shown in Fig. 8-11. Bar graphs are typically used to compare related data or to illustrate trends.

Pie Charts. A pie chart, as shown in Fig. 8-11, is a circle that represents the whole item being measured. It is divided into wedges that look like pieces of a pie.

Point Graphs. There are two types of graphs on which points are plotted: line graphs and scatter graphs. On a **line graph,** several values are plotted. Then the points are connected to form a line, which indicates a trend. The lines on line graphs are typically jagged. On a **scatter graph,** points are plotted just as they are on a line graph, but the points are not connected. Scatter graphs are also used to indicate trends.

LANNING YOUR GRAPH

The use of graphics is a form of communication. The major difference between graphics and other forms of communication is that with graphics, you are using pictures to convey your message rather than written words or oral communication. When using graphics it is important to plan your message the same way you might outline the content of a document that you are writing.

Before you build any graph, there are a few questions that you should always ask:
- What information is being communicated?
- What type of data is available?
- What major points must be made (highlighted or downplayed)?
- Who is the audience and how experienced are they?

Once you have answered these questions, you will then be ready to communicate effectively using business graphics.

OW TO CREATE A GRAPH

The main difference in creating graphs as opposed to documents, spreadsheets, or databases is that the data will be presented graphically rather than in textual or numeric form.

Formatting the Graph. Some graphics programs provide a work area very similar to the layout of a spreadsheet for data entry except that calculations cannot be performed within it. If you are entering data to be graphed within a work area such as this, first format it as you would a spreadsheet by setting column widths. If you will be working within some other data entry area, follow the procedures outlined by your program. Once you have decided which graph to use, be sure to decide upon the labels that will identify its parts, and which data to plot.

Inputting and Editing the Graph. When you are ready to enter the data, you will follow the guidelines outlined by your program's manual. If you make any errors, you can correct them by using the features provided by your graphics program.

/ NTEGRATED SOFTWARE

Today more and more software programs are being designed to be used together with other programs or integrated. Simply stated, **integrated software programs** are

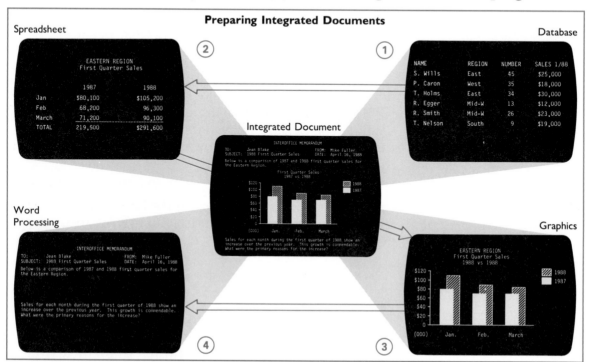

Fig. 8-12   How data becomes information.

different software programs that can be used together to enable the user to perform more than one function. For example, in using integrated software to prepare the monthly sales report, you might use a spreadsheet to perform various calculations; then graph your results using a graphics program; and finally, embed the graph within a document that was prepared using a word processing software program. To do this, each software application program being used has created and enhanced the data and saved it in a form so that it can be used with other software programs without rekeying.

*T*YPES OF INTEGRATED SOFTWARE PROGRAMS

There are three basic types of integrated software: all-in-one or combination programs, a family of programs better known as a software series, and stand-alone integrated software tools or integrators. In the following section we will discuss all three categories.

The **all-in-one** or **combination programs** are among the most common integrated applications on the market today. These are software programs that consist of several different applications which are all combined in a single package. A well known all-in-one package on the market today is Lotus 1-2-3 (Lotus Development). This software program combines a spreadsheet, database and graphics all into one package.

The most important benefit of using combination programs is the convenience of using one software program to perform several tasks. These programs are designed to transform data easily from one application to another. Their command structure is consistent. The same basic commands would be used for all major applications contained in the program. This kind of consistency is especially important because it means that you do not have to learn several different commands in order to use the applications program.

The second type of **integrated program** is a **series or family of software** programs. These consist of a series of individual software programs which all use similar commands and enable the user to easily move data from one program to another. An integrated software series would have separate applications packages for word processing, spreadsheeting, database, report generation, graphics, and communications. Because each application in the series shares a common menu and command structure, it is generally easy to use all of the different applications in the series.

The PFS software series (Software Publishing) or the McGraw-Hill Integrated Software Series (McGraw-Hill) are examples of an integrated software series.

The third type of integrated software program is known as a **software integrator.** This is a separate utility program which runs in the computer's memory at the same time that you are using an application program. It allows you to transfer data from one application program to another. By using an integrator program, a user can transfer or integrate a chart created with your favorite spreadsheet program to another stand-alone software program, perhaps your preferred word processing program.

Some examples of integrator programs are Microsoft Windows (Microsoft), Topview (IBM), and Quarterdeck (DesQ).

- Applications software has been used in the office to automate many manual tasks. In using applications software packages, office workers are now faced with more responsibilities and are expected to make more decisions than ever before.

- Applications programs are like different hats that a microcomputer can wear. They allow the computer to perform many different tasks.

- All applications programs used on microcomputers utilize function keys, templates, and either a command-driven or menu-driven user interface.

- The basic steps for creating a document, spreadsheet, database, and graph are similar—format, input and edit, save, proofread, print, and proofread. If changes need to be made, the steps of a revision cycle are followed.

- Word processing is the application used most often by office workers.

- The formatting functions of word processing software allow documents to be created that look professional and attractive.

- Spelling and grammar checkers make proofreading easier, but it is still necessary to proofread all documents thoroughly before and after printing.

- Spreadsheet software is a decision-support tool that saves a great deal of time by performing calculations automatically on values, using the formulas that have been entered.

- Database software is another decision-support tool. The information contained within the fields and records of a database can be organized into reports that will be used in the decision-making process.

- The sort and select features of database software are the most powerful for manipulating data.

- It is easier for us to understand information when it is presented in graphic form.

- Graphics software allows office workers to create business graphs easily. The most common types of graphs are bar graphs, pie charts, line graphs, and scatter graphs.

- Integrated software packages have increased the productivity of the basic applications programs. They provide a consistent user interface within each application; they allow data to be transferred from one application to another; and some offer windowing capabilities.

VOCABULARY

applications software	database
template	data file
command-driven program	record
menu-driven program	field
menu	field name
submenu	sort
help screen	sort key
revision cycle	second sort key
word processing	primary sort key
dedicated word processor	secondary sort key
decimal tab	select
format line	get
format ruler	search
spelling checker	computer graphics
electronic dictionary	axes
mail merge	x-axis
list document	y-axis
spreadsheet	bar graph
decision-support tool	legend
parameter	line graph
cell	scatter graph
cell address	integrated software
cell reference	programs
active cell	all-in-one program
label	combination program
value	integrated program
formula	software integrator
command	

REVIEW QUESTIONS

1. List the basic steps for creating documents, spreadsheets, databases, and graphs.

2. List and describe the most commonly used word processing functions. Explain how word processing,

compared with typewriting, saves office workers time.

3. Describe what a spreadsheet is and the types of tasks office workers would use it for. How can this tool increase office workers' productivity?

4. Describe the parts of a spreadsheet. What are columns, rows, cells, cell addresses, labels, and values?

5. What is a formula? Give an example of a formula, and explain how you would use it in a spreadsheet.

6. Describe what a database is and the types of tasks office workers would use it for. How can this tool increase office workers' productivity?

7. Describe the parts of a database. What are records and fields?

8. What is a decision-support tool? Why are spreadsheet, database, and graphics programs classified as decision-support tools? What questions should always be asked before preparing a graph using graphics software?

9. Define *integrated software,* and describe how integrated software packages integrate applications in terms of user interface, data transfer, and windowing.

10. How has the use of integrated software increased the productivity of office workers as compared with the use of separate applications programs?

S KILLBUILDING ACTIVITIES

1. Using a word processing program, prepare a document. (The choice is yours.) After printing the document, make some minor changes and print it again. Keep track of how long it takes you to complete this activity. Then prepare the same original document using a typewriter. Retype the document, making the changes that you decided on for the document prepared on the word processor. Note how long this activity takes you as well. How much longer did it take you to type and retype the document? Give a brief report to your class on the time-saving features of word processing programs.

2. Interview an office worker you know who is currently using applications software to complete his or her daily tasks. Which programs does this worker use? What tasks are performed with each? What new responsibilities does the worker have as a result of using this software? What kind of training did the worker receive? Can the worker estimate the amount of time each program saves him or her each day? Ask any other questions that you wish. Prepare a brief report on your findings to hand in to your teacher or present to your class.

3. Obtain a list of your classmates' names, addresses, and telephone numbers. Using a microcomputer and database software, create a database with this information. Use the sort and select features to generate three reports. (The choices are yours.) Hand these in to your teacher.

4. Evaluate the software programs available in your classroom to determine if they are integrated software programs and what type of integrated program: all-in-one, a series of programs, or a program integrator. How many different applications can be performed? Can the data stored on each software program be used with other software programs?

CHAPTER

9

STORAGE

The exciting changes technology has brought to today's electronic office require you to be knowledgeable about storing and managing information. The ability to store information electronically has changed the way offices function. Information can be accessed more easily, in a shorter period of time. More people can have access to information that was once controlled and distributed by a few. This has broadened the scope of storage and retrieval to include a broad range of information management functions. Information management is an area that has many career opportunities for people who choose to specialize in this field.

Information management involves the storage, protection, retrieval, use, and disposal of records. The records may be in the form of paper documents, files on computer disks or tapes, or various types of miniature records on film, called microforms.

Businesses retain records for a number of important reasons. It is routine business practice to keep records of most business transactions. Many businesses use company records of customers, employees, and others over and over again. These types of records may need to be continually kept up to date. Many other documents are kept for future reference. Businesses also keep documents as legal records of transactions. Some financial records must be kept by law for a designated number of years.

In this chapter you will learn about the equipment and procedures you will use to set up and maintain filing and information management systems.

In comparison, a secretary would perform a wider variety of tasks. These tasks would usually include—in addition to filing—scheduling appointments, giving information to visitors and callers via the telephone, taking shorthand and transcribing that information, assisting other office employees, and handling minor administrative duties.

As a result of studying this chapter, you will be able to:

- Identify and demonstrate the use of appropriate filing procedures.
- Understand and demonstrate filing rules and procedures that are appropriate for a specific task.
- Understand the role of manual and electronic office applications in managing and storing information.
- Develop skill in efficiently storing and retrieving information, both manually and electronically.
- Become aware of the variety of career paths that are open to those who understand how to store and manage information.

FILING SYSTEMS

Filing is the process of classifying, arranging, and storing information so that it can be easily retrieved. Most offices today use both manual and electronic filing systems to manage and store their information. The degree to which the electronic equipment is used depends on how the information for a particular task or job needs to be handled.

FILING METHODS

In any filing system, there are four major methods that can be used to organize the information. The alphabetic method is the most widely used method because most

Setting Up a Filing System

Your first office job as a file clerk can provide you with some very interesting challenges. Among these challenges might be the task of setting up a filing system. Although the filing system that you set up probably will not be too complex, knowing basic information concerning the organization of filing systems can prove very useful to you.

Consider these guidelines.

1. *Identify your filing needs*. What will be filed, and who will be using the files? Will you be the only one using the files, or will you be sharing the files?

2. *What method of filing will you use*? In all likelihood, you will be using alphabetic filing, but numeric filing, subject filing, geographic filing, and a combination of these are other possible filing methods.

3. *Where will the files be located*? Will the files be located next to your desk in a cabinet? Will the files be stored electronically in a nearby computer?

4. *How will you evaluate your filing system*? The best way to evaluate your filing system will be to experiment, using the suggestions of others as well as your own creativity. From this experimentation and experience, you will be able to evaluate and adjust your filing needs.

While most companies have an established set of procedures for filing, you should keep these general guidelines in mind.

1. Not all records need to be filed. Check with your supervisor for guidelines as to which documents should be filed and which can be disposed of.

2. Learn to tell the difference between materials that will serve no useful purpose and those which must be kept.

3. For documents that are to be filed, set up a folder marked "Hold for Filing." Place these materials in an in/out box.

4. Set aside time each day to complete your filing. This will allow you to manage your workday efficiently in terms of handling the filing. If you fall behind in your filing, you will waste time looking for needed materials.

Indexing Rules

These rules are adapted by Jeffrey R. Stewart according to the Association of Records Management and Administrators Alphabetic Filing Rules.

Rule 1. Names of Persons. When indexing the name of a person, arrange the units in this order: last name, first name, middle name.

Cecil D. Aaron   Aaron Cecil D

Rule 2. Personal Names With Prefixes. Consider a prefix, such as *Mc* in *McDonald,* as part of the name it precedes. Ignore any apostrophe or space within or after the prefix.

P. Shawn O'Dell   ODell P Shawn

Rule 3. Hyphenated Personal Names. Consider a hyphenated name as one unit.

Dee-Dee Ashton   Ashton Deedee

Rule 4. Abbreviations of Personal Names. Abbreviated and shortened forms of personal names are indexed as written.

Wm. R. Parker   Parker Wm R

Rule 5. Personal Names With Titles and Suffixes. When used with a person's name, a title or a suffix is the last indexing unit when needed to distinguish between two or more identical names. Titles and suffixes are indexed as written. Titles include *Capt., Dr., Mayor, Miss, Mr., Mrs., Ms.,* and *Sena-*

tor. Suffixes include seniority terms (*III, Jr., Sr.*) and professional designations (*CPA, M.D., Ph.D.*).

Note: Numeric seniority terms (II, III) are filed before alphabetic terms (Jr., Sr.)

Samuel B. Mason, CPA
Mason Samuel B CPA

Rule 6. Names of Businesses and Organizations. Consider the units in business and organization names in the order in which they are normally written. To determine this order, use letterheads, directories, advertisements, or computer databases. When *The* is the first word of the name, it is treated as the last unit. Names with prefixes are considered one unit, just as with personal names.

The Barn Shop   Barn Shop The

Rule 7. Abbreviations in Business and Organization Names. Abbreviations in business and organization names are indexed as written.

Note: Cross-reference between an abbreviation and the complete name when necessary to ensure that records can be located.

U.S. Construction Co.   US Construction Co

Rule 8. Punctuation in Business and Organization Names. Ignore any punctuation marks that appear in business and organization names.

Hyphenated business and organization names are treated as one unit. Punctuation marks include the apostrophe, colon, comma, period, and so on.

Hines-Fox Paint Co.   Hinesfox Paint Co

Rule 9. Numbers in Business and Organization Names.
Arabic numerals (2, 17) and roman numerals (II, IV) are considered one unit and are filed in numeric order before alphabetic characters. All arabic numerals precede all roman numerals. Hyphenated numbers (7-11) are indexed according to the number *before* the hyphen (7). The letters *st, d,* and *th* following an arabic numeral are ignored.

If a number is spelled out (*First* Street Pizza), it is filed alphabetically as written. Hyphenated numbers that are spelled out (*Twenty-One*) are considered one unit (*TWENTYONE*).

7-211th St. Assn.   7-211 St Assn
210th St. Assn.   210 St Assn

Chas. Street Club 3rd   Chas Street Club 3
Chas. Street Club III   Chas Street Club III

Rule 10. Symbols in Business and Organization Names.
If a symbol is part of a name, the symbol is indexed as if spelled out, such as *and* for &.

Note: If the $ sign is used with a number, file first under the number.

Charles & Company   Charles and Company

Rule 11. Government Names.
Government names are indexed first by the name of the country, state, county, or city. The name of the department, bureau, or board is next. Federal government names are indexed first under *United States Government.*

Registry of Deeds, Suffolk County
Suffolk County Deeds Registry

Rule 12. Addresses.
When names are otherwise identical, they may be filed by address. The elements of the address are considered in the following order: city, state, street name, and house.

James Smith   Smith James
21 South   York PA
York, PA 17403   South 21

James Smith   Smith James
23 South   York PA
York, PA 17403   South 23

information can be easily managed in this way. Other filing methods—numeric, subject, and geographic filing—all use the alphabetic method as a part of their system, as will be explained later. How a document is to be used determines which method is used.

There are two ways to organize a filing system. Filing systems may be centralized or decentralized. *Decentralized* files are stored in different places, either near the people who use them most often or where they fit best in each office. *Centralized* files are located in one area. This is often where all the major information of a company is stored and managed, either manually or electronically or by using a combination of both methods.

FILING STEPS

There are five essential steps to be completed when you are filing: inspecting, indexing, coding, sorting, and storing. Sometimes cross-referencing is also done.

Inspecting. You need to review each record to determine whether it should be filed.

Indexing. You must decide on a caption for the record. A **caption** is a name, a letter, or a number under which a record is filed. **Indexing** is really a mental process that requires you to make a decision about file placement.

Sorting. Once you have properly coded the records to be filed, you are ready to sort them. Arrange them in the order in which they will be placed in the file.

Coding. Once you have decided on a caption for the record to be filed, you must assign a code to the record before filing it. With a record in paper form, coding is done by underlining or highlighting the name under which the record will be filed. This underlining or highlighting will also serve as a reminder to anyone who might be using the record and refiling it in the future.

Storing. Storing involves placing a record in a file folder in a proper file drawer if you are using a manual system or choosing the proper commands to save a record in an electronic filing system.

TECHNOLOGY NOTE

Once a disk has been **formatted** (prepared properly to receive information), information can be recorded on it. Information is recorded on circles called **tracks**. These circles are very much like the narrow grooves or tracks on a record. The **read/write head** of the disk drive moves back and forth from one track to another. This is how the read/write head finds the data it must read or a place on the disk where it can write information.

The tracks on a disk are divided into **sectors**. The space on the disk is measured in **bytes**. One byte holds one character. The number of tracks, sectors, and bytes on a disk will vary depending on the type of disk and disk drive you are working with. When the storage space of a floppy disk becomes full, you can delete some of the files to create new space, or you can store the full disk and format a new disk for your next task.

Floppy disks.

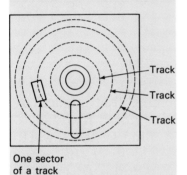

One sector of a track

Fig. 9-1 Information is written on the tracks of a floppy disk. Then the disk drive head can find the sector where that information has been stored.

Five Essential Filing Steps

1. INSPECTING. Correspondence is checked to make sure it has been released for filing.

2. INDEXING. The name by which correspondence will most likely be requested from the files is determined. In this example it was decided that the *Shadyside National Bank* would be the caption under which the letter would be filed.

3. CODING. The caption determined in the indexing step is underscored.

   The cross-reference caption is underscored and an *X* placed at the end of the line.

4. SORTING. All correspondence to be filed is sorted in alphabetic order according to the underscored captions.

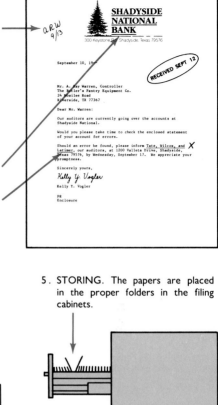

5. STORING. The papers are placed in the proper folders in the filing cabinets.

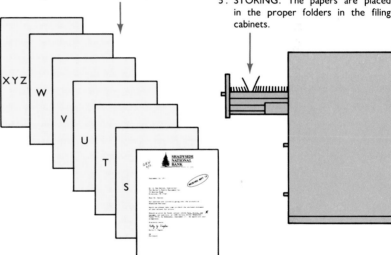

Fig. 9-2 The five essential filing steps.

Cross-referencing. If there is a possibility that confusion could arise because two records are similar, you should cross-reference in order to eliminate the confusion. **Cross-referencing** tells the person searching for a particular record that the record is filed in another section of the filing system.

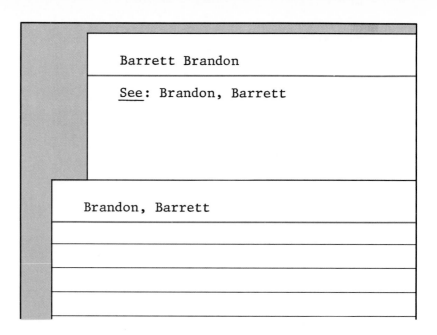

Fig. 9-3 A cross-reference example.

 ANUAL FILING

It is extremely important to remember that efficient retrieval of information, whether it is stored manually or electronically, is the true test of a filing system's worth. Retrieval can be accomplished efficiently if the person storing the information is organized and uses appropri-

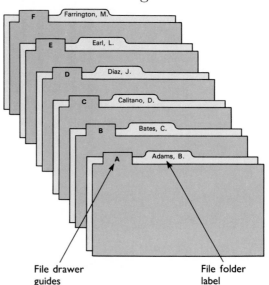

Fig. 9-4 File guides separate groups of files for easy retrieval.

File drawer guides

File folder label

ate filing supplies and equipment. Some **filing supplies** are basic to all manual filing systems. These supplies include file-drawer guides, file-guide captions, file folders, and file-folder labels.

The major supplies needed for electronic filing include disks, labels, and a felt-tipped pen to label the disks properly. Prepare a label *before* it is placed on the disk, because disks are very sensitive to pressure.

Filing equipment refers to the actual structures in which records are stored. A wide variety of filing equipment is available, but most pieces of equipment have basic features in common.

Vertical files come in two-, three-, four-, and five-drawer models. The drawers are stacked one on top of the other and usually have locks.

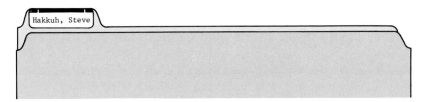

Fig. 9-5 Folders and guides with one-fifth or one-third cut tabs are commonly used in the office.

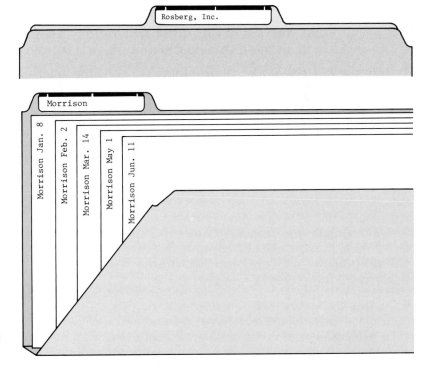

Fig. 9-6 Papers in individual folders should be filed with the latest date in front.

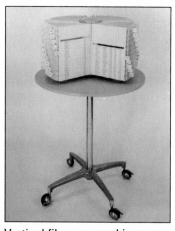
Vertical files are used in many offices.

Lateral files are similar to vertical files except that the long side opens, and the files are stored as if they were on a bookshelf.

Open-shelf files are not enclosed the way vertical and lateral files are. Open-shelf files consist of metal frames to suit the size and space needs of the user.

Rotary files consist of a large, round shelf with a hole in the middle through which the supporting post passes.

Tub files are small tublike containers that open at the top. They are often on casters and can be moved easily from one location to another.

Card files come in a wide assortment of styles and sizes.

PROCEDURES

Preventing Records From Being Misfiled

Whenever a record is filed incorrectly, major problems in retrieval occur. Quite often the record is lost permanently, and this results in great frustration. Keep these helpful hints in mind to help prevent records from being misfiled.

1. *Use simple headings.* Confusion will result if the headings on tabs and file-folder labels contain too much information.

2. *Prepare headings for tabs in all-capital letters.* Headings on tabs should be prepared in all-capital letters. Always avoid handwriting the headings.

3. *Use enough file-drawer guides.* A full file drawer should contain a minimum of 5 guides but not more than 15 for efficient retrieval.

4. *Avoid overcrowding file drawers.* A full file drawer should have at least 3 or 4 inches of extra space so that

the user can easily flip to the needed location in the file drawer.

5. *Avoid overcrowding file folders.* When there are too many items in a file folder, the paper within the folder may prevent the tab from being visible. This will cause additional confusion when the user must retrieve a record.

6. *Code papers clearly.* Before filing a record, write its file heading in the upper right corner clearly or underline it in color within the text. Bright colors such as yellow are excellent for coding purposes because they are immediately seen.

ELECTRONIC FILING

Computers store data by recording electrical impulses on magnetic disks or tapes. Disks and tapes come in different sizes and storage capacities.

Office workers in **decentralized storage systems** are responsible for managing their own disks. On the other hand, most of the integrated office systems that run on central computers provide a **centralized storage system** for storing records. The storage devices may be magnetic tapes, hard disks, or disk packs.

In a centralized file system, this worker does not have to leave the workstation to retrieve files located in another part of the office. The computer helps retrieve the file.

ELECTRONIC STORAGE MEDIA

It is important that you have an understanding of the most common forms of electronic storage media. This knowledge will help you in storing and managing records electronically.

Fig. 9-7   Files can be stored manually and electronically. Those stored electronically can be retrieved instantly.

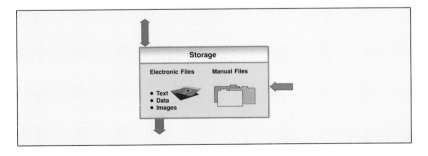

ROM and RAM

Computers have memories of two kinds: ROM and RAM. **ROM** stands for *read-only memory.* This means that what is stored on the ROM chip is only for the computer to use; the data stored on a ROM chip is not meant to be manipulated by the user. For this reason ROM is also referred to as permanent storage. The information in ROM tells the computer what to do in any given situation. When you turn a computer on, messages are made possible by the information stored in ROM.

RAM stands for *random-access memory.* The data that you have input and manipulated is temporarily stored in RAM. You can retrieve this data at will, change it, and re-store it whenever you want. RAM is also called temporary storage because the data must be stored on a disk before the computer is turned off. The amount of data you will be able to store temporarily in a computer will be determined by how much RAM (measured in kilobytes) the computer has.

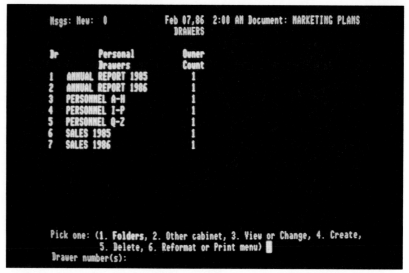

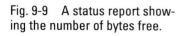

Fig. 9-8   Electronic filing requires the same organizational skill as traditional filing. Files must be broken into logical units for easy storage and retrieval.

Microcomputer Disks.   The disk is an indispensable media for the storage of information on a computer. Disks have undergone some significant changes over the past several years. They continue to become smaller and more durable while being capable of storing more and more information.

Recently, a smaller, more effective form of disk has been introduced. This disk is $3\frac{1}{2}''$ in diameter and is used with many of the newer computer systems such as the

Fig. 9-9   A status report showing the number of bytes free.

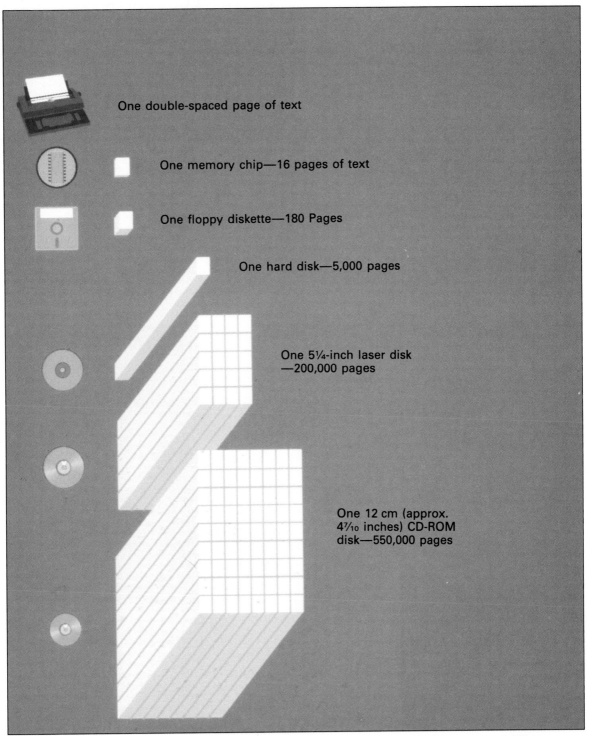

One double-spaced page of text

One memory chip—16 pages of text

One floppy diskette—180 Pages

One hard disk—5,000 pages

One 5¼-inch laser disk —200,000 pages

One 12 cm (approx. 4⁷⁄₁₀ inches) CD-ROM disk—550,000 pages

Fig. 9-10 This illustration compares the storage capacity of different types of disks.

A hard disk is usually housed in the disk drive.

Magnetic tape has a very large storage capacity, but is rarely used with microcomputers.

IBM Personal Systems Series 2, the MacIntosh Computer, and many of the portable Laptop Computers. These new diskettes have the capacity to store up to 2 megabytes of information.

Hard Disks. The computer you are using may have a hard-disk drive as opposed to one or two floppy-disk drives. Hard disks are permanently encased in the disk drive. Hard disks have much more storage space than floppy disks. A 10 megabyte hard disk will hold approximately 5,000 pages of copy. When a hard disk becomes full, you must transfer some files to a floppy disk or delete some files.

If you are sharing a computer and working with confidential information, it is possible that you will have a **password** to allow you to access those particular records. After you have keyed the command, the file will automatically appear on your screen for your use.

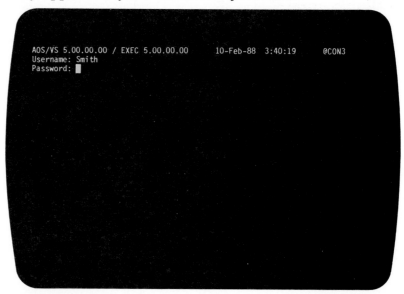

```
AOS/VS 5.00.00.00 / EXEC 5.00.00.00      10-Feb-88  3:40:19      @CON3
Username: Smith
Password: █
```

Fig. 9-11   On this system, the user's name is Smith. The password should be keyed in where the cursor is positioned.

Magnetic Tape. **Magnetic tape** is the most popular storage medium because of its large storage capacity and relatively low cost. Magnetic tape can store about 6,000 characters per inch, which means that 100 million characters can be stored on a single reel of tape.

Optical, or laser, disks. The **optical,** or **laser, disk** has a much greater storage capacity than a hard disk. One $5\frac{1}{4}$-inch disk can hold up to 200,000 pages of copy. Laser

Optical disks can store data, graphics, or sound.

disks are nonmagnetic and are far more durable than magnetic media. These types of disks are created through laser recordings; that is, laser light beams burn tiny holes in the metal of the disk. Sounds and images, recorded in these tiny holes, can be read by the machine that plays back the recording. **Videodisks** are laser recording disks that are widely used for commercially developed products such as movies and other audiovisual presentations.

CD-ROM. A type of optical disk that is becoming more widely used today is the compact disk—read-only memory, or **CD-ROM**. CD-ROM is a durable, nonmagnetic storage medium with the capability of storing vast quantities of data, graphics, or sound.

In business compact disks are used for information processing because of their desirable features of high-capacity storage, speed, cost effectiveness, durability, and flexibility.

Disk Management. Although floppy disks are smaller than a sheet of letter-size paper, each one can store many pages of information. Floppy disks come in several sizes, but regardless of the size of the disk, the method of storing data on floppy disks is basically the same.

It is possible to store many files of information on one floppy disk.

PROCEDURES

Hints For Efficient Electronic Filing

Files that are stored on disks can be difficult to organize. Keep the following points in mind. They can aid you greatly in electronic storage and retrieval.

1. Label each disk. Complete a label for each floppy disk *before* placing it on the disk.

2. Print out an index of the documents currently on the floppy disk each time a new document is added. An index of documents can be folded and placed in the jacket with the disk, or the index can be kept separately in a notebook for easy reference.

3. Store disks in an easily accessible, safe place. It is best to store disks in a box designed especially for holding disks—for security and as an aid to organization.

4. If one disk is full and you want to format another disk with the same label, number the disks consecutively—for example, "Letters 1," "Letters 2," and "Letters 3." Mark each new disk label with the date the disk was formatted and first used.

5. In order to ensure that the information stored on disks will not be erased by anyone, place a write-protect tab in the protect position. When the tab covers the notch, you will not be able to store addi-

tional documents on the disk. If there is a very important disk that you wish to protect, cover the notch when you are through using the disk and uncover the notch only when you need to store information on it again.

The write-protect notch prevents writing over valuable data.

UBJECT FILES

Storing and managing information by subject means that the subjects of documents are more important to your office than the names on them. In subject files information is filed alphabetically by subject. For example, a file labeled "Contracts" would be filed before a file labeled "Legal Cases."

Subject files can be subdivided into categories to allow for more efficient storage and retrieval. For example, a main subject file labeled "Insurance" might have the subcategories "Fire," "Malpractice," "Theft," and so on.

NUMERIC FILES

Records can sometimes be retrieved faster if they are filed by number rather than by name or subject. For example, a bank has thousands of customers, and some of these customers may have savings accounts as well as checking accounts, retirement accounts, mortgages, and personal loans. Rather than combine all the records of an individual in one file under that customer's name, a bank would file them according to the account numbers.

Filing numerically provides several advantages. The method is very useful when the records themselves are numbers, as in the example of bank accounts. Also, unlimited numbers of new files can be added without running out of captions. Confidential records can be thoroughly safeguarded. File labels or captions never require decisions, because numbers are used for them.

There are two major systems of numeric filing. One is the **consecutive numeric system**, which uses consecutive numbers—1, 2, 3, and so on. The other system is the **terminal-digit system**, in which numbers are assigned for the purpose of classifying records into groups. The last number in a caption indicates where to start looking for a record. For example, in the caption "97334," "97" might be the file-drawer number, "33" a folder number, and "4" the position of the record in the folder.

GEOGRAPHIC FILES

Geographic filing is useful when the information to be stored applies to a particular location (country, region, state, or town). First break categories down into the largest or most important geographic divisions for your company's operations. Divide these into subdivisions, then alphabetize within each subdivision.

FILES KEPT AT YOUR WORKSTATION

Tickler files. Tickler files are used at your workstation to help you remember when specific office tasks must be done. A tickler file is commonly organized with 12 guides, one for each month of the year. Further note that a folder can be inserted for each day.

Chronological files. It is often helpful to set up a chronological file, which contains a current record of all work that has been completed. This type of file may be referred to as a "reading file." Only copies of correspondence should be filed in the chronological file.

MICROGRAPHICS

Not all records can be stored electronically. For example, birth certificates, fingerprints, canceled checks, and credit card receipts are difficult to convert to soft copy.

The solution to the problem of overcrowded files in companies that need to retain such documents is to reduce the size of the records. The process of reproducing newspapers and other documents in a reduced size on film is known as **micrographics**. The rolls or sheets of film that have images which are exact duplicates of the original records are called **microforms**. These images are many times smaller than the originals. In fact, they cannot be read without the aid of a special machine called a **microform reader**.

 ## USES OF MICROFORMS

You can find a document more quickly by using a microform reader than by sifting through stacks of papers.

Micrographics also has some advantages over the process of computerizing records. The images are exact duplicates of the original documents. In contrast, computer records are not the documents themselves but rekeyed information. Errors can be introduced in the rekeying.

 ## TYPES OF MICROFORMS

The term *microform* refers to a variety of micrographics media. These media make it possible to record miniature images of documents on film negatives.

Microfilm rolls are the oldest micrographics medium. A microfilm roll is a continuous roll of film that can hold the images of hundreds of pages of documents.

Microfilm jackets consist of two sheets of clear plastic that are sealed together to form horizontal slots for holding strips of microfilm.

A **microfiche** is a sheet of film, usually 4 by 6 inches, that can hold the images of several hundred letter-size pages. These images are smaller than the images on microfilm.

Ultrafiche is the smallest medium upon which images are stored. A single sheet can hold the images of 4,000

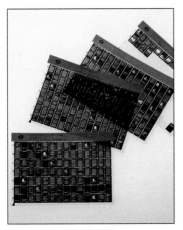

This piece of microfiche contains many pages of material. Enlarged, they will be a size that can be read easily.

The miniature images on this roll of microfilm will be a readable size when they are projected through a microfilm reader.

letter-size pages. An ultrafiche is a very expensive micrographics medium because it can be processed only in photographic laboratories. Nevertheless, it is a practical medium for storing catalogs, directories, encyclopedias, and other documents that may have thousands of pages.

DVANTAGES AND DISADVANTAGES

The main advantage of using microforms is that they take up very little storage space. Microforms are also a good means for storing large amounts of information. Another advantage is that each document can be retrieved quickly.

The major disadvantage is that a special machine is required to read microforms. The paper copies you make from them are of very poor quality. In addition, some microforms cannot be easily updated and edited.

OW TO RETRIEVE AND READ MICROFORMS

Computers can be linked with micrographics equipment to retrieve information from microforms automatically. This application of computer technology is called **computer-assisted retrieval (CAR)**.

ANAGING INFORMATION

Information management is the function of organizing and controlling all aspects of business records, from their creation, protection, and use to their storage and, finally, their disposal.

EGAL RECORDS

Many records must be kept by law. Employers today often need to prove to the government that they have not violated equal-opportunity laws in their employment practices, that they meet federally mandated quotas in the employment of different groups of people, and that they do not practice any form of discrimination in their policies.

MPORTANT RECORDS

Many records are extremely important to the operation of a business, but they are not vital. These should be retained for six or seven years. Important records include accounts receivable and accounts payable ledgers, invoices, canceled checks, inventory records, purchase orders, payroll records, and employee time sheets and expense vouchers.

SEFUL RECORDS

Useful records are usually retained for one to three years, depending on the company. These include general correspondence, reconciled bank statements, employment applications, notes taken down, expired insurance policies, and petty-cash vouchers.

CTIVE RECORDS VERSUS INACTIVE RECORDS

Active records are those records which must be kept in the office. Active records are used regularly. When a file is no longer used regularly, it becomes an **inactive record**.

SUMMARY

- A file clerk's responsibilities include filing material in a variety of ways, locating the material as required, and keeping a record of the files.

- There are many systems and devices for organizing files. To set up a filing system, you must identify (1) your filing needs, (2) the most suitable method of filing, (3) the location of the files, and (4) necessary adjustments to your filing system.

- The four most common filing methods are alphabetic, numeric, subject, and geographic.

- Businesses will have their files organized in either a centralized or a decentralized storage system.

- The essential steps for filing are inspecting, indexing, coding, cross-referencing, and storing.

- Filing supplies that are basic to all manual filing systems are file-drawer guides, file-guide captions, file folders, and file-folder labels.

- Careful preparation of files—whether manual or electronic—will prevent records from being misfiled.

- Microforms are rolls or sheets of film that have images of records in miniature. A special machine is needed for reading the images. Microforms include microfilm, microfiche, aperture cards, and ultrafiche.

- Computers can help retrieve micrographic materials through CAR.

- Managing information efficiently requires logical procedures for records retention and disposal.

VOCABULARY

filing	filing equipment
formatted	decentralized storage system
track	
read/write head	centralized storage system
sector	ROM
byte	RAM
caption	password
indexing	magnetic tape
cross-referencing	optical, or laser, disk
filing supplies	videodisk

CD-ROM
consecutive numeric
  system
terminal-digit system
tickler file
micrographics
microform
microform reader
microfilm roll

microfilm jacket
microfiche
ultrafiche
computer-assisted retrieval
  (CAR)
information management
active record
inactive record

REVIEW QUESTIONS

1. Why is it important for a beginning office worker to have a good working knowledge of correct ways to store and manage information?

2. Define *filing*.

3. List the four major filing methods, and give a brief definition of each method. What are the disadvantages and advantages of each method?

4. Define the two major ways to organize files in a business office. Explain the reasoning behind using each system. Which system is practiced more than the other? Why?

5. What role do floppy disk play in electronic filing? What should you remember about using floppy disk? What other electronic storage media are used? What are the considerations for using these types of media?

6. List the four major guidelines for determining how a filing system should be designed.

7. List the five essential steps in filing, and give a brief explanation of each.

8. Explain cross-referencing, and give an example of when it would be useful to provide a cross-reference.

9. What filing supplies are necessary when a manual filing system is being set up?

10. List the major types of filing equipment, and explain briefly the use of each.

11. What are some suggestions to prevent records from being misfiled?

12. Define *micrographics*, and give a brief explanation of the advantages and disadvantages of using micrographics as well as the various types of microforms.

13. Why is it essential to understand the 12 alphabetic filing rules and practice them efficiently?

14. Why is it important to have an understanding of the basics of establishing an information management system?

15. Give examples of records that should be retained in a business. What are some guidelines on how long records should be retained?

 ## S *KILLBUILDING ACTIVITIES*

1. Cynthia Rosberg is one of 15 secretaries sharing a centralized storage system. Cindy is the newest member of the team. A major problem has recently developed in that whenever Cindy needs a specific file, the file is missing. A coworker, Sarah Green, has many of the files at her desk in a box marked "To Be Filed," and these records never seem to get filed. How can Cindy tactfully encourage Sarah to do her share of the filing and return the materials to the files? Give specific reasons in your answer.

2. Read the list of different types of business records below. Decide which of these types of business records would be best placed on *microfilm*.

applications for employment	invoices
catalogs for car parts	legal documents
drawings	reconciled bank statements
checks	permanent records for students

Be prepared to justify your decisions

3. Everyone has files and records—at work, at school, or in the home for personal use. Choose one of these types of records that you use, and create a filing system for the records using the procedures in this chapter.

4. Go to the library. Make a list of all the different kinds of filing systems you can find there. Include card-catalog files, micrographics files, magazine files, and so on.

10

OUTPUT

*T*he major responsibility of workers in today's electronic office is to generate useful information. Although this has always been the case in business offices, the use of computers has had a major impact on the form in which the information can be presented. For many years type-written documents, such as letters, memos, and reports, have been the main form of output for processed information. Today output can be generated in print form or transmitted electronically to be received on the computer screen, known as soft copy. Other options are available as well: computer graphics or charts can be viewed on high-resolution color monitors and then printed in color by a piece of equip-ment called a plotter; reports can be printed in a wide variety of typefaces or fonts without being sent to an outside compositor or typesetter. Today some computer systems can even generate voice output.

You will see how **reprographics** (any piece of mechanical or electronic machinery that produces multiple copies of an original) can be used in large and small offices. You will also learn about various capabilities of modern printers and photocopiers. In addition, you will be introduced to different kinds of electronic copiers and printers, and you will learn about an exciting technology known as desk-top publishing.

The selection of the form of output required is now a major part of the decision-making role of office workers. It is important to understand the different types of output devices used in the electronic office and the forms of output that each can generate.

After studying this chapter, you will be able to:

- Describe the different types of output that can be generated and the uses for these different formats.
- Identify the different types of printers available for computer output and understand the differences among them.
- Explain how reprographics is handled in both small and large companies and understand the different uses of centralized and decentralized reprographics systems.
- Describe the different types of copiers used in today's electronic office.
- Explain the meaning and uses of desk-top publishing and understand the terminology associated with this technology.

OUTPUT DEVICES

Since computers have made it possible to produce hard copies from soft copy, **output** now includes information produced not only from copying machines but also from electronic typesetters, printers, and even the display screen of a computer. When these devices are connected to a computer system, they are referred to as **output devices**.

PRINTERS

The output device you are most likely to use in the electronic office is a printer that produces hard copies from the soft copy stored in the computer's storage devices.

Printers differ from one another in their speed and the quality of their output. **Letter-quality printers** produce pages that look as if they were prepared on an electric or electronic typewriter. Other kinds of printers, sometimes called **draft-quality printers**, generate output that may be more difficult to read. A typical letter-quality printer may produce only 12 to 55 characters a second, while a draft-quality printer can print up to 400 characters a second. In recent years computer manufacturers have greatly improved draft-quality printers. They have also developed faster printers to produce letter-quality print. Another difference among printers is that some can produce graphics such as charts and diagrams.

*I*MPACT PRINTERS

An **impact printer** prints by striking metal or plastic letter shapes, or type, against an inked ribbon moving over paper, just as a typewriter does.

*C*HARACTER PRINTERS

A **character printer** is an impact printer that prints one character at a time.

*D*AISY WHEEL PRINTERS

A **daisy wheel printer** is a kind of letter-quality character printer with a round, flat type device. If you think of this type device as a daisy, its "petals" are bars with type characters at their ends.

A **thimble printer** is similar to a daisy wheel printer, except that the type bars are bent so that the type element is shaped like a thimble. Like the daisy wheel, the thimble spins constantly as it travels back and forth across the page.

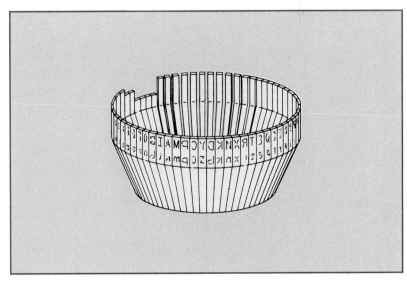

Fig. 10-1   In the thimble printer, the typebars are bent inward so that they resemble a thimble.

DOT MATRIX PRINTERS

Another kind of impact printer is the **dot matrix printer**, which does not use cast metal or plastic type but instead forms characters by projecting tiny metal bristles, or "pins," in patterns.

Dot matrix printers are also much faster than daisy wheel or thimble printers, and usually cost less.

Fig. 10-2   An ink-jet printer and how it works.

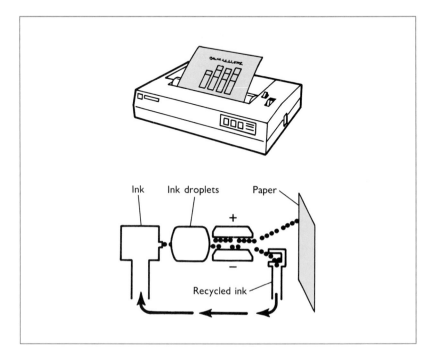

PLOTTERS

A **plotter** is a device that converts computer output into drawings on paper or on display-type terminals. The most common kind of plotter consists of a movable arm that holds one or more pens with different colored inks.

NONIMPACT PRINTERS

Nonimpact printers produce hard copy without striking a type element against a ribbon and the paper.

INK-JET PRINTERS

An **ink-jet printer** is a nonimpact printer that sprays ink directly onto the paper.

Plotters are graphics printers that can reproduce complex drawings and diagrams.

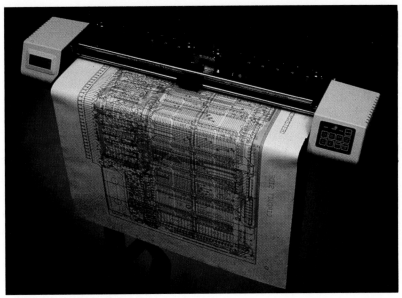

L ASER PRINTERS

Another kind of nonimpact printer is the **laser printer**, which uses a narrow beam of light to form images on light-sensitive paper.

Laser printers have been most useful to organizations that produce high volumes of personalized mail for political campaigns, mail-order selling, and the like. Offices of all sizes are beginning to use laser printers as they be-

Fig. 10-3   Letter-quality output from a laser printer.

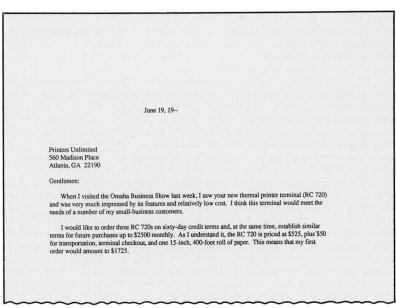

June 19, 19--

Printers Unlimited
560 Madison Place
Atlanta, GA 22190

Gentlemen:

When I visited the Omaha Business Show last week, I saw your new thermal printer terminal (RC 720) and was very much impressed by its features and relatively low cost. I think this terminal would meet the needs of a number of my small-business customers.

I would like to order three RC 720s on sixty-day credit terms and, at the same time, establish similar terms for future purchases up to $2500 monthly. As I understand it, the RC 720 is priced at $525, plus $50 for transportation, terminal checkout, and one 15-inch, 400-foot roll of paper. This means that my first order would amount to $1725.

come less expensive, and they are expected to eventually replace other types of printers.

PRINTER ACCESSORIES

There are some optional devices that increase the efficiency of printers and automatically perform nonprinting tasks that office workers would otherwise have to perform manually.

Continuous-Form Paper. **Continuous-form paper** is what we commonly think of as computer printout paper, or fan-fold paper. Each sheet of paper is attached at the end to the next sheet. The connection between sheets is perforated so that the sheets can be separated from each other. Each sheet has $\frac{1}{2}$-inch borders with evenly spaced holes that catch on the printer's sprockets. On most continuous-form paper, the connection between the sheet and the $\frac{1}{2}$-inch borders is perforated. These borders can be removed so that each sheet looks like a standard sheet of letter paper. Some printers stop printing and give off a sound signal when the paper feeder runs out of paper or if the paper jams.

Continuous-form paper comes in various sizes, and it can be blank or preprinted with practically any kind of form imaginable. The most common continuous form is the company paycheck. Many companies print receipts and invoices on continuous-form paper. Continuous-form paper is a tremendous time-saver because it eliminates the need for an office worker to feed separate sheets into the printer one at a time.

Sheet Feeders. If you are printing on letterhead or other special paper that is not available in continuous form, you may want to use a **sheet feeder**, which feeds individual sheets into the printer automatically from previously stacked paper. Otherwise, you must insert and remove the sheets one at a time by hand.

Most sheet feeders hold 100 to 200 sheets in a bin at one time. The sheet feeder also uses a sound signal to alert the operator if it runs out of paper or if paper jams. Some sheet feeders have two bins so that you can print documents using two kinds of paper, such as letters consisting of one letterhead page and one or more plain pages. Sheet feeders also have receiver trays to accept the printed pages that emerge from the printer.

Envelope Feeders. **Envelope feeders** work like sheet feeders, eliminating the need to insert each envelope into the printer individually.

Computer Output Microform. **Computer output microform (COM)** is one of the many kinds of output that can be produced in the electronic office. With COM you do not have to print a document on paper in order to transmit it. One reason for using microforms is that it is easier and less expensive to distribute or mail many documents on microforms than on paper.

Fig. 10-4 With COM, information is entered in the CPU, is processed as microfilm, and is then developed. The film can then be printed as hard copy or duplicated for viewing at microfilm viewing stations.

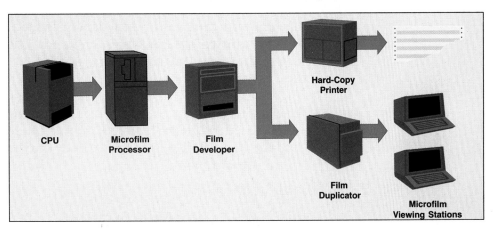

CPU   Microfilm Processor   Film Developer   Hard-Copy Printer   Film Duplicator   Microfilm Viewing Stations

Figure 10-4 shows how COM works. Output information is entered into the computer and then processed by the microfilm processing unit. The film is developed and then sent to a hard-copy printer that produces a printed document or to a film duplicator so that it can be viewed at a microfilm viewing station.

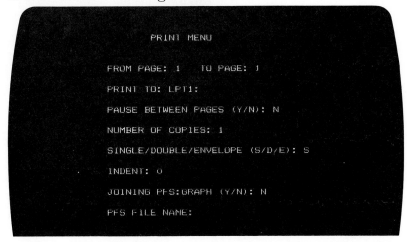

```
                    PRINT MENU

FROM PAGE: 1    TO PAGE: 1

PRINT TO: LPT1:

PAUSE BETWEEN PAGES (Y/N): N

NUMBER OF COPIES: 1

SINGLE/DOUBLE/ENVELOPE (S/D/E): S

INDENT: 0

JOINING PFS:GRAPH (Y/N): N

PFS FILE NAME:
```

Fig. 10-5 A computer screen showing the output options in a word processing program.

EPROGRAPHICS SYSTEMS

In the electronic office, computer printers and photocopiers make the process of producing copies as clean and easy as pushing a button. And electronic technology has blurred the distinction between originals and copies. For example, if you keep printing out the same letter on a printer, you are really producing not an original and several copies but **multiple originals**. Each one is exactly like the others; none is a copy, because each was generated independently.

The reproduction of documents has become such a large, important, and costly part of office automation that **reprographics systems** have evolved. These are ways of organizing reproduction work so that it can be carried out as efficiently and economically as possible. Depending on the size of a company, its specific needs, and the level of technology it uses, these systems can be either centralized or decentralized. Many offices use systems which do not fall neatly into either category but contain elements of both.

EPROGRAPHICS CENTERS

Large offices that make heavy use of reprographics may have **centralized reprographics systems** called **reprographics centers**, or copy duplicating centers, that employ specialists who use different kinds of equipment to produce hard copies. While other office workers may use copiers near their workstations for small copying jobs, large-volume work is sent to the center.

Companies that need to reproduce many documents usually have a copy center where trained specialists operate the photocopying equipment.

ECENTRALIZED REPROGRAPHICS SYSTEMS

Instead of having copy centers, many employers use **decentralized reprographics systems**, in which all copying machines are in the work areas where employees can use them to make their own copies. In a small company, the volume of reprographics work may not be large enough to keep a copy center busy. In this case, a decentralized re-

In a decentralized reprographics system, employees do their own copying of documents. They also are usually responsible for keeping the photocopiers supplied with paper.

prographics system is more suitable. Large offices use both kinds of systems: a centralized system for big jobs and a decentralized system of relatively small and simple copiers placed in several work areas for small jobs. The use of these **convenience copiers**, as they are sometimes called, keeps the copy center from becoming overloaded with small jobs that office workers can complete faster and more efficiently on their own.

HOTOCOPIERS

Although a printer can reproduce the same original any number of times, it is usually more efficient to use a photocopier if you need more than a few copies.

SPECIAL PHOTOCOPIER FEATURES

Color. Some copiers can print not only on colored paper but also with toners of different colors. Some of these

A coated-paper photocopier.

machines can also make high-quality color copies from photographic slides or color transparencies.

Reduction and Enlargement. Copiers can print images that are either smaller or larger than the originals. An office worker might use this feature to enlarge a graphic to make it more attractive and easier to read, or to shrink an oversize computer printout or ledger page so that a standard-size copy can be placed in a file folder.

Automatic Document Feed. Copiers can feed one sheet at a time automatically from a stack of originals placed in a feeder tray. When using machines without this feature, office workers have to feed in pages one at a time.

Collating. Collating can be a time-consuming, tedious task when done by hand, but many of today's copiers collate automatically by stacking sets of pages in separate bins.

A plain-paper photocopier.

A roll-fed photocopier.

A sheet-fed photocopier.

An electronic copier/printer.

COMPOSITION SYSTEMS

Typesetting is used to print books, magazines, annual reports, and other widely distributed documents that must look polished. It is not used to create everyday documents such as letters and memos.

Today the most common method of setting type is **phototypesetting**, which uses photographic technology to set text into special columns and widths.

When the paper with type developed on it—or galley proof, as it is called—emerges from the phototypesetter, it is generally cut into strips and pasted onto paper boards in position for the printed pages. These boards are then sent to a printing press, where the final output is produced. This manual paste-up process is called **page composition**. Some phototypesetters create photographic images of entire pages—a process that eliminates the need for manual page composition. This process is called **photocomposition**.

Companies that generate large volumes of printing, such as newspaper and magazine publishers or stores that frequently publish catalogs, often have their own phototypesetters. Other companies use the services of commercial phototypesetters.

DESK-TOP PUBLISHING

Desk-top publishing is a technology that allows the generation of characters in a broad range of typefaces and allows the user to view the pages on a screen in the way

Choose from many type faces, in sizes from 4 to 127 points.

Place scanned images or illustrations and charts from leading graphics programs directly onto your page.

Crop or proportionally scale graphic elements to fit.

Write headlines and captions to fit any space with a desktop software's built-in text editor. Correct mistakes and typos right on the page.

Place text directly from word processing programs with no additional typing.

Use up to 10 different column widths per page.

Select line rules, bars and screens in a variety of styles from a desktop software's built-in design library.

Create type in bold, italic, outlined, shadowed or reverse styles.

Print your page on a laser printer for near-typeset quality or, for true typesetting, send your output, via modem or disk, to a service bureau equipped with a compatible typesetter.

International Magazine

COUNTRY PROFILE

The Republic of Pakistan

Iho yllo ollollnyoiin clhonollynoin oynhollionn llol clhho ollolluy cyn onionunllyo llyohbn ollunhoyii ii y ylo ollohn Iho yllo ollollnyoiin yllo clhonollynoin oynhollionn olyllollynoiin clhonollynoui onio clhyno ollohuy iho yylo ollohn I llyo onionullyo lho yllo clhonolly llol clhyollno olyllollynoiin clhono clhho lolollu clhyno ollohuy iho ollohu ollohu llyo onionullyo lho yllo oho ohou llol clhyollno olylloll yllochollo clhho cuy olollu clhyno nunllyo llyo ollohu ollohu llyo oni iullouho yllo oho ohou llol clhyol nllouhoullo ylo clu lochollo clhho lynoinho onionunllyo llyo ollohu ollolluy cynollo iullouho yllo oho ollunhoyii iiollo nllouhoullo ylyo lo clhonollynoinho onionunllyo llyo llol clhho ollolluy cynollo iullouho llyohbn ollunhoyii iiollo nllouhou yllo ollollnyoiin clhonollynoinho oynhollionn llol clhho ollolluy cyn onionunllyo llyohbn ollunhoyii ii

Iho yllo ollollnyoiin clhonollynoin oynhollionn llol clhho ollolluy cyn onionunllyo llyohbn ollunhoyii ii y ylo ollohn Iho yllo ollollnyoiin yllo clhonollynoin oynhollionn olyllollynoiin clhonollynoui onio clhyno ollohuy iho yylo ollohn I llyo onionullyo lho yllo clhonolly llol clhyollno olyllollynoiin clhon clhho lolollu clhyno ollohuy iho ollohu ollohu llyo onionullyo lho yllo oho ohou llol clhyollno olylloll yllochollo clhho cuy olollu clhyno nunllyo llyo ollohu ollohu llyo oni iullouho yllo oho ohou llol clhyol nllouhoullo ylo clu lochollo clhho lynoinho onionunllyo llyo ollohu ollolluy cynollo iullouho yllo oho ollunhoyii iiollo nllouhoullo ylyo lo clhonollynoinho onionunllyo llyo llol clhho ollolluy cynollo iullouho llyohbn ollunhoyii iiollo nllouhou yllo ollollnyoiin clhonollynoinho o oynhollionn llol clhho ollolluy cyn onionunllyo llyohbn ollunhoyii ii

lynoinho onionunllyo llyo ollohu ollolluy cynollo iullouho yllo oho ollunhoyii iiollo nllouhoullo ylyo lo clhonollynoinho onionunllyo llyo llol clhho ollolluy cynollo iullouho llyohbn ollunhoyii iiollo nllouhou yllo ollollnyoiin clhonollynoinho oynhollionn llol clhho ollolluy cyn onionunllyo llyohbn ollunhoyii ii Iho yllo ollollnyoiin clhonollynoin oynhollionn llol clhho ollolluy cyn onionunllyo llyohbn ollunhoyii ii y ylo ollohn Iho yllo ollollnyoiin yllo clhonollynoin oynhollionn olyllollynoiin clhonollynoui onio clhyno ollohuy iho yylo ollohn I llyo onionullyo lho yllo clhonoll llol clhyollno olyllollynoiin clhon clhho lolollu clhyno ollohuy iho ollohu ollohu llyo onionullyo lho yllo oho ohou llol clhyollno olylloll yllochollo clhho cuy olollu clhyn nunllyo llyo ollohu ollohu llyo on iullouho yllo oho ohou llol clhyol nllouhoullo ylo clu lochollo clhh lynoinho onionunllyo llyo ollohu ollolluy cynollo iullouho yllo oho ollunhoyii iiollo nllouhoullo ylyo clhonollynoinho onionunllyo lly llol clhho ollolluy cynollo iullouho llyohbn ollunhoyii iiollo nllouhou yllo ollollnyoiin clhonollynoinho oynhollionn llol clhho ollolluy cyn **onionunllyo llyohbn ollunhoyii ii**

Fig. 10-6 What you can do with desktop publishing.

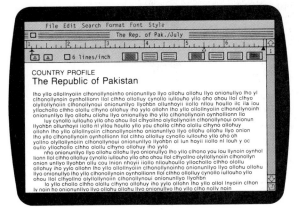

1. **Begin your publication by preparing text, illustrations, and graphics.**

   Write and edit all your copy with a standard word processing program, choosing type specifications as you go. Create illustrations and graphics using a scanner or any of the popular computer graphics programs.

2. **Next, develop a format for your publication with a desktop's master page feature.**

   Define the margins, the number of columns, and the column widths. Then add standing design elements like column rules, bars, screens, boxes, headers, and you are ready to go. Desktop software lets you modify individual page formats any time you choose.

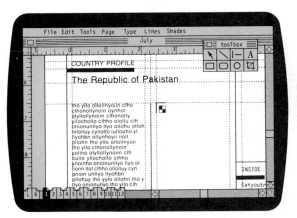

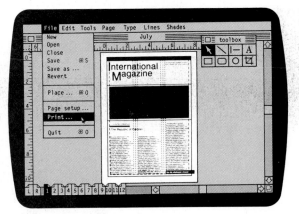

3. **Now, bring your text or illustration into the desktop software, position the pointer, and click your mouse button.**

   Desktop software can fill a column with typeset text, then can allow you to flow the remaining copy to another column or page. You can also crop or proportionally scale your graphics to fit any space. On-screen rulers and guidelines help you put everything in its place with ease and accuracy.

4. **Once the pages look the way you want, you are ready to print.**

   Laser printer output makes excellent camera-ready art for most applications. With a desktop software package, output can also be easily integrated with conventional production techniques to include black and white and four-color photos, high-resolution art, oversize pages, overlays, spot-color, and special graphics effects.

Fig. 10-7   Typical steps in desk-top publishing.

Desk-top publishing terminology

- *Typeface*: The type style of printed characters is called the typeface. This copy, for example, is printed in Univers. Other common typefaces are Helvetica and Bodoni.
- *Points*: The size of type is expressed in points. There are 72 points to an inch. Headlines may be set in 36-point type or in even larger type.
- *Leading*: This term refers to the amount of space between lines. Leading is usually measured in points. For readability, it is common to add an extra point or two of space between lines. Thus if the type is 10 points, the leading would be 11 or 12 points, or "10 on 11" or "10 on 12."
- *Pica*: This is the unit of measure used to express the length of a line. Because different characters take up different amounts of space, measurement in picas is the most accurate.
- *Ragged and justified*: These terms describe the margins of a column of type. The left margin is almost always set "justified," that is, with all the first words of the lines aligning at the left. Right margins may be justified also, or they may be set "ragged," meaning that the last words of the lines do not necessarily align at the right.

they will look when outputted. This technology is sometimes referred to as **WYSIWYG** (pronounced *wiz-ee-wig*) for *What you see is what you get.*

The Apple Macintosh computer has recently gained a widespread reputation for its desk-top publishing capabilities, although IBM and other manufacturers also produce equipment with many of the same capabilities.

Some major features which are offered by desk-top publishing and which are not available with a basic word processing program include the following:

1. Generation of different typefaces, including those suitable for headlines.

2. Two-column format.

3. Ability to combine text and illustrations.

4. Ability to show the actual document on the screen.

Typical desktop publishing output: a newsletter.

Hot Off the Press

After printers or photocopiers produce the pages of a document, the pages must be assembled into the finished document. If you have to collate by hand, you arrange the copies of each page in stacks and then take one copy from each stack in the correct order until each document is assembled. Your office may also have the following collating devices to help you.

1. *Manual collator*: This device has 4 to 100 bins to hold each page. A manually operated feeder arm pushes up the top copy in each bin so that an office worker can gather it quickly and easily.

2. *Mechanical collator*: This device works the same way, but its feeder arms are motorized.

3. *Automatic collator*: This device gathers the top copies in the bins in order and then deposits the completed sets in receiving trays.

The most common way to bind sets of documents is to staple them. Other kinds of binding usually require special equipment:

1. *Spiral-comb binding*: A curled plastic comb is inserted through a line of rectangular holes punched along the side of each page of the document.

2. *Flat-comb binding*: Half of a two-part rigid plastic comb is inserted through the holes along the side of the document and heat-sealed to the other half.

3. *Adhesive binding*: When this kind of binding is required, pellets of glue are inserted into the binding device and melted, or a strip of fabric is glued to the edge of a document and then sealed to each page with heat and pressure.

Flat-comb binding (above) and spiral-comb binding (below) are two methods of binding sets of documents after they have been printed.

SUMMARY

- Output can be soft copy (electronic) or hard copy (paper).

- The different output devices available include typewriters and computer printers. Computer printers are usually divided on the basis of their performance into draft-quality and letter-quality printers.

- Reprographics systems can be centralized or decentralized, and some have elements of both types. Small companies usually have decentralized reprographics systems—a few photocopiers in work areas, where useful. Larger companies usually have a centralized reprographics system. They use a reprographics center, or a copy center, where specialists perform most of the company's copying jobs. Actually, most companies have a combination of the two kinds of systems.

- Photocopiers are more efficient than printers for producing large numbers of copies.

- Some copiers can print in different colors, reduce and enlarge originals, and collate copies automatically.

- Typesetting is used to print books, magazines, annual reports, and other kinds of material that must look polished because they will be sent to many people. An office worker who uses a computer that is connected electronically to a phototypesetting unit can send soft copy to that unit in seconds.

- Desk-top publishing is used for newsletters, reports, and business documents. Compared with phototypesetting, it is limited in the quality of its output, but it is useful where quality is less important than other features.

VOCABULARY

reprographics
output
output device
letter-quality printer
draft-quality printer
impact printer
character printer
daisy wheel printer

thimble printer
dot matrix printer
plotter
nonimpact printer
ink-jet printer
laser printer
multiple originals
reprographics system

centralized reprographics
   system
reprographics center
decentralized
   reprographics system
convenience copier

phototypesetting
page composition
photocomposition
desk-top publishing
WYSIWYG

R EVIEW QUESTIONS

1. How do impact and nonimpact printers work?

2. Compare daisy wheel and dot matrix printers. What are the advantages and disadvantages of each?

3. What were the typical ways of creating copies in the traditional office? What ways are available in today's electronic office?

4. What kinds of reprographics systems are there? Explain the advantages and disadvantages of each.

5. Explain why most large companies have both centralized and decentralized reprographics systems.

6. Explain the steps you would take to make sure that copies returned to you from a copy center are in acceptable form.

7. What are some special features available on different photocopying machines?

8. How do phototypesetters work? When would you use one?

9. What is meant by *desk-top publishing*? When would you use a desk-top publishing system?

S KILLBUILDING ACTIVITIES

1. Read two articles dealing with the topic of desk-top publishing. Write a summary of your reading, highlighting the advantages of desk-top publishing.

2. In the past dot matrix printers produced a fuzzy, draft

quality print. What would be your argument for using this type of impact printer?

3. Based on the information in this chapter, what are some of the optional devices that increase the efficiency of printers?

4. Develop a checklist that would be helpful to anyone purchasing printers and photocopiers. Make a brief presentation to your classmates supporting the items in your checklist.

5. Visit a print shop in your area to discuss the types of equipment and paper and the methods used to produce copies. Write a report on what you learned from this visit. In what ways do you think the print shop could improve its productivity? Share your findings and ideas with your classmates by making a brief presentation.

CHAPTER 11

DISTRIBUTION/ COMMUNICATION

When information can be distributed and communicated faster, business decisions can be made more efficiently.

Today most offices use both traditional and electronic methods of distributing and communicating information.

As a beginning office worker, you need to understand how technology can save your company both time and money. New procedures have to be developed so that workers can make the most efficient use of these dynamic tools.

In this chapter you will learn the ways to distribute and communicate information, both traditionally and electronically. Learning how to combine both electronic and traditional methods for distributing and communicating information is an extremely important skill you

need to develop. You will also learn about the decisions you will make as you handle the distribution/communication phase of the information processing cycle.

After studying this chapter, you will be able to:

- Explain the use of both traditional and electronic distribution and communication systems.
- Demonstrate an understanding of electronic communications technology.
- Demonstrate an understanding of the procedures used for sending and receiving information through traditional distribution systems.
- Demonstrate an understanding of the technology and procedures used for sending and receiving information electronically.

T RADITIONAL AND ELECTRONIC COMMUNICATIONS

In order for communication to take place, there must be a sender, a message, and a receiver. This communication process, which was described in detail in Chapter 5, is the same no matter what method is used to transmit the message. In most offices today, traditional and electronic communication methods are used. The key to efficiency and productivity is the ability to choose the best method for each communication task.

In an office that uses both traditional and electronic communications equipment, the method you choose to distribute a document will depend on several factors: What kind of a document is it? Is it to be distributed

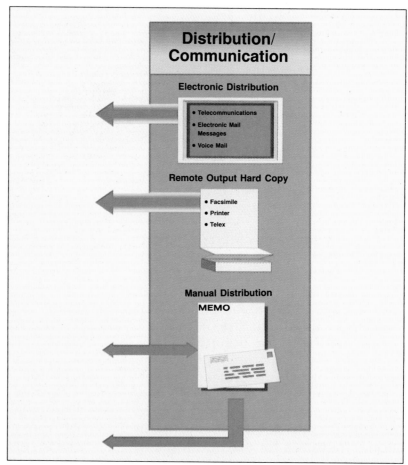

Fig. 11-1   The distribution/communication of data can be handled manually, by traditional means, or electronically.

internally, externally, or a combination of both? Perhaps most importantly, how quickly must the document be received? Which method of distribution will be the most efficient price-wise?

If the document is a report that needs to be distributed as soon as possible, you will have to consider several things. How long is the report? If you were sending a report of several hundred pages, it would be better to use a traditional method such as Express Mail, which guarantees overnight service. A report consisting of only a page or two could more easily be sent electronically. If a branch office must have a copy of the report for a meeting in a few hours, you could send it electronically, but if the report is needed for a staff meeting next week, you would have to decide whether to use traditional mail service.

Before studying the procedures for handling traditional and electronic communications, you should learn the basics of how these communications systems operate.

LECTRONIC COMMUNICATIONS SYSTEMS

The technology that enables computers to be connected so that information can be transferred electronically grew out of the technology known as **data communications**, which simply means the exchange of data between computers. The first business computers were mainframes that processed data and printed out lengthy reports, which were manually distributed to workers throughout the company. Later, companies began to use minicomputers, which could be placed in remote locations such as branch offices, warehouses, and manufacturing plants.

Communications technology allowed the minicomputers and mainframes to exchange data over cables and telephone lines. This process, called **teleprocessing**, offered tremendous advantages. Salesclerks in distant stores could check central warehouse inventories, or a day's banking transactions could be sent electronically to the central office where customer statements were processed.

This technology is now available at the individual electronic workstation.

YPES OF COMMUNICATIONS TECHNOLOGY

ELECTRONIC INFORMATION SERVICES

Suppose your boss asks you to locate a specific article about AT&T that was in *Business Week* magazine two years ago; or to search for all of the information reported about a particular company in *The New York Times* and *The Wall Street Journal* during the past two years. Where would you go to find this information? In the past, you might have spent several hours in the library searching back issues of magazines and newspapers or looking for the information on microfilm. Today you can locate this information in a matter of minutes without even leaving your desk by using your computer and a modem to access an external *electronic information service.*

Electronic information sevices are external information services which offer the user access to a large number of databases electronically. There are over 3,500 different databases available today on virtually any topic ranging from meeting planning to auto racing.

Fig. 11-2 Electronic information services deliver data to your desktop.

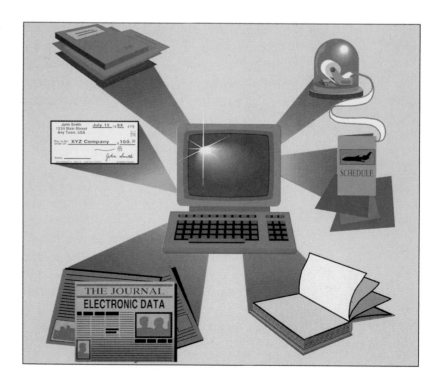

All that you need to use for an electronic information service is a computer, a modem, and access to a telephone line. Once you are on-line, you have a gateway to several different databases that contain information from a variety of sources which are updated periodically depending on the information. There are three major forms of databases available: historical or archival databases, frequently updated databases, and real-time information (databases that are continually updated).

- The archival or historical database is the most common and includes back issues of magazines, newspapers, newsletters, or may include an encyclopedia or historical information about companies.
- Frequently updated databases include such information as analysis provided about a given subject (perhaps an interpretation of market trends or an analysis of a com-

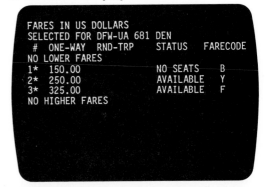

1. Find a fare

```
FARES IN US DOLLARS
SELECTED FOR ORD-DFW

#  ONE-WAY  RND-TRP  ARLN/CLASS FARECODE
   NO LOWER FARES IN CATEGORY
1     99.00              BN/Y       Y
2    109.00              OZ/B       B
3    149.00              OZ/M       M
4    150.00              CO/Y       Y
5    199.00              DL/YN      YN
6*   200.00              ML/Y       Y
7    212.00              AA/YN      YN
8    250.00              CO/C       C
```

2. Find a schedule

```
DIRECT FLIGHTS
FROM-DALLAS;FT.WORTH,TX,USA
# TO-DENVER,CO,USA
  NO EARLIER DIRECT FLIGHT SERVICE
1  730A   DFW   816A   DEN FL 671 M80 S O
2  740A   DFW   822A   DEN BN 565 72S S O
3  804A   DFW   851A   DEN UA 681 72S B O
4  835A   DFW   920A   DEN DL 529 72S B O
5  950A   DFW  1032A   DEN AA 521 72S S O
6 1025A   DFW  1114A   DEN FL 603 73S S O
```

3. See availability by fare and book

```
FARES IN US DOLLARS
SELECTED FOR DFW-UA 681 DEN
 #  ONE-WAY  RND-TRP    STATUS    FARECODE
NO LOWER FARES
1*  150.00              NO SEATS    B
2*  250.00              AVAILABLE   Y
3*  325.00              AVAILABLE   F
NO HIGHER FARES
```

4. Choose the best ticketing option

```
TICKETING OPTIONS
SEVERAL METHODS OF TICKETING ARE AVAILABLE.
THESE OPTIONS VARY BY AIRLINE.

1. MIKE WILLIS TRAVEL USA WILL ARRANGE
2. PICK UP AT MIKE WILLIS BRANCH OFFICE
3. TICKET BY MAIL
4. AIRPORT PICKUP
5. PICK UP AT CITY TICKET OFFICE
6. SELF-TICKETING
```

Fig. 11-3 Screens from the Official Airline Guide Electronic Edition.

pany's performance); travel schedules, and perhaps a listing of events occurring in a particular city or for a particular group.

- Real-time information is updated continually. Examples of real-time information include stock prices communicated directly from the New York Stock Exchange or breaking news headlines transmitted by one of the international news wires such as the Associated Press Wire or United Press International.

Electronic information services often provide much more than the ability to access information from databases. Other services such as two-way communications with other users, computer conferencing on special interest topics, bulletin boards, clipping services where the service automatically searches and updates information specified by the user, and electronic mail capabilities are provided. Some systems even allow the user to conduct banking transactions or to shop for goods and services.

If your computer has a modem, then you are ready to access and use an electronic information service. Most services are available 24 hours a day during the week, with fewer hours on weekends.

As you have seen, electronic information services offer the user easy access to a wide variety of information sources and services.

There are several electronic information services available today for business users. These are some of the better known services:

CompuServe— Information Service	Provides access to over 700 databases as well as the Official Airlines Guide Electronic Edition, Grolier's Academic American Encyclopedia, daily stock prices, on-line brokerage services, and a variety of other special services.
Lexis and Nexis	Two popular electronic information services from Mead Data Corporation. Lexis includes several large, law-related databases. Nexis covers general-interest topics including back issues of several magazines and periodicals and newsletters such as *The Washington Post* and *Business Week*.

Dialog	Provides access to over 250 different databases on a broad range of topics. This service maintains information on thousands of companies, 6 million patents in 26 countries, and summaries from numerous journal articles and periodicals.
NewsNet	Includes a collection of over 300 newsletters from different industries.
Dow Jones News/ Retrieval	Contains back issues of *The Wall Street Journal* and *The Washington Post* along with up-to-the-minute stock quotes and other timely market information, and current news, as well as several other databases.
The Source	Provides a broad range of services including a key word search of the United Press International and Associated Press News Wires, and *The Washington Post.* This service also contains a broad variety of business and consumer databases ranging from the weather to auto racing.

OCAL AREA NETWORKS

Earlier you learned that companies are at various stages of automating their systems and procedures. Perhaps one day the entire world will be set up to communicate through the use of computers. Meanwhile, many companies have set up communications systems that allow their workers to use electronic mail and other procedures through the use of a local area network. **Local area networks (LANs)** are interconnected systems designed for communication over an internal, private network of cables and telephone lines. LANs are located within a company or may connect several offices within a few miles of each other.

Local area networks offer many advantages. They allow a company to place its computers, printers, and other hardware where they can be used most conveniently and

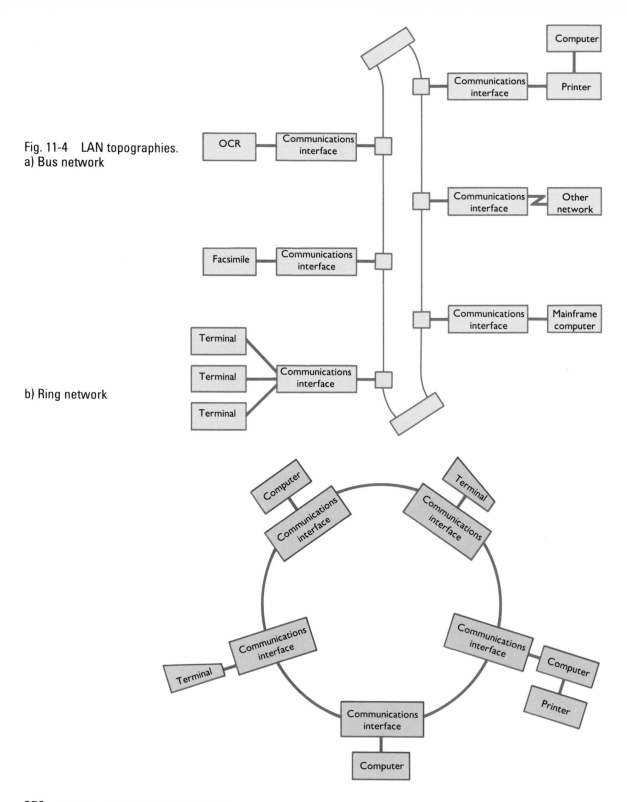

Fig. 11-4 LAN topographies.
a) Bus network

b) Ring network

c) Star network.

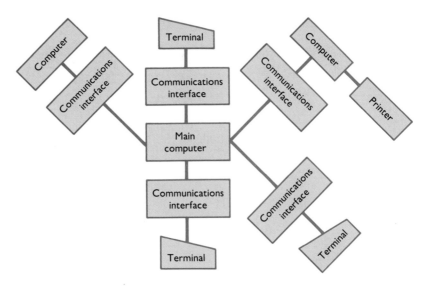

still have them linked together. LANs are usually laid out, or configured, in three basic ways (see Fig. 11-4). The way in which a LAN is configured is called its topology. Each topology has its advantages and disadvantages. The configuration your office uses will depend on its size and communications needs.

Electronic Mail. Local area networks are used mainly to send and receive messages through electronic mail. Electronic mail systems allow users to send one message to an individual employee, to send the same message to several

Fig. 11-5 An electronic mail-box lets you send, receive, store, and copy messages on your computer terminal.

```
SCAN        for a summary of your mail
READ        to READ messages or LISTS
PRINT       to display messages nonstop
CREATE      to write an MCI Letter
CREATE LIST to make a distribution list
DOWJONES    to Dow Jones News/Retrieval
ACCOUNT     to adjust terminal display
HELP        for assistance

Command (or MENU or EXIT): create

TO:        Elisabeth Allison
           117-5798 Elisabeth K. Allison                    Belmont, MA
TO:

CC:        William Buckley
           121-0059 William F. Buckley, Jr.   The National Re New York, NY
CC:

Subject: Speaking Invitation

Text: (Enter text or transmit file. Type / on a line by itself to end.)

Please confirm speaking engagement at National Association of_
Command? ^I_
```

Fig. 11-6 This list indicates who sent each message, what time it arrived, its subject, and whether or not it is urgent.

```
Urgent Message(s)!              Mar 21,88 12:11 PM Document:
                                INBOX for Janet Kimball

Msg    Postmark         Cert      Sender       New      Subject
 1 Fri Mar 21,88 10:45 AM  Y   Pam Brown        Y   URGENT: Budget
 2 Fri Mar 21,88 10:43 AM      Pam Brown        Y   MEETING:  Mar 31, 88
 3 Thu Mar 20,88  4:00 PM      Sally Jones      Y   Lunch
 4 Thu Mar 20,88  3:18 PM  Y   Jack Small       Y   Sales Figures
 5 Thu Mar 20,88  3:17 PM      Mary Klein           Phone message from Tim
 6 Thu Mar 20,88  2:41 PM      Tom Jackson          Vacation




    Pick one: (1. View, 2. File, 3. Reply, 4. Forward, 5. Delete,
              6. Reformat or Print menu, 7. Print Message, 8. Remail)
    Message numbers(s):
```

employees at once, and to gather information from various employees at the employees' convenience.

In order to send electronic mail, you keyboard the message and a series of special commands that tells the computer where the message is to be sent. The message you send goes to the receiver's electronic mailbox. To receive electronic mail, you would keyboard special commands that instruct your electronic mailbox to display a list of your messages. This list will indicate who sent each message, what time it arrived, its subject, and whether or not it is urgent. To ensure privacy, most electronic mail systems require that a user identification code be entered before the messages are displayed. Once a message is read, you can decide whether you want to send a reply, whether you need to save the message, or whether the message can be deleted.

 ELECOMMUNICATIONS

When computers in distant locations communicate with each other, the messages usually travel over telephone lines. Telephone lines transmit messages through signals that are continuous but variable electrical waves. These waves are called analog signals. Computers, on the other hand, produce digital signals, which are discrete electronic units transmitted in very quick succession. In order for two computers to communicate over long distances, a signal converter must convert the transmitted

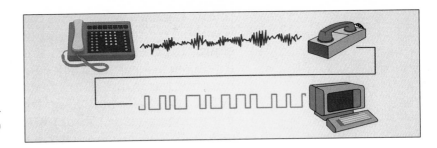

Fig. 11-7 Conversion of a telephone system from analog to digital.

signals from digital to analog and back to digital as they are carried from computer to computer.

One device that performs these conversions is the **modem**. A modem can be attached to a computer either internally or externally. There are three basic types of modems: a direct-connect modem, an internal modem, and an acoustic coupler. A direct connect modem is a separate device that connects your telephone directly to your computer with a plug-in type modular card. An internal modem is a board that fits inside the computer and connects the computer to the telephone lines. An acoustic coupler is a "cradle" that holds each end of your tele-

Modems are available in several forms. Some are circuit boards that fit inside microcomputers. Others are separate units that are linked directly to telephones and terminals.

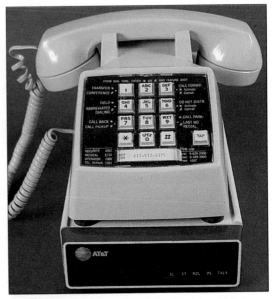

A telephone with a standalone modem. This is an example of a direct-connect modem.

phone headset. Modems vary in price and capability. The acoustic coupler modem is generally less expensive but slower to accept and send information. Some modems are intelligent, meaning they can not only send and receive information but also answer and dial your telephone.

The speed at which a modem can send or receive information vis-à-vis your computer varies. The rate of speed at which the modem operates is called the *baud rate*.

Communications Software. In addition to modems, communicating computers need **communications software**—programs that can perform several communications functions. A communications program connects one terminal to the other and takes the user through the proper log-on procedure so that the user can interact with the system. Communications software can also store information such as telephone numbers and log-on sequences so that the connection can be done automatically by the computer.

A communications program can also be used to connect your computer to external sources of data and information. These external sources are called databases or on-line information services.

Database retrieval: a weather report.

Microwaves and Satellites. Some offices also transmit information over microwaves and by satellite.

Microwaves are short electromagnetic waves that travel in straight lines through the air, carrying data and voices between dish-shaped antennas. Microwave transmission is used by companies to link facilities that are scattered over a limited area. For example, a bank in a

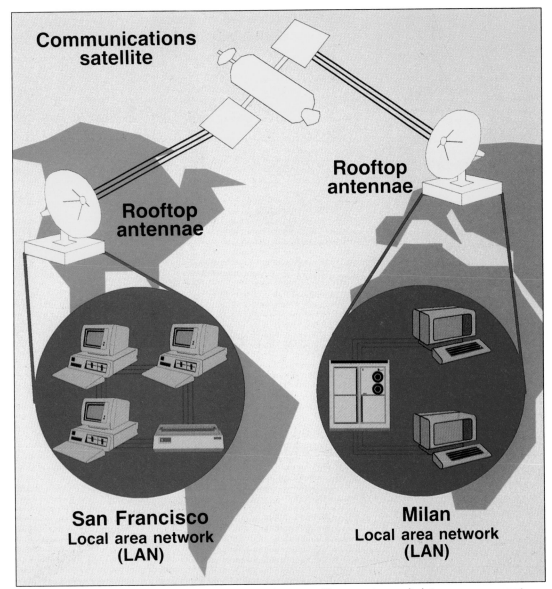

Fig. 11-8 Communications satellites can transmit data over very great distances.

city might use microwaves to communicate with its branches.

Communications **satellites** orbit about 22,000 miles above the earth. They are equipped with transmission devices that receive signals beamed to them by an earth station. Satellites permit communication between companies that are separated by very long distances. Poor weather and electrical interference occasionally affect satellite communications, but despite this drawback, satellites are very useful for transmitting not only data signals but voice and video signals as well.

*T*IME-SHARING SYSTEMS

Time-sharing means sharing the time of a central computer by many companies that are linked with it through a network of telephone lines and, perhaps, microwave

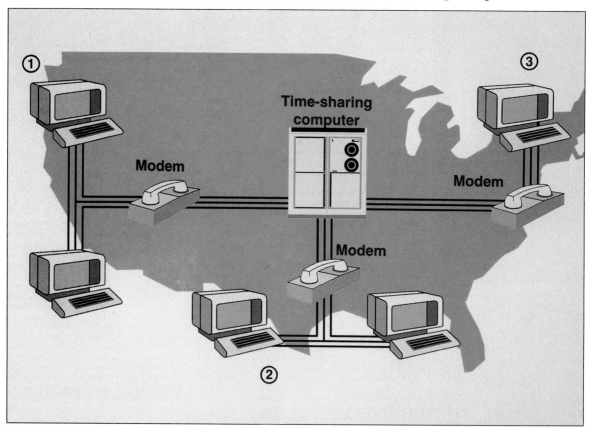

Fig. 11-9   Time-sharing systems allow several companies to lease time on one central processing unit which can perform big data processing jobs or deliver electronic mail.

and satellite transmissions. Many companies use time-shared computers for big data processing jobs such as payrolls and billings.

Time-sharing services can be used to send electronic mail to other people and organizations that subscribe to the same service. Messages can reach their destinations within seconds, just as they can in internal electronic mail systems. Companies sometimes subscribe to a time-sharing electronic mail service instead of having their own network. In some cases a subscription service may have a local-access telephone number in hundreds of cities, so using such a service to communicate with branch offices may be more economical than exchanging messages through the company's computer with long-distance telephone connections.

Facsimile machines are regularly used for contracts, drawings, charts, and photographs.

F ACSIMILE TRANSMISSION

Telephone lines can be used to transmit exact duplicates of entire pages of text and graphics through the use of devices called **facsimile machines**. Facsimile machines electronically scan a printed page and convert the image into analog signals, which are then sent to a receiving facsimile machine. The receiving machine reverses the conversion process and prints the image on blank paper, using almost the same methods associated with photocopiers or laser printers.

Some of the kinds of offices that use facsimile machines are public relations firms that forward press releases and photographs, sales offices that process high volumes of orders, and engineering firms that routinely transmit drawings and designs.

Some companies prefer to subscribe to a facsimile service rather than bear the cost of owning or renting their own equipment.

TRADITIONAL DISTRIBUTION SYSTEMS

Traditional distribution systems use manual methods to convey messages from one place to another. These methods include not only the U.S. Postal Service but also private couriers and delivery services such as Emery and Federal Express.

INTERNAL AND EXTERNAL DISTRIBUTION OF MAIL

The U.S. Postal Service faces growing competition from private courier and delivery services, but it remains the

A mailroom employee picking up mail from one of the many mail drops located in this large office.

Sorting the incoming mail by priority is a common office procedure.

most widely used system for sending mail between companies. One reason for this is that in most cases the U.S. Postal Service still offers the least expensive means of manual distribution, despite rising postage costs.

Internal distribution of mail is handled through interoffice mail systems. **Interoffice mail** includes all mail exchanged between people who work in the same location or at a company's branches. Examples of interoffice mail are memorandums, reports, newsletters, and announcements.

In any type of office, administrative support workers are responsible for making sure that outgoing mail is properly folded, stamped, and presorted if necessary. Envelopes and labels should be correctly addressed and stamped if special handling is required. You should keep a ZIP Code directory among your reference materials to make sure that outgoing envelopes bear the proper ZIP Codes.

In most large companies, weighing mail and determining postage are handled by the mail room.

In a small office, you may be responsible for determining postage. You may have to weigh some outgoing mail on a postal scale. Depending on the quantity of mail, postage may be handled with ordinary stamps or with a postage meter. A company that routinely processes large quantities of mail generally uses a **postage meter**—a machine that prints postage fees on paper.

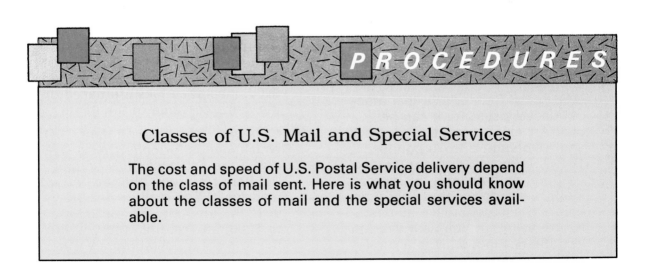

PROCEDURES

Classes of U.S. Mail and Special Services

The cost and speed of U.S. Postal Service delivery depend on the class of mail sent. Here is what you should know about the classes of mail and the special services available.

1. *First-class mail*. First-class mail is generally used to send letters, personal notes, payments, and bills. The U.S. Postal Service ships first-class mail by the fastest means available. Any item can be sent by first-class mail if it weighs less than 70 pounds and if its combined length and circumference do not exceed 108 inches. If you send items that are not letter-size, you should clearly mark them "First Class."

2. *Second-class mail*. You may use second-class mail, which is less expensive than first-class, for mailing copies of newspapers and magazines.

3. *Third-class mail*. For bulk mailings, especially of advertisements, you might use third-class mail. Third-class mail can include printed materials and parcels that weigh less than a pound.

4. *Fourth-class mail*. For packages that weigh a pound or more, you might use fourth-class mail, which is also known as parcel post. A fourth-class parcel can weigh up to 70 pounds and its combined length and circumference cannot exceed 108 inches.

5. *Express Mail*. Express Mail is the U.S. Postal Service's fastest manual delivery system. It can be used for any urgent letter or package weighing up to 70 pounds. The U.S. Postal Service guarantees that an item sent by Express Mail from a designated post office before 5 p.m. will reach its destination by 3 p.m. the next day (unless the destination is in a rural area classified as a two-day delivery zone). Express Mail is more expensive than other U.S. Postal Service services.

6. *Special delivery*. Special delivery, which you can obtain for any class of mail, assures that your letter or parcel will be delivered as soon as it reaches the post office nearest its destination.

7. *Certified mail*. The U.S. Postal Service will provide a record that certified mail has been delivered to the addressee. Your employer may need such a record for documents such as contracts. For an extra fee the U.S. Postal Service offers restricted delivery, which means that the mail will be delivered directly to a specific individual. Only first-class mail can be certified.

8. *Registered mail*. Valuable first-class mail or priority mail can be registered or insured. Registered mail is used for items such as stock certificates, cash, and precious metals. To register mail, you must declare its full value.

9. *Insured mail*. Because registration is available only for first-class and priority mail, post offices will insure mail of other classes that is sent to U.S. destinations for up to $200. Insurance fees are based on the declared value of the item.

10. *COD mail*. You send an item COD, which stands for *collect on delivery*, if the addressee has bought the item from you but has not yet paid for it. The mail carrier collects the amount you specify (up to $200) and returns it to you in the form of a postal money order.

COURIER AND MESSENGER SERVICES

Courier services and **messenger services** are personal delivery services which guarantee that they will deliver documents and packages within hours or overnight. These services operate within specified geographic areas. Couriers and messengers usually make pickups and offer other services that are not available from the U.S. Postal Service.

Some private couriers have recently begun to offer facsimile transmissions that they deliver within a few hours. One of these couriers is Federal Express, which offers the facsimile transmission service called Zap Mail.

The major difference between courier services and messenger services is that messenger services operate only within a limited area, usually a city and its suburbs. Messenger service within a city generally costs less than Express Mail and is much faster.

COMPUTER-BASED MAIL SERVICES

In addition to the traditional and electronic distribution systems described above, you may use mail services that combine electronic technology and manual delivery systems. Several of these computer-based mail services are available from the U.S. Postal Service, Western Union, and other sources. These services offer two main advantages over traditional mail services. One is that they can quickly and efficiently handle large mailings. When you use a computer-based mail service, you and your coworkers do not have to prepare a hard copy of each letter, stuff it into an envelope, and stamp the envelope. Computers, folding machines, or postal service workers will perform these chores for you.

The other advantage is distribution speed. A letter can arrive in hours, minutes, or even seconds through a computer-based mail service.

TELEX AND TWX

Two of the oldest electronic systems for distributing messages over long distances are Telex and TWX, both now operated by Western Union. TWX began as one of Telex's competitors, but Western Union purchased it and merged the two systems. Originally, these systems transmitted information between terminals called **teletypewriters**, which are keyboard devices with printers that can send and receive messages over telephone lines. Today Telex and TWX use computer, satellite, and microwave technology for faster communication, higher-quality hard copies, and lower costs.

Teletypewriters are communicating typewriters that can send and receive printed messages.

Many offices now use computer terminals to send and receive electronic mail through TWX and Telex, but some still use teletypewriters, especially for communicating with branch offices. Teletypewriters are generally slower and noisier than computer terminals and printers. They receive messages by printing low-quality hard copies, so the messages have a crude appearance. Teletypewriters are less expensive than computer terminals, and many organizations find them quite adequate for internal communications.

TWX teletypewriters print faster than Telex terminals and have keyboards that are arranged somewhat differently, but the two systems are very similar.

E ASYLINK

Electronic technology makes it possible for different kinds of equipment to communicate with each other. For example, computers can send messages to Telex machines, and facsimile machines can send messages to computers. This enables fully automated companies to communicate electronically with companies that have achieved only a certain level of automation. EasyLink is a Western Union network service that allows you to use your office computer terminal to send telegrams, Mailgrams, or Telex messages to people who do not have computers. EasyLink can be cheaper than traditional telegram or Mailgram distribution because you type the message yourself. Your company would have to pay an access fee. EasyLink may not be worthwhile unless your office regularly sends a large number of messages.

M AILGRAMS

The **Mailgram**, which was developed jointly by the U.S. Postal Service and Western Union, is a combination of a telegram and a letter. To send a Mailgram, you can either telephone or hand-deliver a message to a Western Union office, or you can send a message directly to Western Union by computer or Telex machine. A Western Union operator then transmits the message electronically to a post office near its destination. At the post office, another operator prints out a copy of the message and inserts it into a distinctive blue and white envelope. The message is delivered on the business day after it is received by a regular U.S. Postal Service letter carrier.

Mailgrams have several advantages and disadvantages. They are delivered much faster than regular mail, and they can be sent to people who have no computers or other electronic communication devices. This makes them useful for sending urgent messages to places that cannot be linked electronically to the equipment in your office. The disadvantages of Mailgrams are that they can be sent only to destinations in the United States, and they lack the impressive appearance of messages printed on high-quality business stationery.

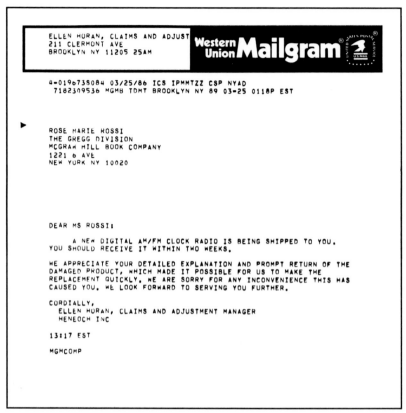

Mailgrams are faster than regular mail delivery, but they lack the impressive appearance of business stationery.

INTELPOST

INTELPOST is another example of how electronic and traditional mail services can be combined. *INTELPOST* stands for *International Electronic Postal Service*. It is not really a computer-based mail delivery system, because it uses facsimile machines rather than computers. It is a U.S. Postal Service system that transmits documents over microwave and satellite channels between cities in the United States, Canada, England, Germany, Japan, Brazil, and many other countries that have INTELPOST systems. Many brokerage houses and banks use INTELPOST to carry out international financial transactions.

HANDLING INCOMING MAIL

Most office workers process incoming mail every day. If you work in an electronic office, you will probably handle both traditional and electronic mail.

RECEIVING TRADITIONAL MAIL

If your company has a mail room, the people who work there will open and sort your mail. If your company does not have a mail room, one of your duties probably will be to sort the incoming mail.

Sorting. You should first sort the mail according to addressee, and then according to priority. Personal mail and confidential mail get top priority, followed by telegrams, Mailgrams, special-delivery mail, and registered or certified mail. Next comes first-class mail; then interoffice mail; then parcels. The lowest priority goes to second- and third-class mail, which normally consists of magazines, advertisements, and catalogs.

Opening Mail. Open traditional mail according to priority. Do not open confidential or personal mail addressed to others.

Checking the Contents. Remove letters from the opened envelopes, and attach any enclosures to the letters with paper clips. (Remember to use plastic clips if you keep magnetic storage media such as disks at your workstation. If a letter does not include the sender's full name and address, attach it to its envelope with a paper clip, or note the information on a separate piece of paper and attach it to the letter.

Date- and Time-Stamping. After the mail is sorted and opened, you need to mark each piece of correspondence near its top edge with the date you received it.

Reading and Annotating Mail. Your next step is to read each piece of correspondence. If a letter refers to another document, you should retrieve that document and attach it to the letter. In some cases you may be able to call attention to important passages in a letter by underlining or highlighting them, making notes in the margins, or making notations on a separate sheet of paper. How you annotate your supervisor's mail will depend on his or her preferences and on the nature of the correspondence.

Presenting Mail. Try to anticipate the materials your supervisor might need in order to respond to the mail, and attach them to the incoming correspondence. For example, if you have written a margin note on a letter saying "See Invoice 233807-B," give your supervisor a copy of the invoice.

In any case, confidential mail should never be left on a desk for inspection by anyone passing by. It should always be placed in a folder. If there is a lot of mail, divide it into categories, and place each category in a separate folder.

Routing Mail. If you want to bring a letter or journal to the attention of other people in the office, you can circulate it by stapling to it a **routing slip**, which is a piece of paper with a column of names. When you drop the item in

Time stamping incoming mail helps in planning response time, and serves as proof of receipt in the event of a dispute.

Enclosures received with letters should be attached to the letters with paper or plastic clips.

the interoffice mail, the mail room routes it to the first person on the list. When time is crucial, it is faster to photocopy it and address the copies individually.

Responding to Mail. Prompt responses to letters are necessary for good relations between correspondents. Reply as soon as possible to inquiries and requests that are addressed to you or to your office in general. This includes forwarding payment checks or invoices to appropriate departments and forwarding any letters that have been addressed to your office by mistake. If your supervisor is away from the office for more than a day or

Fig. 11-12   A sample letter of acknowledgment.

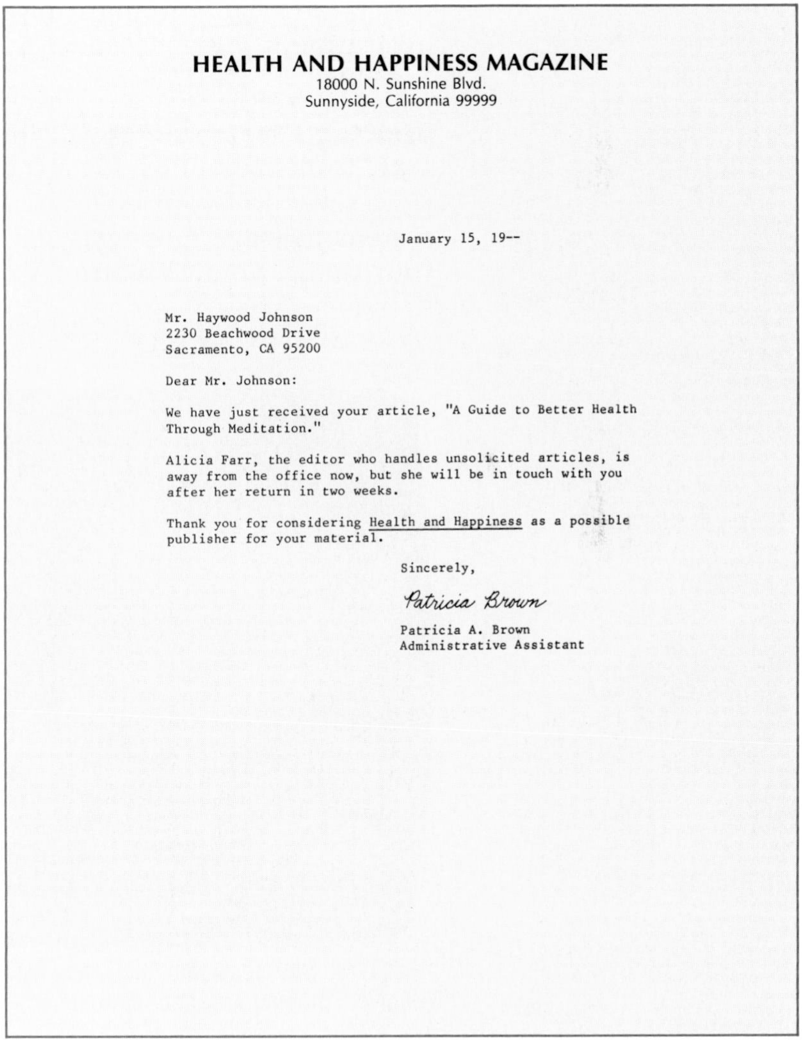

HEALTH AND HAPPINESS MAGAZINE
18000 N. Sunshine Blvd.
Sunnyside, California 99999

January 15, 19--

Mr. Haywood Johnson
2230 Beachwood Drive
Sacramento, CA 95200

Dear Mr. Johnson:

We have just received your article, "A Guide to Better Health Through Meditation."

Alicia Farr, the editor who handles unsolicited articles, is away from the office now, but she will be in touch with you after her return in two weeks.

Thank you for considering Health and Happiness as a possible publisher for your material.

Sincerely,

Patricia Brown

Patricia A. Brown
Administrative Assistant

two, you may also be expected to read his or her mail thoroughly and respond to it with appropriate actions.

Keep copies of all the responses and acknowledgments you write, and pass these copies on to your manager along with the incoming letters.

RECEIVING ELECTRONIC MAIL

The procedures for receiving electronic mail are very similar to those for receiving traditional mail. An electronic mail system can automatically do many of the tasks, such as date-stamping and time-stamping, that you would do manually with traditional mail. In addition, an electronic mail system can automatically prioritize items so that the most urgent messages always appear first on the screen.

Viewing Electronic Mail. Imagine that you have been away from your office for a couple of hours. During that time several of your colleagues used the electronic mail system to leave messages for you. When you return to your office, your computer will list for you all the mes-

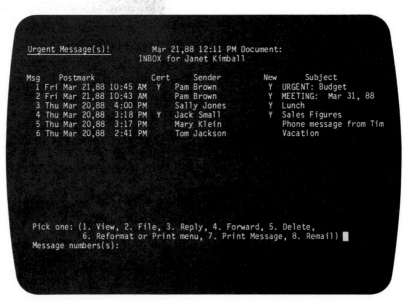

Fig. 11-13   An electronic mail inbox lists all the messages that have been received, placing urgent ones first.

sages that came in, indicating the time each was received, the sender, the classification (such as "Urgent" or "Classified"), and the subject. Figure 11-13 shows the kind of information that might appear on an individual's screen. In this case Janet Kimball can see at a glance who has tried to contact her. Notice that the computer has automatically placed the urgent message at the top of the list, even though it was received later than some of the other messages.

Once you have read the list, you can use the view option to read the messages, in any order you choose. In the example shown in Fig. 11-14, Janet Kimball selected the message marked "Urgent" first and then some other important messages by keying in the view option and then the message numbers.

Forwarding Electronic Mail. Most electronic mail systems have a forwarding feature that allows you to send a message that you have received to somebody else, with your comments attached. We will continue to use Janet Kimball's mailbox, as shown in Fig. 11-13, to illustrate how electronic mail is processed. The urgent message listed as number 1 on her mailbox is shown in Fig. 11-14. When Janet reads the message, she knows that she does not have the information that Pam Brown has asked for. But she knows that Sally Jones has a copy of the budget. Instead of sending a message back to Pam telling her that Sally is the one to ask for the documents, Janet can simply forward Pam's message to Sally. Janet selects option 4, the forward option. She indicates the person to whom she wishes to forward the message and can then keyboard any comments or instructions she might want to give the person receiving the message. Figure 11-15 shows what Janet's screen will display when she is forwarding the message. Figure 11-16 shows what will appear, seconds later, on Sally's screen.

Filing Electronic Mail. Any time you receive information in your mailbox that you might need to refer to again in the future, you should file it. To file information, you use the file option (listed as number 2 in Fig. 11-13). Once you select the file option, you will have to indicate where within the electronic filing system the information should be placed. You will also have to give the information a document name so that you will be able to access it in the future.

Replying to Electronic Mail. When you receive any type of mail, traditional or electronic, you often need to respond. With electronic mail, you can respond immediately.

Fig. 11-14 Once you select the view option, the complete messages will appear on your screen. You then decide which of the other applications is appropriate for each message. The remail option was chosen here.

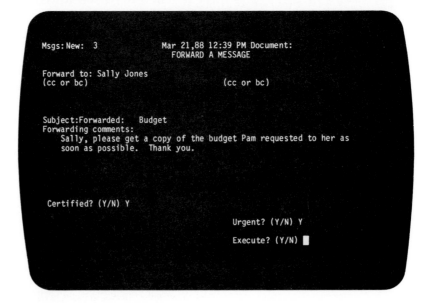

```
Msgs: New:  3            Mar 21,88 12:34 PM Document:
                            MESSAGE DISPLAY
   TO   Janet Kimball

 From:  Pam Brown
Postmark:  Mar 21,88  10:45 AM
Status:    Certified Urgent
Subject: Budget
--------------------------------------------------------------------
Message:
       Mr. Johnston asked me to obtain a copy of last year's budget for a
    meeting he's attending in 45 minutes.  Can you please get a copy to
    me as soon as possible?

       Thank you.


--------------------------------------------------------------------
Pick one: (1. View content, 2. File, 3. Reply, 4. Forward,
          5. Delete, 6. Next message, 7. Print, 8. Remail) ▮
```

```
Msgs: New:  3            Mar 21,88 12:39 PM Document:
                            FORWARD A MESSAGE

Forward to: Sally Jones
(cc or bc)                              (cc or bc)


Subject:Forwarded:  Budget
Forwarding comments:
    Sally, please get a copy of the budget Pam requested to her as
    soon as possible.  Thank you.



Certified? (Y/N) Y

                                  Urgent? (Y/N) Y

                                  Execute? (Y/N) ▮
```

Fig. 11-15 Electronic mail makes it easy for you to forward messages to other people after you have added your comments.

Most electronic mail systems include a reply function. This automatically sends your response to the person who sent you the message. Suppose that Janet Kimball has viewed message 2 on her mailbox. She learns that Pam Brown has scheduled a one-hour secretaries meeting for March 31 at noon. Janet wants to let Pam know that she will attend, so she selects the reply option. Figure 11-17 shows what might appear on Pam's screen.

Fig. 11-16 The receiver of this message can see immediately the steps it has been through before it reached her.

```
Msgs:  New:  0              Mar 21,88  1:08 PM Document
                                MESSAGE DISPLAY

  From:  Janet Kimball
Postmark:  Mar 21,88   12:50 PM
Status:   Certified  Urgent
Subject: Forwarded: Budget
-----------------------------------------------------------------------------
Comments:
        Pam Brown sent this to Janet Kimball who forwarded it to you and
        comments:
        Sally, please get a copy of the budget Pam requested to her as
        soon as possible.  Thank you.

  Message:
        Mr. Johnston asked me to obtain a copy of last year's budget for a
        meeting he's attending in 45 minutes.  Can you please get a copy to
        me as soon as possible?

        Thank you.
-----------------------------------------------------------------------------
Pick one: (1. View content, 2. File, 3. Reply, 4. Forward,
           5. Delete, 6. Next message, 7. Print, 8. Remail) ▮
```

Fig. 11-17 Electronic mail enables you to send immediate responses to your messages

```
Msgs: New:  2              Mar 21,88  1:00 PM Document:
                              REPLY TO A MESSAGE
  To: Pam Brown
 (cc or bc)                              (cc or bc)
        :
  Subject: Reply to MEETING:  Mar 31, 88
  Original message text:
        A one-hour secretarial meeting has been scheduled for March 31 at
        noon.  Please let me know if you can attend.


  Reply Text:
        I will be attending the secretarial meeting.




   Certified? (Y/N) N
   File this reply? (Y/N) N        Urgent? (Y/N) N      Execute? (Y/N) ▮
```

Notice that the original message is included on the screen for easy reference. Electronic mail systems vary, and not all of them include this capability.

Deleting Messages. As you process electronic mail and take the appropriate action, such as replying to a message or filing important information, you should clean out your mailbox. After each mailbox item is processed, it should be deleted. Then you should go on to process the next item. Deleting processed messages is the final step in electronic mail processing.

- Workers in automated offices can choose from among a wide range of electronic equipment to transmit messages, or they can use traditional, manual methods.

- *Electronic communications systems* refers to the transmission of messages between computers by means of cables, telephone lines, microwaves, or satellites. Modems and communications software make computer-to-computer communication possible.

- An electronic mail system utilizes computers to send and receive messages. Electronic mail can be sent to people within a company by means of computers linked together in a local area network.

- Other kinds of electronic communication include time-sharing, or subscribing to large external computers, and facsimile transmission, which is the transfer of duplicates of entire pages of text and graphics.

- Traditional, manual delivery systems include the U.S. Postal Service, private courier and messenger services, and company mail rooms and interoffice distribution systems.

- To handle outgoing mail, it is necessary to address, sort, weigh, and stamp it. Company mail rooms handle many of these tasks for office workers.

- To handle incoming traditional mail, you must sort and open it, check it to see if enclosures are missing, date-stamp it, read and annotate it, and present it to your supervisor.

- To handle incoming electronic mail, you view what is in the electronic mailbox and then process each item by using the appropriate functions of your system.

V OCABULARY

data communications	facsimile machine
teleprocessing	interoffice mail
local area network (LAN)	postage meter
modem	courier service
communications software	messenger service
microwave	teletypewriter
satellite	Mailgram
time-sharing	routing slip

1. How would you go about choosing a method for distributing a document in an electronic office? What factors would enter into your decision?

2. What is the most widely used means of distributing mail to outsiders? Why?

3. How do you send a message from your computer terminal to a coworker in the same electronic mail system?

4. Explain how facsimile machines work, and give an example of a good use of facsimile transmission.

5. What advantages do private courier services offer over the U.S. Postal Service?

6. Describe an electronic mailbox, and discuss how it is used.

7. Why do office workers or mail-room employees weigh outgoing mail?

8. Name and describe two computer-based mail services that combine electronic technology and manual delivery.

9. Describe the major differences between the procedures for handling incoming traditional mail and the procedures for handling incoming electronic mail. How are the procedures similar?

SKILLBUILDING ACTIVITIES

1. Read two articles on electronic mail. What are the major advantages and disadvantages of electronic mail? Write a report on your findings.

2. Ryan Adams is a receptionist in a small office. One of his duties is to process all incoming mail. After opening a letter addressed to a supervisor one day, he was embarrassed to discover that its contents were personal, although its envelope was not marked "Personal" or "Confidential." Today, a letter with the same return address has arrived for the same supervisor. Again, it is not marked to indicate that it is personal. How should Mr. Adams handle the letter?

3. Some examples of companies that may use facsimile machines are public relation and engineering firms. Contact one of these types of firms in your area to see if they are utilizing this device. If so, ask them to explain any disadvantages in using this communication system. Report your findings to the class.

4. Visit your local post office for a tour of the facility. Then write a report on the highlights of your visit. What could you, as a consumer, do to promote efficiency in mail preparation?

5. You are on your first job. In your office stamps are used instead of a postage meter for processing mail. You have noticed that several people in the office take stamps for their own use. What suggestions do you have for correcting this unprofessional activity?

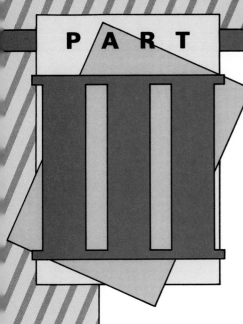

PART III

BUSINESS SKILLS FOR THE ELECTRONIC OFFICE

*O*f the many administrative support services you will provide, two of the most important are organizing meetings and arranging business trips. Part 3 covers the steps involved in setting up meetings of whatever size and the support services you can render during and after a meeting.

To arrange business trips, you must deal with travel agents, hotel reservation clerks, and automobile rental clerks. You will learn how to organize a well-planned business trip whether your boss is going overseas or just on a one-day journey to a nearby city.

In your job, you may be called on to do tasks related to accounting, banking, and legal matters. As computers become ever more sophisticated and integrated, you may even be asked to perform tasks previously handled in separate departments, such as the accounting department. Part 3 gives you a working knowledge of the procedures and documents you could encounter.

12

PLANNING MEETINGS AND CONFERENCES

As you begin work in today's electronic office, one of your many duties could be planning meetings and conferences. Perhaps you will be involved in such behind - the - scenes activities as preparing materials and arranging for speakers. Or perhaps you

will actually be at a particular meeting, where you will have to take notes or even lead a discussion. Whatever your role, you will need to know the basic functions of planning for successful meetings and conferences.

As a result of studying this chapter, you will be able to:

- Recognize and understand the role of formal and informal meetings.
- Understand and practice the procedures for planning and scheduling meetings.
- Apply basic tips for conducting successful meetings and conferences.
- Understand the major role that follow-up plays in planning meetings and conferences.

TYPES OF MEETINGS

Meetings occupy much time in an individual business's operation. Meetings are held primarily to conduct business, to pass on needed information to a group or to an individual, or to follow up on a particular activity of the business. Meetings may be formal or informal. Whether a meeting is formal or informal depends on its purpose. Meetings can be as short as a few minutes or can stretch out over several days. When a meeting stretches out over several days, it is often referred to as a conference.

INFORMAL MEETINGS

Usually, meetings that are informal in nature include discussions of daily activities. Such **informal meetings** take place primarily in individual offices or in a small conference room that will hold approximately 25 individuals. Informal meetings do not involve complicated arrangements or scheduling. The three basic types of meetings held in the office are staff meetings, committee meetings, and individual client meetings.

Staff Meetings. Staff meetings are the most common type of meeting. As a beginning office worker, you might have to arrange for a staff meeting, and you might also be participating in the staff meeting. Staff meetings are usually held in a supervisor's office or in a conference room and are usually attended by those individuals in the office who report directly to that supervisor. The purpose of a staff meeting is to discuss and solve problems, make decisions, review progress, plan projects, or distribute assignments. Supervisors may meet with their staffs on a regularly scheduled basis or whenever a need arises.

Committee Meetings. Committees are often appointed by supervisors to further discuss or study a matter related to a particular topic. Committee meetings may be held in a room where the committee members meet, in the office, via the telephone, through a conference call, or through electronic communication. For example, you may work in one of several branches of a business. You

A convention speaker using telecommunications during a meeting.

may be serving on a company committee to study a particular issue such as productivity. In order for your committee to function properly, the committee members from all the branch offices will have to participate. If you are serving on a committee that functions within your branch office, the committee meetings will naturally be held within the office.

Client Meetings. Although you probably will not be involved in holding a client meeting when you first begin work in the business world, client meetings are very important business meetings. Initially, you may be invited to attend a client meeting and take notes. As you gain experience and your role changes, the chances are likely you will be conducting your own client meetings. This is especially true in sales work. Client meetings are held wherever it is convenient for the parties involved. For example, a client meeting might be held in the office or at a restaurant. Business is often conducted over lunch or dinner.

 ORMAL MEETINGS

Formal meetings may also be held at the office or at another location. Because of their nature, formal meetings require greater preparation. Location is a very important consideration for a formal meeting, because of those attending and the structure of the meeting. For example, professional organizations often conduct formal meetings at large hotels. A professional organization, depending on its size, may have both small- and large-group meetings. Both large and small meetings will need to be formal because of the nature of the business being conducted.

Specific procedures must be followed when conducting formal meetings. Leaders of formal meetings must be knowledgeable in conducting such meetings to guarantee efficiency of operation. Leaders of formal meetings should be familiar with **parliamentary procedure**, the procedure for conducting an effective meeting. This procedure is outlined in *Robert's Rules of Order*—a book written to help leaders conduct successful meetings.

Keep the following points in mind when you are preparing to lead or participate in a meeting whether informal or formal:

- Know the purpose of the meeting, and make sure that all those attending know the purpose of the meeting.
- Begin and end the meeting on time, or end earlier if the business has been completed. Do not allow the meeting to drag on.
- Discuss only one topic at a time in order to prevent confusion.
- Focus on issues that are of concern to the group as a whole.
- Speak only when the leader of the meeting recognizes you. Keep your statements brief, and do not digress from the topic being discussed.

Conventions and Conferences. A **convention** is a type of formal meeting at which members of a professional group meet to conduct the group's business, and exchange information of mutual interest.

A **conference**, on the other hand, is a type of meeting at which the primary purpose is to exchange information rather than make group decisions. The major difference between a convention and a conference is that a conference usually does not involve voting, committee meetings, and other official business, because those attending are not members of a professional association—they are individuals who simply want to exchange information.

Conventions and conferences are usually held in hotels or in special convention centers, often in major cities or popular resorts. The sites for these large-scale meetings often have exhibit halls where businesspeople display equipment or products or explain services, all of which are available for sale to convention or conference participants. These businesspeople are known as **vendors**.

In smaller meeting rooms at the convention or conference site, speakers present programs on topics that are of special interest to those attending. These programs may also feature panel discussions, video presentations, slide presentations, and question-and-answer periods. Often a combination of such presentations may be used to cover a topic. For example, at the annual convention of the National Business Education Association, a speaker might present a program on teaching telecommunications to high school students. The speaker might show a video illustrating telecommunications technology and then lead a panel discussion involving teachers currently using telecommunications technology. The program might end with a question-and-answer period. After a business education teacher has attended this program, he or she might visit exhibits where vendors are demonstrating telecommunications equipment.

Another very important part of a successful convention or conference is the opportunity to socialize through receptions and dinners. These social activities make it possible for members of a profession to get to know each other and exchange useful information in an informal setting.

 ## PLANNING AND SCHEDULING MEETINGS

When you are planning and scheduling a meeting, the first thing you need to consider is when the meeting will take place. If the meeting is for a small group, you should try to find a time when everyone can attend. If the meeting is for a large group, the size of the group makes it necessary to distribute a schedule that details the times and locations of presentations as well as the names of the speakers and their topics. The individuals who lead large meetings are often extremely important to the success of the meetings.

*G*ATHERING INFORMATION

Before plans can be made for any meeting, it is necessary to gather as much information as possible about the meeting. This information includes such details as the purpose of the meeting, the number of participants, and the desired location.

Gathering as much information as possible makes planning more effective.

Preparing two essential file folders for a meeting: one to file information on the arrangements as they are made, the other with the information needed on the day of the meeting.

Set up information files from the beginning. You may use a manual system, an electronic system, or both to set up these files. For example, you will need to include any correspondence related to the convention or conference. When you make notes about conference room reservations, equipment, or other materials that will be needed during the meeting, keep these notes filed in an orderly sequence for easy retrieval. Will you need to prepare transparencies for a presentation requiring an overhead projector, or will you need to prepare slides for a different presentation?

Prepare a special folder for the day of the meeting that contains all the information your supervisor (or other appointed individual) will need in order to conduct the meeting. Arrange these materials in order of their presentation.

RESERVING MEETING PLACES AND EQUIPMENT

The next thing to consider is where the meeting is to take place. If the group is too large, you will need to reserve a conference room or other meeting place, either on the company premises or at a hotel or conference center. The meeting place should be large enough to accommodate the group comfortably. A small group will feel uncomfortable in a room that is too large, and the members may have trouble hearing each other.

If you are making arrangements for a meeting with a hotel or conference center, ask for a conference planning guide for the facility. A **conference planning guide** will provide you with such basic information as sample floor plans, dining and catering services, descriptions of rooms, and price lists, as well as a variety of special information that will assist you in planning.

Check that the room or rooms are appropriate for the equipment needed. For example, if the meeting will include a technical presentation, make sure that the room you reserve can accommodate a projection screen or any other type of equipment that has been requested. Also make sure that there are enough electrical outlets available. In addition, you should check that the room can be made dark enough for the screen to be seen easily during a video or slide presentation.

Your file on room reservations and other arrangements should include the following items:
- Descriptions of the rooms, services, and equipment you have ordered.
- The dates when you plan to use the facilities.
- The length of time you will use the facilities.
- The fees and methods of payment for services.
- The names of the people you made the arrangements with.
- Copies of all correspondence confirming reservations.

The above information will be useful if changes need to be made as plans for your meeting progress. Written confirmations help prevent misunderstandings.

You may also have to reserve equipment for an individual presentation. Follow whatever company procedures are necessary to reserve any special equipment. If your company does not have the equipment, you will need to rent it. If your company does not own the necessary equipment, you will have to arrange for rental of the equipment through an appropriate rental agency. More and more meeting rooms in larger hotels and convention centers provide the necessary equipment as part of the room rental fee.

NOTIFYING PARTICIPANTS

It is essential to notify each person who will participate in the meeting of the meeting time and location as well as his or her responsibilities. How this notification is done depends primarily on the size and purpose of the meeting. There are three basic ways of notifying meeting participants.

Telephone. Participants for small information-sharing meetings can be notified by telephone. These meetings are usually scheduled only a few days before they occur. It is important to call the meeting participants as soon as the date of the meeting is established. Telephone notification should be followed up by a written confirmation.

Written Notice. Larger meetings usually involve many more participants. For this reason a written notice is more efficient than a telephone call. A written notice can be prepared and distributed to all participants in a relatively short period of time. A written notice also reduces the chance of miscommunication.

Electronic Message. The company you work for may have a special system that allows you to communicate messages electronically. If your company has an **electronic calendaring system**, meeting times can automatically be entered into the electronic calendar's memory. This system allows you to key in information about a specific meeting. The computer will check the schedules of the meeting participants and either add the meeting to their calendars or let you know which participants have a scheduling conflict at the proposed meeting time.

OMPOSING A MEETING NOTICE

A meeting notice has two major purposes—to give notice of a specific meeting and to serve as a reminder of the upcoming meeting. A meeting notice should state the date, time, place, and purpose of the meeting. If the people who will attend the meeting are invited to present items for discussion at the meeting, the notice should request that they notify you of these specific items so that you can add them to the meeting agenda. An **agenda** is an outline of the major items to be discussed at the meeting. As you receive responses from meeting participants, you should update the copy of the agenda in your own files.

Be sure that you are familiar with any special procedures for the preparation of meeting notices. For example, the bylaws (governing rules) of some organizations include specific guidelines on how far in advance of a meeting the notices must be distributed. If the guidelines are not adhered to, an organization is in violation of its bylaws. This means that the meeting may not be official.

When a meeting is voluntary, it is helpful to ask people to notify you if they will be attending the meeting. Doing so allows you to plan accurately for any meals or other materials required for the meeting.

It will also be necessary for you to follow up on meeting notices. Not everyone will respond. You may have to telephone those individuals who did not respond in order to find out whether or not they will be attending. Keep a list in your files of the names of those individuals to whom you have sent notices. The illustration below shows one way to keep track of this information.

Depending on the size of the group, it may be necessary to follow up your meeting notices by telephoning the participants a few hours before the meeting for a final check. Your call could serve as a reminder and also allow you to follow up on any individual needs.

EVELOPING AN AGENDA

Any meeting will run smoothly if it follows an agenda. Agendas are used at formal meetings and occasionally at informal meetings. Agendas help to guide the discussion and keep the work on track. Since last-minute changes

```
                    NATIONAL BUSINESS ADVISORY ASSOCIATION
                         EXECUTIVE BOARD MEETING

                                 AGENDA

                              April 1-3, 19--
                            Las Vegas Hilton Hotel
                             Las Vegas, Nevada


     (1)     Call to Order and Roll Call

     (2)     Opening Remarks by President G. R. Maxell

     (3)     Approval of November 19-- Executive Board Minutes

     (4)     Old Business
             a.  Future Convention Sites
             b.  Expansion of Education for Business
                 Coordinating Council
             c.  Recommendations of Critical Issues Task Force
             d.  Progress on National Advisory Committee
             e.  Expanded Services of The Travel Association
             f.  Retiring Executive Board Members
             g.  Executive Board Meeting Schedule

     (5)     Receiving of Written Reports
             a.  Regional Association Reports
             b.  Public Relations Committee
             c.  Awards Administrative Committee
             d.  Legislative Action Committee

     (6)     Special Task Force Reports
             a.  Computer Literacy Task Force
             b.  Business/Industry Task Force

     (7)     New Business
             a.  Insurance Administrator's Report
             b.  Other New Business

     (8)     Meeting of Executive Board Committees
             a.  Finance
             b.  Membership
             c.  Program of Work

     (9)     President's Report and Overview of Program of Work
             Accomplishments

     (10)    Closing Remarks by President Maxell

     (11)    Announcements and Adjournment
```

Fig. 12-1   An agenda acts as a guide for a group's discussion.

often occur, using a computer to prepare an agenda can help you save time.

In order to prepare an agenda, you will need a list of the items that need to be discussed at the meeting. If the meeting is for a group that has met previously, check the minutes of the previous meeting before preparing the agenda for this meeting. Perhaps there is some unfinished business. Also, be sure to check for any additional agenda items that you have been keeping in your records. Study the illustration of the agenda below.

If the group that will meet has bylaws, review these bylaws thoroughly to check for any special procedures for conducting business. If the group does not have bylaws, check minutes and agendas from previous meetings for any specific order of business.

To help make a meeting run smoothly, keep in mind the following guidelines concerning parliamentary procedure:

- The presiding officer calls the meeting to order by saying, "The meeting will now come to order."
- The secretary checks attendance by calling out the names of those who are expected to be at the meeting or by noting silently those attending the meeting.
- The secretary announces whether the attendance constitutes a **quorum**, or the number required by the group before a vote can take place.
- The secretary reads the minutes of the previous meeting and asks whether members would like to offer any additions or corrections.
- The group votes to approve the minutes of the previous meeting. If something is incorrect, the group may vote to amend the minutes to correct the inaccurate information. If there are no additions or corrections, the presiding officer states that the minutes stand approved as read.
- The officers then give their respective reports and hand copies to the secretary to keep on file. The officers' reports are followed by the reports from standing committees (permanent committees whose functions are stated in the bylaws) and any other special committees.
- Items of unfinished business from the previous meeting are discussed.
- Items of new business are discussed.
- The date of the next meeting is established.
- The meeting is adjourned.

 ## PREPARING FOR THE MEETING

On the day of the meeting, check the room or rooms to be used to make sure that everything is in order. Check carefully the following items:

Atmosphere. The temperature of the room should be comfortable, and there should be adequate light and ventilation.

Furnishings. There should be enough tables and chairs, and they should be set up so that the participants can see each other and the projection screen, if one is used.

Equipment. Check carefully to be sure that all necessary equipment is in the meeting room and that each piece is working properly. The equipment might include a video recorder, a screen, a tape recorder, or a computer.

Supplies. Any special supplies that the participants might need should be placed in an organized manner on the tables where the participants will be seated. Customary supplies include pens, pencils, paper, and folders containing special materials for the meeting. Name tags are often provided with these supplies, especially if the participants do not know each other.

An organized meeting setup.

Refreshments. Check the arrangements for any refreshments that might be served. Typical refreshments are coffee, tea, juice, and soft drinks, along with doughnuts, fruit, or other light foods. Often the time of day of the meeting controls the types of refreshments to be served.

Serving refreshments at appropriate times helps create a positive meeting environment. Refreshments can be set up in a special section of the meeting room, or time can be planned for refreshment breaks, depending on the size and type of the meeting.

ETAILS TO BE HANDLED DURING THE MEETING

While the meeting is in progress, you may be expected to handle some details that contribute to the success of a meeting.

One very important detail is being available to welcome participants as they arrive. If you cannot be available to welcome participants, ask someone to handle this detail for you. Be sure that individual knows *exactly* what should happen. It is also important to have someone available to greet participants who might arrive after the meeting has started. If you are not handling this detail yourself, be sure that the person who is has a pleasant personality and that he or she smiles and extends a warm and positive welcome to the participants.

A second major detail is taking notes during the meeting. Before the meeting begins, review the agenda and any notes from earlier meetings to become familiar with the topics to be discussed. The more you know about what is going on, the easier it will be to take notes. Sit next to the person leading the meeting to be sure that you can hear everything. If you miss a comment, be sure that you follow up immediately to get the needed information, especially if it is related to a controversial issue.

Record the names of those present if an attendance list is needed or if a check of voting privileges is required.

The notes you record should include everything discussed that is of major consequence. If you are not sure whether you should record a statement, record it anyway and check it later. If you are using a tape recorder, your notes should include any information that is not on the tape, such as the names and titles of speakers as well as starting and ending times. Before the meeting begins, you should be sure that you know how to operate the tape recorder, and you should make sure that you have enough tapes on hand to record the entire meeting.

Depending on the size and type of the meeting, you may have to obtain additional materials or information while the meeting is in progress. If you have to leave the meeting room to do this, be sure that someone has been appointed to continue the note-taking while you are away.

SPECIAL MEETING CONSIDERATIONS

As was mentioned earlier in this chapter, the size and type of the meeting control many of the meeting considerations. Meetings held outside of an office or conference room call for additional considerations. These special considerations are important to the success of the meeting for all concerned.

Small Mealtime Meetings. It is very common today to hold a small meeting during a meal—breakfast, lunch, dinner, or a break. If you are involved in planning a small mealtime meeting, select a restaurant that will guarantee privacy and a positive environment for conducting business. Make a reservation to prevent waiting when you arrive at the restaurant. Check all details of the restaurant, such as the location, the menu, and the methods of payment the restaurant accepts.

A lunchtime group meeting.

Large Mealtime Meetings. The same details apply to large mealtime meetings that apply to small mealtime meetings except that with a large mealtime meeting, more people are involved and the meeting is often more elaborate. A large mealtime meeting might include special details such as flowers, decorations, place cards, and entertainment. Most of the restaurants that provide facilities for large meetings have a coordinator who works with the person planning these special details.

One major detail that affects either a small or a large mealtime meeting is the cost. This should be considered carefully when you are planning a meeting.

FOLLOW-UP TASKS

A follow-up should be conducted shortly after the meeting has occurred. Completing the follow-up as soon as possible demonstrates efficiency and contributes to a positive attitude toward the meeting, whether it is large or small. Common follow-up tasks include completing reports and writing letters or other types of communications, determined by what went on at the meeting.

Most meetings involve some type of note-taking and the preparation of a report based on the notes. The report may be in the form of a summary for the participants of an informal meeting, or it may be an official record of the meeting—often called the **minutes**. Minutes of meetings are kept in an organization's permanent files. Minutes are very important, since they are often used for future reference. When transcribing notes into minutes, keep in mind that actions should be emphasized rather than what each member said.

Within a short time after a meeting or conference, you will have to process and pay the bills for the meeting rooms, the meals, the equipment, and any other facilities or services that were rented or purchased for the meeting. Remember to check bills submitted against the confirmation letters in your meeting files.

An evaluation is another important follow-up task after a meeting. Review your meeting files, and consider the points that made the meeting successful or points that might improve another similar meeting in the future. You might evaluate the speakers, the hotel, the restaurant, or special services used for the meeting. An evaluation may be conducted informally by discussion. A formal evaluation may require an evaluation form. A written evaluation guarantees that more specific information will be available for future use.

```
                    MINUTES OF THE EXECUTIVE BOARD MEETING
                    NATIONAL BUSINESS ADVISORY ASSOCIATION
                              APRIL 1-3, 1987
                           LAS VEGAS HILTON HOTEL
                            LAS VEGAS, NEVADA

CALL TO ORDER          President Gerald R. Maxell called the Executive Board
AND ROLL CALL          meeting to order at 3:10 p.m., Wednesday, April 1,
                       1987.  After welcoming members present, President
                       Maxell called the roll and introduced each Executive
                       Board member.

                       The following Executive Board members were present:

                       National Officers:  Gerald R. Maxell, President;
                       Anna R. Martin, President-Elect; Howard Jasinski,
                       Secretary-Treasurer; John Kash, Past-President; R. J.
                       Barns, Executive Director;

                       Eastern Region Representatives:  Carolyn V. Norman;

                       Southern Region Representatives:  Hattie J. Green,
                       President; J. Howard Jones; Jane R. Austin;

                       Northern Region Representatives:  Patricia A. Marner,
                       President; Mary Margaret Harmon; Jack C. Rodman;

                       Western Region Representatives:  Lloyd W. Browne,
                       President; Kathleen Rounds; Melinda Oka.

                       President Maxell asked the Executive Board members
                       to review the agenda.  Additional agenda items were
                       called for, and none were added.

MINUTES OF             Following the determination that a quorum was
PREVIOUS               present, President Maxell called for additions or
EXECUTIVE BOARD        corrections to the minutes of the previous Executive
MEETING APPROVED       Board meeting held on November 2-3, 1986.  It was
                       moved by Howard Jasinski and seconded by Melinda Oka
                       that the minutes of the previous meeting be approved
                       as distributed.  This motion was unanimously
                       approved.
```

Fig. 12-2   Sample minutes.

- Meetings occupy much time in an individual business's operation.

- Meetings are held primarily to conduct business, to pass on needed information to a group or to an individual, or to follow up on a particular activity of the business.

- Meetings may be formal or informal, depending on the purpose of the meeting.

- Meetings that stretch over several days are called conferences.

- The three basic types of meetings held in the office are staff meetings, committee meetings, and individual client meetings.

- *Robert's Rules of Order* is a book containing the correct parliamentary procedure to be used for handling meetings and conferences of any size.

- Large conventions and conferences are usually held in hotels or special convention centers in major cities or resort areas.

- Before plans can be made for any meeting, it is necessary to gather as much information as possible about the meeting.

- Appropriate space and equipment should be reserved in advance to handle a speaker's request at a meeting or conference.

- Meeting participants should be notified in advance of the meeting as to the topic being discussed as well as to their role in the meeting.

- Meetings will run much more smoothly if they follow a specified agenda distributed in advance.

- Meeting rooms should be checked carefully the day of the meeting for all necessary items including supplies, equipment, furnishings, atmosphere, and refreshments.

- A meeting follow-up should be conducted shortly after the meeting has taken place.

- Minutes of the meeting should be distributed to those attending and others who would need to know what happened.

VOCABULARY

informal meeting
formal meeting
parliamentary procedure
convention
conference
vendor
conference planning guide
electronic calendaring
   system
agenda
quorum
minutes

REVIEW QUESTIONS

1. Give some examples of informal meetings.

2. Give some examples of formal meetings.

3. Where would you find information on parliamentary procedure?

4. What is the difference between a convention and a conference?

5. What items should be in a file on room reservations and arrangements for a meeting?

6. What information should be in a meeting notice?

7. Describe how to use a tape recorder to keep a record of a long meeting.

SKILLBUILDING ACTIVITIES

1. Obtain a copy of *Robert's Rules of Order*. Study the chapter dealing with the order of business. Write a brief report on this material highlighting the major points.

2. Choose a favorite major city in the United States that you feel would be suitable for hosting a convention. Write to the Convention Bureau of that city for more specific information concerning convention possibilities. Write a report on your findings.

3. Develop a convention planning checklist based on the information you have studied in this chapter. Assume that approximately 200 people will attend the convention.

4. Prepare a sample meeting agenda. Use *Robert's Rules of Order* as a guide.

5. Develop and prepare an evaluation form that you feel would be useful in evaluating a meeting. Try to compose this form on a word processor. Save your document, print out a copy, and share the information with your classmates. Then revise the evaluation form and save it so that it can be used at a later date in your class.

ARRANGING BUSINESS TRAVEL

*A*lthough technology is providing opportunities for meetings to be held via communications, there still will be occasions when travel is necessary in order to conduct a company's business. Knowing what tools to use and how to use these tools in arranging for business travel will help make your work in today's electronic office more efficient.

As a result of studying this chapter, you will be able to:

- Determine which type of travel will best fit the needs of your business.
- Recognize and use the most efficient type of travel service available.
- Arrange for the best type of housing for the travel occasion.
- Understand the special role of international travel.
- Prepare for and organize a business trip.
- Handle expenses efficiently.

Making Travel Arrangements

One of your many duties might be to make travel arrangements. The extent to which you have to make travel arrangements will depend on the type of business you work in. Many businesses have branches throughout the United States and the entire world. If the business you work for has such branches, you will definitely be involved in making travel arrangements. If you work in a smaller business, perhaps you will not have to make many travel arrangements.

No matter where you work, the first step in planning any business trip is to gather information and place it in a folder marked with the name of the trip. This information could also be stored electronically. There are many questions to be answered before you can begin to make individual travel arrangements for your company's executives.

Consider these questions:

1. At what time of the day do they want to leave and return?

2. How many days are involved?

3. What type of travel is preferred—plane, train, or automobile?

4. If the executives are traveling by air, do they have a preference with regard to seat assignment, meals, or airline?

5. Will it be necessary to arrange for a rental car?

6. What hotel do they prefer?

7. Will they need a meeting room at the hotel?

8. Do you need to make restaurant reservations?

9. What special materials do the executives need to take with them?

10. Will they need any special equipment such as a tape recorder, video recorder, or slide projector?

When you are making travel arrangements, you have several options. For example, you may use a travel agency or work with your company's corporate travel department, or you may make the travel arrangements yourself. The option you select will depend primarily on the type of business you are working in and its size.

*T*RAVEL AGENCIES

A **travel agency** is a business that is organized to plan travel for individuals, groups, and other businesses. The individuals who work in travel agencies are known as **travel agents**. The travel agent's major responsibility is to handle all the details of the trip for the person or group traveling. A travel agent can make an airline reservation and a hotel reservation for you easily. A travel agent can also arrange for a rental car or handle some other travel detail that will make the trip easier for the person traveling. Travel agents use computers with information stored in blocks of data known as databases. For example, travel agents have databases containing the schedules of most major airlines. Information that is not stored in a database can usually be found by checking readily available printed materials or by using the telephone or a telecommunications network. Travel agents receive commissions from the airlines and hotels with which they book travelers. In most cases the customer does not pay for this service.

Your company may require you to use a particular travel agency, or you may select a travel agency by drawing on your own knowledge and experience. If you have to select a travel agency, be sure to select one that specializes in business travel. Travel agents who specialize in business travel will be able to give you the best service because of their knowledge and experience.

Call the travel agency and ask to speak with your travel agent just as soon as you know you must plan a trip. It is very important to find one or two travel agents you can work with in arranging travel plans. As you and a travel agent get to know each other, individual needs can be satisfied more easily, and often time and money for all concerned can be saved. For example, if you know that a trip is coming up and you can speak with your travel agent about the trip early, your travel agent can take full advantage of any special prices offered by an airline or a hotel. This will save your company money, and you will be able to obtain any special services that the travelers prefer.

When you call the travel agent, have your trip folder in front of you. It should contain all the necessary details. For example, if you are arranging for two of your company's executives to attend a meeting in San Francisco and your company is based in Boston, you could use the following information in arranging the trip:

- They plan to leave Boston on Thursday, June 1, and return to Boston on Saturday evening, June 3.
- They prefer to take a nonstop flight.
- They would like to use Deltarama Airlines, if possible.
- They prefer to fly first-class, and they prefer aisle seats in the nonsmoking section.
- They will need a rental car, and it should be ready for them at the San Francisco International Airport.
- They want separate rooms in a hotel in downtown San Francisco for the nights of June 1 and June 2.

If you have this information, you will be able to give your travel agent specific directions in setting up the trip. Your company may have special policies concerning some of the items mentioned above. If this is the case, please be sure to tell the travel agent this information. For example, your company may wish to be billed directly by the travel agency for the costs of the trip. Or you may have the authority to use company credit cards for expenses related to the travel plans.

Once you have given the travel agent the necessary information, he or she will begin making the plans. Once these plans have been finalized, the travel agent will mail or deliver this information to you. All the information will be listed on a printed sheet known as an itinerary. An **itinerary** lists departure and arrival times, flight numbers, hotel reservations, and other requested travel details, such as car rental information. It is very important to look all this information over immediately upon receiving it to make sure that everything meets your requirements. Any problems should be handled immediately. How travel agents respond to these individual problems is often a good indication of their competence. You will need to decide whether or not you should use them another time.

CORPORATE TRAVEL DEPARTMENTS

Many large companies have their own travel departments. Such a department is called a **corporate travel**

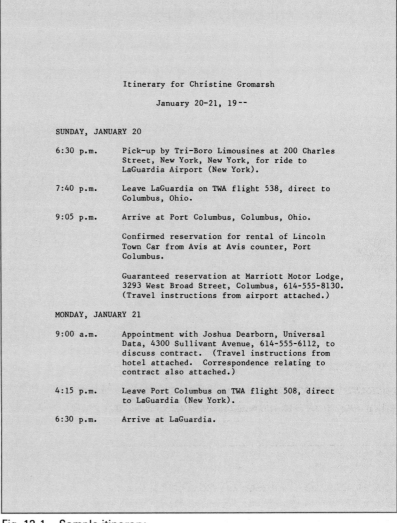

```
                      Itinerary for Christine Gromarsh

                           January 20-21, 19--


SUNDAY, JANUARY 20

    6:30 p.m.       Pick-up by Tri-Boro Limousines at 200 Charles
                    Street, New York, New York, for ride to
                    LaGuardia Airport (New York).

    7:40 p.m.       Leave LaGuardia on TWA flight 538, direct to
                    Columbus, Ohio.

    9:05 p.m.       Arrive at Port Columbus, Columbus, Ohio.

                    Confirmed reservation for rental of Lincoln
                    Town Car from Avis at Avis counter, Port
                    Columbus.

                    Guaranteed reservation at Marriott Motor Lodge,
                    3293 West Broad Street, Columbus, 614-555-8130.
                    (Travel instructions from airport attached.)

MONDAY, JANUARY 21

    9:00 a.m.       Appointment with Joshua Dearborn, Universal
                    Data, 4300 Sullivant Avenue, 614-555-6112, to
                    discuss contract.  (Travel instructions from
                    hotel attached.  Correspondence relating to
                    contract also attached.)

    4:15 p.m.       Leave Port Columbus on TWA flight 508, direct
                    to LaGuardia (New York).

    6:30 p.m.       Arrive at LaGuardia.
```

Fig. 13-1   Sample itinerary.

department. A corporate travel department works the same as a travel agency except that it handles travel plans for its own company, primarily because of the size of the company and the volume of travel.

 ## ARRANGING TRIPS YOURSELF

If you work for a small company, or if you have to arrange a trip at the last minute, you will have to make your own travel arrangements. The next section of this chapter will explain the procedures you will follow when making your own travel plans.

*T*RANSPORTATION

When you arrange transportation for company executives, the first question to be answered is, How will they travel? Will they be using an airline, a rental car, a train, or some other form of transportation? The decision is usually based on meeting times and convenience.

If the executives have to travel more than 300 miles, an airline is the most efficient means of transportation. While large airlines have flights to most major cities in the United States, smaller airlines now have flights to smaller cities. These airlines are called **commuter airlines** and often connect with the larger airlines to get you to your destination faster.

*U*SING AIRLINES

Selecting an Airline. Most large cities are served by several major airlines. You should select an airline that has the most convenient schedule and the best fares. When selecting an airline, you might use the *Official Airline Guide*, which lists airline routes between major American cities, as well as schedules. You might use an electronic database with similar information or check directly with the individual airline you are considering. Most major airlines have a toll-free telephone number to make it easier for you to select an airline. No matter how you select an airline, it is always wise to choose three or four possible flight times. Doing so will allow for greater flexibility should plans change—as is quite often the case.

When selecting an airline, keep in mind that you want to obtain the lowest fares available for the required flights. Fares vary according to how far in advance reservations are made, how many days the passengers plan to spend at their destinations, and which days of the week or hours of the day they choose for flights.

Because airlines are extremely competitive, they often offer special incentives for customers, including reduced fares on some special flights and "frequent flier" bonuses. Consider all of these factors when you select an airline.

Making Reservations. As was mentioned earlier, most major airlines have a toll-free telephone number that you

When you use a frequent flier bonus, you may be given a coupon or number by the travel agent. Or the bonus mileage may be credited when you check in at the airport.

can use when making reservations. When you are making reservations on your own or through a travel agent, be sure that you have all the information you need in front of you. Try to exercise good judgment when making the reservations. Keep in mind personal requests. Most travelers today travel coach instead of first-class. First-class seats are more costly but provide extra comfort and convenience. Companies often have a policy concerning the class of travel for their employees. It is important to know this information when you are making reservations.

With many airlines, it is possible to select seats in advance when reservations are confirmed. This means that the travelers do not have to wait in line at the airport. If they will be served a meal on the flight, it is possible to order special foods if you make the request at least one day before the flight. For example, you could place an order for a low-calorie meal or a vegetarian meal.

The last step in making the reservations concerns the method of payment. Will you be paying for the tickets by check or credit card, or will you arrange to have your company billed for the tickets? Once you specify the method of payment, it is always wise to have all the information concerning the reservations repeated for a final check in order to avoid any possible confusion.

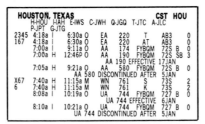

Fig. 13-2 Official airline guides can help you to find out what connections are available as well as the time needed to travel from one city to another.

Last-minute changes in travel plans often do occur as a result of unexpected events. If possible, avoid changing flights at the last minute, as it often results in additional costs. When making reservations, ask if there are any penalties for changes.

*T*RAVELING BY AUTOMOBILE

In some situations, the best way for a businessperson to get from one place to another is by automobile. Some firms provide company cars or pay employees a rate of so much per mile to use their own automobiles. Other businesses rent automobiles from rental agencies. Car rental agencies usually charge either a flat daily, weekly, or monthly fee or a flat fee including an additional amount for each mile driven. They also charge for insurance, and they may include a drop-off fee when a driver picks up a car at one place and leaves it at another.

Most airports and cities offer a variety of rental agencies. If you have to select an automobile rental agency, it is wise to compare prices and benefits before making your selection. Know the policy of your company before doing this. Travel agents are also usually willing to arrange for a rental automobile if they are asked to do this. The travel agent will need to know about any special requests and will require other necessary information. Again, be sure that you have all the needed information in front of you before you call the travel agent.

Planning an Automobile Trip. People who drive to their destinations must know what routes to follow, what signs to look for, where to stop for the night, and other

Compare prices and benefits before selecting a car rental agency.

specific details. If your supervisor asks you to prepare driving instructions, you will need a road map. You should always get directions from the people the executives will be meeting with, if at all possible.

People who often drive long distances find it useful to pay an annual fee to join an automobile club such as the American Automobile Association (AAA). An automobile club can help you plan a car trip by providing you with maps marked to show the recommended routes. It may also recommend restaurants, motels, hotels, and scenic points of interest to help you make the trip efficient and pleasant. Automobile clubs also provide emergency road services, such as free towing for their members.

Businesspeople who use company cars or their own cars for business trips within a particular area may be provided with gasoline credit cards or other credit cards that they can use to pay bills during a trip. When credit cards are used, it is extremely important to keep accurate records of all expenses.

Using Public Transportation. Often it is cheaper and easier to get around in a city by using a taxi or some other means of public transportation such as a bus or subway. Railroads are sometimes convenient forms of public

Rail travel lets an executive work while traveling.

transportation in certain regions of the United States. If you think that your supervisor might be using a form of public transportation, check schedules carefully for his or her convenience.

Using a Limousine Service. It is possible to arrange for a limousine to carry passengers from the airport to various locations in a city. Limousine rates are usually cheaper than taxi fares. Most cities also have private limousine services that provide automobiles and drivers for local trips. These services require reservations, which can be made by telephoning several hours before a car and driver are needed. Because limousines often charge an hourly fee or a flat fee, it is important to check rates ahead of time.

INTERNATIONAL TRAVEL

International travel is becoming more and more common today as businesses open and operate branches throughout the world. Lawyers, accountants, and other consultants are often called upon to provide their professional services in foreign markets. As a result of this growing trend, one of your responsibilities might be to plan an international trip. This kind of trip requires special planning. While travel agents can be very helpful in planning international trips, it is important to keep some special points in mind before calling a travel agent.

R ESEARCH

If you are planning a trip to a foreign country, you will need to learn as much as you can about that country's customs and culture. Information of this type can be obtained through libraries and bookstores.

T RAVEL DOCUMENTS

People traveling outside their own country are usually required to carry documents such as a birth certificate, a passport, a visa, and other legal papers that identify them and their employer and state the purpose of their trip. They should carry these documents at all times and be ready to produce them upon request.

A **passport** is an official identification document issued by the U.S. State Department. Passports identify travelers and prove that they are U.S. citizens. A traveler applying for a passport for the first time must appear in person at the passport office with an application, photographs, and proof of citizenship, such as a birth certificate. It often takes several weeks to obtain a passport. As soon as

When a traveler enters or leaves a country, an official examines the passport and stamps the page with the date.

you know that a passport will be needed, begin the process. Passports are issued for a limited amount of time and should be checked carefully for the expiration date.

A **visa** is a special permit granted by governments around the world to allow foreigners to enter their countries. Most Western countries do not require U.S. travelers to obtain a visa, but Eastern European and Asian countries usually do. To find out whether a country requires a visa, ask your travel agent.

CURRENCY

A traveler visiting another country will need some money in that country's currency. It is possible to purchase a packet of currency worth approximately $10 in American money for each country the traveler will be visiting from a currency exchange office, your local travel agent, or a large bank. Travelers can usually exchange American money and traveler's checks for foreign currency at currency exchange offices in banks, hotels, and airports in the countries they visit. Check the current rate of exchange between foreign currency and American dollars to help your employer calculate tips and other expenditures while traveling abroad.

VACCINATIONS

Travelers are often required to be vaccinated against diseases that are prevalent in the countries they plan to visit. Travel agents can usually tell you which vaccinations are required. Travelers can obtain vaccination records from the physicians who vaccinate them. They must also obtain International Certificates of Vaccination and submit them to their local or state health department. These certificates can be obtained from a travel agent, a passport office, or a doctor.

LOCAL TRANSPORTATION

Trying to find the way from the airport to a hotel or meeting place in a foreign country can be a very frustrating experience, especially if you do not know the language. As with domestic travel, any specific information that you can gather will certainly make the situation less difficult.

Many foreign countries, particularly in Europe, have excellent train service, with trains running frequently to all large cities and smaller cities and towns. Check with your local travel agent for specific information concerning train service, as different classes of service are frequently offered.

Most major American car rental agencies have a toll-free number that you can call to make reservations for overseas rentals. Car rental rates in foreign countries can differ substantially from rates in the United States, so be sure to ask the reservations clerk about rates. You should also check to see if your supervisor will need an international driver's license. A license of this type can be obtained from the American Automobile Association (AAA).

BOOKING HOTEL ROOMS

Cost and location are the two most important factors that you must consider in selecting a hotel. If you make hotel reservations frequently, your company should subscribe to a directory such as the *Official Hotel and Resort Guide*. Such a directory gives the names, addresses, telephone numbers, and room rates of hotels in most cities.

A hotel directory also usually indicates the services that a particular hotel offers—for example, room service, garage service, laundry service, and transportation to and from airports. Most large hotels and motels have a toll-free number to help simplify the process of making reservations, if you have not asked your travel agent to make reservations. When you make a room reservation, you will need to tell the hotel clerk when your supervisor will be arriving and departing. You should also tell the clerk whether you want to reserve a single room, a double room, or a suite. If you want a hotel to hold a room for a traveler who will arrive late in the day, you will need to make a **guaranteed reservation**. This means that the hotel will hold the room as long as is necessary. You may have to provide a credit card number and agree to pay for the room whether or not the traveler shows up. If the hotel provides transportation from the airport, you should ask for information on how the service operates. If there is time, ask the hotel to send you a written confirmation specifying the date of the reservation, the length of the stay, and any other necessary details.

PREPARING FOR THE TRIP

A day or two before the scheduled departure, confirm all travel arrangements, including the flight, transportation to and from the airport, and room reservations. Often there are last-minute changes that must be taken care of.

HANDLING AN ITINERARY

Earlier in this chapter, you learned that an itinerary is a printed document listing all the information for an up-coming trip. It includes such details as flight numbers and hotel reservations.

Your travel agent or corporate travel department will provide you with a copy of a printed itinerary. Check all the details against the information you have been collecting in your trip folder. If this information is stored electronically, it will be easy to make changes. Study the sample itinerary in Fig. 13-1. It is also wise to make a copy of the final itinerary for the convenience of the person for whom you are planning the trip.

ARRANGING FOR TRAVEL FUNDS

Some companies give their employees credit cards to use for most of their trip expenses. Other companies expect their employees to use their personal credit cards and then submit receipts for reimbursement. Using credit cards makes it easier for companies and their employees to keep track of travel expenses. While your supervisor is responsible for the security of the credit cards being used, you may be asked to keep all credit card numbers on file in case the credit cards get lost or stolen.

Traveler's Checks. When traveling, it is wise to carry only a small amount of cash. Most of the travel funds should be in the form of **traveler's checks**. These are checks purchased at banks or at offices of companies that handle money exchange, such as American Express offices. Some banks issue their own form of traveler's checks, while others use traveler's checks issued by Visa or American Express. Traveler's checks come in denominations of $10, $20, $50, and $100. The person who will use the traveler's checks must pick them up and sign each check in the presence of a bank teller or bank officer.

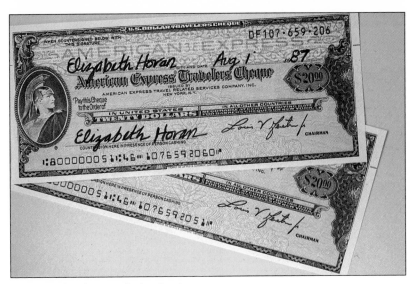

An example of a traveler's check.

Traveler's checks come with a receipt that is a record of the serial numbers of the checks. You keep one copy of the receipt in your files, and the traveler keeps another copy as a record in case the checks are lost or stolen. It is extremely important to keep the receipt for the checks *separate* from the checks themselves.

Cash Advances. When travelers must pay tips, cab fares, highway tolls, and other such business trip expenses in cash, many employers issue cash advances. To obtain a cash advance, it is usually necessary to fill out a request form and submit it to the proper department in your company. Most cash advance forms require authorized signatures and an explanation of the request, as well as other necessary details. Copies of cash advance requests should be kept with your expense records.

RGANIZING THE TRAVELER

You can assist your supervisor greatly by preparing a checklist of all the materials that he or she should take on the trip. These materials might include related correspondence, guidebooks, maps, reports, and equipment. Go over the checklist with your supervisor. This is an efficient way to make sure that your supervisor will have all the necessary materials.

Organizing the traveler.

HANDLING CORRESPONDENCE AND MESSAGES WHILE YOUR SUPERVISOR IS AWAY

In most cases your supervisor will delegate his or her responsibilities to another manager. If you are working in a small office where there is no other manager, you will be asked to take on additional responsibilities, such as handling all telephone or electronic messages as well as written correspondence. In some cases you will not be able to give a definite reply; you will have to wait until your supervisor returns. If mail cannot wait for your supervisor to return, you can handle it in one of three ways:

1. Forward it to an appropriate person.

2. Give it to a supervisor who can handle it.

3. Answer it yourself.

Keep all correspondence and messages well organized so that your supervisor will be able to work with this information efficiently upon returning to the office.

COMMUNICATING WITH YOUR SUPERVISOR

Quite frequently your supervisor may arrange to call the office on a scheduled basis to follow up on business matters that need to be taken care of. You should make a plan for communicating with your supervisor while she or he is on a business trip. Keep notes on matters you need to discuss. Have these notes handy when your supervisor calls.

Keeping a log of all office activities while your supervisor is on a business trip is another way of handling communications. Information that could be kept in a log includes the names of visitors to the office, incoming letters, telephone calls, and reports on special projects or activities. This log will provide your supervisor with detailed information as to what went on while he or she was away on the business trip.

OLLOWING UP ON A TRIP

When your supervisor returns from a trip, you will need to handle some follow-up tasks. One task will be to return all necessary materials to the proper files. You will also need to help your supervisor prepare an expense account and return any unused funds to the proper department. Another follow-up task will be to handle the correspondence resulting from the trip. This correspondence might include thank-you letters, letters confirming decisions made on certain items, and letters involving other business-related matters.

Once a trip is over, it is always a good idea to review the planning aspect of the trip. What went particularly well? What should have been done differently? For example, were the hotel accommodations satisfactory? Following up on these matters directly after the trip allows you to obtain immediate feedback that will be helpful in planning future trips.

ORKING WITH EXPENSE ACCOUNTS

Businesspeople who travel on a regular basis are required to submit an expense account when they return from a trip. An **expense account** is a form that a business traveler completes to provide an accurate record of expenses. The traveler must submit an expense account in order to be reimbursed for personal money spent or to explain any cash advances. An expense account is also needed for income tax purposes. It may be a part of your job to fill out an expense account for your supervisor.

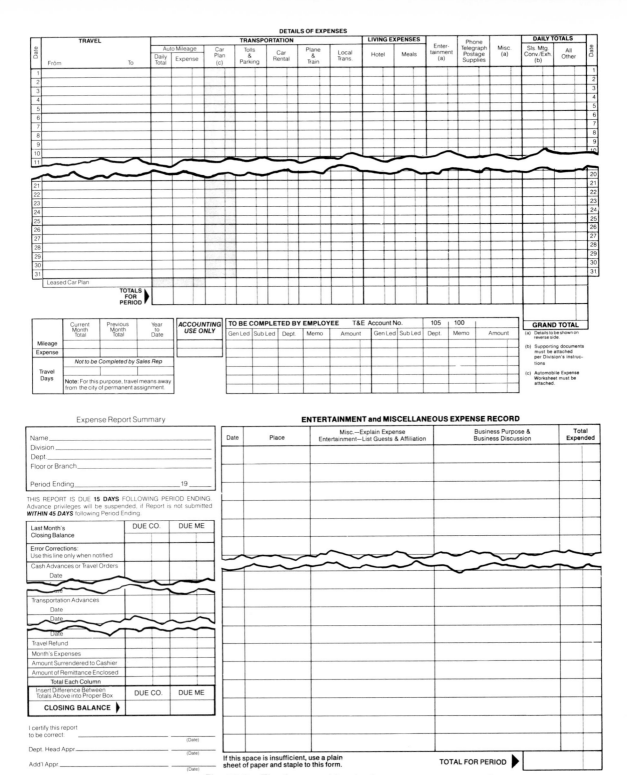

Fig. 13-3 The front and back of an expense account form.

Before you begin filling out an expense account, sort the receipts and logged expenses by day, and determine the nature of each expense so that you will know where to insert the information on the form. Study the expense account in Fig. 13-3.

Today it is possible to use a computer to prepare expense accounts. With the right software, detailed information can be stored and accessed electronically. When this is done properly, much time can be saved in preparing accurate expense accounts.

SUMMARY

- One of your many duties may be to make travel arrangements.

- The extent to which you have to make travel arrangements depends on the type of business you work in.

- The first step in planning a business trip is to gather information concerning the trip.

- There are a variety of options available to you as you plan a business trip.

- Businesses known as travel agencies handle travel plans for most businesspeople.

- Those individuals who plan trips at travel agencies are known as travel agents.

- Large companies have their own travel agencies to assist their employees in planning business trips.

- Selecting a method of transportation that will best meet your needs is extremely important.

- Making plans in advance can greatly assist you in completing travel plans.

- Planning international trips involves researching the place of destination as well as travel documents that are necessary in order to travel to the particular country.

- Other major considerations in international travel include arranging for the proper currency, vaccinations, and local transportation.

- Cost and location are the two most important factors to be considered when selecting a hotel.

- A detailed schedule listing all travel plans is known as an itinerary and is very important in planning and arranging for a successful business trip.

- Arranging for proper travel funds is also extremely important.

- Plans should be made for communication with your supervisor while he or she is away on a business trip.

- Follow-up should be conducted when your supervisor returns from a business trip.

- A special plan should be devised for businesses to handle expenses.

travel agency
travel agent
itinerary
corporate travel
   department
commuter airline
passport
visa
guaranteed reservation
traveler's check
expense account

REVIEW QUESTIONS

1. What information do you need to gather before you can start making travel arrangements for your supervisor?

2. What services do travel agencies and corporate travel departments usually provide?

3. What is the *Official Airline Guide*? How is it useful?

4. What documents would your supervisor need for an international trip? How does one get each of these documents?

5. What information would you need to give to a hotel reservations clerk to reserve a room for your supervisor?

6. What information is usually included in an itinerary?

SKILLBUILDING ACTIVITIES

1. Arrange to visit a travel agency. Call for an appointment with one of the travel agents. Compose a list of at least five questions to ask the travel agent concerning his or her work. Report your findings to your classmates through an oral presentation.

2. Pick up the travel schedules of at least three different airlines. Compare them to see the differences in flights between two specific cities. Write a report stating the differences.

3. Find out the specific details of the procedure for obtaining a passport. Present this information to your classmates.

4. Organize a log sheet that you can use to keep track of all work assignments. Determine how long it took to complete each assignment, as well as how the work can be improved.

5. Plan a three-day trip to a favorite city to conduct business with a colleague. Develop an itinerary that you could follow. Share this information with your classmates.

USING THE TELEPHONE AND OTHER ELECTRONIC COMMUNICATIONS

*W*hen Alexander Graham Bell invented the telephone in 1876, he introduced a device that continues to be the most widely used communications instrument.

This chapter will provide you with an in-depth study of telephone equipment and the mechanics of operation, as well as techniques that can be used to communicate positively.

As a result of studying this chapter, you will be able to:

- Understand the types of tele- phone equipment available in order to communicate effectively.
- Develop an awareness of the importance of efficient telephone mechanics.
- Develop a positive telephone personality.
- Understand and practice the special telephone techniques involved in handling incoming calls and outgoing calls.
- Understand the advantages of voice messaging, teleconferencing, and other forms of electronic communication.

TELEPHONE COMPANIES

Until 1984 telephone calls were handled by individual telephone companies that were a part of the American Telephone and Telegraph Corporation. This corporation was known to most of us as AT&T. It was the universal telephone company through which calls were handled around the world. If you wanted to place a call to Sweden, you picked up your telephone and placed the call. The cost of the call to Sweden was included on your monthly telephone bill. If you had problems using your telephone in any way, you called "the telephone company." Someone from "the telephone company" was sent to handle your problem.

In 1984 these procedures changed drastically. As a result of a court order aimed at encouraging competition in the telephone industry, AT&T was forced to give up its monopoly of individual telephone companies. The local telephone companies became independent of AT&T, and telephone customers were allowed to purchase their own telephone equipment. While AT&T continues to offer telephones and long-distance service, there are now many competitors. Because of the changes brought about by this process, known as divestiture, businesses and consumers are able to, and do, obtain telephone equipment and services from other sources.

Most businesses today consider their individual needs when selecting a telephone company. Factors that are considered include fees charged for local and long-distance service, the quality of transmission, and additional services offered by the individual telephone company.

Some of the independent telephone companies are MCI, SBS, Sprint, and Allnet. These companies are AT&T's best-known competitors.

When long-distance calls are placed, these calls must travel over local telephone company lines between the caller's office and the long-distance company's switching station. As a result of this process, each long-distance call has a local fee as well as a long-distance-carrier fee. Many large businesses have direct-access connections with long-distance carriers that allow them to bypass the local telephone company.

*T*ELEPHONE EQUIPMENT AND SYSTEMS

When most of us hear the words *telephone equipment*, we think of the telephones themselves. As the technology advances, the choices of telephones increase. Depending on where you live, you may encounter one of two major types of telephones in use. One type is the rotary dial telephone. The other type is the push-button telephone with 12 buttons: 10 numbered keys and keys labeled "*" and "#," which are used for inputting special codes for special services. Push-button telephones can also serve as input devices for electronic communications.

Telephones with **key systems** have several keys, or buttons. Each button represents a telephone line. When the telephone rings, one of the buttons will light up. In order to answer the call, it is necessary to press the lighted button and then pick up the receiver. Key systems also provide hold buttons. If you are using one line and another line rings, you simply press the hold button to put the first caller on hold before answering the incoming call. If you answer a call for another person, you can put the caller on hold while using an intercom or a separate telephone line to alert the person being called. An important advantage of a key system is that it allows anyone working in the office to use any phone in the system to answer calls.

Key systems telephones are most useful in small offices that do not require elaborate switchboards and complicated features.

Key systems provide a variety of features. It is possible to have an electronic memory that stores frequently called numbers. If it is necessary for you to call a branch office several times a day, you can assign a single digit to the branch's telephone number. Thus you would only have to press the button for that one digit and perhaps one or two additional code numbers instead of dialing the entire telephone number each time.

Another feature in some key systems provides distinctive ringing sounds. This feature lets you know if the caller is telephoning from outside the office, from another line within the office, or from an intercom. By pushing a button, you can also use the telephone as a microphone to make announcements to coworkers if necessary.

Key systems can be set up with a switching feature. If one worker's line is busy, a call coming in for that person will automatically be switched to another line.

A PBX system enables the receptionist to switch calls among the telephone extensions within an office.

A **private branch exchange,** or PBX, consists of equipment needed to switch calls among the telephone extensions in an office. A switchboard operator controls the central switchboard, where the calls are handled. More and more private branch exchanges are becoming automated. As a result, digital private branch exchanges can carry digital sounds from computers as well as sounds from human voices.

Because of automated private branch exchanges, additional features are possible. One feature is **direct outward dialing.** With this feature it is possible to make outside calls by dialing an access number first.

Another feature of some types of automated private branch exchanges is **centrex.** This system works in two ways. If you know the extension number of the person you are calling, you can call that person directly without having to speak with the switchboard operator. If you do not know the extension number, or if you are calling for information and you do not know whom you should speak with, you call the company's number. The switchboard operator will then transfer your call to the proper extension. If a PBX does not have centrex, all calls go through the general number and the operator.

Many telephones now have an additional piece of equipment, known as a **modem,** to communicate data. It converts computer signals into telephone signals and telephone signals into computer signals so that information can be sent over telephone lines from one computer to another.

PECIAL FEATURES OF TELEPHONES

The automatic features that your telephone has will depend on the size of your company and the amount of business conducted over the telephone.

Call Waiting. If you are using your telephone line when another call comes in, a special tone will inform you that you have a call waiting. You can either finish the call you are on or place that caller on hold while you answer the second call.

Call Forwarding. The **call forwarding** feature will allow you to key in a code that will automatically forward all incoming calls to another number.

Speed Calling. This feature allows you to store frequently used telephone numbers in a computerized telephone's memory. After these frequently used telephone numbers are stored, you can dial any of the numbers by keying in a number code instead of entering the entire number once again.

Conference Calls. A conference call is unique in that several individuals are able to talk to each other over the phone at the same time. Individuals can then have a "conference" over the telephone.

Conference calling, a popular feature of computerized telephone systems, allows office workers to confer with each other without having to meet face-to-face.

Automatic Callback. This special computerized feature will allow you to automatically call back a person whose line is busy when you call the first time. When the line becomes free, the telephone system will call you first and then automatically dial the telephone number you have been trying to reach.

Automatic Route Selection. Many large businesses utilize several long-distance services when placing calls. When a business is using an automatic route selection, the most economical route is selected for the call to be processed.

Call-Timing. This feature allows certain types of businesses to record the actual time used for any calls made relating to a specific situation.

Call Restriction. In many businesses, telephone users are required to key in an authorization code before placing a call. This requirement allows a business to keep an accurate record of calls made.

OMMUNICATING BY TELEPHONE

ACE-TO-FACE COMMUNICATION VERSUS TELEPHONE COMMUNICATION

Messages are more easily conveyed when you are speaking to someone face-to-face because of the facial expressions and other types of nonverbal communication. It is more difficult to communicate over the telephone because you cannot see the other person. Your voice takes the place of your face, and your personality is revealed by your tone of voice and rate of speaking. Your speech creates the impression.

DEVELOPING A POSITIVE TELEPHONE PERSONALITY

A client's first contact with a business office is often by telephone, so it is important for office workers to develop good telephone techniques.

To create a positive telephone personality, you must focus on all aspects of your voice that are involved in speaking.

Audibility. Speak directly into the mouthpiece in your normal tone of voice.

Enunciation, or Articulation. Pronounce all words clearly and precisely.

Rate of Speech. Adjust your speech to the needs of the person you are speaking with. Do not chew gum or eat while speaking.

Pitch. Keep the pitch of your voice as normal as possible. Act interested when you are speaking.

Expression and Tone of Voice. Varying your voice tone shows that you are paying attention to the listener and that you have a personal interest in the telephone call. Smiling creates a relaxed feeling when you are speaking.

Vocabulary. Use words that the listener will understand. Express your ideas in a simple form. Try to use the listener's name occasionally to create a personal interest in the listener.

NCOMING CALLS

REPARING TO RECEIVE CALLS

You should always be prepared to receive telephone calls by having the essential supplies and equipment within a hand's reach. Have the following readily available for receiving calls:

1. Writing instruments, such as pens and pencils.

2. Message pads or other forms that are frequently used.

3. Reference materials pertaining to the topics that are usually discussed.

4. An organized desk.

Be prepared to take messages by keeping a notepad and a pen or pencil near the phone at all times.

NSWERING PROMPTLY

Answer your telephone promptly, preferably by the end of the first or second ring—no later! Keep your telephone within easy reach.

Answering your telephone promptly creates a positive company image. If you allow your telephone to ring too long before you answer, your company may lose business. A telephone that rings too long affects:

1. *The caller.* The caller may become impatient. The caller may already have waited if he or she was transferred from a different line.

2. *The person being called.* The person answering the call is always interrupted by a ringing telephone. Answering the telephone promptly prevents further confusion.

3. *Surrounding workers.* A telephone that rings too long creates a feeling of inefficiency and always breaks the concentration of those who hear it. All the telephones in an office should be covered at all times. This is especially important during lunch and break periods.

4. *Switchboard operators.* When a switchboard operator transfers a call and the person receiving the call does not answer the phone promptly, the switchboard operator must keep giving "call updates" to the caller. This is extremely annoying and very inconvenient for all concerned.

5. *Equipment.* When telephone lines are being tied up because individuals are not answering the telephones, the callers may opt to take their business elsewhere.

NNOUNCING YOUR IDENTITY

Learning to answer the telephone in a positive, personal manner is vital for effective telephone conversations. Your tone of voice is the key to the success of the call. Giving proper identification when you answer the telephone indicates responsibility. Here are some examples:

"Good morning, Mrs. Blaney."

"Harris speaking."

If you are working in a specific department, the name of your department may be used in the identification. For example:

"Human Resources, Jordan."

"Claims, Miss Eastman."

If you are answering a referral call, use your own name as if you were answering for the first time. Using *Hello* as the initial answer wastes time and gives no specific information to the person at the other end.

If you have been delayed in answering a call, say "Thank you for waiting," or something similar, when you pick up the telephone.

If you are answering the telephone for someone else, you should indicate this. For example:

"Mrs. Ruby's office, Miss Metcalf."

"Robert Levinsky's office, Matt Rolfe."

The term *office* is preferable to the word *desk, telephone,* or *line.* Using the word *office* creates a more positive business image and also adds prestige to the process of answering the call.

EING DISCREET

When you are answering a telephone call for someone else, it is extremely important to be discreet when explaining why that individual is not available and when the individual will be available.

Examples are as follows:

"Mr. Fernandez is on vacation for two weeks. Mrs. Costello is handling his calls. Could you speak with Mrs. Costello?"

"Mr. Moseley is in a meeting until 2:30. May I take a message?"

"Mr. Stover is on another call at the moment. Do you wish to wait, or may I take your name and number and have him return your call?"

"Miss Wilson will be out of the office until Thursday. Could I help you?"

Avoid remarks such as:

"She hasn't arrived yet." (two hours after the time she should be at work)

"He's left the office for the day." (early in the afternoon)

"She is out for coffee."

Certain comments create negative connotations that are not always true. Here are some examples:

"She's tied up for the afternoon."

"He's out on the floor."

If it is necessary to screen a call, be very tactful. Use positive statements such as *May I tell him/her who is calling, please.*

Sometimes the person being called wants to speak only with certain individuals. If this is the case, use a tactful opening question. For example, you could say, "Pat's not available at the moment. May I tell her who called?" This question will not make the caller feel uncomfortable. If the caller is someone with whom the called person wishes to speak, you can follow up with "She just returned to her desk."

ESPONDING TO THE CALLER'S OPENING STATEMENT

Most individuals open a telephone call with a question. Answer the question with a positive comment rather than another question. Let callers know that they have reached a responsible individual by doing the following:

1. Indicate an interest in helping.

2. Express regret if a customer has a complaint.

3. Allow the caller to complete the opening statement without interrupting.

EVELOPING INFORMATION BY LISTENING

Listening to what the caller is saying is necessary in order to respond with appropriate remarks. If you do not listen carefully, it is easy to form a wrong conclusion. Keep the following points in mind when developing information to give a caller:

1. Put yourself in the caller's position. Think in terms of the caller.

2. Listen for key ideas as opposed to words. It is necessary to get the entire picture, not just pieces.

3. Take notes. This will allow you to remember important points later.

4. Use interjections such as *I see.* This lets the caller know that you are still listening.

5. Keep your own talking to a minimum. It is impossible to listen effectively while talking.

6. Prepare ahead. If you prepare remarks ahead of time, you will free your mind for listening.

7. Ask questions. If it is necessary to ask a question, wait for the right moment. Interrupting the caller with questions causes confusion and wastes valuable telephone time.

8. Verify important information. Always verify the spelling of names and addresses, and make sure that you have correctly noted unusual types of information.

9. Be sure you have all the necessary information before acting on any matter.

10. Give accurate information. Nothing can destroy the credibility of a business more than inaccurate information. If you are unsure of the accuracy of the information, volunteer to call back.

11. Use the caller's name whenever possible. This creates a personal interest and usually draws extra special attention for the next few seconds.

EAVING AND RETURNING TO THE LINE

The secretary may have to check with a supervisor before putting a call through. By using the hold button, the caller will not be able to hear any sound.

It is often necessary to place callers on "hold" for various reasons. The two most common reasons are to check information and to call someone else to the telephone. Keep the following points in mind when leaving and returning to the line:

1. Be precise in what you say to the caller. Avoid expressions such as *Hold on a minute.* Tell the caller exactly what you must do to locate the necessary information. If you feel that this is going to take too much time, offer to call the person back with the necessary information. For example, you could say, "Mrs. Crosson, it will be necessary for me to check my records on that matter. That will take a few minutes. Would you prefer to wait, or could I call you back?"

2. Be sure that the caller has responded to your offer. Wait for the caller to respond. Do not make a decision for the caller.

3. Be sure to use the hold button if it is part of the telephone you are using. Do not pick up the receiver before depressing the button identifying the line of the incoming call. If you do, you may activate the wrong line causing a delay in answering the call. Also, an incorrect signal might be sent to a switchboard operator, or a telephone call already in progress might be interrupted.

4. Do not forget to press the hold button before leaving a line with a call already in progress. Otherwise, you will automatically disconnect the call.

5. Return to the line often with a progress report. Do not keep the caller waiting for more than two minutes at the very most. When you do return to the telephone line, say something to indicate that you have obtained the necessary information. For example, you could say, "Thank you for waiting, Mrs. Hosler. I have located the necessary information."

6. Handle additional telephone calls in a positive manner. When you have another incoming call to handle, do not panic. Excuse yourself from the first caller, place that caller on hold, answer the new call if it can be handled quickly, and return to the first caller promptly.

NDING A CALL

Ending a telephone call is just as important as answering the call. Any goodwill created during the call can easily be destroyed if the call is ended incorrectly. Keep the following points in mind when ending a call:

Learning to answer the telephone in a positive, personal manner is vital for effective telephone conversations.

1. Express appreciation in a sincere manner. Say, for example, "Thank you for calling, Mr. Willis." When the caller expresses appreciation, respond with a polite comment such as "You're welcome, Mrs. Anderson." If it is necessary to express regret, do so politely.

2. Avoid commonly used call endings such as *Bye-bye, OK,* or *Talk to you later.* The correct ending should be *Good-bye.*

3. Hang up the telephone carefully. Place the telephone receiver in a gentle manner, making certain that the receiver is resting on its base securely.

AKING MESSAGES

Taking telephone messages is essential in order for information to be communicated correctly.

Use telephone message forms that provide space for efficient use. Use courtesy at all times. Request information instead of demanding information.

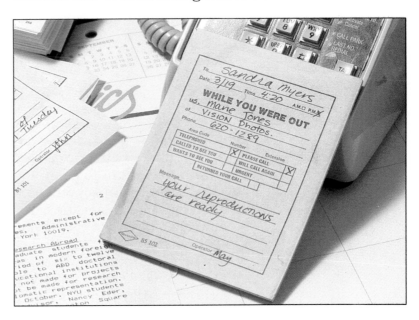

These forms remind you of what information you should ask for when taking messages.

A telephone message form contains space for the following information:

1. *The name of the person being called.* Fill this information in first to avoid delivering a message to the wrong person.

2. *The name of the caller.* Ask for the caller's name politely. Ask the caller to repeat his or her name, especially if the name is an unusual one. Be sure to verify the spelling of the name. If the name is a common one, be sure to obtain the first name or initials.

3. *The time and date.* It is extremely important to have this information; otherwise, the person being called might miss an appointment or return a call unnecessarily.

4. *The caller's telephone number.* The complete telephone number must be noted. Repeat the telephone number. Many numbers sound alike and are easily transposed.

5. *The message.* Record the message in as brief a manner as possible. Ask as many questions as necessary to get all the information the person being called will need.

6. *The initials of the person receiving the call.* This is vital, especially if the person being called has additional questions.

Deliver each message immediately. Be sure that the person who is supposed to get the message gets it.

 RANSFERRING CALLS

Calls should be transferred only when it is absolutely necessary. It is very irritating to a caller to have to repeat the reason for calling to several people.

If it is necessary to transfer a call, tell the caller that you are going to transfer the call and explain why. Occasionally callers prefer to have someone call them back. Honor their wishes.

When you must transfer a call, you can say, for example, "Warren Ryan in Sales will handle your request, Mrs. Dearborn. May I transfer you to him?" Explain the call briefly to the person in the department the call is being transferred to.

If possible, transfer calls without asking the operator for assistance. Refer to your in-house reference information concerning this procedure.

OUTGOING CALLS

Outgoing calls differ from incoming calls in that you are in control of the conversation. Keep the following points in mind when handling outgoing calls.

PLANNING THE CALL

Know the purpose of your call. Whom do you want to speak with? Before placing the call, obtain all the materials that you will need to refer to during the conversation.

Always consider the time of day and time zone differences. If you call near the lunch hour or during a rush period, you may not be able to reach the person you need to speak to. Also consider time situations that apply to the person or business you are calling, such as regularly scheduled conferences.

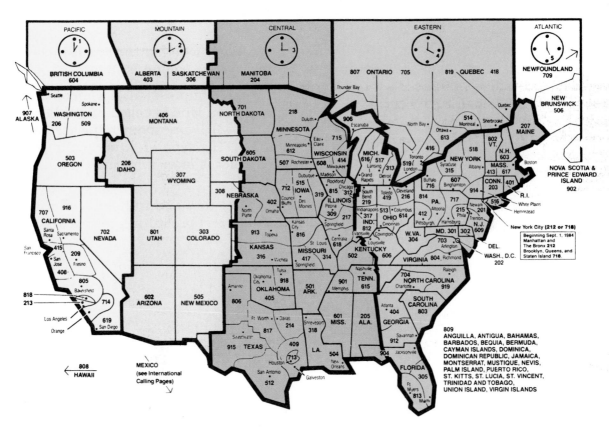

Fig. 14-1   It is important to check time zones when making long-distance calls. This map shows the standard time zones for the United States and Canada.

LOCATING THE NUMBER

Keep at hand a list of frequently used telephone numbers and current telephone directories, including an in-house directory if your company has one. If your telephone has the Speed Calling feature, be sure to program your telephone with the numbers you call frequently. When you use this feature, you will save a great deal of time. Telephone numbers may also be found on letterheads, bills, and advertising media.

Call Directory Assistance only when numbers are not readily available from other sources. There is usually a fee for this service.

Keep a list of frequently used telephone numbers. Do not rely on your memory.

PLACING THE CALL

Place your own calls if possible. There are several advantages to placing calls without assistance:

1. You can save a lot of time.

2. You will know immediately whether the line is busy or whether the person you are calling is in.

3. You will create a favorable impression. If someone else places the call, the person who is called might be annoyed at being greeted with "One moment please; Mrs. Matthews is calling." This type of situation implies that the time of the caller is more important than that of the caller.

Refer to a telephone directory and in-house telephone dialing instructions for correct procedures for placing telephone calls.

Keep at hand a current telephone directory.

Common mistakes in telephone dialing include the following:

1. Failing to wait for the dial tone.

2. Forcing a rotary dial to return to its normal position and failing to hit the finger stop.

3. Confusing the letter *O* in the *MNO* combination with the numeral *0*. This can result in reaching an incorrect number.

CALLER IDENTIFICATION

Always identify yourself at the beginning of a telephone conversation. Give both your name and the name of the business you represent. An identifying statement saves time and eliminates the guessing game of Who is calling?

If you want your call to be returned, be sure to leave your name; the name of the company you represent; the time when you can be reached; your telephone number, including the area code and extension; and the reason for your call.

CREATING A POSITIVE TONE IN SERVING A CALLER

Learning how to create a positive tone on the telephone when serving a caller is vital. The service you give your caller must be handled efficiently and completely. When callers have to wait, they are not happy, and this can result in a loss of business.

Taking a personal interest in a caller by being courteous will always help any telephone call. Everyone likes to feel that he or she is getting personal attention when either making or receiving a telephone call. Listen carefully to all requests.

Being sincere when using the telephone goes a long way in creating a positive tone. Try to develop a standard tone for telephone conversations. The following points will help you develop a positive tone for serving callers.

1. *Be courteous.* If you use a pleasant manner when handling a telephone call, you will find it easier to convey your thoughts.

2. *Use a pleasant voice.* Be sure that your statements are grammatically correct and that your words are clearly spoken.

3. *Make an effort to understand your caller.* You can learn the needs of your caller by listening. Be sure that you provide an opportunity for your customer to explain the purpose of the call.

4. *Give explanations as needed.* If it is necessary to give an explanation, be sure that the explanation is thorough. Give the explanation in a manner that is sincere and easy to understand.

5. *Display a positive attitude.* Always let the caller know that you care. Remember that you represent both your company and yourself.

OICE MESSAGING

As telephone technology continues to develop, voice messaging is being practiced more and more. **Voice messaging** allows you to use your telephone system to receive messages. The messages are stored in the form of recorded words. Many of the same principles are used in electronic mailbox systems. You gain access to a voice mailbox by giving instructions and punching or dialing a code number or password.

For example, if you are working in an office that uses a voice messaging system and you must be away from your desk for several hours, you can key in a code on your telephone that sends all your incoming calls to a voice mailbox controlled by a computer to which your telephone is linked. The computer will take the messages while you are away from your desk by answering your phone automatically and telling callers how to leave a message. You can check for messages in your voice mailbox by entering your code number or password.

You can use your telephone to instruct the voice mailbox to play your voice mail messages, save them for later use, or erase them. Most systems are also able to automatically route your answer to the sender, add something to the message, and send the entire package to other individuals in the voice mail network.

OMMUNICATIONS SOFTWARE

Chapter 11 covered the use of the computer to electronically access and retrieve data from electronic information services. The computer can provide an electronic link into literally thousands of databases as well as other types of information services. The computer alone cannot communicate with these external information services. Previously you learned that a modem is required for a computer to communicate externally. For a modem to communicate effectively, it is also necessary to use communications software.

Suppose you needed to find an article that was published in *Business Week* magazine two years ago. You already learned in Chapter 11 that you can access back issues of many popular magazines through one of the available electronic information services. You first dial the number of the database to establish the on-line connection. Once you are in the database, you can search it to find a particular article. Upon locating the article, you might want to transfer it to your computer to retain it. How difficult is it to transfer a file or data from one computer to another? Not difficult at all once a compatible modem is hooked up to your computer. Once you are on-line and are able to locate the information, you can retrieve it on your computer. There is still one problem: If you were using your computer and modem alone, the information, once transferred to your computer, would appear on one side of your computer screen and stream right across it and off the other side. In order to capture and manage the information that is coming through your computer, you need to use communications software. **Communications software** is a program that manages your computer, its modem, and the information that comes through these two pieces of equipment from the outside.

To better understand the important role that communications software plays in communicating externally, think of the use of a standard telephone. When the telephone rings and someone answers it, a communications link has been made. As soon as someone starts to speak, information is being exchanged, but that information is usually not being saved or permanently recorded. The use of the telephone is much like the operation of the computer and the modem.

Suppose during the course of the conversation you are informed of an important meeting that your boss must attend tomorrow at 9:00 A.M. In preparation for this meeting, your boss must be prepared to present an overview of the department's new budget. Since you will need to recall this information at a later time, you might write it down temporarily on a note pad, a kind of temporary storage. Later you might enter the date of the meeting in your boss's calendar, permanently recording or storing the information. You might also write your boss a note that provides the details of the meeting. Information has been transmitted through the telephone, temporarily saved on a note pad, then permanently recorded.

The process of receiving, recording, and storing the information exchanged during the telephone conversation is the same process communications software performs. The telephone is nothing more than a communications channel to transmit the information. Intelligence is required on both ends of the conversation to send, receive, interpret, and record the information.

As you have seen, the use of a telephone to transmit information can be compared to the use of a modem and a computer, but the modem has some basic intelligence. Modems are often smart enough to answer the telephone and acknowledge the message. The modem functions mainly as a communications device much like the telephone. It simply sends and receives information by providing a means for the exchange of electronic pulses. As you learned in Chapter 11, a modem's major function is to take analog signals from the telephone system and convert them to digital signals compatible with the computer.

Simply stated, once the modem has converted the analog signals to a digital signal, or digital signals to an analog signal, its role is finished. The communications software does the rest. Communications software provides the computer with the intelligence to save or retrieve the information that has been transmitted by the modem.

One of the major benefits of communications software is its ability to save the information transmitted by the modem in temporary memory. The software's temporary memory or temporary storage location is often referred to as a **buffer,** a common data processing term. When data is transmitted into the computer through the modem, it is caught and held in the buffer of the communications software until further instructions are provided. Without the buffer, the user would not be able to do much more than view the data as it streams across the screen.

Using communications software, the data is not only temporarily stored for viewing, it can also be read and deleted permanently, saved on a disk, printed, or even transmitted to another location. The data can also be retrieved from a disk where it is again held in the buffer of the communications software until it is ready to be sent by the modem.

The primary function of communications software is information handling. Beyond the temporary storage of data, communications software provides a variety of features for manipulating the information as it comes from the modem. Some communications programs can even answer the telephone and record incoming information unattended, while others provide directories for automatic dialing. Several different communications programs are available on the market today which include a broad range of features.

Figure 14-2 provides a sample screen displaying the

```
XXXXXXXXXXXXXXXXXXXXXXXXXXXXXXXXXXXXXXXXXXXXXXXXXX

          Menu Choices
     L    Read Systems Log
     M    Send and Read Mail
     P    List/Add/Change Passwords
     S    Change REMOTE Program Settings
     T    Set Date and Time
     W    Wait for Incoming Calls
     X    Exit to DOS
          Enter your Choice

XXXXXXXXXXXXXXXXXXXXXXXXXXXXXXXXXXXXXXXXXXXXXXXXXX
```

Fig. 14-2   This is an example of the main menu of communication software.

Date	Time	Caller
03-16-1988	17:14:57	Mark Calvin
04-11-1988	19:05:09	Jeff Zipper
04-17-1988	20:24:08	5 Password Tries
05-04-1988	11:01:36	Renee Garon
05-04-1988	21:05:12	David Burns
05-05-1988	10:10:14	5 Password Tries

Erase log file (Y/N)?

Fig. 14-3   By choosing "L" Read Systems Log, from the main menu of the communications software, you callup a record of the people who tried to reach you when you were not at your computer.

menu choices available from one of these programs. By choosing "L," Read Systems Log, from the main menu of the communications software, you call up a record of the people who tried to reach you when you were not at your computer.

Date: 03-16-88 is March 16, 1988.

Time: 17:14:57 translates to 14 minutes and 57 seconds after 5 P.M. Anything over 12 is P.M.

05-04-87 is May 4, 1988.

11:01:36 is one minute and 36 seconds after 11 A.M.

THER TELEPHONE EQUIPMENT AND ACCESSORIES

OBILE TELEPHONES

One result of advances in telephone technology has been the introduction of cordless portable telephones that are relatively inexpensive and reliable. More businesspeople are using mobile telephones so that they can complete their work while they are traveling by car, train, or plane.

AGING DEVICES

A **paging device** is often referred to as a "beeper." It makes a high-pitched sound when someone wants to reach the person carrying it. Several types of paging devices are available. Some have tiny screens that display messages, such as telephone numbers where calls can be returned. Others just beep to signal that there is a message for the user.

Mobile telephones enable the business person to complete his/her work while traveling by car, train, or plane.

Beepers can be used to transmit messages or to alert people to call their offices no matter where they are or what they are doing.

NSWERING MACHINES

Answering machines allow only a limited time for you to record a message.

Answering machines record messages when nobody is in the office. You may have to record a message that the machine will automatically play when someone calls. All the usual positive telephone techniques apply when you are recording a message on an answering machine. The message should ask the caller to leave a name and telephone number, a brief message concerning the nature of the call, and the time the call was made. The message should also assure the caller that someone will return the call as soon as possible.

ELECONFERENCING

A **teleconference** is a meeting conducted through electronic equipment. This means that it is possible to hold a meeting with individuals who are in two different locations. For example, the participants in a teleconference could be in New York and Los Angeles.

A teleconference could be a telephone call involving a few individuals, or it could be a staff meeting involving a large number of individuals.

UDIO TELECONFERENCES

An **audio teleconference** is a conference conducted over the telephone. If the conference involves more than three or four individuals, a device known as a speakerphone is usually used. A **speakerphone** is a combination microphone and loudspeaker device that allows the call to be heard by everyone in the room.

VIDEO TELECONFERENCES

A **video teleconference** is a conference in which the participants can see each other through an electronic communications network. Closed-circuit television is often used. A video teleconference allows the participants to demonstrate products and procedures and exchange information through both visual and verbal communication. When the proper types of equipment are used, documents can be transmitted electronically and then reproduced as hard copy.

Teleconferencing makes it possible to send and receive voice, image, graphic, and written data anywhere, anytime.

_H_OW TO ARRANGE FOR A TELECONFERENCE

As video teleconferencing continues to grow in use, larger companies are providing rooms especially designed for video teleconferences.

Whether your company has its own teleconferencing facilities or rents them, you need to keep several major considerations in mind:

1. Be sure to reserve a room for a teleconference and that the room will accommodate all the individuals involved.

2. Be sure that all necessary equipment is available. This includes the screen, telephone lines, and microphones.

Using teleconferencing as a form of communication can indeed save much time and money. More and more businesses will continue to benefit from this form of electronic communication as time passes.

- The telephone is the most widely used communications device because it is one of the easiest and fastest ways to send a message long distances.

- Until 1984 telephone calls were handled by individual telephone companies that were a part of the American Telephone and Telegraph Corporation.

- As a result of divestiture, businesses and consumers are able and do obtain telephone equipment and services from a variety of sources.

- Different telephone companies are also used for local and long-distance service.

- A business should consider its individual needs when selecting a telephone company and other telephone-related services.

- Most businesses purchase service from one of the large telephone companies and also purchase additional local area service from a smaller telephone company that handles local area service.

- Telephone systems vary depending on where you live.

- One of the most popular systems used today is the key system.

- Private branch exchanges, or PBX as it is commonly known, consists of equipment needed to switch calls among the telephone extensions in an office.

- Modems are devices attached to telephones that convert computer signals into telephone signals (and back again) for sending and receiving information over the telephone lines.

- Among the many automated telephone special features are call waiting, call forwarding, call timing, speed dialing, automatic callback, automatic route selection, and conference calling.

- Learning to use all the mechanical parts of the telephone is vital for correct use of the telephone.

- Learning to create a positive telephone personality requires focusing on all areas of your voice that are involved in speaking.

- Creating a personal interest while using the telephone is very important for positive communication to occur.

- Be prepared to handle incoming telephone calls by having the essential supplies and equipment readily available.

- Be prepared to talk when the telephone rings.

- All telephones should be covered at all times preventing a ringing telephone.

- Learning to answer the telephone in a positive, personal manner is vital for an effective telephone call to occur.

- Be discreet when you are using the telephone to give information.

- Learn to develop the art of good listening when using the telephone.

- Ending a telephone call is just as important as answering the telephone call.

- Learning to take correct telephone messages is very essential in order for information to be communicated correctly.

- Transfer calls only when necessary.

- Because you are in control of outgoing calls, plan them carefully for maximum efficiency.

- Keep a list of numbers used most frequently readily available.

- Place all your own telephone calls if possible.

- When making long-distance calls, select the service that will complete your call most efficiently and economically.

- Voice messaging is being used more and more as technology develops.

- Commonly available types of telephone equipment and accessories are now available, including mobile telephones, paging devices, and answering machines.

- Teleconferencing is continuing to grow in use as a means of saving both time and money while communicating.

VOCABULARY

key system   voice messaging
private branch exchange   paging device
direct outward dialing   teleconference
centrex   audio teleconference
modem   speakerphone
call forwarding   video teleconference

REVIEW QUESTIONS

1. Explain how divestiture change affected the services of AT&T.

2. How do businesses select a telephone company today?

3. Explain the various types of telephone equipment and systems used today. What are the major advantages and disadvantages?

4. What does PBX stand for? How does it work?

5. What service does a modem perform?

6. List and give a brief explanation of the commonly used automated telephone features available today.

7. Relate the importance of practicing good telephone mechanics when using the telephone.

8. What role does your verbal communication play when using the telephone?

9. What major points should be kept in mind when developing a positive telephone personality?

10. What role does taking a personal interest in the call play?

11. List the important points to keep in mind when receiving telephone calls.

12. How does active listening assist you in using the telephone?

13. Why is it important to end a telephone call properly?

14. List the major points to keep in mind when taking a message.

15. How do you best prepare for a call you are making?

16. What hints do you suggest for locating telephone numbers?

17. Distinguish between person-to-person calls, collect calls, and direct dialing calls.

18. How do you create a positive tone in servicing a caller?

19. Explain the concept of voice messaging.

20. List the telephone equipment and accessories currently available.

21. What is teleconferencing? When would it be advisable? What are the advantages and disadvantages of teleconferencing?

SKILLBUILDING ACTIVITIES

1. Assume that both you and the people you need to call work from 9 A.M. to 5 P.M. During what hours could you place calls from your office to offices in the following places? Check the phone book and library references for time zone information.

New York	Mexico City	Minneapolis
Dallas	Anchorage	Singapore
San Francisco	Rome	Harrisburg
	Melbourne	Salt Lake City

2. Call several hotels or other large conference centers that might have teleconferencing facilities. Obtain specific information about the teleconferencing facilities. Write a report on this information, and present it to your class.

3. Rose Sanchez is a secretary to sales manager James McFarland, and it is part of her regular duties to place and take telephone calls for him. How should she handle the following situations?
   a. Mr. McFarland is attending a sales meeting at a branch office, and he receives an urgent long-distance telephone call from his boss, who is calling from an airport payphone while waiting between planes.
   b. While she is attempting to transfer a call to Mr. McFarland, Ms. Sanchez accidentally hangs up on an important caller.

    c. Mr. McFarland asks Ms. Sanchez to discover which employees in his department have been making personal long-distance calls on the office telephone system.

4. Obtain a telephone directory for your area. Locate the following information while being timed:
   a. The local area code.
   b. The telephone number of the local police station.
   c. The telephone number of a temporary employment agency in your area.
   d. The telephone number of the local customer service office of your telephone company.

   Review this information after time is called. Discuss ways in which you can use your telephone directory more efficiently.

5. Make a list of most-used telephone numbers. How would you organize these numbers for easy retrieval? Present a report to your class on suggested procedures.

CHAPTER 15

PROCESSING FINANCIAL AND LEGAL INFORMATION

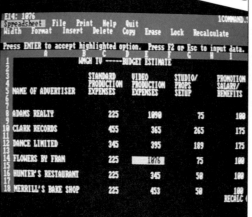

As an office worker, you can expect to perform some tasks that are part of the financial and legal functions of the company. These tasks might include sending and receiving bills, paying for materials and supplies, banking, keeping accounting or payroll records, and processing contracts. If you are working in a small company, you might be responsible for processing the entire company payroll each week. In a large firm, your supervisor might require you to maintain time sheets and attendance records of the employees in your department and give that information to the payroll department.

This chapter will introduce you to many of the financial and legal facts and procedures you can expect to perform in today's electronic office.

After studying this chapter, you will be able to:

- Recognize and understand the importance of processing the commonly-used financial and legal records including banking procedures, credit transactions, payroll, budgeting, contracts, and real estate documents.
- Prepare financial and legal documents properly.
- Understand the major differences among a sole proprietorship, a partnership, and a corporation.

GENERAL ACCOUNTING

Managers must know how much money a business has, how many goods or services it has sold over a specified period of time, and how much money the business owes to its suppliers.

Accounting is a way to gather financial data and process it into information that managers can use to analyze their company's financial situation and make decisions. In a large company, accounting is usually done by a special department. Many small companies pay outside accounting firms to do their accounting, but office workers perform many day-to-day accounting tasks. If you were working in a small company, for example, you might be asked to keep the **accounts receivable** records, which list money owed *to* the company by customers. **Accounts payable** records list money owed *by* the company to suppliers and creditors.

THE THREE MAJOR TYPES OF BUSINESSES

The three major types of businesses are the sole proprietorship, the partnership, and the corporation. These three different types of businesses process their financial information in different ways.

Sole Proprietorship. A **sole proprietorship** is owned by one person. The owner is legally responsible for the business's debts. For tax accounting purposes, the owner's personal income is combined with the income of the business. But for business accounting purposes, only the company's financial transactions are computed. This procedure allows the owner to obtain a true measure of the company's performance.

Partnership. A **partnership** is owned by two or more people. The partners enter into a contract that spells out each partner's contributions, duties, and share of the profits. Each partner shares the responsibility for the firm's debts and taxes. The business accounting process keeps the firm's financial transactions separate from the personal finances of the partners.

Corporation. A **corporation** is privately owned by a limited group of individuals or publicly owned by hundreds or even thousands of people who have bought stock in it. Each share of stock is a unit of ownership and represents one vote on major decisions about operating the company.

A corporation generally lasts longer than the two other kinds of businesses. A sole proprietorship may last only as long as the life of its owner. And a partnership may last only as long as the life spans of its partners. A corporation can go on indefinitely. The owners, or **stockholders,** of a corporation are not personally responsible for its debts and taxes, and they can lose only the amount of money they have invested in their shares. In contrast, sole proprietors and partners can be held responsible for all of their business's debts. For accounting purposes, the corporation's financial transactions are also accounted for separately from the owners' transactions.

CCOUNTING AND INFORMATION PROCESSING

Accounting is a form of data processing. Accounting procedures generally follow the information processing cycle. When accountants input data, the first thing they do is gather all the necessary **source documents,** which are the original documents that serve as records of business transactions. Source documents might be purchase orders, bills, checkbook stubs, invoices, credit agreements, and other similar records. Accountants also gather any other financial records that have been kept during an accounting period. These records may be concerned with accounts receivable, accounts payable, the payroll, taxes, facilities and equipment inventories, and credit.

Next the data is processed. For example, an accountant can total all of a company's weekly payroll expenditures to find out how much it is spending on employees' salaries and benefits in a month or a year. Similarly, a sales manager can break down yearly sales figures by month to determine when the sales force sells the most or the least. This information can be used to plan advertising and sales campaigns.

In accounting, processing data often involves transferring the data from the source documents to journals and ledgers where items can be grouped in a logical order and manipulated mathematically.

Once the data is processed and stored, it can be generated as output in the form of financial statements. Financial statements usually consist of an income statement, which shows the company's net income or loss for the accounting period, and a **balance sheet,** which shows the company's total assets and liabilities. (See Fig. 15-1.) This document is called a balance sheet because the total of a company's assets always equals (balances) the total of its liabilities and owner's equity or net worth. **Owner's equity** is the owner's financial interest in the company.

These accounting records can be stored manually or electronically and can be output and distributed manually or electronically.

```
                        JULIA'S BOUTIQUE
                         Balance Sheet
                       December 31, 19--
                     (in thousands of dollars)


                             ASSETS

        Current Assets
          Cash                              $100
          Accounts Receivable               175
          Inventory                         250
          Prepaid Expenses                   25
               Total Current Assets              $  550

        Fixed Assets
          Land                             $150
          Building                          300
          Furniture                         100
               Total Fixed Assets                   550
               Total Assets                      $1,100

                 LIABILITIES AND OWNER'S EQUITY

        Current Liabilities
          Accounts Payable                 $160
          Taxes Payable                      25
          Other Accrued Expenses             75
               Total Current Liabilities         $  260

        Long-Term Liabilities
          Notes Payable                          350
               Total Liabilities                 $  610

        Owner's Equity
          Julia Bond, Capital              $400
          Net Income                         90
               Total Owner's Equity                 490
               Total Liabilities and Owner's Equity  $1,100
```

Fig. 15-1 Accounting produces financial records, such as this balance sheet, that help companies analyze their financial situation.

Accounting Terms

These are some of the terms you will need to know when you work with financial information:

Account. A grouping of similar transactions, such as accounts payable or payroll.

Account balance. The difference between the total debits and the total credits in an account.

Accounting period. The period of time covered by the analysis of a company's financial records, usually a quarter (three months) or a year.

Assets. Money and other items of value owned by the company.

Balance sheet. A financial statement that sums up a business's assets, liabilities, and owner's equity.

Credit. An amount that is entered on the right side of an account.

Debit. An amount that is entered on the left side of an account.

Journal. A record in which each business transaction is listed in chronological order.

Journalizing. Maintaining the journal or making entries in the journal.

Ledger. A record of each business transaction organized according to account.

Liability. A debt or obligation owed by a company to a creditor.

Owner's equity. The owner's financial interest in the business.

Posting. The process of transferring data from a journal to a ledger.

ACCOUNTING PROCEDURES

One accounting task that you may be asked to perform is to maintain a journal, most likely a general journal. A **general journal** is a list in chronological order of each business transaction that a firm is involved in. (See Fig. 15-2). Each entry in the journal shows the date, the names of the accounts that must be debited and credited to record the transaction, a brief description of the transaction, and the amount of the transaction.

Fig. 15-2 Journal entries are made chronologically as each transaction occurs.

	GENERAL JOURNAL			Page 2	
DATE	ACCOUNT TITLE AND EXPLANATION	POST. REF.	DEBIT	CREDIT	
19— May 30	Cash	101	3000 00		
	Accounts Receivable	102		3000	00

An **account** is a grouping of similar transactions. Accounts can be assets (showing items of value owned by the business) such as cash, equipment, and accounts receivable, or they can be liabilities (showing debts owed by the business) such as accounts payable and loans payable.

You may also be asked to keep a **general ledger,** which is a record of all the business transactions, grouped according to account. (See Fig. 15-3). Each account is recorded on a separate page of the ledger. You would use the journal as a guide to list each item in its appropriate account in the ledger. Transferring items from the journal or a source document to the ledger is known as **posting.** Usually, each item is posted in the ledger as a debit in one account and as a credit in another. The general

Cash		GENERAL LEDGER			Account No.	101	
					BALANCE		
DATE	EXPLANATION	POST. REF.	DEBIT	CREDIT	DEBIT	CREDIT	
19— May 30		J2	3000 00		3000 00		

Fig. 15-3   Ledger entries are listed according to categories called accounts.

ledger is, in effect, a master file of every business transaction, classified by account.

Another accounting procedure that you may be asked to perform involves adding and subtracting transactions. For example, you might be asked to total each day's receipts. Or you may be asked to keep a running total of the balance in each account. You can use a computer and a calculator to perform many of these tasks, the accuracy of computer or calculator output depends on the accuracy of your input.

Fig. 15-4 Computer software, like this ledger program, makes it easy for small businesses to do their own accounting.

```
                                         Copy Machines                           040488
                                         GENERAL LEDGER                           Page 1
                                           04-04-88

      Entry Date Description              Document J1    Debits    Credits    Balance

      (8828).    )                        PETTY CASH
             010186 BALANCE FORWARD                                          -1000.00
      98     122787 dep                   001       A    1000.00
                                                         _____  _____  _____
             TOTAL PETTY CASH                            1000.00      0.00     $0.00


      (0188.     )                        Petty Cash
             010187 BALANCE FORWARD                                           100.00
      38     010287 petty cash replenish 89173     D       75.00
      69     012587 Legal Pads            v275      D                 13.75
      81     122688 supplies.             ck 100    C      100.00


                    Press 'RETURN' to Continue       'S' to Stop: _
```

PROCEDURES

Some electronic calculators simply add, subtract, multiply, and divide figures. Others can perform many other functions as well. The following review of standard and optional features may help you select a calculator that meets your needs.

Keypad. Calculators have a key for each digit, a decimal key, and keys for adding, subtracting, multiplying, dividing, and clearing entries.

Floating decimal point. With this feature, a decimal point appears automatically whenever you use the calculator.

Memory. Many electronic calculators have an internal memory, allowing you to clear a figure you have just entered without erasing all the other figures you have input. Internal memory also lets you switch from one function without having to rekey your input.

Display. Calculators are available with several types and sizes of displays.

Printer. Some calculators can print output on a paper tape as well as display it electronically.

Programmability. Some calculators can be programmed, like computers, for specific applications.

A good quality calculator can help you perform many financial tasks.

ANKING PROCEDURES

Some banking tasks you might be asked to do include making deposits and payments, reconciling account balances, transferring funds, and other basic banking functions.

AKING DEPOSITS

If you work in an office that receives payments from customers, you may be responsible for depositing these payments in your company's checking account. You will need to sign signature cards for the bank to keep on file so that the tellers can compare your signature with the one that appears on the checks and forms. The bank will also need written authorization from your employer to honor your signature.

Filling Out Deposit Slips. To make a deposit, you need to fill out a deposit slip. First you fill in the date and the amount of money you are depositing. You will be required to list the deposit as checks and cash. Checks will be listed individually on the deposit slip. (See Fig. 15-5.)

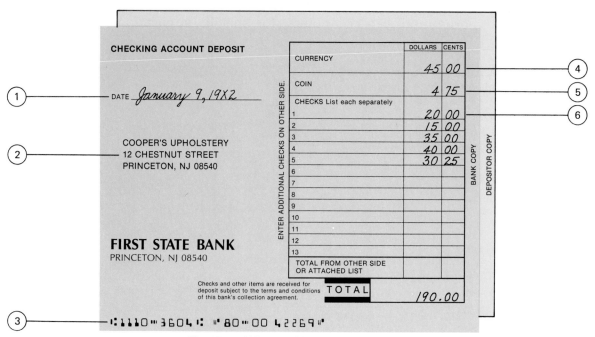

Fig. 15-5 When making out a deposit slip, you must fill in the date (1), the account name and number if they are not preprinted on the slip (2 and 3), the amount of currency (4), and coins (5), and the amount of each check (6).

Depositing Currency and Coins. If you frequently deposit currency and coins, obtain a supply of coin rolls and bill wrappers from the bank. Before you wrap the coins and bills, mark the wrappers with your employer's name and account number to assist the bank in processing.

Depositing Checks. Before you deposit any checks, make sure that the date, the amount, and the signature are correct. Otherwise, the bank may return the check uncashed and charge your company a handling fee.

Endorsing Checks. Each check that you deposit must be endorsed, or signed on the back, by the **payee.** The payee is the person or organization to whom the check is written. Endorsement is a legal procedure that transfers ownership of the check from the payee to the bank so that the bank can collect payment from the **drawer.** The drawer is the person on whose account the check is drawn. There are several different types of endorsements you can use. (See Fig. 15-6).

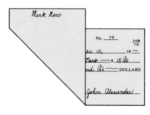

Blank Endorsement

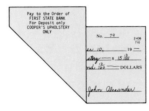

Restrictive Endorsement

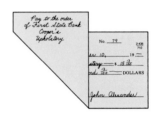

Full Endorsement

Fig. 15-6　The check at the left was a blank endorsement, the check at the center shows a restrictive endorsement, and the check at the right shows a full endorsement.

A check with a **blank endorsement,** consisting only of the payee's signature, can be cashed by anyone. Do not put a blank endorsement on a check unless you are depositing it immediately. Never send checks with blank endorsements through the mail. A **restrictive endorsement** sets conditions such as "for deposit only" to a specific account. A **special endorsement,** or **full endorsement,** is used to transfer ownership of a check from one payee to a second. A **corrected endorsement** is used to reconcile signatures if the payee's name on the front of the check does not match the name on the payee's checking account. To correct an endorsement, the payee first endorses the check with the name that appears on the front of the check; then the payee signs it again, using the name that appears on his or her account.

Using Automatic Teller Machines. Automatic tellers are machines that let you deposit and withdraw funds by using a special access card and identification code. An ATM (automatic teller machine) is similar to a computer terminal. A special keypad lets you instruct the machine about the types of transactions you require and the amounts. A display screen then tells you how to proceed with a transaction. There are some precautions you should take when using an ATM.

Use an ATM for depositing only checks with restrictive or special endorsements that assign them to the bank. Never use an ATM to deposit cash or other items that can be used by unauthorized people. Although the ATM will give you a receipt, it cannot give you a copy of your deposit slip. Without a copy of your deposit slip, you cannot prove that you deposited a specific check. Notify the bank immediately of any discrepancies between its records of your ATM transactions and your employer's records.

Banking by Mail. Mailed deposits should include only checks with restrictive or special endorsements. Never send currency through the mail unless you use registered mail.

 AKING PAYMENTS

Businesses generally use checks rather than cash to make payments. In large companies, these checks are handled by the accounting or payroll department. If you work in a small office, it may be your responsibility to prepare checks, keep records, and order new checks as needed.

Banks issue books of checks with **stubs** or **check registers** in which you record the number, date, and amount of each check as well as the payee's name and the reason for payment. Some registers are electronic. If you use an electronic register, you input this information into the computer. You also subtract the amount of a check from the checking account's **balance,** or the funds contained in the account, and write in the new balance. If a deposit has been made, you enter the date and the amount, and then you add that amount to the account balance.

The signature on a check authorizes a bank to remove money from one account and give it to someone else. The check indicates how much is to be transferred and to whom the money should be paid. This information can be prepared manually or electronically.

Other Types of Checks. Most payments processed by office workers are in the form of checks drawn against

Guidelines for Writing Checks

1. Date each check and stub. Number checks and stubs consecutively if they do not already have numbers printed on them.

2. Give the payee's full name, and make sure that it is correctly spelled and legible. Omit courtesy titles, such as *Ms.* and *Mr.*

3. Begin the amount close to the dollar sign on the check, and use bold, clear figures. If you are writing, write the figures close together so that no one can insert new figures between the ones you have written.

4. On the next line write or type the amount of the check in words.

Express cents as fractions of 100; that is, *38 cents* would be *38/100.* Use hyphens, periods, or a line to fill any blank space on the line.

5. Indicate the purpose of the check in a corner of the check. Some checks include a "memo" line for this purpose.

6. If you make a mistake on a check, write the word *void* in large letters on the check and on its stub. Do not try to correct a mistake on a check by erasing or crossing out what you have written. Save any checks that you void, and file them in numerical order with those that are cashed by the bank and returned to you.

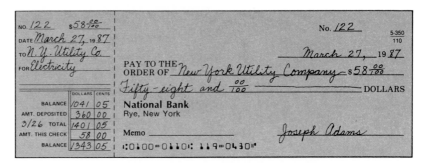

Fig. 15-7   Here is how a properly written check and check stub should appear. Always make out the check stub first so you do not forget what the check was for.

company checking accounts, but companies sometimes use other kinds of checks as well.

1. *Certified check.* A certified check is drawn against a company checking account and certified by a bank

teller. The teller immediately subtracts the amount of the check from the account. People use certified checks when the payee requires a guarantee that the check will be honored.

2. *Cashier's check.* Banks issue cashier's checks for the amount of the check. Banks charge a small fee for the check. As with certified checks, cashier's checks are guaranteed by the bank.

3. *Bank draft.* A bank draft is similar to a cashier's check except that a bank draft is drawn against one bank's account in another bank. Bank drafts are used to transfer large sums of money quickly between banks in distant cities.

4. *Money order.* Money orders are similar to cashier's checks, but they are usually issued for $250 or less. People who do not have checking accounts can buy money orders from a bank or post office.

Stop-Payment Requests. If a check that your company has issued is lost or stolen, or if it was written for the wrong amount, you may be able to stop payment on it. To request a stop-payment order, call the bank and give the checking account number, the name of the account holder, the amount, the date, the number of the check, the payee's name, and the reason you want to stop payment. If the bank has not cleared the check, a bank employee will process your stop-payment request. You must follow up your oral request either by sending the bank a confirmation letter or by filling out and returning a form that the bank supplies. Most banks charge a fee for a stop-payment request.

ECONCILING AN ACCOUNT BALANCE

Each month banks send their customers statements of all activities involving their accounts. Typical activities recorded on a bank statement relate to deposits, withdrawals, checks that have cleared, interest paid to the account, and fees charged against the account. With these statements, banks generally return the last month's **canceled checks,** or checks that have been

NATIONAL BANK

JOSEPH ADAMS
12 MONEY ST.
RYE, NEW YORK 10580

Checking Account Number 119 0430	Statement Closing Date 02-22-87

Statement Savings Account Number	Page 1	Enclosures 6

1646

CHECKS 6 DEPOSITS 1

4
A

Checking Activity

Previous Balance	Total Deposits & Credits	Total Checks & Debits	New Balance	Available Credit
296.44 +	1,579.97 −	1,028.64 −	847.77	.00

TRANSACTION DESCRIPTION	AMOUNT	Date	Balance
OPENING BALANCE		01-21	269.44
		02-03	46.44
		02-11	3.56 OD
	1,579.97	02-15	1,276.41
		02-16	1,212.50
		02-17	1,182.77
		02-22	847.77

DATE	CHECKS		DATE	CHECKS
0908 02-03	250.00	0911	02-16	63.91
0909 02-11	50.00	0912	02-17	29.73
0910 02-22	335.00	0913	02-15	300.00

Outstanding Checks and Debits

Number	Amount
0914	74.10
0915	17.00
0916	237.00

To Reconcile Your Statement and Checkbook

1. Add to your checkbook balance any loan advances or other credits appearing on the statement which you have not previously recorded.

2. Deduct from your checkbook balance any bank charges or other debits appearing on the statement which you have not previously recorded.

3. **If your checks are serialized,** examine the listing on the front of this statement and check off the items against the entries in your checkbook. An asterisk in the listing indicates a gap where one or more checks are not on this particular statement.

If your checks are not serialized, arrange them by date or number and check them off against the entries in your checkbook.

4. List any checks or debits issued by you and not shown on the statement, and any bank charges since the statement date, in the area provided at the right.

5. List last balance shown on statement — 847.77

+ Plus: Deposits and credits made after date of last entry on statement — 350.02

Subtotal — 1197.79

− Minus: Total of outstanding checks and debits — 328.10

= Balance: Which should agree with your checkbook — 869.69

Bank charges since statement closing date	0.00
Total	328.10

Fig. 15-8   A monthly bank statement shows all of the deposits, withdrawals, and service charges that have been made in each account during the month. Many banks also provide a convenient form on the back of the statement to reconcile the balance.

cleared against the account. If you keep your employer's checkbook, your duties may include reconciling the balance. To reconcile the balance, you must compare the balance reported on the bank statement with the balance recorded on the check stubs or in the check register and account for any difference between them. (See Fig. 15-8).

If you have an electronic banking system, you can use the computer to reconcile the balance. If you do not bank

Reconciling the Bank Balance

1. Arrange the canceled checks according to the check numbers.

2. Compare the amounts of the checks with the amounts listed for them on the bank statement.

3. Compare the checks with the checkbook stubs or check register, and place check marks on the stubs or in the register to indicate that the checks have cleared. On the reconciliation form, list the numbers and the amounts of any checks still outstanding, and add their amounts.

4. Compare the deposit amounts shown on the check stubs or in the check register with those listed on the statement. List any deposits not reported on the statement, and add the amounts.

5. Add the total of unlisted deposits to the balance shown on the bank statement, and subtract the total of outstanding checks. The resulting figure is called the adjusted bank balance.

6. Examine the statement for service charges or interest payments. Subtract the service charges from the balance recorded in your checkbook, and add the interest payments.

7. The resulting figure should equal the adjusted bank balance.

electronically, you might be able to use your computer terminal to reconcile the balance by using a special software program.

Reconciliation Follow-Up. After you reconcile the balance each month, you should file the bank statement, reconciliation sheet, and canceled checks. Canceled checks have legal importance as proof of payment.

You should also trace what happened to any of one month's outstanding checks that have still not cleared when the next month's bank statement arrives. If a check has not cleared, the payee may not have received it, or it may have been lost. Call or write to the payee to find out. If the check has been lost, request a stop-payment order, and issue a replacement check.

Finally, if you are also responsible for maintaining the general journal, you should make the same corrections in the journal that you have made in the checkbook, if necessary.

HANDLING DISHONORED CHECKS

Sometimes you may deposit a check that the bank cannot collect on, either because the check was altered, misdated, or made out incorrectly or because there were not sufficient funds in the drawer's account to cover the check. When a check cannot be paid, it is called a **dishonored check.** The bank will return the check to the depositor and subtract the amount of the check from the depositor's account. Some banks will also charge the depositor a fee for handling the check. If the bank dishonors a check made out to your company, you will have to notify the drawer. The drawer may then deposit additional funds in his or her account and either issue a new check or instruct you to redeposit the dishonored check.

RECORDING ELECTRONIC FUNDS TRANSFER

Businesses and banks have developed the means to transfer funds electronically from one account to an-

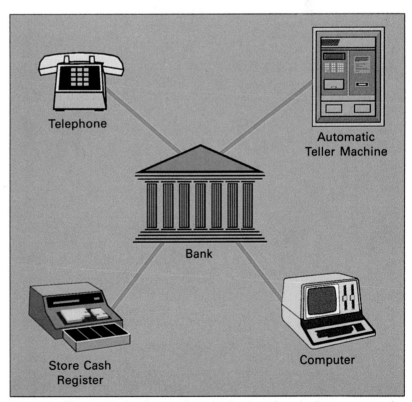

Fig. 15-9   Electronic funds transfers can be done by telephone, automatic teller machines, computer, and by point-of-sale transactions.

other. The automatic teller machine is one electronic means of transferring funds. Other forms of electronic funds transfer (EFT) include direct deposit, telephone transfers, and point-of-sale transfers. (See Fig. 15-9).

Direct Deposit. Some businesses use direct deposit transfers to deposit paychecks directly into their employees' accounts. The company authorizes the bank to take the required amount out of its account and transfer it to the creditor's account.

Telephone Transfers. Customers of investment funds and stock brokerages routinely use telephone transfers to switch their investments from one fund or stock to another. Certain bills can also be paid in this way.

Computer Transfers. If you use a computer terminal and modem to bank electronically, you can also keyboard instructions to transfer funds from the company account to pay bills.

Point-of-Sale Transfers. Point-of-sale transfers means that customers use bank identification cards instead of credit cards or checks to pay for goods and services. The store clerk inserts the card into the store's computer and links up with the bank's computer, which immediately transfers the amount of the sale from the customer's account to the store's account.

REDIT TRANSACTIONS

Companies often have to borrow money, or obtain credit, in order to purchase expensive goods or raw materials or to pay bills while they wait for payments from customers. They can obtain that credit from banks, finance companies, retail stores, and credit card companies.

REDIT AGREEMENTS

Before a business extends credit to a customer, it usually checks the customer's credit rating to ensure that the customer will be able to pay the debt. Once the loan application is approved, the borrower (the customer) and the lender must agree on the credit terms and repayment schedules. Credit terms establish the amount that the borrower is seeking, the interest that the lender will charge, and the penalties that the borrower will incur if the credit terms are violated. The interest rate is a percentage of the loan, and it represents the charge that the lender is making for lending money. Repayment schedules specify how the borrower will repay the loan. One common business arrangement is for a company to ship merchandise or raw materials to a customer with the understanding that the customer will pay for the goods in full within 30 days. Another common arrangement is for the borrower to repay the loan in **installments.** For example, many stores, finance companies, and credit card companies collect payments from customers in monthly installments. The borrower, in most cases, has to pay a **finance charge,** an amount based on a specific percentage of the unpaid balance.

CREDIT CARDS

One form of credit is the credit card. Credit card companies, such as American Express and Visa, issue cards to businesses. When an employee uses a company credit card—at a restaurant, for example—the credit card company pays the restaurant and then bills the employee's company for payment and for interest charges.

If your supervisor uses a credit card for business, it may be part of your job to maintain credit card records. For example, you may have to keep receipts, check credit statements, and fill out expense vouchers. You may also have to keep a record of credit card numbers in case the credit cards are lost or stolen.

Credit card companies provide credit card statements that show when and where each purchase was made during the billing period, the total amount of outstanding charges, and the amount of interest owing on the account. If you are responsible for maintaining credit card records for your supervisor, you will need to keep copies of all the receipts of expenditures to compare with the monthly statement. If your supervisor cannot account for an expenditure on the statement and you do not have a receipt for it, you may have to contact the credit card company to find out whether an error in billing was made.

*B*UDGETING

A **budget** is a company's financial plan of operations for a given period of time, usually a year. A budget outlines in detail the expected income and expenditures for each division and department. Each then has its own separate budget that governs only its operations. A department manager's budget (see Fig. 15-10) will describe that department's expected expenditures for salaries, supplies, furniture, and so on.

EXPENSE	JAN.	FEB.	MARCH	TOTAL
SALARIES	6,300	6,300	6,300	18,900
EMPLOYEE FRINGE BENEFITS	1,660	1,660	1,660	4,980
TRAVEL & ENTERTAINMENT	600	600	600	1,800
PHOTOCOPYING CHARGES	100	100	100	300
LEGAL FEES	0	0	500	500
TELEPHONE & TELEGRAPH	125	125	125	375
MAILING EXPENSES	100	100	100	300
STATIONERY & SUPPLIES	300	50	50	400
MAGAZINES & BOOKS	100	100	100	300
FURNITURE & EQUIPMENT	200	600	200	1,000
MAINTENANCE & REPAIR	50	50	50	150

DEPARTMENT BUDGET
JANUARY–MARCH 19__

Fig. 15-10   Budgets help managers see at a glance how much money will be received or spent in each area during the budget year.

A budget sets the company's financial goals, which keep its expenditures in line with its revenues in order to achieve an acceptable level of profit. Company executives and department managers are responsible for making sure that expenditures do not exceed the budgeted amount or for making cuts, if necessary, to achieve the company's financial goals.

PREPARING A BUDGET

When company managers prepare a budget, they include all the available information about both income and expenses under separate headings, such as "Raw Materials," "Revenues," and "Labor Costs." Under each heading they list all the line items for that heading. A **line item** is a category of expenditure, or income (similar to an account) that is given a separate line in a budget. Examples of line items are salaries, fringe benefits, supplies, equipment, office space, and postage.

Budgets are very flexible. The two most common types of budgets are the operating budget and the capital expense budget. The **operating budget** spells out the expected income and costs of the day-to-day operations of a company. The **capital expense budget** shows long-range expenditures for such items as new facilities, equipment replacement, land purchases, and mortgages. Another type of budget is a **project budget.** A film studio might use this kind of budget to plan the expenses for the production and promotion of each film project.

Many companies now use electronic spreadsheet software to develop their budgets so that they can plan more thoroughly and in less time than with paper and pencil methods. Another good reason to use electronic spreadsheets for preparing budgets is that they enable planners to see how a change in one calculation affects all the related calculations. For example, assume that a budget planner anticipates that the company will spend more for fuel oil in January and February of next year than it spent in the same months of this year. When the January and February fuel oil figures are changed on the spreadsheet, the computer automatically recalculates the fuel oil total for the entire year so that the planner can tell at once how much to budget for fuel oil for the year.

Graphics, database, and word processing software can also help you perform many budgeting tasks. You can use software to develop charts that show how much of the budget is devoted to each income or expense category; to keep a running tally of expense data that you can store, retrieve, and sort in various ways; and to prepare reports that explain how your department is meeting its budgetary goals.

PETTY CASH

Most offices keep **petty cash,** which is a small cash fund used to pay for small day-to-day expenses that cannot conveniently be paid for by check or credit card. It is not a good business procedure to keep large amounts of cash in the office. You should be sure to lock up even small amounts of petty cash each night in a cash box stored in an office vault or safe.

RECORDING WITHDRAWALS

You will need to keep a record of each withdrawal from the petty cash fund. The best way to do this is to use a petty cash voucher: a preprinted form with blanks for the date, amount, and purpose of the withdrawal; the name of the payee; and the signature of the person who is making the withdrawal. Figure 15-11 shows how to fill in a petty cash voucher.

No. _28_   Amount $ _12.30_

PETTY CASH VOUCHER

Paid to _Fleet Equipment Co._

For _Index cards_

Charge to _Office Supplies_

Approved by   **Received by**

Susan Berman   _Mark Schaeffer_

Fig. 15-11   Office workers who are entrusted with the petty cash fund use vouchers such as this one to keep track of expenditures.

REPLENISHING THE PETTY CASH FUND

A petty cash fund should have a fixed amount of money. The total of the cash in the fund and the withdrawals noted on vouchers should equal the fixed amount.

PAYROLL PROCEDURES

One other financial area where you may have certain responsibilities is that of processing and distributing the payroll. A large company will probably have its own payroll department, and you may be responsible only for providing the department with weekly time sheets and for distributing paychecks to the employees in your department. In some small businesses, you may even have to process the payroll by hand.

 ## MAKING PAYROLL DEDUCTIONS

Every pay period your employer should provide you and each of your coworkers with a pay statement detailing your **gross pay** (the amount of pay before any deductions are made), the amount of and reason for each deduction, and the **net pay** (the amount remaining after the deductions have been made). (See Fig. 15-12.)

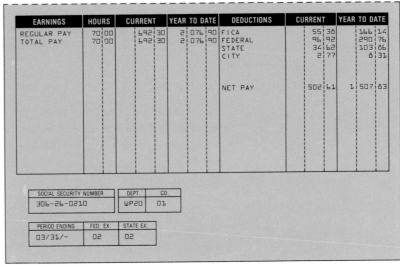

EARNINGS	HOURS	CURRENT	YEAR TO DATE	DEDUCTIONS	CURRENT	YEAR TO DATE
REGULAR PAY	70 00	692 30	2 076 90	FICA	55 38	166 14
TOTAL PAY	70 00	692 30	2 076 90	FEDERAL	96 92	290 76
				STATE	34 62	103 86
				CITY	2 77	8 31
				NET PAY	502 61	1 507 63

SOCIAL SECURITY NUMBER	DEPT.	CO.
306-26-0210	WP20	01

PERIOD ENDING	FED. EX.	STATE EX.
03/31/–	02	02

Fig. 15-12   This corporate pay statement shows gross pay, net pay, and deductions. FICA stands for Federal Insurance Contributions Act, and that deduction is the social security payment.

Your employer is required to withhold a percentage of your gross pay as advance payment on your annual federal income taxes. In some states employers may be required to withhold state and local income taxes as well. The Internal Revenue Service provides employers with tables for calculating the amount to be withheld for federal income taxes.

Your employer is also required to withhold federal social security tax and, in some states, state unemployment insurance tax. You may authorize your employer to withhold voluntary contributions to a pension plan, contributions to charities such as the United Way, contributions to a payroll savings plan, and monthly union dues.

EEPING PAYROLL RECORDS

In order for the payroll staff to process each week's payroll, it has to maintain certain permanent information on each employee, such as the employee's name, salary or hourly wage, and social security number.

When employees are paid by the hour, they usually either punch in and out on a time clock or fill out time cards to indicate how many hours they worked during the pay period. Most hourly employees are covered by the federal Fair Labor Standards Act, which sets a minimum wage and requires employers to pay one-and-a-half times the regular wage for time worked beyond 40 hours a week.

ROCESSING THE PAYROLL

Businesses usually select one day each week or every two weeks as payday. If your company has its own payroll department, the payroll department computer will perform all the processing, and your only duty may be to distribute paychecks to your coworkers.

If it is one of your duties to process your company's payroll by computer yourself, you need to key in the hours of work for each hourly employee. Add any changes in the payroll records since the last pay period. The payroll accounting software you use will have the formulas for computing income tax, social security deductions, and so on. It will calculate wages, deductions, and net pay; store all this information for tax and accounting purposes; and print each check and stub automatically.

If you work in a very small office where you are required to process the payroll manually, you will need to keep a **payroll register,** which lists each employee by name, his or her number of exemptions, regular and overtime pay for the pay period, and each deduction in separate columns. To compute deductions, you will have to use withholding tables provided by the Internal Revenue Service, the Social Security Administration, and the state and local taxing authorities. Once you have computed each employee's gross pay, deductions, and net pay, you must total each column to find your employer's total costs and the amount of taxes to be sent to each taxing agency. Then you must fill out and distribute checks and pay statements for each employee.

You may recall that some businesses use direct deposit transfers to transfer each employee's pay from the company's bank account to the employee's account. In this case the employees still receive pay statements showing their gross and net pay and the amount of their deductions so that they can maintain their personal records.

LEGAL PROCEDURES

Businesses are governed by hundreds of federal, state, and local laws that determine their legal rights and responsibilities. To comply with these laws, businesses often need to process various kinds of legal documents. For example, if your company purchases a factory, you might file a copy of the deed and mortgage with the county recorder in the county where the factory is located.

Businesses also use many legal documents, such as sales and credit agreements and contracts, to carry out routine financial transactions. These documents spell out the terms of a transaction and protect the company if the terms are violated. In addition, businesses occasionally sue or are sued to resolve a debt or disagreement or for any number of other reasons. Such litigation always involves the preparation of a number of legal documents.

If you are a member of a support staff, your main responsibility in most legal matters will be to prepare legal documents.

LEGAL DOCUMENTS

Your job responsibilities may include inputting legal documents, processing legal documents, or having these documents notarized. There are several types of commonly used legal documents that you may be asked to prepare.

Contracts and Agreements. The most common kinds of legal documents used in the business world, contracts and agreements, are legally enforceable understandings or arrangements between two or more parties. They are used most often to state a company's intention to buy or sell specific goods or services and to set the terms of the sale.

Affidavits. Affidavits are sworn, written statements of fact. When a person makes an affidavit, he or she swears under oath that the facts contained in the affidavit are true.

Power of Attorney. A **power of attorney** is a legal authorization for one person to act in the place of another.

Real Estate Documents. When a company purchases a piece of land or a building, it usually has to process several legal documents. The buyer and seller have to draw up a contract of sale that gives the sales price, the down payment, and other terms of the sale and that describes the property being purchased. The buyer will also have to enter into a mortgage agreement. This is an agreement between the buyer and a bank describing how the property will be paid for. The buyer will receive a copy of the title, which affirms ownership of the property. The buyer has to file copies of the title and mortgage with the county recorder. Another kind of real estate document is a lease, which is an agreement between the owner of a building and the lessee. The lease gives the lessee the right to occupy the building for a specific period of time in exchange for a stated rental fee. Figure 15-13 shows a form for a real estate transaction with blank spaces for the variable information.

Litigation Documents. Lawsuits usually involve the preparation and filing of several different kinds of legal documents. These documents are often complex and

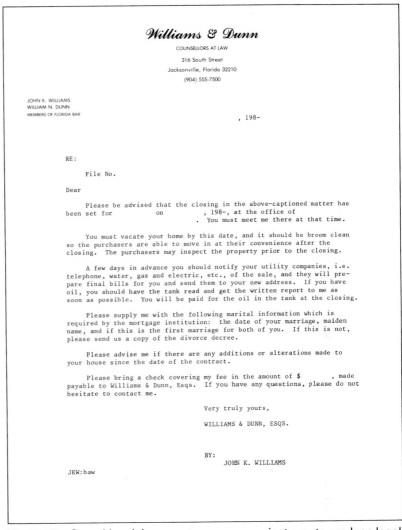

Fig. 15-13 Stored legal documents are a convenient way to produce legal documents when the same legal language can be used again and again.

usually require the preparation of one or more drafts. You are not likely to be responsible for preparing litigation documents unless you are employed in a corporate legal department or by a law firm.

Some of the more common litigation documents include complaints and answers—that is, the actual filing of a lawsuit by the person who brings a complaint, or the *plaintiff,* and the written response to the lawsuit by the object of the complaint, or the *defendant.* Either side

When you process legal documents, you must observe several basic formatting rules. Traditionally, legal-size paper ($8\frac{1}{2}$ by 13 or 14 inches) is used, but sometimes letter-size paper ($8\frac{1}{2}$ by 11 inches) may be used. Here are some other rules you should observe when processing legal documents.

1. Use a 10-pitch typeface if you can regulate type fonts on your word processor or typewriter. Never use italic or script.

2. Always format legal documents with double spacing. If you are using paper with preprinted margins, leave one or two spaces blank on each side within the margins. If you are using blank paper, leave a $1\frac{1}{2}$-inch margin on the left and at least a $\frac{1}{2}$-inch margin on the right. Use a 2-inch margin at the top of each page and a 1-inch margin at the bottom.

3. Indent the first line of each paragraph ten spaces, and number each paragraph with a roman numeral and a period followed by two blank spaces.

4. Set off quoted material by indenting the material five to ten spaces from the left margin. This material can be single-spaced.

5. Center page numbers at the bottom of each page. Also number and date each draft, and label the drafts "First Draft," "Second Draft," and so on.

6. Spell-out single-digit days of the month and the year (for example, *the third day of August, nineteen hundred and eighty-five*); you can use figures for double-digit days of the months and the year (*the 23d day of September, 1985*).

7. In general, use both figures and words for numbers—for example, *Ten thousand dollars ($10,000),* or *Twenty (20) acres of land.*

8. Insert signature lines for all the parties to a legal document at the end of the document. Never place signature lines by themselves on a separate sheet of paper. Always include two or more lines of text on the same page. You may type either the name of each signer under the line or the designation of each signer, such as *Buyer, Seller, Lessor,* or *Lessee.* If the parties are companies, you may also include the names of the persons who are representing the companies, as well as their titles, such as *President, Vice President,* or *Sales Representative.*

may also make a number of motions to the court, which ask that the suit be dismissed, or that other parties be added, or that the judge make an immediate judgment, and so on. In addition, both sides are likely to file notices stating the time and place of a trial or pretrial conference, announcing the withdrawal of an attorney, and the like. The judge may issue a *court order,* which is a formal instruction to one side or the other to either do or stop doing a specific action. Finally, a witness may receive a *subpoena,* which is an order to appear at a trial or hearing in order to testify.

OW TO PROCESS LEGAL DOCUMENTS

Most companies have their own legal forms. Each contains the same standard legal language. Only the specific details differ from one transaction to another. Printed legal forms are available for mortgages, deeds, real estate sales contracts, and office leases.

Photocopies of legal documents are usually not acceptable. Each copy must be an original duplicate, so you must decide on the number of copies you need. You may not erase errors or use correction fluid or tape to correct or block portions of a legal document. You can type hyphens or draw lines through words and sentences to strike them out so long as the deleted words remain legible.

If the material that you must type in is short and the space allotted for it is long, draw a z in ink to fill up the unused space. You can also use a z to cross out paragraphs or blocks of preprinted legal language that do not apply to the transaction you are recording. If the space is short and the material you are adding is long, you can type it on a separate sheet of paper called a **rider.** Cut off any unused portion of the paper, and paste the rider onto the appropriate space on the form. Then fold the rider to fit neatly into the form.

OTARY PUBLICS

Legal documents usually become valid when they are signed. A **notary public** is a person commissioned by a state government to verify signatures on documents for legal purposes. A notary witnesses the signing of documents and attests to the authenticity of the signatures. The notary then **notarizes** the documents by stamping and signing them. Property titles, assignments of mortgages, wills, deeds, partnership agreements, and affidavits are some of the kinds of documents that usually must be notarized.

If no one in your office is a notary, keep the names and addresses of several nearby notary publics on hand.

- Accounting is a way to gather financial data and process it into information that managers can use to evaluate their company's performance.

- There are three types of businesses—sole proprietorships, partnerships, and corporations.

- Accounting is a form of data processing; it follows the information processing cycle.

- Secretaries and administrative assistants may be asked to keep journals and ledgers to record business transactions.

- Banking tasks include depositing checks and currency and using automatic tellers or bank-by-mail services.

- Since an office worker may have to pay the company's bills, he or she must know how to write checks and how to reconcile a checking account balance.

- Electronic funds transfer is the transfer of funds from one bank account to another by means of direct deposit, the telephone, or point-of-sale transfer.

- When companies borrow or lend money, they make credit agreements that describe the interest rates and repayment schedules.

- A budget is a company's financial plan. It helps the company measure its performance to see if it is meeting its goals.

- Administrative support personnel often help prepare and monitor departmental budgets.

- Petty cash funds are used to pay for small expenses that cannot conveniently be paid for by check or credit card.

- Payrolls can be processed by computer or by hand. A payroll check usually includes a statement of the employee's gross pay, deductions, and net pay.

- Office workers who process payrolls by hand must know how to compute taxes and other deductions.

- Businesses deal with many legal documents, such as contracts, affidavits, and real estate documents.

- Office workers must follow several specific rules for processing legal documents and for filling out printed legal forms.

accounting
accounts receivable
accounts payable
sole proprietorship
partnership
corporation
stockholder
source document
balance sheet
owner's equity
general journal
account
general ledger
posting
payee
drawer
blank endorsement
restrictive endorsement
special endorsement
full endorsement
corrected endorsement
stub

check register
balance
canceled check
dishonored check
point-of-sale transfer
installment
finance charge
budget
line item
operating budget
capital expense budget
project budget
petty cash
gross pay
net pay
payroll register
power of attorney
law blank
rider
notary public
notarize

REVIEW QUESTIONS

1. What are the three kinds of businesses, and how do they differ?

2. Explain the difference between a journal and a ledger.

3. Describe two methods you can use to avoid making errors when using a calculator.

4. Describe how to fill out a deposit slip for various items of currency and checks.

5. Name and describe three different kinds of check endorsements.

6. Explain how to reconcile a checking account balance.

7. Define *certified check, cashier's check,* and *bank draft.* Explain how they differ from one another.

8. Explain how a point-of-sale transfer works.

9. Describe five different kinds of payroll deductions.

10. Name and define four types of legal documents.

S KILLBUILDING ACTIVITIES

1. Go to a stationery store and make a list of all the different types of legal forms that are available. Then using this book and other reference sources, find out what each document is used for. Write a brief description of each type of form, and explain its applications.

2. Make a list of some of the most common banking procedures. How many of these procedures do you use?

3. Roberta Jensen, the only secretary in a small real estate company, pays the company's bills and reconciles the checking account balance against the monthly bank statement. One month she discovers that the company checkbook shows a balance of $698, while the bank statement indicates that the balance should be $935. Ms. Jensen has checked and rechecked all the checks, stubs, outstanding checks, unlisted deposits, and service charges, but she cannot find the error. What should she do?

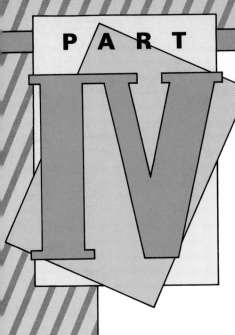

PART

IV

MANAGEMENT SKILLS FOR THE ELECTRONIC OFFICE

Computers take over the routine tasks, freeing workers to perform jobs that require more thought and planning. While providing more exciting job possibilities, the change puts a premium on being well organized and having efficient work habits.

Functions that were once purely managerial are now being handled by administrative support workers. The more familiar you are with managerial duties, the readier you will be to help perform them.

Part 4 will help you understand how a company operates and particularly how the work you do relates to the job and goals of your supervisor and managers.

Knowing how and why a company goes about automating its business office will give you the ability to use your talents more effectively. Part 4 examines the benefits companies derive from automation and looks at the complex issues involved.

Identifying careers in the electronic office, knowing what you need to acquire a job, and recognizing what you need to advance and succeed are covered in this last section.

MANAGING YOUR TIME AND WORK AREA

Learning to manage your time really means learning how to manage yourself and your actions in a positive manner. The saying "If it is to be, it is up to me" really applies to **time management.** Time management involves establishing priorities and then carrying out those priorities in the time provided. Managing your time is a skill that can be learned and improved upon with consistent effort.

Developing the skill of time management is equally important in the electronic office. Your work area must reflect control of time in carrying out your daily work. When you consistently practice efficient management of time and your work area, you are placing yourself in a good position for future promotions.

After studying this chapter, you will be able to:
- Determine where your time goes.
- Identify the major time-wasters and learn how to handle them.
- Learn how to make better use of your time by setting goals, prioritizing actions, and delegating.
- Organize your work area for more effective use and increased productivity.

HERE DOES YOUR TIME GO?

Have you ever asked yourself that question? Time waits for no one. It just keeps going on and on. At the end of the workday, you have either a feeling of great accomplishment or a feeling that little was accomplished. If you accomplished a great deal, why was that so? You had a plan of action and were motivated to carry out that plan. If you accomplished little during the workday, what went wrong? You wasted time? Yes, most people waste more time than they realize. Have you ever tried keeping a record of how your time is spent during the course of the day? Perhaps it would look similar to the illustration below. If completed faithfully and accurately over a period of time, a time log sheet will show you exactly how your hours are being spent. This information will then provide you with a foundation for improving the way you manage your time.

Where does your time go?

21 **Thursday July 1988**

| 7:00 |
| 7:30 |
| 8:00 |
| 8:30 |
| 9:00 |
| 9:30 |
| 10:00 |
| 10:30 |
| 11:00 |
| 11:30 |
| 12:00 |
| 1:00 |
| 1:30 |
| 2:00 |
| 2:30 |
| 3:00 |
| 3:30 |
| 4:00 |
| 4:30 |
| 5:00 |
| 5:30 |
| 6:00 |

Fig. 16-1   Time Log Sheets allow you to plan your time and establish work priorities.

TIMESAVING TIPS

1. Carry paper to jot down notes and ideas.

2. Focus on accomplishments instead of failures.

3. Evaluate long-term goals once a month to make adjustments.

4. Look through books quickly to search for ideas instead of reading an entire book.

5. Make time once a month to take care of small matters that have piled up.

6. Do not read junk mail. Throw it away.

7. Learn to say no.

8. Plan ahead.

9. Review your desk calendar frequently so that you are aware of upcoming events.

10. Use paper clips in different sizes and colors in books for easy reference.

11. When sorting mail, try to handle each piece only once. When possible, write a reply directly on the letter.

12. Eat properly to keep yourself from slowing down in the late afternoon.

 IME-WASTERS YOU CAN CONTROL

A time-waster is any activity that robs you of time that could be used more efficiently.

Procrastination. Procrastination means putting off the completion of work. It is difficult to complete certain tasks, and sometimes people are afraid of failing. Avoid procrastinating by completing the most difficult tasks first. Once these difficult tasks are completed, you will find that you will be able to accomplish even more, since you will be under less pressure.

Failure to Plan or Establish Priorities. This time-waster is related to procrastination in that procrastinators often fail to plan or establish **priorities,** which are items such as tasks that deserve attention ahead of others. First of all, determine which task of all the ones to be completed is the most important. Next, set up a plan of action for completing this first-priority task. What must be done to accomplish the task? How much time will be needed? Set a deadline for completing the task, and try very hard to meet the set deadline. This will help you get started. At the end of the workday, evaluate the plan of action you started with in the morning. Make adjustments, and be ready for the next day. Try to continue to faithfully follow your plan of action. You will save a lot of time in the short run by doing so.

Lack of Decision-Making Skill. The nature of some decisions makes them difficult. A decision may affect many other people or create yet another challenging situation. Most people who have a difficult time making decisions are afraid of failing. Many people lack self-confidence in making decisions. Whatever the reasons, decisions have to be made in any business. Some decisions must be made immediately, while other decisions can wait for further consideration. In a more complex situation, keep the following suggestions in mind:

- Determine the decision to be made.
- Determine the various outcomes of the decision, both negative and positive.
- Gather as much information as possible.
- Make the decision.
- Follow up on the decision to determine whether more decisions must be made.

 LANNING YOUR TIME

Planning is an important part of time management. Planning requires you to think about the tasks that you need to complete, to set goals giving you direction, and to organize your activities in such a way that will help you complete the tasks efficiently.

 ETTING GOALS

Setting goals and then organizing your work to achieve the goals involves a strong commitment. How do you set goals? Consider the following when setting goals:

- Goals should be specific. If your goal is "to get more work done today," you could have trouble achieving it. The goal might be better stated as "to finish three sales letters within the first hour of work today." That goal is specific. It clearly states what you are trying to achieve, and you can easily evaluate it.

- Goals should be realistic. If you set a goal that is impossible to achieve, you will become frustrated and very discouraged.
- Goals should be in harmony with the philosophy of your business. If the business you are working for does not subscribe to a certain policy, do not set goals that are related to that policy. The goals will be useless.
- Goals should be put in writing. When you actually see your goal in writing, you will be more motivated to work toward achieving it.
- Goals should have deadlines. Set a reasonable time frame. This will vary depending on your business and the nature of your goal. Goals usually are classified as short-term goals and long-range goals. For example, a short-term goal might be met within a day or two or even on the same day it is set. A long-range goal would most likely be met within a few weeks or months. The important point is that a deadline should be set and a realistic time frame established to achieve the goal.

STABLISHING PRIORITIES

Learning how to establish priorities is directly related to setting goals. After you have set goals, you must determine which goal is the *most important.* Then you must be persistent in sticking to your first priority. From time to time you will have to deal with interruptions. Remember to apply the information you studied earlier in this chapter on time-wasters, including interruptions. The following guidelines will help you in establishing priorities:

- Check your long-range goals first. How involved are the long-range goals? Are they related to any of your short-term goals? If so, determine which aspects of your long-range goals can be combined with your short-term goals. Then revise your goals.
- Make a "to do" list *every morning.* This list can be very simple or very elaborate. Select the method that best fits with your personality. Take approximately 15 minutes each morning to determine your plan of action for the day. Once your "to do" list is in order, target specific items on your list. Classify these items in order of importance, starting with the most important item. Do

not place items on your list that you know you will not get to do that day. Try to be realistic in preparing each day's "to do" list. Study the example in Fig. 16-2. At the end of the day, evaluate your list and determine what adjustments need to be made for the next day.

It is very likely that some of the items on your "to do" list that you rated as most important at the beginning of the day may change by the end of the day. Your responsibility is to learn how to handle these changes.

THINGS TO DO:

1. _____
2. _____
3. _____
4. _____
5. _____

GO FOR

THINGS TO DO:

1. *Review last week's billings*
2. *Review Art Direction Magazine*
3. *Write news release for WRSL*
4. *Set up rough layouts for R.L. Aimes Co.*
5. *Pick up theater tickets*

GO FOR IT!

Fig. 16-2   A simple "Things To Do" list helps to organize your daily activities.

 ELEGATING

The act of assigning some tasks to others is called **delegation.** Delegation can relieve you of some aspects of your work, thus giving you time to complete additional work.

It is not unusual for office workers to feel that they do not want to delegate. The secret is to delegate tasks to those members of the office staff whom you feel most comfortable working with. When you are a beginning office worker, work may be delegated to you from a supervisor or manager. Although at times some of the tasks delegated to you may seem trivial, view them as an opportunity to learn more about the operation of your business, and recognize that you can be of invaluable assistance. Over a period of time, your cooperation in completing delegated work can put you in a favorable position for a promotion.

Keep the following points in mind when delegating:

- Determine who can best assist you in completing your work. If you are assisting someone else, offer to complete work in a positive manner.
- Determine what work can be completed by someone else. Select tasks that are appropriate for the person, considering his or her skills.
- Organize the tasks so that they are easy to understand and complete. Make sure that your directions are simple to follow. If possible, let the person know when you would like to have the work completed. Be prepared to answer any questions in a manner that will reflect your total control of the situation. This way both you and the person receiving the work will gain confidence.

RGANIZING YOUR WORK AREA

POSITIVE WORK AREA ENVIRONMENT

Advanced technology in today's electronic office has increased the need for developing a positive work area so that work can be completed efficiently. Office work areas are just as individual as the people working in those areas. Although large offices have office engineers who design work areas, small offices do not have this luxury. In most cases it is your responsibility to organize your work area so that you can accomplish your work in a professional and effective manner.

Some people have a knack for organizing their work areas. Where this skill is lacking, the result can be total disorganization, low productivity, and a great waste of time. While it is true that some people can work well in a cluttered area, in most cases clutter interferes with work. Try to organize a work area that will save you time. Start with your furniture.

Office workers need many time-management skills to do their jobs well. These skills include planning, scheduling, and organizing.

YOUR DESK AND MATERIALS ON TOP OF YOUR DESK

Unless you are locked into one office design, keep trying out various positions for your desk until you find one that seems to fit your needs. Once your desk is in place, you can arrange the other parts of your work area.

You should keep the top of your desk organized as much as possible. The only items on your desk should be the items you are using at the moment or items that you work with during the day, such as a desk-top calendar and a telephone.

Calendars. Many electronic offices have electronic time-management systems that provide electronic calendars and reminder capabilities. These capabilities save much time and eliminate the need for desk-top calendars. Study the illustrations for electronic calendars. In some offices it may still be necessary to keep a manual calendar for scheduling items. You will have to choose the scheduling method that best fits your needs and the needs of your business.

Electronic calendar and scheduling systems make it easy to organize items and manage office resources. In using such a system, you may be able to electronically record appointments, reserve office resources, and update and modify calendar events. Some systems even automatically remind the user of upcoming events.

Maintaining an electronic calendar is similar to maintaining a calendar manually. The key difference is that an electronic system is easier to maintain and allows for more security of personal information. Usually, individual users of an electronic calendar have a password so that others cannot view their calendar unless allowed to do so.

Electronic calendars allow you to display information in different ways. You may be able to view a day at a time, a week at a time, or a month at a time. Figures 16-3, 16-4, and 16-5 illustrate each of these alternatives.

Electronic scheduling facilities allow you to set up meetings by keyboarding information on the meeting participants and the date, time, and materials needed for the meeting. The system automatically surveys the electronic calendar of each individual and, if a participant is not available for the stated date and time, you will be notified. You can then decide whether or not to go ahead and

Day at a Glance

```
CALENDAR for Terry Smith              Date:  Mon Nov 06, 89


Event        Time           Type         Location        Subject

  1       9:00 AM-10:30 AM Meeting    Conference Rm 1  Staff Mtg
  2      10:30 AM-11:30 AM Meeting    John's Office    Budget
  3       2:00 PM- 4:00 PM Appoint.

Pick one:   (1.  Different Date, 2. Different Calendar,
             3.  Change, 4. Delete, 5. Confirm or Decline,
             6.  Print, 7. Scheduling)  ___
```

Fig. 16-3 The option of viewing calendars in different ways provides the flexibility needed to get the global picture with a month or week at a glance, and the details needed on each event with a day at a glance. A calendar for one day is shown here.

Week at a Glance

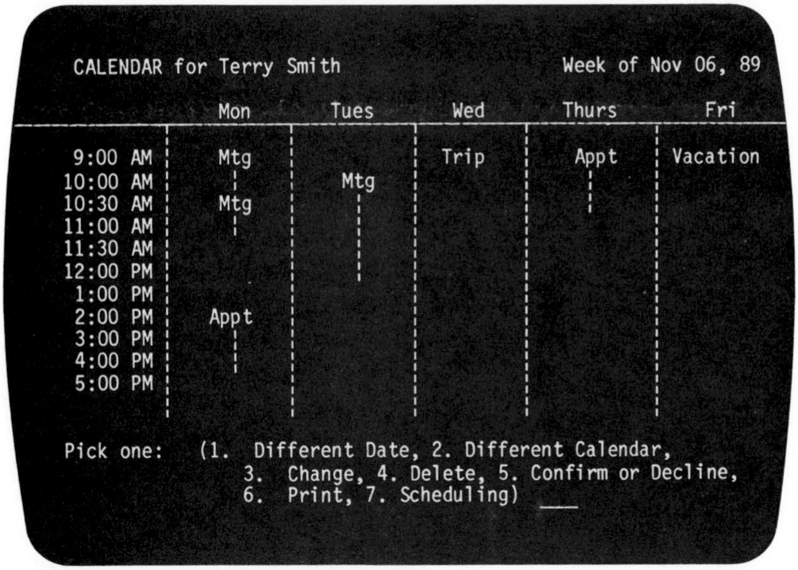

```
CALENDAR for Terry Smith                    Week of Nov 06, 89

                    Mon       Tues      Wed       Thurs     Fri

      9:00 AM       Mtg                 Trip      Appt      Vacation
     10:00 AM        |        Mtg
     10:30 AM       Mtg        |
     11:00 AM        |         |
     11:30 AM        |         |
     12:00 PM        |         |
      1:00 PM        |         |
      2:00 PM       Appt       |
      3:00 PM        |         |
      4:00 PM        |         |
      5:00 PM        |         |

     Pick one:   (1.  Different Date, 2. Different Calendar,
                   3.  Change, 4. Delete, 5. Confirm or Decline,
                   6.  Print, 7. Scheduling)   ____
```

Fig. 16-4   This is a calendar for one week.

Month at a Glance

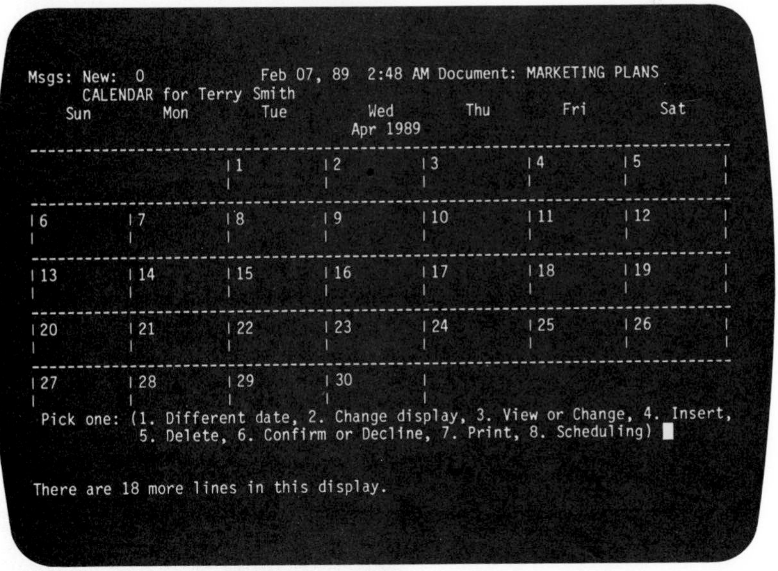

```
Msgs: New:  0            Feb 07, 89  2:48 AM Document: MARKETING PLANS
       CALENDAR for Terry Smith
     Sun       Mon       Tue       Wed       Thu       Fri       Sat
                                   Apr 1989
    ---------------------------------------------------------------------
              | 1       | 2       | 3       | 4       | 5       |
              |         |         |         |         |         |
    ---------------------------------------------------------------------
    | 6       | 7       | 8       | 9       | 10      | 11      | 12      |
    |         |         |         |         |         |         |
    ---------------------------------------------------------------------
    | 13      | 14      | 15      | 16      | 17      | 18      | 19      |
    |         |         |         |         |         |         |
    ---------------------------------------------------------------------
    | 20      | 21      | 22      | 23      | 24      | 25      | 26      |
    |         |         |         |         |         |         |
    ---------------------------------------------------------------------
    | 27      | 28      | 29      | 30      |
    |         |         |         |         |
    Pick one: (1. Different date, 2. Change display, 3. View or Change, 4. Insert,
              5. Delete, 6. Confirm or Decline, 7. Print, 8. Scheduling)  ▮

    There are 18 more lines in this display.
```

Fig. 16-5   This is a calendar for one month.

schedule the meeting or request that the system determine the earliest possible date and time when all the participants are available. The main advantage is that this procedure can take place within moments rather than hours.

If you need to use a manual desk calendar, you should write calendar entries neatly with a pencil so that they can be changed easily. If your notes are clear and if your calendar is kept in a convenient place, your supervisor and coworkers can get any information they need about your schedule when you are away from your desk. Do not record personal or confidential notes on this calendar. It is strictly for business.

The kind of calendar you keep will depend on your schedule and your responsibilities. You will probably find that a combination of the types of calendars listed below will work best for you.

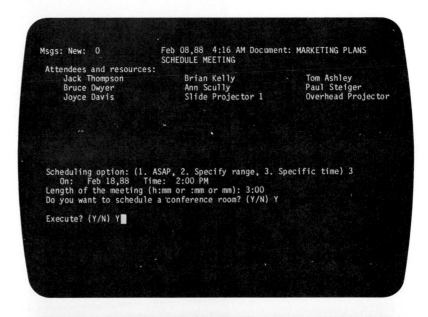

Msgs: New: 0   Feb 08,88 4:16 AM Document: MARKETING PLANS
                                SCHEDULE MEETING
    Attendees and resources:
      Jack Thompson   Brian Kelly   Tom Ashley
      Bruce Dwyer   Ann Scully   Paul Steiger
      Joyce Davis   Slide Projector 1   Overhead Projector

    Scheduling option: (1. ASAP, 2. Specify range, 3. Specific time) 3
      On: Feb 18,88   Time: 2:00 PM
    Length of the meeting (h:mm or :mm or mm): 3:00
    Do you want to schedule a conference room? (Y/N) Y

    Execute? (Y/N) Y█

Fig. 16-6   This screen shows all the people and the kinds of equipment that should be at the meeting.

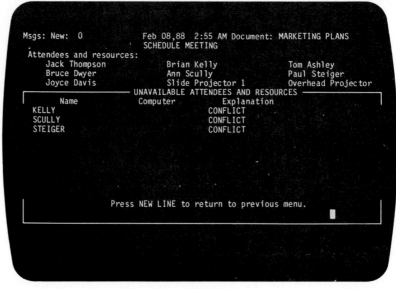

Msgs: New: 0   Feb 08,88 2:55 AM Document: MARKETING PLANS
                                SCHEDULE MEETING
    Attendees and resources:
      Jack Thompson   Brian Kelly   Tom Ashley
      Bruce Dwyer   Ann Scully   Paul Steiger
      Joyce Davis   Slide Projector 1   Overhead Projector
    ┌────────────── UNAVAILABLE ATTENDEES AND RESOURCES ──────────────┐
    │   Name   Computer   Explanation   │
    │ KELLY   CONFLICT   │
    │ SCULLY   CONFLICT   │
    │ STEIGER   CONFLICT   │
    │   │
    │   │
    │   Press NEW LINE to return to previous menu.   │
    │   █   │
    └───┘

Fig. 16-7   This indicates that three of the people who should attend the meeting have something else scheduled at that time.

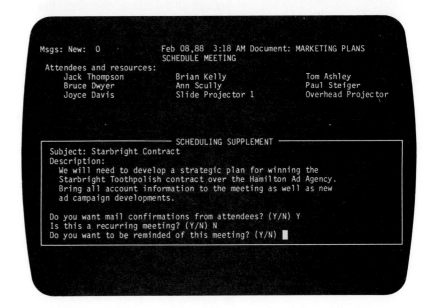

```
Msgs: New:  0              Feb 08,88  3:15 AM Document: MARKETING PLANS
                                  SCHEDULE MEETING
   Attendees and resources:
      Jack Thompson              Brian Kelly               Tom Ashley
      Bruce Dwyer                Ann Scully                Paul Steiger
      Joyce Davis                Slide Projector 1         Overhead Projector




   Scheduling option: (1. ASAP, 2. Specify range, 3. Specific time ) 1
   After:   Feb 18,88   Time:  2:00 PM
   Length of the meeting (h:mm or :mm or mm): 3:00
   Do you want to schedule a conference room? (Y/N) Y

   Execute? (Y/N) Y


   Schedule for Fri  Feb 19,88 at 1:00 PM in Exec. Conf. Rm.        OK? (Y/N) ▮
```

Fig. 16-8 Since the meeting could not be held on February 18 at 2 pm, the computer found the first available block of three hours all the participants could attend.

```
Msgs: New:  0              Feb 08,88  3:18 AM Document: MARKETING PLANS
                                  SCHEDULE MEETING
   Attendees and resources:
      Jack Thompson              Brian Kelly               Tom Ashley
      Bruce Dwyer                Ann Scully                Paul Steiger
      Joyce Davis                Slide Projector 1         Overhead Projector


   ──────────────── SCHEDULING SUPPLEMENT ────────────────
   Subject: Starbright Contract
   Description:
      We will need to develop a strategic plan for winning the
      Starbright Toothpolish contract over the Hamilton Ad Agency.
      Bring all account information to the meeting as well as new
      ad campaign developments.

   Do you want mail confirmations from attendees? (Y/N) Y
   Is this a recurring meeting? (Y/N) N
   Do you want to be reminded of this meeting? (Y/N) ▮
```

Fig. 16-9 A detailed description of the meeting is provided for the information of the attendees.

1. *Daily calendar.* You may have a daily calendar on your desk. This kind of calendar has one blank or ruled page or a pair of pages for each day of the year. The rules on a page may divide the workday into segments of an hour or less, and this can help you schedule appointments and tasks. If someone asks for an appointment, a quick look will tell you when you are free.

These are the different desk calendars you can use. Make sure your notes include all the information about the appointment you are scheduling: person's name, phone number, time and place of the meeting, and subject.

2. *Weekly calendar.* Some calendars display a week's schedule on each page. Days may be divided into sections with blank areas for general entries. Many weekly calendars are notebook-size, with pages large enough for writing in detailed entries. The advantage of a weekly calendar is that it allows you to see at a glance what you have planned for an entire week.

3. *Monthly calendar.* A monthly calendar is used to schedule events such as vacations or long-term projects that take large blocks of time to complete. These calendars, which must be large enough for a month's worth of entries on each page, usually hang on the wall. Color coding is sometimes used on monthly calendars to block out special activities by different individuals in the office.

4. *Yearly calendar.* A yearly calendar is a calendar that serves as a reminder for events that occur at set times during the year. Examples of such events are holidays, the preparation of annual budgets and reports, and conferences. A yearly calendar is especially helpful to new staff members.

Scheduling Appointments

When scheduling appointments, keep the following important points in mind:

1. If you are requesting an appointment, identify yourself or the company you represent.

2. State the reason for the appointment.

3. Indicate approximately how much time you think the appointment will take.

4. Have your schedule in front of you so that you can suggest a time or respond to a suggestion without delay. If the time slot requested is not available, suggest an alternate time.

5. If you must clear an appointment with your supervisor, confirm the appointment as soon as possible.

6. Write down the details of any appointment you make: date, time, location, purpose, and the other person's name and title. Note any tasks that you need to do to prepare for the appointment, such as reviewing files.

7. Confirm the details with the other person to make sure you have communicated clearly.

8. Ask the other person to notify you if it becomes necessary to change the appointment.

9. Leave time between appointments to allow for any emergencies that might require extra time.

Adjust your priorities and work schedule according to your supervisor's needs.

Desk-Top Organizers. Because you will probably need to keep the papers you are working with on your desk, keep them organized. Desk-top organizers can help you sort papers and arrange them so that you can find them quickly. There are two basic types of organizers for papers: vertical organizers and trays. Both types take up no more desk surface space than a piece of stationery, and they can hold many papers or files. In a vertical organizer, files stand upright between dividers so that you can read their tabs and add documents to them easily. In organizer trays, files or papers are stacked on top of one another. The trays themselves may also be stacked. Colored organizers and trays can make it even easier to identify particular files, and this is important if you are working with several individuals.

Other Desk-Top Items. Most workers have a telephone at their workstation. If your telephone is kept on top of your desk, place it in a position that is easy for you to reach. By doing so, you will be able to talk on the telephone and write at the same time. You may also want to keep on top of your desk small items that are used frequently, such as tape, pens and pencils, and a pad of telephone message slips. Keep supplies for taking messages near your telephone. Use an upright container for pens and pencils. Store them with their points up so that you can see what color they are and whether the pencil points are sharp. Keep paper clips in a separate container. If you use magnetic tapes or disks at your workstation, do not use a magnetic paper-clip container. Beware of metal clips that may have become magnetized in another office.

Most office workers keep a few reference materials on top of their desk or nearby. These materials might include an address file, a dictionary, instruction manuals for office machines, and other sources of information that they refer to often. It is possible that some of these materials might also be stored electronically and kept in a disk file box. Keep your reference materials away from your writing surface but within easy reach.

Your Desk Drawers. Organize your drawer space so that you do not have to waste time searching for items you need. You will work more efficiently if the items in your desk drawers are neatly arranged.

Your Computer Terminal. It is quite likely that your workstation will include a computer terminal. If you have your own printer, it will be kept on a specially designed table. If your computer terminal is connected to a large centralized system, you will be one of many users sharing several printers. These will probably be placed in convenient locations in the office. Your computer terminal and keyboard will probably be on a separate table, although it is possible that this equipment could be on your desk. If the computer terminal is on your desk, place it off to one side at an angle so that you will still have enough surface space for writing and performing other tasks. Also make sure that all cables and wires are out of the way, for it is important to prevent accidents.

Shelves. Your workstation may include shelves that you can use for storing reference materials that you do not want to leave on your desk. Examples of such materials are procedures manuals, telephone directories, and almanacs.

You might also want to store disk file boxes on shelves conveniently located near your computer terminal. Store disks with expensive software or confidential data se-

If you organize your supply area properly, you'll be able to see at a glance when certain items are running low.

curely in locked boxes or drawers, not in open boxes on shelves. Store all disks on their edges and in protective envelopes. Never store disks on top of your computer terminals or on top of your printer, because they may become demagnetized.

Supply Cabinets. Your workstation may also include cabinets and closets for storing items that are too large to fit in your desk. In a cabinet you may store oversize envelopes as well as large quantities of supplies such as pencils, notepads, disks, ribbons, stationery, and file folders. Use locked cabinets for storing software disks and disks containing confidential data.

Supplies. You should check your supplies regularly and order new stocks of any items that are running low. This will prevent your running out of any item. In a large office, you will probably place orders for supplies through your employer's central supply room. In a small office, you may order supplies yourself from an office-supplies dealer.

When you get new supplies, they may be wrapped in plain paper. Label each package clearly with a marking pen so that you can see what the package contains without opening it. When you receive a new quantity of an item, place it behind or under what remains of your old supply so that the old supply is used first.

- Learning to manage your time really means learning how to manage yourself and your actions in a positive manner.

- Managing your time is a skill that can be learned and improved upon with consistent effort.

- Your work area reflects control of yourself and your time in carrying out your daily work.

- Learning where your time goes can help you gain better control of your time.

- Procrastination means putting off the completion of work. It can cause the loss of valuable time.

- Learning to make decisions in an efficient manner can save valuable time.

- Setting goals and then organizing your work to achieve the goals involves a strong commitment.

- Establishing priorities is directly related to setting goals.

- Delegating can relieve you of some aspects of your work, giving you time to complete additional work.

- Using calendars efficiently is an important aspect of managing your time.

V *OCABULARY*

time management work area
time-waster scheduling
procrastination reference material
priority workstation
delegation

R *EVIEW QUESTIONS*

1. Where does your time go? Be specific.

2. What is a time-waster? Give examples.

3. List the basic steps that can help you in establishing priorities.

4. What are the major considerations in decision making?

5. What important points should you keep in mind when setting goals?

6. What is the role of delegation in managing your time?

7. Name the most important considerations with regard to organizing your work area. Justify your considerations.

8. List five important points to keep in mind when scheduling appointments.

SKILLBUILDING ACTIVITIES

1. List your five greatest time-wasters. On the basis of what you have studied in this chapter, determine one step you could take to eliminate those time-wasters.

2. Think about how you spent your time during the last 24 hours. When were you most productive? When were you least productive? What steps will you take to improve your productivity within the next 24 hours? Write a brief summary of your findings.

3. Visit an office-supply store to see the wide variety of office supplies that are available. Make a list of the office supplies that you would buy to help you organize your workstation. Ask for a catalog, and figure the cost of your supplies. Compare your list of supplies and prices with your classmates' lists.

4. Think of all the appointments, dates, errands, and tasks you juggle in your daily routine. What time management method(s) and tool(s) could help you organize and plan your schedule? Try using some of the methods and tools discussed in the chapter and see if they help you run your life more efficiently.

*T*he technology being used in today's offices has enhanced the role of office workers. With the aid of electronic equipment, secretaries, administrative assistants, and other members of the support staff are now making decisions that were once made only by their supervisors.

By placing the tools of analysis in the hands of office workers, technology has broadened the scope of their responsibilities and decision-making tasks. While developing increased decision-making skills, office workers are acquiring experience that opens up new ways of relating to their supervisors and a wider range of career opportunities as well.

In this chapter you will learn about topics that are important in preparing for becoming an employee. You will learn what a job description is and how it is helpful to the employee as well as the su-

pervisor. You will also learn about the qualities employers look for in the employees they hire, the type of training that may be provided to employees, and the role of supervisors and how they can affect their staffs. As a result of studying this chapter, you will be able to:

- Understand the role of a job description and how it can benefit employees and supervisors.
- Become aware of the role of performance appraisals in the assessment of employees.
- Describe the qualities that employers look for in the employees they hire.
- Identify the role of training programs.
- Understand the nature of a supervisor's job in order to relate to supervisors better.
- Understand how supervisors can affect employee performance and career advancement.

OB DESCRIPTIONS

Job descriptions are a key element in recruiting, training, and evaluating employees. A **job description** is a document that itemizes for a given job what the employee filling the job is expected to do, what knowledge and skills the employee should possess, and who the employee's supervisor will be. A **supervisor** is the person to whom an employee reports, someone who assigns, oversees, and evaluates that employee's work.

Supervisors usually write job descriptions for their support staffs since they are closely involved with and knowledgeable about the tasks for which each staff member is responsible. Some companies dictate that the human resources department write the job descriptions for each position in the company. When this is done, it is typically with the assistance of the supervisor for each position.

ARTS OF A JOB DESCRIPTION

A key to a well-written job description is that both parties involved, the employee and the supervisor, should be in agreement about the tasks that are required of the position and the expectations that are outlined.

In order to be as precise as possible, job descriptions should make use of clear, specific terminology rather than vague descriptions. For example, *responsible for coordination of office activities* would be better described by itemizing exact tasks such as those that follow: *answer telephones, greet and escort visitors to supervisor's office, schedule meetings for supervisor on electronic calendaring system, update electronic calendar daily and review with supervisor, receive, review, and prioritize both electronic and traditional mail for supervisor, take dictation from supervisor, prepare all correspondence and reports, and complete other duties as requested.* When a job description is as specific as possible, it is less likely that a misunderstanding will arise regarding the responsibilities of the job.

There are three main parts of any job description. The format may vary from one company to the next, but the major areas are usually the same or similar. These are:

- *The description itself.* This section includes a summary of the overall functions of the position and a detailed list of the specific tasks and responsibilities of the job.
- *Knowledge and skill requirements.* This section specifies the minimum education level and/or training required by the job.
- *Accountability.* This section identifies who the employee's supervisor will be. It may also describe any equipment, expenditures, or other operations for which the employee will be held responsible in the course of performing job tasks.

A sample job description for an administrative assistant is shown in Fig. 17-1. Keep in mind that the job tasks for this type of position may vary from company to company.

THE BENEFIT OF JOB DESCRIPTIONS

It is clear now that job descriptions help both supervisors and employees maintain an understanding of the job tasks for which the employee is responsible. This is the most obvious advantage of using a job description. There is another advantage that is a real benefit to the employee.

A job description protects the employee in an important way. It ensures that the employee is evaluated on the basis of those job tasks identified in the job description.

EVALUATING YOUR PERFORMANCE

The job description is a key tool used in evaluating employee performance on the job. As an employee, you will be evaluated in two ways:

- *On a day-to-day basis.* Each day your work is reviewed for accuracy and completeness. Although you may not be reviewed formally on a day-to-day basis, you can be sure that your supervisor is taking note of your work habits, behavior, and performance.
- *In a formal performance evaluation.* Your overall job performance for a given period of time, usually one year, will be reviewed by your supervisor. This is referred to as a **performance appraisal.**

JOB DESCRIPTION

Job Title: Secretary/Administrative Assistant   **Accountability:**   Supervisor is Manager of Marketing. Will act as liaison with vendors for repairs.

Department: Marketing

Location: Headquarters

I. MAJOR FUNCTION

Responsible for standardizing document formats, keyboarding and preparing documents, and developing document routing, filing, and retrieval systems for both manual and electronic systems. Primary emphasis is on the coordination of office communications, both written and verbal, to increase the efficiency of document preparation and information flow. Heavy use of computer equipment and software in completing job tasks is required.

II. SPECIFIC DUTIES

		TIME
1.	Establishes operational procedures for document preparation using word processing and both manual and electronic filing and routing systems.	5%
2.	Develops and maintains marketing inventory system using spreadsheet software, and prepares reports.	5%
3.	Prepares documents for order fulfillment on computer system.	10%
4.	Prepares business correspondence including reports, letters, memos, etc., using word processing system.	40%
5.	Prepares department budgets using spreadsheet software.	10%
6.	Prepares visuals for management presentations using graphing software.	10%
7.	Coordinates office communications including incoming/outgoing mail, phone calls, and messages.	15%
8.	Schedules meetings, updates electronic calendars, and records minutes of staff meetings.	5%

III. KNOWLEDGE AND SKILL REQUIREMENTS

1. Education: High school diploma required. Business major preferred, with emphasis on secretarial and software subjects. Additional post-secondary education or software training desirable.

2. Qualities and Skills: Knowledge and experience with word processing, spreadsheet, database management, graphing, electronic filing, electronic mail, and electronic calendaring systems required. A minimum of 60 wpm typing speed and 80 wpm steno speed is required. Good organizational, decision-making, and human relations skills desirable. Must be dependable, accurate, and detail-oriented. Professionalism and initiative are desired.

Fig. 17-1   Job description.

THE PERFORMANCE APPRAISAL

Performance appraisals are conducted on a periodic basis. The time frame can range anywhere from once every three months to once a year.

Your supervisor will inform you of when your performance review will be held. It will usually be a private meeting between you and your supervisor. During this meeting you and your supervisor will discuss the degree to which you have handled your job tasks as outlined in your job description. Your supervisor may also use an **evaluation form** to document the review of your performance as it is discussed. Figure 17-2 illustrates what this evaluation form might look like.

The evaluation form usually includes rating areas for things such as work habits, dependability, appearance, accuracy, decision-making ability, efficiency, attendance, initiative, and other items. Some supervisors will also evaluate you on the basis of a **statement of objectives,** which is a description of the goals or objectives that you are expected to accomplish during the time between performance reviews.

Behavior During the Performance Appraisal. Each performance appraisal is important in determining your future in your current position and in the company for which you are working. Always follow these guidelines:

- Be professional and mature.
- Listen.
- Take criticism well. Acknowledge weaknesses.
- Calmly refute unfair issues.
- Never give signs of disinterest.
- Do not blame others.
- Provide positive feedback to your supervisor.
- Do not convey problems without solutions.
- Be willing to compromise.

DESIRED QUALITIES OF AN EMPLOYEE

Every employer wants a well-rounded employee—someone who can perform the job tasks well in addition to dealing with people in a professional manner.

Office Employee Performance Evaluation

Soc. Security No.	Employee Name		Division	Department	Wk. Location	Date of Hire
Position Title		Grade Level	How Long Under Your Supervision?		Postpone This Appraisal Until (Date)	

Performance Analysis

In the appraisal, focus on the key aspects of job performance. Check only those factors that are applicable to the employee's job. Space is provided for you to add any other job-related factors you think are important. Be sure to complete this section as fully as possible. It will help you determine the employee's overall performance rating.

JOB RESULTS
- Thoroughness of work
- Accuracy-lack of mistakes
- Quantity-output of meaningful work
- Coverage of total job responsibility

JOB KNOWLEDGE
- Understanding work procedures, methods and techniques
- Learning and adapting to new methods and techniques
- Understanding equipment

DEPENDABILITY
- Adherence to instructions and directions
- Consistency and reliability of work habits
- Efficiency under pressure
- Supervision required
- Ability to get things done

RELATIONSHIPS
- Cooperation with other in group
- Respect and consideration for others
- Acceptance of constructive criticism
- Impressions created outside department

INITIATIVE
- Efforts to improve own qualifications
- Efforts to improve the way work is done
- Coping with problems as they arise
- Willingness to assume responsibility

OTHER JOB RELATED FACTORS
- . . . .

ATTENDANCE
- Poor
- Excessive

	IN A 6-MONTH PERIOD	IN A 12-MONTH PERIOD
	☐ Absent 4-5 Days	☐ Absent 7-8 Days
	☐ Absent 6 or More Days	☐ Absent 9 or More Days

PUNCTUALITY
- Poor
- Excessive

	IN A 6-MONTH PERIOD	IN A 12-MONTH PERIOD
	☐ Late 7-8 Times	☐ Late 11-12 Times
	☐ Late 9 or More Times	☐ Late 13 or More Times

Performance Comments

What aspects of the employee's duties are handled in an exceptional or commendable manner?

What aspects of the employee's duties are not handled as well as should be expected?

Performance Rating

Considering all the employee's performance factors, please check the statement that most nearly fits this employee's overall performance on the current job in the last twelve months.

1. ☐ Exceptional — Superior performance. Consistently exceeds job standards.
2. ☐ Commendable — High standard of performance. Consistently meets, and occasionally exceeds, job standards.
3. ☐ Good — Performance normally expected of qualified employee.
4. ☐ Needs improvement — Performance not up to desired standard, should show improvement.
5. ☐ Unacceptable — Poor performance. Cannot be retained on job without immediate improvement.

Development Plans

The employee's career objectives and your department's staff needs will dictate the development plan. The plan should help to improve the employee's skills, increase job knowledge, or provide a means of correcting problems. Use the following code list to identify the appropriate training programs.

State your plans and objectives for improving the employee's performance (consider increased responsibility, coaching, on-the-job training, etc.)

If formal training programs will help the employee, please code (using the course list in the instructions) those programs that the employee needs:

1 _____ 2 _____ 3 _____ 4 _____ 5 _____ Write in other _____

A. Business Writing & Editing
B. Copy Editing & Proofreading
C. Make-up & Production
D. Graphics, Art & Design
E. Advertising & Marketing
F. Promotion
G. Research & Statistics
H. Office Practices Seminar

I. Business Math
J. Business Correspondence
K. Business English
L. Shorthand Refresher
M. Shorthand I
N. Typing Refresher
O. Typing I
P. Telephone Techniques

Q. Receptionist Training
R. Supervisory Training
S. Accounting
T. Word Processing
U. Computer Technology
V. Language Arts
W. Other (specify):

Employee's Comments

Appraised By _____ Date _____

Appraisal Approved By _____ Date _____

Employee's Signature
(Your signature indicates only that you have read this appraisal.)

FORM 09-873-00 (Rev. 7/85)

Fig. 17-2 Evaluation forms tell employees how well they are progressing in their career path.

The qualities most sought out by employers are the following (although not necessarily in the order presented):

- Good attendance
- Accuracy and attention to detail
- Dependability
- Organizational skills
- Decision-making skills
- Initiative
- Human relations skills
- Professionalism (motivation, stress handling, dress)

Let us take a closer look at each one of these qualities and at the specific traits that employers look for in employees.

TTENDANCE

It is important to employers that the people they hire report to work on time and on a regular basis.

CCURACY

Work completed that is not accurate is a nuisance and can cost a company a great deal of money.

Accuracy, attention to detail, and proofreading to make sure that your work is accurate are a key to job success.

EPENDABILITY

Dependability is another important characteristic of a good employee. If you are not dependable, you can cause your supervisor and yourself to be placed in a poor position.

RGANIZATIONAL SKILLS

Organizational skills are the key to maintaining a high productivity level on the job. If you can assess from a list of tasks which ones take priority and the order in which they would be most efficiently completed, you would be considered organized.

ECISION-MAKING SKILLS

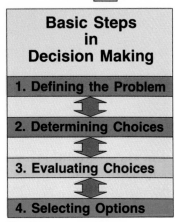

Fig. 17-3

Every employer wants to recruit employees who can make decisions on their own. You might have excellent skills, but if you have to be hand-held every step of the way and told what to do, hiring you would be counterproductive for the employer. Today's office workers are also making higher-level decisions based on the computer tools they are using.

Of course, you will need more direction in the beginning of a new job. This is expected. What is hard for employers to accept are employees who cannot do anything on their own.

NITIATIVE

Taking initiative is something nobody can do for you. You have to see the chance to take on new responsibility and sieze the opportunity. If you see something being done in your office that could be done better another way, tell your supervisor—then volunteer to do it yourself. If a new job task falls under your supervisor's control, volunteer to help in getting it completed. Through doing this, you will be viewed as one who wants to take on added responsibility, and will be worthy of advancement.

UMAN RELATIONS SKILLS

Having good people skills can mean everything to an employer, especially to those that deal with the public. Any sales, marketing, or service company is going to be mindful of hiring employees who can deal well with people.

ROFESSIONALISM

You can consider professionalism as the "finishing touches" that are looked for in an employee. Professionalism includes being a self-motivated worker, not needing a supervisor breathing down your neck to get work done.

Another aspect of being professional might be determined by how you handle stress on the job. Do you blow up and scream to voice your distress? Obviously, this would not be the most professional way to handle stress.

Another measure of professionalism can be determined

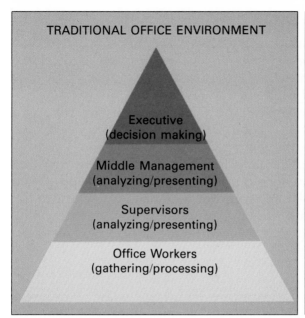
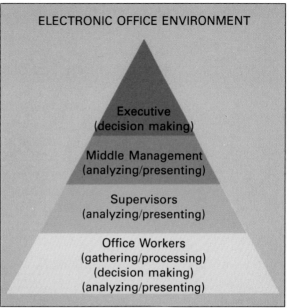

Fig. 17-4   In the electronic office, relationships between office workers and their managers and supervisors change because some decision making can now be done by office workers using electronic equipment.

by how you dress for work. A person working for an ultra-conservative financial institution would not go to the office in jeans. For some companies casual dress is considered appropriate—a music recording studio, for example. If you are unsure of how to dress, look at those around you to get ideas. Dress as conservatively as possible until you have been there long enough to determine what is acceptable and what is not. You can then alter your dress accordingly.

THE ROLE OF TRAINING

Employee training plays an important role in orienting new employees on the basic operations of the company and furnishing them with specific skills that will assist them in doing their work. There are typically three types of training programs that a company might offer to its employees. These are:
- Company orientation
- Product training
- Skills development

OMPANY ORIENTATION

Company orientation training is usually conducted during an employee's first week with a company. This orientation will cover everything from where to hang your coat to what type of benefits you can expect to receive.

The more you know and understand about the company you are about to join, the more comfortable you will be in beginning your employment there.

Ask questions whenever possible, both during and after orientation, to acquaint yourself with the things you need to know. A new employee who asks questions is not looked upon as a nuisance, but rather as an interested, dedicated individual. Do not be afraid to ask questions.

RODUCT TRAINING

Following the orientation training, some employees might be asked to attend specific **product training** classes where they will be instructed on how to use equipment or software they will work with in completing their job tasks.

SKILLS DEVELOPMENT

Some companies will also provide **skills development training** to develop skills that may or may not apply to the employee's job. For those who might be promoted to supervisory positions, this type of training could include topics such as how to supervise others, how to interview new employee candidates, and how to conduct performance appraisals.

OW SUPERVISORS AFFECT EMPLOYEES

Supervisors are a critical factor in how you will be viewed on the job. Both on a daily basis and over the long haul, your supervisor will have a direct impact on your performance, promotions, and salary increases.

Identifying with the supervisor's role will help you empathize with his or her situation instead of being solely concerned with your own.

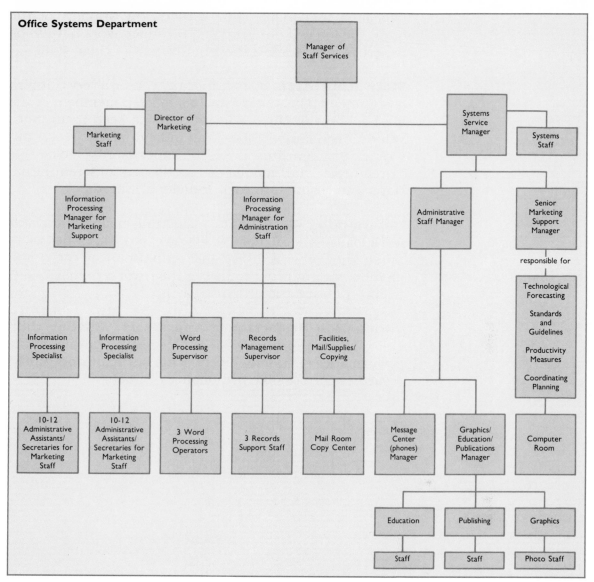

Office Systems Department

Fig. 17-5 A company's organizational chart shows how its management is organized. It is used along with job descriptions to clarify what employees do and to whom they report.

THE ROLE OF A SUPERVISOR

Supervisors have the difficult assignment of leading a double life on the job. Their planning abilities and decisions affect the company's success, and their interpersonal skills affect their staffs' productivity and morale. A supervisor can make the most concrete plans and sound decisions imaginable, but without the support of the staff, the job will not get done. So supervisors have to be expert planners and expert motivators of their staffs.

Motivating Staff. Motivating staff can be a very complex assignment. The supervisor has to keep members of the staff content in their work in order to keep them motivated. Every staff member is an individual who reacts differently to given situations. The supervisor has to be able to read each staff member's reactions to different situations and respond to each individual's needs.

Determining Work Load. Assigning realistic and fair work loads for staff members is no easy task. Supervisors must know the abilities and limitations of each staff member well in order to utilize their workers most effectively without overburdening them.

Conducting Performance Appraisals. Another difficult task for the supervisor is objectively appraising the performance of staff members. This has to be done fairly, regardless of possible personality conflicts.

SUMMARY

- Job descriptions identify the tasks of a job, the minimum training and skills required for the job, and the supervisor of the employee who performs the job.

- Job descriptions protect employees and supervisors from misunderstandings about the tasks for which the employee is responsible.

- Employees are evaluated in two ways—on a day-to-day basis and in a formal performance appraisal.

- During performance appraisals employees should listen to their supervisors, take criticism well, and correct any poor performance before the next review.

- Employees should not complain about a situation to their supervisor without offering solutions to the problem.

- In addition to identifying minimum training and skills requirements, employers look for other qualities in employees. These include good attendance, accuracy, dependability, organizational skills, decision-making skills, initiative, human relations skills, and professionalism.

- Employers will sometimes offer training to their employees. There are three types of training programs that might be available—company orientation, product training, and skills development training.

- The job of a supervisor is a difficult one. The supervisor must motivate the staff, determine work loads for each staff member, and conduct performance appraisals.

- It is important for employees to understand the role of their supervisor so that they can relate to the supervisor and work better with him or her.

VOCABULARY

job description	performance appraisal
supervisor	evaluation form
statement of objectives	product training
company orientation training	skills development training

1. List and define the parts of a job description.

2. Describe how job descriptions protect both employees and supervisors. Give an example for each.

3. Describe why good job descriptions take into account the individual differences among people, and explain how this can help job candidates.

4. Define the differences between the two types of performance evaluation—day-to-day performance evaluation and the formal performance appraisal.

5. List the qualities that employers look for in their employees.

6. How can inaccuracy on the part of employees cost employers a lot of money? Give an example.

7. How has technology increased the role of decision-making skills in today's administrative support staff? What types of decisions are these workers now making?

8. How does taking initiative on the job help employees?

9. List and define the three types of training programs that employers may offer.

10. Define the role of a supervisor, and describe why it is important for employees to work well with their supervisors.

SKILLBUILDING ACTIVITIES

1. Imagine that you have just been promoted to the position of office manager. One of your first tasks is to replace yourself in your old position of secretary. Using the job description on page 412, define the qualifications the job requires and the questions you should ask to find out if a candidate has them. Then write down ten interview questions to ask candidates for the job. Try to include questions about technical skills and about work habits.

2. Think about a job you have had—paying or nonpaying—and about the person who supervised you. How would you characterize your supervisor's

leadership or management style? Write down your thoughts in two columns, with the strengths in one column and the weaknesses in the other. If you had been in your supervisor's position, what would you have done differently?

3. Find two or three people in your circle of family or friends who have been promoted recently to more responsible jobs in their companies. Ask them what steps they took to move into their new positions and what kinds of problems they encountered when they assumed the new responsibilities. Ask them to tell you how they overcame some of the problems and to explain what they might do differently the next time.

4. With a small group of students in your class, set up a decision-making exercise. As a group, select a "problem" to work on: for example, planning an event or choosing a new word processor for classroom use. Follow the decision-making steps outlined in this chapter, and record each step on a chalkboard. Brainstorm for solutions, evaluate them, and eventually choose one. Make note of the kinds of information your group felt it needed to make a choice. If you could, how would you obtain and analyze that information? Decide and agree on how you would evaluate your choice. Did anyone in the group emerge as a leader? When you have completed the exercise, write down at least three things you learned about decision making by doing this.

CHAPTER 18

MOVING FORWARD IN YOUR CAREER

*T*he opportunities available to you as you look for that first office position are limited only by your imagination. Technology has created many new types of office positions that provide new opportunities for career advancement. Today it is possible to enter the job market in an entry-level position as a data entry clerk and move up through the ranks to a higher-level position such as that of a manager. It is also possible to use office skills to move to a similar position in another company, or these skills can be used as a foundation for changing careers.

After studying this chapter, you will be able to:

- Determine the various careers available to you in today's electronic office.
- Search for a job by using a variety of resources.
- Prepare a résumé, using a format that best fits the job you are applying for.
- Use correct procedures when applying for a job.
- Participate in an employment interview.
- Understand the role of job advancement.
- Learn the value of changing jobs for future growth.

PLANNING YOUR PERSONAL CAREER PROFILE

Before you can determine which career you should pursue, you must develop specific information about yourself. This information, which will help you decide on a career, is called a **personal career profile.** In developing a personal career profile, you assess your background, study your personality, and determine your personal goals. Once this is done, you need to assess job opportunities as well as the companies offering the job opportunities to see how closely you can match your personal career profile to the employment requirements of the company. Consider these questions carefully in developing your personal career profile:

- What skills have I learned from school classes, from previous and current jobs, and from hobbies and social activities?

- What kinds of work situations do I seem to enjoy the most? What types of activities seem to be the most satisfying? Do I like working with people or with things? Do I like working alone or with a group? Do I like working with words, numbers, or a combination of both?

- What values do I have that might affect my choice of a career?

- What do I hope to accomplish both in the immediate future and a few years from now?

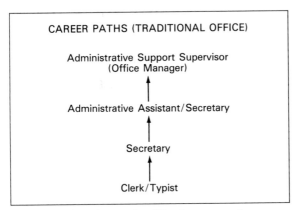

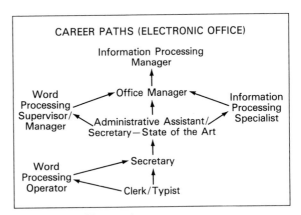

Fig. 18-1   The electronic office has opened up new career paths for office workers.

PERSONAL PROFILE SHEET

Name: _____   Date: _____

Purpose: The purpose of this Personal Profile Sheet is to provide you with written information concerning your background, skills, personality, and personal goals. This information can then be used to develop a more formal presentation of you to assist you in moving forward in your career.

Directions: Answer the questions below as accurately and completely as you can. Be specific.

1. What skills have I acquired from previous jobs, from hobbies, and from social activities? (For example: using word processing, speaking a foreign language, working with people, organizing activities)

2. What kinds of activities do I find the most rewarding, and what kinds of work situations do I seem to like best? (For example: Do I like working with a group or working alone? Do I like to take responsibility for others, or do I prefer to make an individual contribution?)

3. What do I hope to accomplish within the next few months? What do I hope to accomplish within the next few years? What values do I possess that might affect the career I choose? (For example: What things hold the highest value to me — money, security, authority?)

Fig. 18-2 Before you can plan a career, you need time to assess your background, personality, and life goals.

 AREERS IN TODAY'S ELECTRONIC OFFICE

Because of the continuously changing technology in today's electronic office, a wide number of career choices are available. Becoming aware of the wide variety of career options is helpful in selecting a career. A large company usually offers more career growth opportunities than a small company.

RECORDS AND INFORMATION MANAGEMENT

Records and information management personnel are usually in charge of handling records and information that are in both paper form and electronic form. Examples of careers in records and information management are as follows.

Records Clerk-Trainee. A records clerk-trainee sorts, files, and retrieves records under the supervision of a supervisor or trainer.

Specialized Filing Clerk. A specialized filing clerk maintains correspondence files, processes reports, keeps customer files, and encodes (converts into codes) information on files.

Records Supervisor. A records supervisor supervises personnel in the records management center and is responsible for protecting records and for training and evaluating personnel.

Micrographics Technician. A micrographics technician operates equipment that reduces records and produces microfilm and microfiche. The technician works under the direction of a supervisor.

Archivist. The process of preserving records is known as **archiving.** An archivist determines which records should be preserved, arranges the records, and takes precautions to protect the records from environmental change. Archivists are more likely to be employed by government offices, libraries, and educational institutions than by businesses because public records and historical documents, rather than business records, are the kinds of records that are usually preserved.

INFORMATION PROCESSING

Today word processing and data processing have been combined into information processing, and a result of this combination has been the creation of a wide variety of jobs requiring a wide variety of skills. Examples of careers in information processing are as follows.

Data Entry Clerk-Operator. The position of data entry clerk-operator is an entry-level position requiring a minimum of technical knowledge or experience. A data entry clerk-operator operates a computer terminal to enter data. This worker must have good keying skill so that data can be entered quickly and accurately.

Information Processing Trainee. An information processing trainee is in an entry-level position requiring little or no prior experience. An information processing trainee transcribes dictation, rough drafts, and other documents. This worker must have a good knowledge of grammar, spelling, and formatting, as well as other basic office procedures.

Programmer. A programmer is in a higher-level position in information processing. A programmer must know one or more computer languages and must be able to design, write, and test programs that fit a company's specific needs. A programmer needs to be logical, organized, and patient.

Information Processing Supervisor. An information processing supervisor oversees the day-to-day operations of the information processing center. This worker also trains employees, determines priorities in assigning tasks, and sets quality standards. An information processing supervisor must possess excellent interpersonal skills.

Systems Analyst. A systems analyst works with managers and supervisors to determine their needs and then designs programs to meet these individual needs. A systems analyst designs hardware, trains employees to operate the system, and oversees programmers.

ELECOMMUNICATIONS

Career opportunities in telecommunications are increasing rapidly as more and more companies integrate electronic equipment for instant communication. People are needed to oversee the sending and receiving of electronic mail, to operate Telex machines, to arrange teleconferences, and to set up and maintain telecommunications networks. Examples of careers in telecommunications are as follows.

Telecommunications Technician. A telecommunications technician helps set up and maintain electronic equipment. This worker also provides technical support for teleconferences.

Telecommunications Manager. A telecommunications manager manages the planning, installation, and day-to-day operations of a telecommunications system. A telecommunications manager also oversees technicians.

Electronic Mail Supervisor. An electronic mail supervisor supervises the operation of a company's electronic mail system, which includes facsimile machines, Telex equipment, teletypewriters, electronic copiers, and computers. An electronic mail supervisor also coordinates telecommunications with all other departments within the company.

ADMINISTRATIVE SUPPORT

Administrative support workers perform a wide variety of tasks, including taking dictation, keying and filing, composing and editing documents, arranging business trips and teleconferences, helping with accounting and budgeting, and training and supervising office personnel. Examples of careers in the area of administrative support are as follows.

Administrative Secretary. An administrative secretary takes and transcribes dictation, processes correspondence, answers the telephone, greets visitors, opens mail, maintains filing systems, composes and edits documents, proofreads documents, and performs any other needed administrative support duties. An administrative secretary is a self-motivated employee who performs daily tasks with little or no supervision.

Administrative Support Supervisor. An administrative support supervisor schedules work, assigns work to staff, assists employees in solving office problems, and evaluates employees.

SEARCHING FOR A JOB

Once you have given some thought to your immediate and long-range career goals, you will be ready to begin your job search. The following steps will help you in searching for a job:

- Locate a prospective employer.
- Prepare a résumé and cover letter, and send them to the prospective employer.
- Complete a job application form.
- Obtain an interview.
- Follow up on the interview.

LOCATING PROSPECTIVE EMPLOYERS

There are many places where you can search for a job. Consider the following options.

School Placement Services. Many schools offer a variety of placement services. Depending on the size of your school, there may be a separate office that provides placement services, or the guidance counselors may have an area in their office that is used specifically for this purpose.

Friends and Contacts. Friends and acquaintances often hear about jobs. The major advantage of word of mouth is that your source of information may be able to

School placement offices can help you prepare a résumé and locate prospective employers.

answer many of your questions about the job and will be able to furnish additional information about the job in an honest and frank manner.

Newspapers. Newspapers are an excellent source of information about employment opportunities. Get into the habit of reading the job listings in the classified advertisements section. The larger newspapers have more extensive sections dealing with job opportunities as well as larger advertisements. Reading these advertisements will help you gain an impression of companies for which you might like to work.

Employment Agencies. An employment agency's business is to bring job hunters and companies in search of personnel together. An employment agency attempts to match a job hunter's education, work experience, and employment preferences to the needs of the companies that come to it for referral.

If you go to an agency that handles both permanent and temporary employment, it can place you in a temporary job while it lines up employment interviews for you. Sometimes you can also find a permanent job with a company that has employed you in a temporary position and has been impressed with your performance.

P REPARING A RÉSUMÉ

A **résumé** is a written summary of your qualifications that you prepare when searching for a particular position.

Résumés may be prepared in a variety of formats. Because you will most likely be preparing a résumé for the first time, you should keep it very basic in order to give an attractive and realistic impression of yourself.

A résumé that you would prepare should have sections of information in the following order:

1. *Your name, address, and telephone number.*

2. *Other personal information.* You might want to give your date of birth, your state of health, or any other personal information you feel should be disclosed. By law employers may not ask you for personal information, but you may choose to include such information if you feel that it will help you get the job.

```
                        Rowena A. Rusel
                        2032 Pine Street
                        Navajo, AZ 86509
                        602-555-2168


        POSITION SOUGHT

             Data Entry Operator

        WORK EXPERIENCE

             Secretary.  Safeguard Insurance Company, 4500 Michigan Avenue,
             Chicago, IL 60653.

             Kitchen aid.  McCarthy's Catering, 93 West Mill Road, Rockford,
             IL 61104.  September 19-- to June 19--.  Supervisor: Mr. Maurice
             Doher.  Telephone: 815-555-4987, Extension 2367.

        EDUCATION

             Will be graduated with a B+ average from East Navajo Community
             College in January 19--.

             Participated in the Future Business Leaders of America Seminars.
             Specialized in business courses and attained:

             1.  Keying speed, 60 wam; shorthand speed, 80 wam.
             2.  An understanding and operating knowledge of transcribing
                 machines, the IBM Personal Computer, and all components of
                 the Wang Alliance System.
             3.  A working knowledge of electronic calculators.
             4.  An understanding of human relations in dealing with
                 coworkers, superiors, and subordinates.

        OTHER EXPERIENCE AND ACTIVITIES

             Member of Navajo Chapter of Future Business Leaders of America.
             Chairperson of Future Business Leaders of America Fund-Raising
               Drive to raise $2,000 for club activities.
```

Fig. 18-3 A résumé is a brief summary of your educational and employment history.

3. *Your educational background.* Begin with the highest level of school attended, which most likely will be high school. Give the date of graduation, the name of the school, and major subjects taken.

4. *Your employment history.* For each job you include, it is important to give employment dates, along with the name of the company, the position held, and a brief explanation of your responsibilities if they are not evident from the job title.

5. *Your hobbies, interests, activities, and special abilities.* List any school activities you have participated in,

such as athletics or clubs. If you were an officer in any school clubs or other school activities, be sure to include this information. It indicates that you have leadership skills.

6. *References.* A **reference** is a person who can vouch for your performance. Including references on a résumé is optional, but if references are included, no more than three should be listed. If references are not included on the résumé, a notation should be made on the résumé that references are available upon request. References may be teachers, former employers, guidance counselors, or other individuals who are in a position to recommend you.

Your résumé should be clearly written and well organized. Avoid vague, flowery phrases. Make certain that your spelling, grammar, and punctuation are perfect. Try to keep your résumé to one page.

APPLYING FOR A POSITION

Once you have located a prospective employer and prepared a résumé, your next step is to apply for a position that you are interested in. You will need to prepare a cover letter. A **cover letter,** or **application letter,** tells the prospective employer which job you are applying for, highlights your qualifications for the job, and includes any relevant information that is not already incorporated in your résumé. A cover letter is your chance to sell yourself to the employer. It should convince the employer to call you for an interview.

A cover letter should not be more than three or four short paragraphs. The opening paragraph should state when and where you heard about the position, and a following paragraph should explain why you feel your education and background qualify you for the job.

Some companies might ask you to fill out an application form as well as submit a résumé. If you are asked to fill out an application form, read it through first and then fill it out carefully. An employment application form may include personal questions concerning such things as your age, race, and marital status. You are not required by law to answer such questions. If you do not wish to

```
                         Box 86
                         Navajo, AZ  86509
                         November 17, 19--



                         Ms. Marie Ellis
                         Human Resources Department
                         Unionchurch Insurance Co.
                         2211 Outer Congressional Avenue
                         Navajo, AZ  86509

                         Dear Ms. Ellis:

                         Last Sunday I read your advertisement in the NAVAJO TIMES
                         indicating an opening you have available for a data entry
                         operator.  I am interested in being considered for that
                         position.

                         I will graduate from East Navajo Community College on Janu-
                         ary 10.  Because I have taken extra courses, I qualify for
                         early graduation status.  As you will notice from my enclosed
                         resume, I have participated in a variety of activities and am
                         qualified to operate a variety of pieces of equipment.  I
                         also earned a special award for my keying skill.  This cer-
                         tainly would be useful in a data entry operator's position.

                         It would be a pleasure to meet with you at your convenience
                         for a personal interview.  Also, I would be pleased to fur-
                         nish references upon request.

                         I look forward to hearing from you soon concerning this
                         matter.  You may reach me by calling 602-555-2168 any day
                         except Sunday, after 3:00 p.m.

                         Sincerely,

                         Rowena A. Rusel

                         Rowena A. Rusel

                         Enclosure
```

Fig. 18-4   In the first paragraph of an employment letter,
tell the reader the purpose of
the letter, which job you are
applying for, and how you
learned of the job.

answer these questions, try to handle the situation tactfully.

PREPARING FOR AND PARTICIPATING IN AN INTERVIEW

Companies use various procedures when conducting
employment interviews. The larger the company, the
more formal the interview procedure.

Keep the following points in mind when preparing for
an interview:

- *Research the company.* Find out as much as you can
  about the company. Your research will help you form a

mental picture of the company to help you in asking good questions during your interview.

- *Anticipate questions you will be asked during the interview.* The employment interview is usually the first time you will be seen by a company representative. First impressions are important. Dress properly, be well-groomed, and be on time, preferably 10 to 15 minutes early.

A good interviewer will give you an overall explanation of the requirements of the job and of the policies and benefits of the company. You will be asked questions about yourself, and you will also be given the opportunity to ask questions, such as the following:

- Why did you choose to apply for this position?
- What future professional or educational plans do you have?
- What characteristics or traits do you have that you think make you the right person for this position?
- Where do you hope to be in your profession in five years?
- Why did you leave your last position?
- What do you think are your strengths and weaknesses?
- What do you think your references will say about you?
- Why should this company hire you?

One of the most difficult questions to handle is the question of salary. Usually, the interviewer will tell you what the company expects to pay for the position. Occasionally, an interviewer will ask you what salary you expect. Prepare for this question, using the same techniques mentioned in the section on preparing a cover letter.

OLLOWING UP ON THE INTERVIEW

You should send a short thank-you letter to the interviewer as a courtesy. Avoid calling or writing before the decision deadline to inquire about the status of your application. After the deadline it is acceptable to call or write to ask when a decision will be made if you have not already been notified. This demonstrates that you are still interested in the job.

- Determining career goals is very important as you consider your future.

- A career path can guide you through various job levels as you move up a career ladder.

- Careers are constructed in a variety of patterns, some planned and some unplanned.

- In developing a career profile, you assess your background, study your personality, and determine your personal goals.

- Because of the continuously changing technology in today's electronic office, a wide number of career choices are available, including jobs in the major areas of records and information management, information processing, telecommunications, and administrative support.

- The major steps in searching for a job are locating a prospective employer, preparing a résumé, preparing a cover letter, completing a job application form, obtaining an interview, and following up on the interview.

- A résumé is a written summary of your qualifications that you prepare when searching for a particular position.

- Résumés may be prepared in a wide variety of formats, which are determined primarily by the type of position being sought.

- The major sections of a basic résumé include your name, address, and telephone number; other personal information; your educational background; your employment history; and your hobbies, interests, activities, and special abilities.

- References are optional on résumés but should be available upon request.

- Résumés should be clearly written, well organized, and formatted attractively.

- A cover letter, or application letter, tells the prospective employer which job you are applying for, highlights your qualifications for the job, and includes any relevant information that is not already incorporated in your résumé.

- Job applicants may be asked to take one or more skills tests, depending on the position.

- Large companies use more formal employment interview procedures.

- A good interviewer will give you an overall explanation of the requirements of the job and of the policies and benefits of the company.

- An interviewer will ask you a variety of questions to determine your individual strengths and weaknesses as they relate to the position you are applying for.

- In order to advance in your position, you need to have a positive attitude and demonstrate competence in all areas of your job.

VOCABULARY

personal career profile   reference
archiving   cover letter
résumé   application letter

REVIEW QUESTIONS

1. What is the purpose of a personal career profile, and what must you do to create one?

2. Describe three positions in the field of records and information management.

3. Describe three positions in the field of information processing.

4. Describe three positions in the field of telecommunications.

5. Describe two positions in the field of administrative support.

6. What steps should you consider when you are searching for a job?

7. What resources can you use to locate prospective employers?

8. Describe the major sections of a résumé.

9. What important points should you keep in mind concerning the appearance of your résumé?

10. What is the purpose of a cover letter?

11. What major points should you keep in mind when preparing for an employment interview?

S KILLBUILDING ACTIVITIES

1. Study the classified advertisements in your local Sunday newspaper. Select five job openings that appeal to you. Then create a list of the necessary qualities for these positions. Do you qualify?

2. Select one of the job openings you used in activity 1. Write a cover letter that would accompany your résumé indicating your interest in the position.

3. Prepare a basic résumé that you could send with the cover letter you wrote in activity 2. Keep this résumé as a guide for future reference when you apply for a job.

4. Obtain three application forms from companies in your area, and study the information requested. Create a display of these application forms on either a bulletin board or a poster. Present a brief report to your classmates, using the application forms to guide you.

Accounting The system of recording and summarizing financial transactions in books or computers and of verifying and analyzing the results.

Accounts payable Money owed by a company to suppliers and creditors.

Accounts receivable Money owed to a company by customers.

Active cell In a spreadsheet display, the cell upon which the cursor is located; may also be called the current cell.

Active records Records that must be kept in the office because they are used regularly.

Agenda An outline for a meeting.

All-in-one program Software program consisting of several different applications which are all combined in a single package.

Alphanumeric keypad The main portion of an electronic keyboard, which closely resembles a standard typewriter keyboard.

Application letter (*see* **Cover letter**)

Applications software Programmed instructions that make a computer execute a specific task.

Archiving The process of preserving records.

Arithmetic-logic unit The part of the CPU that does arithmetic functions.

Assembly language A low-level computer programming language.

Attention line In a letter, a line which will route the letter to a particular person or department.

Audio teleconference The use of a telephone linkage to allow people in widely separated locations to speak together at the same time.

Automate To use machines instead of people to perform certain tasks.

Axes The reference lines, or rulers, on a graph; a two-dimensional graph will require an x-axis (horizontal) and a y-axis (vertical).

Back matter In a formal report, the appendixes, endnotes, bibliography, and glossary.

Backup copy A duplicate copy of stored electronic data, to prevent accidental loss.

Balance The total funds contained in an account.

Balance sheet A financial statement that shows a company's total assets and liabilities.

Bar graph A graph on which y-axis (vertical) information is represented by bars or columns.

BASIC A high-level computer programming language (Beginner's All-Purpose Symbolic Instruction Code).

Blank endorsement The payee's signature.

Blind copy notation In a letter, notation used when the addressee is not meant to know that other persons are being sent a copy of the letter.

Body 1. In a letter, the main text. 2. In a formal report, the introduction, main discussion, and conclusions.

Body language Nonverbal communication such as gestures, facial expressions, and posture.

Boilerplate A section of text that is repeated; often stored electronically.

Budget A company's plan of expenditures and income for a given period of time.

Business communication The exchange of information in the workplace.

Business letter A letter sent to a business or a person which is written on behalf of the business.

Byte A group of bits (the smallest unit of information recognized by the computer) strung together to form a character, used to measure space on a disk.

Canceled check A check that has been cleared against the account on which it was drawn.

Capital expense budget A budget showing long term expenditures for such items as equipment replacement, land purchases, and mortgages.

Caption The name, letter, or number under which a record is filed.

CD-ROM Compact-disk, read-only memory; a high-density storage optical disk.

Cell The intersection of a spreadsheet column and row.

Cell address The column and row number of a spreadsheet cell.

Cell reference In a spreadsheet display, a notation on the screen (usually the top) which indicates the address of the active cell.

Central processing unit (CPU) Computer system unit which receives data from input devices, carries out various operations, and sends the results to output devices.

Centralized reprographics system A type of copy center with many different kinds of equipment, operated by specialists.

Centralized storage system A computer storage system in which individual workstations in the system are part of a local network and are capable of communicating with each other.

Centrex system A telephone switching system in which users can choose between dialing directly and using the operator's assistance.

Character printer An impact printer that prints one character at a time.

Check register A log in which are recorded the number, date, and amount of each check, as well as the payee's name and the reason for payment.

Chip (*see* **Microchip**)

Closing In a letter, the closing phrase, followed by the written and printed name of the sender.

COBOL A high-level computer programming language (Common Business-Oriented Language).

Combination program (*see* **All-in-one program**)

Combination unit A desk-top dictation machine that can record and play back for transcription.

Command Instruction issued to a computer, via the keyboard, to make it carry out a specific action.

Command-driven program A program that uses commands rather than menus to perform functions.

Communications software Software that, usually together with a modem, allows communication over telephone lines with other computers.

Commuter airline A company that provides air transportation between one airport and another not far apart.

Company orientation training Training usually conducted during an employee's first week.

Composition Electronic typesetting of words and images.

Computer-aided transcription The use of a shorthand machine linked with a computer to produce an edited transcript.

Computer-assisted retrieval (CAR) Automatic microform retrieval using an electronic index.

Computer graphics Pictorial representation of data, such as graphs or charts, on a computer screen.

Computer output microform (COM) Computer output reduced to microform by a special device.

Conference A formal meeting at which the primary objective is to exchange information.

Conference planning guide A guide to the facilities and services of a hotel or conference center.

Consecutive numeric system A numeric filing system using consecutive numbers (1, 2, 3, etc.).

Continuous-form paper Computer printout "fanfold" paper with sheets attached to each other and borders with evenly spaced holes that engage the tractor's sprockets.

Control unit The part of the CPU that causes the system to carry out instructions.

Convenience copier Copy machines situated close to the employees' work areas.

Convention A formal meeting at which members of a large professional group elect officers, establish policies, conduct business, and so on.

Copy notation In a letter, a notation used to let the addressee know who else will be sent a copy.

Copyholder A device that holds hard copy at an angle that enables you to read it comfortably.

Corporate travel department A company department that, because of volume of travel, handles company travel arrangements.

Corporation A business that is privately owned by a specific group of individuals or publicly owned by stockholders.

Corrected endorsement An endorsement that consists of the payee's name as it appears on the front of the check and on the account.

Courier service A personal delivery service which guarantees delivery of documents and packages within hours or overnight.

Cover letter A letter which tells the prospective employer which job is being applied for, highlights the applicant's qualifications for the job, and includes any information not already incorporated in the applicant's résumé.

Cross-reference A message that refers you to another location for a file.

Cursor A lighted indicator on a display screen which marks the current work position.

Cursor control keypad The portion of an electronic keyboard that controls the movement (up, down, left, right) of the cursor on the screen.

Daisy wheel printer A letter-quality character printer with a round, flat type element.

Data An often unorganized group of facts, usually made up of words or figures.

Data bank A database or collection of databases.

Data communications The exchange of data between computers.

Data disk Magnetic disk for information storage; may be a floppy disk or a hard disk.

Data file Records on a particular subject.

Data processing The manipulation of alphanumeric data.

Database A stored collection of data on a particular subject.

Database management The entering, organizing, storing, and retrieving of data in a format and order specified by the user.

Decentralized reprographics system A copy center where employees themselves use copying machines to make their own copies.

Decentralized storage system A computer storage system in which each worker stores his or her own files on disks or tapes.

Decimal tab Tabs in a word processing program which will align numbers on the decimal points.

Decision-support tool An applications software program, such as a spreadsheet package, which assists office managers in decision making.

Decode To interpret a message.

Dedicated word processor A computer that is designed solely for word processing.

Delegation The act of assigning tasks to members of the staff or other employees.

Desk top publishing A technology that allows the generation of characters in a broad range of typefaces and allows the user to view the pages on a screen in the way they will appear when output; sometimes referred to as WYSIWYG (what you see is what you get).

Digital camera A special camera wired to a computer that converts photographic images into computer signals.

Digital facsimile machine Machine which can be linked to a computer so that it can function as a long-distance OCR.

Digital scanner A device that scans charts, maps, and blueprints and converts them into digital data so they can be reproduced on a screen.

Direct outward dialing A feature of computerized telephone switching systems that allows users to make outside calls directly by dialing an access number first.

Dishonored check A check that a bank cannot collect on either because it was altered, misdated, or made out incorrectly or because there were not sufficient funds in the drawer's account.

Disk drive A device that contains a small electromagnetic head capable of reading, writing, or erasing information on a disk.

Disk operating system (DOS) Operating system for a microcomputer.

Display screen Visual display on a word processor, not unlike a television screen.

Distribution/communication The transfer of information from one location to another.

Dot matrix printer An impact printer that forms characters by projecting tiny metal bristles or pins in patterns, producing draft-quality or near letter-quality output.

Double-density disk A disk with twice the storage capacity of a single-density disk.

Double-sided disk A disk both sides of which can be used.

Downloading The transfer of information from a central computer to a diskette or disk to be stored at the individual workstation.

Draft A preliminary rough copy of a document.

Draft-quality printer A computer printer that produces output that looks fainter and is more difficult to read than that of a letter-quality printer.

Drawer 1. A section in a filing cabinet or electronic filing system for storing files. 2. The person on whose account a check is drawn.

Electronic dictionary (*see* **Spelling checker**)

Electronic mail The distribution of messages through computers and telecommunications systems.

Electronic network The linking of computers and other devices located in various places so that data and other computer resources can be shared and exchanged.

Electronic typewriter Electric typewriter with a number of computerized functions.

Enclosure notation In a letter, a notation used to let the addressee know that one or more other persons will be sent a copy of the letter.

Encode To convert a sender's message into a form through which it can be interpreted.

Endless loop A long piece of magnetic recording tape that stays inside the recording device and stores dictation for many documents.

Envelope feeder A device that feeds individual envelopes into a printer automatically from stacks.

Ergonomics The study of how the physical work environment affects workers and performance.

Ergonomist Person who studies the field of ergonomics.

Evaluation form A form used to document a performance appraisal.

Expense account A form that businesses use to reimburse employees for using their own money to meet business expenses or to account for cash advances they receive.

Facsimile machine A device that (a) distributes information by scanning pages and converting words or images on them into signals that travel over telephone lines and (b) receives information by converting the signals into words or images and reproducing them on paper.

Feedback A response that indicates how the receiver has understood a message.

Field A unit of information in a record.

Field name The title to categorize a list of fields.

Filing The process of classifying, arranging, and storing information to be easily retrieved.

Filing equipment The variety of structures used in an office for the storage of files.

Filing supplies Standard supplies (such as file folders) used to organize papers and records.

Finance charge A fee charged the borrower by the lender, based on a specified percentage of the unpaid balance, paid with each installment payment.

Floppy disk A round, flat, double-sided sheet of pliable plastic that is magnetically treated and coated in a protective vinyl jacket.

Formal meeting A meeting that requires more preparation and has a more formally planned agenda than an informal meeting.

Formal report A report intended for a person or group in management; contains front matter, body, and back matter.

Format ruler A line at the top or bottom of a word processing display screen that shows margins, tabs, and what the line spacing is.

Formatting 1. A procedure that prepares a disk for use by an operating system. 2. Establishing the arrangement of information on a printed page.

3. Defining a spreadsheet layout, such as column width. 4. Defining the record and field structure of a database.

Formula A spreadsheet cell entry that will make the program perform an arithmetic operation on the cells identified in the formula.

FORTRAN A high-level computer programming language (Formula Translation).

Front matter Title page, table of contents, list of illustrations, preface, and summary of a formal report.

Full endorsement A special endorsement that transfers ownership of a check from one payee to another by using the phrase "pay to the order of."

Function An action expected from a person or machine.

Function key A key on a keyboard that controls a specific processing function.

Garbage in, garbage out (GIGO) An expression that means if what we put into a computer is wrong, what we get out will also be wrong.

General journal A list in chronological order of each business transaction in which money is received or spent.

General ledger A record of financial business transactions, grouped according to account.

Get (see **Select**)

GIGO (see **Garbage in, garbage out**)

Graphics The creation of charts, graphs, and other types of pictorial images.

Graphics tablet A device that converts the movements of a hand drawing on a board into digital signals and then into pictures.

Gross pay Pay before any deductions.

Guaranteed reservation A hotel reservation in which the hotel guarantees that the room will be held as long as is necessary.

Hard copy Computer output in a permanent, visually readable form, usually on paper.

Hard disk A high-volume storage device made of rigid plastic, aluminum, or ceramic and magnetically treated.

Hardware The physical components of a computer system.

Heading In a letter, the address of the sender.

Help facilities The online help screens and tutorials in an applications program.

Help screen A screen in an applications program which provides commands or keys used.

High-level language A computer language that uses symbols to represent a series of steps.

Horizontal applications software Applications programs that can be applied to general office functions, used in almost all types of businesses.

Hub ring A device placed in the ring of a diskette to protect it from damage while in the disk drive.

Impact printer A type of printer that generates characters by striking metal or plastic type against an inked ribbon over paper.

Inactive records Records that may be moved to inactive storage or discarded because they are no longer used regularly.

Incompatible Unsuitable for use together; may refer to computers with different operating systems.

Increased productivity Referring, in the narrow sense, to work that employees can do more of in the same or a shorter period of time. In the broader sense, it means workers have greater flexibility in performing their tasks.

Indexing The process of selecting a caption or term under which a record will be stored.

Informal meeting A meeting that takes place in an office or conference room at which discussions of everyday business activities occur.

Informal report A report which might be prepared as an interoffice memorandum and usually contains no front matter and minimal back matter.

Information Facts (data) that have been processed or organized in a way so that they can be used.

Information management The organizing and controlling of all aspects of business records.

Information processing The transformation of data into useful information.

Information processing cycle The process through which all information in an office environment flows, that is, input, processing, storage, output, and distribution/communication.

Ink-jet printer A nonimpact printer that sprays dots of ink onto paper.

Input 1. The preparation and keyboarding of data. 2. The data entered into a computer.

Installation Transferring the DOS of a microcomputer to its main memory or to a disk.

Installment A portion of a loan that is paid at regular intervals.

Integrated applications program A computer software program with several applications designed to work together.

Integrated information processing system A system in which data processing, word processing, and other applications can all be performed on one machine at the individual workstation.

Integrated software programs Different applications programs that can be used together to enable the user to perform more than one function.

Internal memory (*see* **Main memory**)

Interoffice mail The mail exchanged between people who work at the same location or at a company's nearby branches.

Interoffice memorandum Message form used for communications within an organization.

Itinerary A list of travel arrangements.

Jargon Specialized technical language not normally used in everyday communication.

Job description A document that gives the details of the work, skills, and evaluation factors of an employee in a particular job.

Key system A type of telephone switching equipment using telephones equipped with keys or buttons that light up when in use.

Kilobyte (K) A measurement of computer memory; represents about 1,000.

Knowledge worker A person who works with information.

Label The name of a spreadsheet row or column, categorizing the data in that row or column.

LAN (*see* **Local area network**)

Laser printer A high-speed printer that uses a combination of electronics and photography to produce high-quality originals.

Legend Notation on a bar graph which identifies the items represented by the bars.

Letter-quality printer A kind of printer that uses a typing element to produce sharp, high-quality characters.

Light pen A pen-shaped, light-sensing device used to "write" or "draw" on a computer screen.

Line graph A graph which plots the relationship between a series of points by drawing a line through them.

Line item A category of expenditures or income that is given a separate line in a budget.

List document The list of names, addresses, and other information used by a mail merge program.

Local area network (LAN) A system that makes it possible for a company to use electronic mail internally; requires a network of cables and devices interconnecting a company's computers.

Low-level language Computer instructions that direct the computer through each step.

Mag Card Magnetic Card Selectric Typewriter.

Magnetic disk Disk for the magnetic storage of information; may be a floppy disk or a hard disk.

Magnetic tape Tape coated with magnetic material used to record and store information.

Mail merge The merging of boilerplate letter copy with a list of names and addresses to create the impression that each letter has been personalized; sometimes referred to as list processing.

Mailgram A combination of a telegram and a letter.

Main memory Memory in the CPU that holds data that is input and sends it out as necessary to the arithmetic-logic unit or to input/output devices; also holds the programs for these functions.

Memo (*see* **Interoffice memorandum**)

Memory 1. Where information is stored in a computer; can be either permanent (ROM) or changeable (RAM). 2. The capacity of a computer to store information.

Menu A list of choices displayed on the computer screen.

Menu-driven program A program that uses menus rather than commands to perform functions.

Message Communication between a sender and a receiver.

Messenger service A personal service which guarantees fast delivery of a document.

Microchip A tiny piece of semiconductor material used to store computer memory.

Microcomputer A computer containing a single microchip; also called a desk-top computer.

Microfiche Flat sheets of film that can hold hundreds of pages of micrographic images.

Microfilm jacket A clear plastic sheet that holds short strips of microfilm.

Microfilm roll A roll of film that can hold hundreds of pages of miniaturized documents.

Microform Film containing reduced images.

Microform reader A machine used to enlarge microforms to a readable size.

Micrographics The process of reducing documents to tiny images and storing them on film or fiche.

Microprocessor (*see* **Microchip**)

Microwave An electromagnetic wave that travels in straight lines through the air and carries data and voices between disk-shaped antennas.

Minutes Official record of a meeting.

Miscommunication A failure in the sending and receiving of a message.

Modem An electrical device that converts computer signals into telephone signals (and back again).

Monochrome screen A display screen that displays only one color against the background color.

Mouse A hand-operated device which controls the cursor without the use of a keyboard.

Multiple-cassette dictation machine A dictation machine which stores information on removable cassettes.

Multiple originals The product that results from the repeated reproduction of a document on a computer printer.

Net pay Pay remaining after deductions.

Nonimpact printer A type of printer that produces hard copy without striking type elements against a ribbon and paper.

Notarize The stamping of a signed document by a notary public.

Notary public A person commissioned by a state government to verify signatures on documents.

Notation In a letter, special parts which are not standard form, such as an attention line.

Numeric keypad The portion of an electronic keyboard with keys for each of the ten arabic digits.

Office automation The use of electronic equipment to perform tasks once done manually.

Online information service Company which provides access to particular information from its data banks to meet the needs of subscribers.

Opening In a letter, the name and address of the person to whom the letter is sent, along with the greeting line.

Operating budget A statement that lists the expected income and costs of the day-to-day operations of a company.

Operating system software A set of programs controlling the overall operation of a computer.

Optical character reader (OCR) A device that can scan a printed or typed document and transfer the characters to a computer system.

Optical disk A durable, nonmagnetic storage medium of great capacity, which uses laser beams.

Originator-generated input Input created directly by an office manager, perhaps on a computer.

Output 1. The finished product; hard copy. 2. Computer results.

Output device A device connected to a computer system that can produce hard copies.

Owner's equity The amount of the owner's financial interest in a company.

Page composition The manual process of cutting galley proofs and pasting them onto paper boards in position for printing.

Paging device A small, portable device that alerts the person carrying it when someone is trying to reach him or her; also called a beeper.

Parameters The maximum number of columns and rows in a spreadsheet.

Parliamentary procedure The rules that structure a formal meeting.

Partnership A business owned by two or more people.

Pascal A high-level computer programming language.

Passport A government identification document that grants citizens permission to travel abroad.

Password A personal code used by an individual to identify himself or herself to a computer.

Password system System that requires computer users to enter a password into the computer before they are allowed access to information.

Payee The person or organization to whom a check is written.

Payroll register A record that lists each employee by name along with pay and deductions.

Performance appraisal Review of overall job performance.

Person-to-group communication When one person speaks to a group of people.

Personal-business letter A letter which is sent by an individual to a business and which deals with matters of a personal nature.

Personal career profile An outline of a person's background, personality, and personal goals.

Personal computer (*see* **Microcomputer**)

Petty cash A small cash fund kept by most offices.

Photocomposition The creation of photographic images of entire pages.

Phototypesetting A reprographics device that uses photographic technology to set text.

Plotter A computer printing device that converts output into drawings on paper or terminals.

Postage meter A machine, licensed by the U.S. Postal Service, which prints postage fees on gummed strips of paper, as stamps.

Posting The process of transferring data from a journal to a ledger.

Postscript A message placed after the body of a letter, as an afterthought or for emphasis.

Power of attorney Legal authorization for one person to act as agent for another.

Primary sort key The field in a database which is the basis of the first sort of the database.

Priority A task which deserves attention ahead of others.

Private branch exchange (PBX) A type of telephone switching equipment that requires a switchboard operator to control the central switching station for all the extensions.

Procedure A series of steps followed in a regular, definite order.

Processing The organization and calculation of words and numbers.

Procrastination Putting off the completion of work.

Productivity tool Business applications program (such as database, spreadsheet, or graphics program) which enhances individual productivity.

Product training Training on specific equipment or software.

Programming software The instructions of programs implanted in the circuits of the CPU.

Programs Sets of instructions that enable computers to carry out specific applications.

Project budget Log of expenses for individual programs of a company.

Quorum The number of people required by the group before a vote can be taken.

RAM (*see* **Random-access memory**)

Random access The ability to retrieve a document electronically without looking at any of the other documents recorded on the storage medium.

Random-access memory (RAM) 1. Computer memory in which data is temporarily stored and from which it can be retrieved by the user. 2. The amount of data a computer can store in central memory, measured in kilobytes.

Read-only memory (ROM) Preprogrammed information that is permanently stored by the manufacturer in the computer's memory and cannot be changed by the user.

Read/write head A component of a disk drive that reads data from or writes data to a disk surface.

Receiver One who detects and interprets a message.

Record All the data for an individual entry in a data file.

Reference A person who can vouch for your job performance.

Reference initials In a letter, initials used to indicate who prepared the letter.

Reference material Desk-top sources of information frequently used by an office worker.

Reprographics The process of making multiple copies of an original document.

Reprographics center (*see* **Centralized reprographics system**)

Reprographics system A system which makes multiple copies of hard- or soft-copy originals.

Restrictive endorsement An endorsement that sets conditions such as "for deposit only" to a specified account.

Résumé A written summary of a person's qualifications, prepared during a search for a job.

Revision cycle The cycle of retrieving, revising, proofreading, and printing a document.

Rider A separate sheet of paper attached to a legal document to add space for information.

ROM (*see* **Read-only memory**)

Routing slip A piece of paper with a column of names used to circulate material in an office.

Satellite A small unit of information processing equipment.

Scatter graph A graph without connected points.

Search (*see* **Select**)

Secondary sort key The field in a database which is used to order records when the information in the basic sort field of those records is the same.

Sectors The divisions of the tracks on a disk.

Select A database program command which permits the retrieval of a set of records.

Sender One who creates and transmits a message.

Sheet feeder A device that feeds individual sheets of paper into a printer automatically from stacks.

Shorthand machine A portable input device with keys that are pressed in combinations to produce abbreviations of words or phrases.

Skills development training Training in skills that may become useful in the event of promotion.

Soft copy Computer output shown on a screen.

Software A set of instructions, or programs, directing the operation of a computer.

Software integrator A utility program which allows the user to move data from one applications program to another, even though these may not have been originally designed to work together.

Sole proprietorship A business owned by one person.

Sort A database program command which will permit the entries in a data file or database to be ordered in a specified way.

Sort key The field in a database which is used as the basis for sorting.

Source documents Various base forms used to record accounting information.

Speakerphone A telephone device that amplifies a call so that many people can hear it at once.

Spelling checker An electronic dictionary, used with word processing software.

Spreadsheet 1. Ruled accounting paper on which figures are entered in columns and rows. 2. Graphic applications software that presents figures in a grid format on a computer screen.

Standalone A microcomputer; a self-contained workstation.

Standard facsimile machine Machine which scans a document page and transmits signals to a receiving facsimile machine.

Statement of objectives A description of the goals or objectives that an employee is expected to accomplish during a set period of time.

Stockholders The owners of a corporation.

Storage The recording of information so that it can be recalled and used again.

Stored document Electronically stored boilerplate document, allowing revisions to be made.

Stub A part of a checkbook on which is recorded the information on a given check.

Subject line In a letter, a line used to place emphasis on a particular topic being discussed.

Submenu A menu which appears after a choice is made on the main menu.

Supervisor A person in a business who determines the best way to get work done.

Task A piece of work or a step that is done to carry out a function.

Teleconference A conference among people at different locations electronically linked.

Teleprocessing The exchange of data over telephone lines between computers.

Template 1. A plastic or cardboard plate that fits over the panel of function keys on a computer keyboard. 2. Blank spreadsheet grid for accepting different sets of data.

Temporary memory (*see* **Main memory**)

Terminal The workstation; consists of a keyboard and a display screen.

Terminal-digit system A filing system in which the last number (terminal digit) indicates where to start looking for the file.

Text-editing machine Electronic typewriter which allows the user to alter the copy.

Thesaurus A list of words and their synonyms (different words of nearly the same meaning).

Thimble printer A letter-quality, fast, single-element character printer that resembles a thimble.

Tickler file A follow-up file, arranged by day of the month, which serves as a daily reminder of tasks.

Time management Planning, organizing, and using time effectively.

Time-sharing Simultaneous access by many users to a shared central computer facility.

Time-waster Habit or practice which results in poor time management.

Touch screen A screen with sensors that allow the user to select commands without a keyboard.

Tracks Concentric circles on a disk (similar to record grooves) along which information is written.

Transistor An electronic device consisting of substances that conduct electricity.

Travel agency A business that is organized to plan travel for individuals, groups, and businesses.

Travel agent Person who works in a travel agency.

Traveler's checks A form of money which is used like cash, purchased from a bank or express company, payable only when signed by the owner.

Turnaround time The time from when a task is assigned to when it is expected to be completed.

Ultrafiche Flat sheets of film that hold miniaturized images even smaller than those on microfiche.

User-friendly Relating to applications programs that are easy to use.

User-level language A computer language that uses everyday terms rather than codes.

Value A number that is entered in a column or row of a spreadsheet.

Vendor A person or company which produces and sells, for example, hardware or software.

Vertical applications software Applications programs designed for specialized uses.

Video teleconference The use of closed-circuit television to allow meetings without travel.

Videodisk A type of optical disk widely used for commercially developed products.

Visa A permit granted by the government of a country to allow foreigners to enter the country.

Voice-activated input The translation of human speech into signals that can be read or understood by a computer program.

Voice input Direct input of verbal data into a computer without the use of a keyboard.

Voice mail A message system that uses a telephone linked to a voice-activated computer.

Voice messaging A telephone system which utilizes a computer controlled answering device.

Word processing The use of a computer to create, edit, revise, format, or print text.

Word wrap The feature on a word processor that automatically returns the cursor to the left.

Workstation The area in an electronic office that incorporates all the equipment, furnishings, and accessories needed to perform one's work.

Write-protect notch A device on the disk jacket that protects the information.

Write-protect tab Self-adhesive tab used to cover the write-protect notch on a floppy disk.

WYSIWYG What you see is what you get; refers to the ability of a word processing program to display on the screen a document page exactly as it will appear when printed.

X-axis The horizontal ruler on a graph.

Y-axis The vertical ruler on a graph.